Help Wanted?

PROVIDING AND PAYING
FOR LONG-TERM CARE

Francesca Colombo,
Ana Llena-Nozal,
Jérôme Mercier,
Frits Tjadens

OECD

This work is published on the responsibility of the Secretary-General of the OECD. The opinions expressed and arguments employed herein do not necessarily reflect the official views of the OECD or of the governments of its member countries or those of the European Union.

Please cite this publication as:
Colombo, F. et al. (2011), *Help Wanted? Providing and Paying for Long-Term Care*, OECD Health Policy Studies, OECD Publishing.
http://dx.doi.org/10.1787/9789264097759-en

ISBN 978-92-64-09758-2 (print)
ISBN 978-92-64-09775-9 (PDF)

Series: OECD Health Policy Studies
ISSN 2074-3181 (print)
ISSN 2074-319X (online)

The statistical data for Israel are supplied by and under the responsibility of the relevant Israeli authorities. The use of such data by the OECD is without prejudice to the status of the Golan Heights, East Jerusalem and Israeli settlements in the West Bank under the terms of international law.

Photo credits: Cover © Alexandre Lukin/Shutterstock.com.

Corrigenda to OECD publications may be found on line at: *www.oecd.org/publishing/corrigenda*.

Foreword

There comes a time in many people's lives when their functional and physical abilities decline. To continue to live an active and fulfilling life, people need help – from family, friends, or from people employed to help.

This report is about how countries can provide that help. Most caring is provided by family and friends out of love or duty. Some additional support to such carers can have a big effect, at relatively low cost. Workers to fill caregiving jobs can be found, as long as policy makers and employers take steps to improve the dismal image of caregiving as being low-paid, hard, and low-skilled. Providing adequate financial protection for those needing care is possible, in a way that does not unduly stretch public financing. But getting these policies right needs to start now, because the challenge to implementing sustainable, responsive and fair long-term care policies is only going to get bigger and bigger, as populations age. Learning from other countries' experiences, both good and bad, might save much money and grief.

This book is the result of a two-year project conducted between 2009 and 2010 by the OECD Health Division and Social Policy Division. The study points to key polices and strategies that can help address future demand for care and respond to the implications this will have for long-term care workforce and financing. It highlights examples of useful country experiences, but it also warns about the dearth of evidence on cost-effective policies in a number of areas, making a strong plea for advancing evidence-based research on long-term care (LTC).

The study used a mix of quantitative and qualitative methods. Qualitative information was collected through a fact-finding and policy questionnaire covering 29 OECD countries, complemented by selected country missions. Quantitative data were gathered from OECD databases and longitudinal surveys on health, retirement and ageing in Europe, Australia, the United States, the United Kingdom, and Korea. Projections of LTC costs were based on an update and expansion of earlier projections by the OECD and the European Commission.

Acknowledgements

This book is the result of work undertaken at OECD and the product of truly concerted efforts between the OECD Secretariat, governmental delegates and experts from many OECD countries. Within the OECD Secretariat, two Divisions of the Directorate for Employment, Labour and Social Affairs – the Health Division and the Social Policy Division – collaborated on the project.

The report was developed by Francesca Colombo, who acted as project leader, and by Ana Lena Nozal, Jérôme Mercier and Frits Tjadens. Lihan Wei provided statistical and research assistance throughout the project. Many interns contributed to the analysis and drafting process at various stages, especially Margarita Xydia-Charmanta, as well as Katerina Gousia, Elizabeth Sugarman, Y-Ling Chi, Anna-Mari Viita and Lilian Chi Yan Li. The report benefited from invaluable comments and suggestions especially from Mark Pearson, Monika Queisser and John Martin, as well as Rie Fujisawa and Jonathan Chaloff. Many thanks also to Marlène Mohier for her editorial contribution in preparing the document for publication and to Judy Zinneman for assistance.

The project would not have been possible without the help of country experts and delegates, including representatives from Health and Social Policy Ministries in OECD countries, who provided technical input, background information, and feedback. An expert meeting discussed the draft report on 15-16 November 2010 in Paris. Comments on the report were also received from the European Commission, the World Health Organization, and the Business and Industry Advisory Committee to the OECD (BIAC).

The project was supported by a grant from the Directorate General for Health and Consumers Affairs of the European Commission. It benefited from voluntary contributions from Belgium, France, Japan and the Netherlands.

Table of Contents

Figures

Glossary

Activities of daily living (ADL): include bathing, dressing, eating, getting in and out of bed or chair, moving around and using the bathroom. Often they are referred to as "personal care".

Annuity: series of regular payments over a specified and defined period of time.

Benefit trigger: criteria insurance providers use to determine when an individual is eligible to receive benefits.

Benefit waiting period: specified amount of time at the beginning of a disability during which services are received, but for which the policy will not pay benefits (also referred to deductible period or elimination period).

Care setting: means the place where users of care services live, such as nursing homes, assisted living facilities/sheltered housing or private homes.

Cash (or cash-for-care) benefits: include cash transfers to the care recipient, the household or the family caregiver, to pay for, purchase or obtain care services. Cash benefits can also include payments directed to carers.

Formal care: includes all care services that are provided in the context of formal employment regulations, such as through contracted services, by contracted paid care workers, declared to social security systems.

In-kind benefits: are those provided to long-term care recipients as goods, commodities, or services, rather than money. They may include care provided by nurses, psychologists, social workers and physiotherapists, domestic help or assistance, or special aids and equipment. They might also include assistance to family caregivers such as respite care.

Family carers: include individuals providing LTC services on a regular basis, often on an unpaid basis and without contract, for example spouses/partners, family members, as well as neighbours or friends.

Informal carers: is a terminology used often to refer to family carers, but, strictly speaking, this category includes also "paid" caregivers who are undeclared to social security and therefore work outside the context of formal employment regulations.

Instrumental activities of daily living (IADL): include help with housework, meals, shopping and transportation. They can also be referred to as "domestic care or home help".

Long-term care (LTC): is defined as a range of services required by persons with a reduced degree of functional capacity, physical or cognitive, and who are consequently dependent for an extended period of time on help with basic activities of daily living (ADL). This "personal care" component is frequently provided in combination with help with basic medical services such as "nursing care" (help with wound dressing, pain management, medication, health monitoring), as well as prevention, rehabilitation or services of palliative care.

Long-term care services can also be combined with lower-level care related to "domestic help" or help with instrumental activities of daily living (IADL).

(LTC) at home: is provided to people with functional restrictions who mainly reside in their own home. It also applies to the use of institutions on a temporary basis to support continued living at home – such as in the case of community care and day-care centres and in the case of respite care. Home care also includes specially designed, "assisted or adapted living arrangements" for persons who require help on a regular basis while guaranteeing a high degree of autonomy and self-control.

(LTC) institutions: refer to nursing and residential care facilities (other than hospitals) which provide accommodation and long-term care as a package to people requiring ongoing health and nursing care due to chronic impairments and a reduced degree of independence in activities of daily living (ADL). These establishments provide residential care combined with either nursing, supervision or other types of personal care as required by the residents. LTC institutions include specially designed institutions where the predominant service component is long-term care and the services are provided for people with moderate to severe functional restrictions.

(LTC) recipients (or care recipients): people receiving long-term care in institutions or at home, including recipients of cash benefits.

(LTC) workforce: includes individuals who provide care to long-term care recipients. The formal LTC workers include the following occupations and categories: 1) nurses, as defined by the ISCO-08 classification (2221 ISCO code for professional nurses and 3221 ISCO code for associate professional nurses, providing long-term care at home or in LTC institutions (other than hospitals); 2) personal care workers (caregivers), including formal workers providing LTC services at home or in institutions (other than hospitals) and who are not qualified or certified as nurses. As per the draft definition in the ISCO-08 classification, personal care workers at home or in institutions are defined as people providing routine personal care, such as bathing, dressing, or grooming, to elderly, convalescent, or disabled persons in their own homes or in institutions (other than hospitals).

Nonforfeiture: a nonforfeiture benefit allows a policy subscriber who stops paying premiums to retain some coverage.

Private LTC coverage arrangements: they are primarily distinguished from public coverage programmes by their funding through voluntary non-income related premia, as opposed to taxes or compulsory social security payroll contributions. Typically, private insurers promote and sell the products on the market.

Reimbursement insurance policy: provides for a reimbursement, in whole or in part, of eligible LTC expenses incurred.

Indemnity insurance policy: provides for a fixed indemnity (cash benefit) paid to eligible recipients once they become dependent, regardless of whether LTC services are received.

Reverse mortgage: it is a special type of home equity loan under which one can receive cash against the current value of a home minus outstanding home-secured debt. The loan does not have to be repaid as long as the borrower continues to live in the home and it generally becomes due when the borrower dies, sells the home, or permanently moves out of the home.

Executive Summary

What will be the effects of growing need for long-term care?

*Chapters 1 and 2 examine the growing demand
for long-term care in the context of ageing
societies, discuss demographic projections
and their implications for long-term care labour
markets and expenditure*

In 1950, less than 1% of the global population was aged over 80 years. By 2050, the share of those aged 80 years and over is expected to increase from 4% in 2010 to nearly 10% across OECD countries. This population ageing is being accompanied by family ties becoming looser. The need for community involvement in the care for frail and disabled seniors is growing and will do so ever more rapidly in OECD countries.

This will challenge long-term care (LTC) services and systems. The pool of potential family carers is likely to shrink because more women are working, and social policies no longer support early retirement. Currently, between 1 and 2% of the total workforce is employed in providing long-term care. For many countries, this share will more than double by 2050. Government and private market spending on LTC is as much as 1.5% of GDP on average across the OECD, and will double or even triple between now and 2050.

There is a history in many countries of LTC policies being developed in a piecemeal manner, responding to immediate political or financial problems, rather than being constructed in a sustainable, transparent manner. The future of LTC is more demand, more spending, more workers, and above all, higher expectations that the final few years of life must have as much meaning, purpose and personal well-being as possible. Facing up to this challenge requires a comprehensive vision of long-term care. Muddling through is not good enough. This study examines not only policies for informal (family and friends) carers, but also policies on the formal provision of LTC services and its financing.

Why should family carers be supported? And how?

*Chapters 3 and 4 discuss the role of family carers,
the impact of caring on carers' mental health,
poverty and labour market participation,
as well as policies to support family carers*

Family carers are the backbone of any long-term care system. Across the OECD, more than one in ten adults aged over 50 years provides (usually unpaid) help with personal care to people with functional limitations. Close to two-thirds of such carers are women. Support for family carers is often tokenistic, provided as recognition that they perform a socially useful and difficult task. But supporting family carers effectively is a win-win solution. It is beneficial for carers. Without support, high-intensity caregiving is associated with a reduction in labour supply for paid work, a higher risk of poverty and a 20% higher prevalence of mental health problems among family carers than for non-carers. It is beneficial for care recipients, because they prefer to be looked after by family and friends. And it is beneficial for public finances, because it involves far less public expenditure for a given amount of care than the estimated economic value of family caring. Governments can support family carers by:

- *Providing cash*, although if badly designed, such policies can become counter-productive. Both carer's allowances and cash benefits paid to the care recipients increase the supply of family care, but the state will pay for some cases that would have been provided even in the absence of any financial incentive. Furthermore, carers risk being trapped into low-paid roles in a largely unregulated part of the economy, with few incentives for participating in the formal labour market.

- *Promoting a better work-life balance through more choice and flexibility*. A one per cent increase in hours of care is associated with a reduction in the employment rate of carers by around 10%. Flexible work arrangements in the United Kingdom, Australia and the United States attenuate the risk of a reduction in working hours associated with caring.

- *Introducing support services*, such as respite care, training and counselling. These ensure quality of care at the same time as improving carers' wellbeing. Such services can be arranged for a relatively low cost, especially if leveraging upon the widespread and invaluable contribution of the voluntary sector, as is done already in some countries.

Recognition that both carers and the people they care for are heterogeneous groups with different needs calls for flexibility in designing support measures. Co-ordination between formal and informal care systems is desirable, too. Further evidence on the cost-effectiveness of policies to support carers is badly needed.

How to improve the supply and retention of long-term care workers?

Chapters 5 and 6 review employment and work conditions in formal long-term care labour markets, and consider strategies to attract and retain care workers to the sector

Over-reliance on family carers is not desirable. Many countries need to strengthen the formal LTC sector.

LTC is highly labour-intensive, but working conditions for care workers are poor, few workers remain in their jobs for long and turnover is high. The number of LTC workers per 100 people aged over 80 years varies from slightly over 0.5 in the Slovak Republic to over 3.5 in Norway, Sweden and the United States. Ninety per cent of LTC workers are women and many are relatively old. Typically, the required qualifications are low – and lower in home care than in institutional settings. Between 16% (Japan) and 85% (Hungary) of all LTC workers are nurses, but in most countries fewer than half the LTC workers are nurses. Difficult working conditions and low pay often generate high turnover among workers, contributing to producing a negative image of LTC, and endangering both access to, and quality of, services.

While demand for more LTC workers is growing across the OECD, and many countries are already struggling to meet the challenge, an adequate supply of LTC workers is a manageable goal. Countries can use the following strategies:

- *Improving recruitment efforts (e.g.,* expansion of recruitment pools; recruiting migrant LTC workers). Measures to expand existing recruitments pools and create new potential pools *(e.g.,* young people, long-term unemployed) have however met with mixed success. The inflows of migrant LTC workers is growing in some countries, but the absence of specific reference in labour migration programmes to the labour needs of the LTC sector is conspicuous.

- *Increasing the retention of successfully recruited LTC workers.* High staff turnover is costly. In the United States, turnover costs have been calculated to be at least USD 2 500 per vacancy. Valuing the LTC workforce by improving the pay and working conditions will have some immediate positive spin offs if retention rates increase. There is evidence of good results from measures aimed at upgrading LTC work, for example in Germany, the Netherlands, Sweden and Norway.

- *Seeking options to increase the productivity of LTC workers.* The main avenue has been from the reorganisation of work processes, the use of ICT to reduce indirect workload, and the delegation to nursing assistants of tasks that were previously the responsibility of nurses. However, evidence on productivity improvements in LTC labour markets remains sparse.

In the long-run, improving job quality – for current workers, new hires, domestic and migrant care workers – will be important. High turnover, low quality and low pay do not seem sustainable strategies: not enough workers may be willing to provide care. The flip side of the coin is that "professionalising" a still relatively easy-to-enter sector may raise entry barriers in the future, increasing rigidity in a sector that is regarded by workers as being highly flexible. These measures require investment of resources, too. Cost will go up. This can only be justified if productivity is improved.

What financing policies help to reconcile access to care with costs?

Chapters 7 and 8 analyse, respectively, public and private coverage schemes for long-term care in OECD countries, while Chapter 9 discusses financing policies to improve access while keeping cost under control

Most OECD governments have set up collectively-financed schemes for personal and nursing-care costs. One third of the countries have universal coverage either as part of a tax-funded social-care system, as in Nordic countries, or through dedicated social insurance schemes, as in Germany, Japan, Korea, Netherlands and Luxembourg, or by arranging for LTC coverage mostly within the health system, as in Belgium. While not having a dedicated "LTC system", several countries have universal personal-care benefits, whether in cash *(e.g.,* Austria, France, Italy) or in kind *(e.g.,* Australia, New Zealand). Finally, two countries have "safety-net" or means-tested schemes for long-term care costs, namely the United Kingdom (excluding Scotland, which has a universal system) and the United States. Private LTC insurance has a potential role to play in some countries, but unless made compulsory it will likely remain a niche market.

Moving towards universal LTC benefits is desirable on access grounds. Uncertainly with respect to whether, when, and for how long an individual might need LTC services suggests that pooling the financial risk associated with long-term care is a more efficient solution than relying on out-of-pocket payments. Otherwise, the cost of LTC services and support can rapidly become unaffordable, for even relatively well-off people. Average LTC expenditure can represent as much as 60% of disposable income for all those in the bottom four quintiles of the income distribution.

However, to maintain cost control, it will be important to:

● *Target care benefits where needs are the highest*, for example via cost-sharing policies, and a better definition of the need levels triggering entitlement and of the services included in the coverage. Even within universal LTC schemes, stringent assessment criteria can be in place, as is the case in Korea and Germany, in contrast, for example, to Japan. All countries have user cost-sharing for LTC, although the extent varies significantly. Maintaining flexibility to adjust benefit coverage to changing care needs is desirable on both adequacy and quality grounds.

● *Move towards forward-looking financing policies*, involving better pooling of financing across generations, broadening of financing sources, and elements of pre-funding. Japan, the Netherlands, Belgium and Luxembourg complement payroll contributions with alternative revenues sources. In Germany, retirees are required to contribute premia to social LTC funds, based on their pension. Innovative voluntary funding schemes based on automatic enrolment with opting-out options are being implemented in the United States.

● *Facilitate the development of financial instruments* to pay for the board and lodging cost of LTC in institutions. This cost can be twice or three times as large as personal-care and nursing costs taken together. Home ownership can provide means to help users mobilise cash to pay for such cost, for example via bonds/equity release schemes, public measures to defer payments, and private-sector products, such as reverse-mortgage schemes and combinations of life and LTC insurance policies.

Is it possible to extract better value for money in long-term care?

Chapter 10 reviews options to improve value for money from long-term care services, and to manage more efficiently the interface between health and care

In the face of rising costs, seeking better value for money in long-term care is a priority. Efficiency discussions in long-term care have thus far received relatively little attention and better evidence on what works and under what conditions is needed. Still, the following are possible areas for action:

● *Encouraging home and community care*. This is desirable for users, but there are questions about the appropriateness or cost-effectiveness of home care for high-need users requiring round-the-clock care and supervision, and for users residing in remote areas with limited home-care support. In 2008, institutional care accounted for 62% of total LTC costs across OECD countries, while on average only a third of LTC users received care in institutions.

● *Improving productivity in long-term care.* Pay-for-performance initiatives in long-term care are limited to a few examples in the US Medicaid programme. Sweden, Denmark and Finland have vouchers, enabling LTC users to choose freely among accredited competing providers. Competitive markets have the potential to drive efficiency improvements in care delivery, although evaluation on productivity impact remains sparse. Some research results have shown a positive correlation between technology introduction *(e.g.,* ICT), job satisfaction and productivity, for example in Australia and Finland.

● *Encouraging healthy ageing and prevention.* The most obvious way to reduce cost in long-term care systems would be to reduce potential dependency in later life through lifelong health promotion. In 2006, the Japanese government introduced a community-based, prevention-oriented LTC benefit targeted at low-care-need seniors. In 2008, Germany introduced carrot-and-stick financial incentives to sickness funds that are successful at rehabilitation and moving LTC users from institutions to lower-care settings.

● *Facilitating appropriate utilisation across health and long-term care settings and care co-ordination,* for example by arranging for adequate supply of services outside hospitals, changing payment systems and care pathways to steer LTC users towards appropriate settings, and setting up co-ordination tasks to guide users through the care process.

● *Addressing institutional efficiency,* such as by establishing good information platforms for LTC users and providers, setting guidelines to steer decision-making at local level, the use of care planning processes, and data sharing within government administrations.

Summary and Conclusions

Help Wanted?
Providing and Paying for Long-Term Care

1. The growing need for long-term care has significant financing and labour-market implications

Long-term care need is growing in line
with population ageing...

With population ageing, no clear signs of a reduction in disability among older people, family ties becoming looser and growing female labour-market participation, it is not surprising that the need for care for frail and disabled seniors is growing.* Growth in older age cohorts is the main driver of increased demand for long-term care across OECD countries. Indeed, policy discussion around long-term care reforms is often framed in the context of pressures arising from ageing societies. The statistics speak for themselves. In 1950, less than 1% of the global population was aged over 80 years. In OECD countries, the share of those aged 80 years and over is expected to increase from 4% in 2010 to nearly 10% in 2050.

... and this will have huge effects both
on financing and labour market needs

This rapid ageing of the population and societal changes will have a significant impact on both the delivery and financing of long-term care. On the one hand, they will affect the potential supply of individuals available to provide both formal and informal long-term care. The pool of potential family carers is likely to shrink because people are having to work longer and female participation in the labour market is arising. Currently, full-time equivalent nurses and personal carers represent between 1 and 2% of the total workforce. For many countries this share could more than double by 2050.

On the other hand, LTC expenditure (excluding the value of care provided by family and friends), which currently accounts for 1.5% of GDP on average across the OECD, could at least double by 2050. But this projection could well be an underestimate once due allowance is

---

* The primary focus of this publication is the implications of an ageing population for the labour markets and financing of LTC services. It is important to remember that younger disabled groups also need long-term care and, in some countries, LTC systems cover both target groups. This report does not address specific questions regarding equity between these two groups (*e.g.*, available resources and support for funding the care), the labour market and social integration of younger disabled, or the adequacy of services for younger disabled people.

made for risks and uncertainties. The availability of family carers is expected to decline. This could exacerbate the expected rise in LTC spending, by about 5 to 20% by 2050. With raising real incomes, people demand more responsive and quality services. In a context of declining labour supply, higher demand for LTC workers is likely to push up real wages in the sector and, as a result, push up spending beyond the baseline projections. Taken all uncertainties into account, LTC expenditure could even triple between now and 2050.

*Facing up to these challenges requires
a comprehensive vision of long-term care*

Addressing these future challenges will be difficult but not impossible. It will require a comprehensive approach covering both policies for *informal* (family and friends) carers, and policies on the *formal* provision of LTC services and its financing. Often, policy attention focuses excessively on paid care systems. Less attention is given to the interaction with informal and private structures.

2. Paying more attention to the needs of family carers is a win-win approach

*Family carers, especially women, are the backbone
of any long-term care system*

Whatever the LTC system of a country, most care is provided by family carers (and friends), as part of an ongoing social relationship. Across the OECD, more than one in ten adults aged over 50 provides informal (usually unpaid) help with personal care to people with functional limitations. Much of this informal care is of low intensity: just over half of carers are involved in caring activities involving less than ten hours per week. This low intensity of caring is particularly prevalent in Northern European countries and Switzerland. In contrast, in Southern Europe, the Czech Republic and Poland, more than 30% are intensive carers supplying more than 20 hours per week), raising to over 50% in Spain and over 60% in Korea. This large variation signals not only different government policies on family obligations, but also cultural and societal attitudes.

Close to two-thirds of family carers are women, typically caring for close relatives such as their parents or their spouse, but more man become carers at older ages. One in five adults aged 50 years and above suffering from one limitation of daily activities receives informal care. This proportion doubles in the case of people with two or more limitations. These data show that family carers (and friends) are the major sustaining factor behind long-term care services.

*Paying more attention to family carers
is a potentially win-win-win solution*

Support for family carers is often provided as recognition of the fact that they perform a socially useful and difficult task. But more than a gesture is needed. While caring responsibilities should not be forced upon families and next of kin, supporting carers is an arrangement where all parties can benefit. There are at least three potential "wins" from supporting carers:

- For the care recipient, because LTC recipients prefer to be looked after by family and friends.

● For the carer, because carers provide care out of love or duty, despite the fact that they incur economic, health and social consequences as a result.

● And for the public finances, because supporting the supply of family care can help maintain the public, formal parts of the system, affordable. The estimated economic value of informal caring exceeds by far that of formal care. According to some estimates, the economic contribution of family carers in the United States could amount to USD 375 billions in 2007 (around 2.7% of GDP). Significant reductions in family caring would put public LTC systems under financial strains.

Data suggest that there is, potentially, some scope for increasing the intensity of informal caregiving. But high-intensity caregiving is associated with a reduction in labour supply for paid work, a higher risk of poverty and increased prevalence of mental health problems among family carers. For example, on average, high-intensive caring is associated with a 20% higher prevalence of mental health problems than for non-carers, reaching even 70 or 80% higher in Australia, the United States and Korea. All these considerations suggest a role for governments in supporting family carers. This, however, immediately begs the question: What should be the policies?

Cash support is one way to support carers,
but the trade-offs are difficult to manage

Financial support for carers – such as allowances paid directly to carers and cash benefits paid to the care recipient – recognise and compensate carers for their effort, but targeting of support to those facing the highest health and labour market risks, and defining appropriate compensation, remains a challenge.

Carer's allowances are cash benefits providing carers income support replacing lost wages or covering expenses incurred due to caring. In the Nordic countries, the payment to carers is akin to a remuneration, offering compensation for caring efforts while representing a relatively low wage. In some English-speaking countries (Australia, Canada – Nova Scotia, Ireland, New Zealand, and United Kingdom), allowances are targeted to carers with income below a set threshold, or carers who provide a minimum amount of hours of care.

While recognising the societal value of caring, carers' allowances raise difficult design issues, for example how to fix an appropriate compensation level, which offers carers a reasonable reward without discouraging labour market participation for working carers. Means-testing and eligibility conditions, for example, may result in disincentives to work. Eligibility criteria need to be clearly spelled out, but the definition of who is the primary carer and the measurement of carer's efforts are prone to errors. Strict eligibility requirements help to avoid abuse, but can be costly to administer and be viewed as arbitrary. There are trade-offs between how many carers can be compensated, and the amount of the compensation that can be afforded by public authorities.

Paying the recipient of care has some advantages

Cash benefits paid to the care recipient offer direct support to the person who is most in need, but are not only or necessarily used to compensate carers. Such cash benefits exist in nearly all OECD countries that have public LTC benefits, with only a few countries relying solely on an *in-kind* system (Australia, Hungary, Japan and Mexico). Many provinces and territories in Canada have well-established self-managed care schemes, providing eligible users with cash benefits to manage care delivery, including by paying family carers and friends.

Cash benefits paid to the care recipients have some advantages, because they avoid having to define who the primary carer is. Moreover, the amount of the cash benefit can be more closely related to need. But they also leave carers dependent on the care recipient for compensation of their effort and may change family ties into a relationship where money is the driving factor. Requiring family carers to be employed under formal contracts (*e.g.*, as in the case in Germany, France for relatives other than spouses) has the advantage of clearly identifying the primary carer.

Both types of financial supports have the potential to help maintain informal caring by increasing the supply of care by family, but also involve some deadweight loss, *i.e.* the state will pay for some cases that would have been provided in the absence of any financial incentive. The extent to which cash benefits are used to reward family carers is nevertheless influenced by, among others, how flexible are the conditions for utilisation of the benefit. Here, there can be trade-offs between maintaining incentives for family caring and controlling for inappropriate use of cash benefits, or for the emergence of unregulated grey labour markets (*e.g.*, Italy, Austria).

A second trade-off regards the risk of trapping family carers into low-paid roles with few incentives for participating in the labour market. In this respect, designing financial incentives for carers might be especially delicate when care needs increase or a relatively high allowance is needed to provide sufficient financial support. As most carers are aged over 45 years, it will be important to minimise incentives for pre-retirement by avoiding offering too-high replacement rates or guaranteed pension and unemployment contributions. Policy should also not encourage women's withdrawal from the labour market for caring reasons. Last, reliance on a cash-benefit system where there is little supply of formal LTC workers can discourage the emergence of formal provider markets, unless the use of the cash is regulated to discourage black or unregulated markets.

For all the reasons mentioned, financial support should not be regarded as the sole policy option to support family carers. Services are also needed. For example, cash benefits should be seen in the context of a personalised care plan, which could include basic training for the family member, work reconciliation measures, and other forms of support to carers, including respite care.

Supporting carers also involves addressing work-life balance issues through more choice and flexiblity…

While caring does not lead to reduced work hours in case of low caring responsibilities, the impact of caring increases with care intensity. A 1% increase in hours of care is associated with a reduction in the employment rate of carers by around 10%, while a 1% increase in hours of care translates, on average, into slightly more than a 1% decrease in hours of work. Care leave and flexible work arrangements help carers address the balance between workplace obligations and caring responsibilities, and so can induce the supply of both.

Two-thirds of the OECD countries for which information is available have statutory rights to leave to care for people with chronic conditions or LTC needs. Paid leave is restricted to slightly less than half of the countries, and typically limited to less than one month or to cases of terminal illness, while the amount paid is often so low that use is limited. As in the case of parental leave, it can be difficult to set the appropriate duration of care leave. Long leave may damage the labour market position of the carers, while a short leave might not be enough and could encourage workers to withdraw from the labour force.

Care leave conditions are generally restrictive relative to parental leave to care for children, which is available widely and is paid in nearly all OECD countries. Regulations also make it easier for employers to refuse care leave than for parental leave. There are reasons for this disparity. Higher predictability – in terms of timing and duration of parental leave – makes it easier for employers to manage parental leave in a stage of the employee's working life where productivity and career opportunities are growing. Still, considering the expected future growth in LTC needs and that many carers might be caught between dual caring responsibilities (for children and for old parents), there could be advantages if caring roles were better recognised.

Flexible work conditions can reflect variation in the availability of formal care and in care needs. The United Kingdom, Australia and the United States have flexible work arrangements which appear to be effective in attenuating the risk of a reduction in working hours associated with caring. While in eight out of ten OECD countries, parents can request part-time work, rights to work part-time for carers of the frail elderly exist in fewer than two-thirds of the 25 OECD countries for which information is available.

... and offering flexible support services to carers
which have to go beyond respite care

Some support services, such as respite care, training and counselling, can contribute both to ensure quality of care and to improve carers' wellbeing. Besides, such policies are of prime importance because many carers – particularly siblings and partners – are becoming older themselves and possibly frailer. Although there is a dearth of evidence on cost-effectiveness, such services can be arranged for a relatively low cost, especially if leveraging upon the widespread and invaluable contribution of the voluntary sector, as is done already in some countries.

Respite care provides carers with a break from caring duties and an opportunity to get trained to care better. Often, this is the only and most prevalent form of carers' support, although there can be shortage of services as signalled by waiting lists in some countries. Most often, families are the main funders of short-term respite care, but there can be means-tested subsidies or full financial support for respite as in Denmark. A few countries provide a legal entitlement to respite of varied duration (a few days per month in Finland, 4 weeks per year in Germany and Austria). Respite is of vital importance to reduce risk of carers' burnout. Effectiveness is the highest when services are targeted to high-intensity carers or those with the highest perceived burden, those in paid employment, and for night-care respite. Flexible services or combination of services are more likely to be appropriate to adapt to diverse carers' needs. As many carers are reluctant to seek temporary respite, financial support or geographical proximity of service facilitate access to respite.

Counselling can be effective at relieving carer's stress, and carers often lament the lack of psychological support. Sweden promotes a comprehensive and integrated counselling system. In Ireland, training for family carers is available, while the Netherlands offers preventive counselling and support services. Germany provides legal rights to individual care counsellors. In the United States, a national programme organises support groups and individual counselling. However, these services tend to be hard to access, small-scale, and often unfunded.

One-stop shops for carers and their families, or arrangements that link information on public, private, and voluntary organisations, can inform carers of available services and help to plan medical and social care. Care managers, too, can be a real asset in advising carers and helping them co-ordinate services. Assessment of carers' needs, as in Australia, Sweden and the United Kingdom, is a first important step to identify carers and advise them on appropriate services. Researchers in several countries have developed various assessment tools to this end. Nurses and General Practitioners broadly can also play a key role in identifying carers' distress early and suggest appropriate remedies.

More evidence on the relative cost-effectiveness
of alternative ways to support carers is needed

While addressing carers' needs requires targeted policies, it is important to maintain a focus on the recipients' care needs when targeting support. This is a practical matter – it is easier to identify the care recipient than the carer – but it will also enable the authorities to modulate support to the needs of the care recipient. Recognition that both carers and the people they care for are heterogeneous groups with different needs calls for flexibility in designing support measures, and adapting them to the individual circumstances of both the person being cared for and the carers, and over time. Co-ordination between formal and informal care systems is desirable, too. Ultimately, however, it will be vital to strengthen the evidence-base on the cost-effectiveness of policies to support carers. As the cost of support policies will likely go up in the future, evaluation of their effectiveness in mitigating the detrimental health and labour-market effects of caring will be highly valuable.

3. All OECD countries need a system providing formal LTC services

Although family carers are the backbone,
all OECD countries need well-performing formal
LTC systems

While family carers provide the bulk of caring services, there are limits to what they can do, especially when dependency is very severe. Over-reliance on family carers has undesirable social, health, and labour market consequences. All OECD countries need formal LTC services, including both institutional, home-based, and community services, and good partnership between formal and informal care systems. Future demands for care will put higher pressure on governments and the private sector to deliver high-performing long-term care services. Setting the public and private financing mix and organising formal workforce supply are key elements that all governments need to address. Models and approaches vary greatly.

4. LTC workforce challenges appear manageable

Long-term care is a highly labour-intensive sector
with often poor working conditions

Some workers get considerable satisfaction from working in the LTC sector. However, relatively low pay and difficult working circumstances discourage many others. Turnover is high and retention is low. As a consequence, some OECD countries struggle to match growing demand for LTC workers with available supply. Shortages of LTC workers could endanger access and quality of services.

Long-term care is a highly labour-intensive sector, but the density of LTC workers (an indicator of development of LTC supply that measures the number of LTC workers per 100 people aged over 80 years) varies widely across the OECD. While the Slovak Republic has the lowest density of LTC workers per 100 people aged 80 or over (slightly over 0.5), Norway, Sweden and the United States have the highest densities (over 3.5 per 100). Between 27% (Switzerland) and 82% (Korea) of LTC workers work in home care. Not surprisingly, density ratios are higher in institutional settings than in home care. Worker density in residential care varies from 0.1 full-time-equivalent (FTE) worker per care recipients in the Slovak Republic, to 0.8 in New Zealand.

The share of qualified nurses working in the sector varies greatly across countries. LTC workers are predominantly women (90% of all LTC workers), and many are relatively old. Typically, the required qualifications are fairly low, and lower in home care than in institutional settings. In some counties, however, qualified personnel accounts for a major part of the personnel employed in the sector, such as in Germany. There is no clear skill mix. Between 16% (Japan) and 85% (Hungary) of all LTC workers are nurses, but in most countries fewer than half the LTC workers are nurses. The average age of care workers tends to be relatively high in most OECD countries. More than half of the Australian care workers enter the LTC workforce after the age of 40, and one in ten enter after the age of 50.

For low-qualified care workers, entering an LTC job – especially in home-care settings – does not require high credentials, but difficult working conditions and low pay often generate high turnover among workers. High turnover contributes to producing a negative image of LTC, and endangers both access to, and quality of, services.

Turnover and shortages of nurses in the LTC sector are high, too, and may have negative outcomes for heath and quality of life of LTC users. Working conditions and benefits for nurses in LTC settings are generally poorer than in acute care.

Achieving an adequate supply of LTC workers
is a manageable challenge

Even if the supply of family carers remains large and the economic downturn has eased labour market tightness in some countries, demand for LTC workers is growing across the OECD, and many countries are already struggling to meet the challenge. Projected declines in the working age population due to population ageing will add to the challenge. Nevertheless, an adequate supply of LTC workers is a manageable goal. This will require a multipronged approach, as well as better evaluation of success stories and encouraging examples. Countries will need to use the following strategies:

- improving recruitment efforts, including through the migration of LTC workers, in some OECD countries, and the extension of recruitment pools of workers;
- increasing the retention of successfully recruited LTC workers, by improving the pay and working conditions of the LTC workforce; and
- seeking options to increase the productivity of LTC workers.

Migrant LTC workers reach destination countries through a variety of channels; improvements in migrant care workers' jobs quality are desirable

The presence of foreign-born workers in the LTC sector is uneven across the OECD. While Japan has very few foreign-born care workers, in the United States nearly one in every four direct care worker is foreign-born. Italy and Israel have an overrepresentation of foreign-born LTC workers compared with other low-skilled sectors in the economy. Demand keeps growing. Between 2008 and 2009, over half of the 6% increase in residential-care employment in the European Union was accounted for by foreign-born workers. In the United States, the social-assistance sectors have experienced the fourth largest growth in foreign-born workers over the period 2007-09.

Although most OECD countries have restricted managed-migration programmes for low-skilled workers, there are many immigrant low-skilled LTC workers in the OECD area. Migrant care workers reach destination countries through diverse channels. In Sweden, Spain, Portugal and Italy, some care workers may migrate under general regimes (often subject to a labour-market test). Canada, Israel, Germany, Italy, the United Kingdom and France have specific programmes, visa, regularisation measures, exemptions, or bilateral agreements targeting migrant care workers. In addition to free movements of labour across EU member states, irregular migrants in some EU countries such as Italy and Austria have entered the LTC sector via unmanaged migration channels, such as via overstay or illegal border crossing. Finally, some migrant carers arrive under family reunification schemes.

The diversity of channels and labour market conditions of migrant LTC workers makes it difficult to draw generalisations regarding the phenomenon. Nevertheless, it is possible to identify some specific challenges. First, in light of the growing inflows of LTC workers in some countries, the absence of specific reference in labour migration programmes to the labour needs of the LTC sector is conspicuous. Where irregular care migrants are numerous and growing, the question of adequacy of official migration channels to match supply with demand for care workers arises. Using agencies to match demand for workers with supply can create new problems, such as high agency rents and oversight of agency practices.

Although many LTC workers experience poor work conditions, there can be specific issues linked to job conditions for migrants. Where job quality is lower than for native-born in similar jobs, improving labour market conditions for migrants seems a priority. Training strategies, including language training, can help improving integration and labour market outcomes. Finally, over the longer term, dependence on migrant LTC workers to fill domestic "shortages" can signal inadequacy of domestic recruitment and retention policies, and raise equity concerns about the impact on sending countries.

Broadening recruitment pools can be a successful strategy but numbers reached tend to be small and evidence on outcomes poor

Measures to expand recruitments pools for LTC workers, including both existing workforce pools and new potential pools, have met with mixed success. Germany and the United States have measures seeking to encourage young people into LTC training and jobs. Economic incentives directed to LTC workers have been employed in several countries, such as financial support for re-training workers for LTC jobs in Germany, and bonuses for nurses going into LTC in Australia. Efforts to re-hire LTC workers who had exited the LTC sector exist in Germany, the Netherlands and Australia. Other countries have re-activation measures targeting long-term unemployed and those economically inactive (*e.g.*, Japan, New Zealand, Finland, the Netherlands and the United Kingdom).

There is generally little evidence on long-term cost and effects of policies aimed at increasing entry and retention from new target groups. But, where it exists, evidence suggests that such recruitment efforts have had mixed outcomes or, where successful, only concerned relatively few people. In addition, re-activation measures have often targeted work in itself, rather than work in the LTC sector, without lasting improvement in job retention in the sector.

Valuing the LTC workforce will have positive spin offs on retention and recruitment; this requires emphasis on improving working conditions

No strategy to develop new recruitment pools or make better use of existing pools will be successful if job retention and job quality is poor. Mass exit of LTC workers reduces returns on investment in recruitment and training, and depresses quality of care. Unattractive work conditions lead more workers to quit which, in turn, further increases the work burden and stress on those who remain – a vicious spiral. In the United States, turnover costs have been calculated to be at least USD 2 500 per vacancy. Measures to keep the workforce in place are therefore of utmost importance.

Investing in higher remuneration and benefits, better working conditions, training opportunities, more responsibilities on-the-job, feedback support and supervision, have all been found to be important ingredients of a successful LTC job attraction and retention strategy. Health and safety concerns are another area of paramount concern, and possibly one more difficult to manage in home-care settings, a consideration that also applies to reducing work pressure and improvement in management.

Training can be a route to upgrading the status of LTC work as a profession. Most OECD countries do not have compulsory training or qualification requirements for care workers, although many have locally organised or nationally-set training schemes for LTC workers. There is little proof of nurses in training being prepared for a potential career in LTC (*i.e.*, gerontology knowledge, managerial skills, and internships). LTC managers should be trained in leadership skills.

There is evidence of good results from measures aimed at upgrading LTC work. Dutch and German LTC-workers' retention rates, for example, are higher than in the United States and the United Kingdom, as workers in the former countries appear to be more satisfied with their working conditions and responsibilities. Sweden, Denmark and Norway also appear to be success stories on this front. The introduction in Germany of elderly care nurses led to a redesign of tasks and responsibilities for nurses, with a positive impact on attractiveness of the sector for nurses. This suggests the importance of specific measures to improve career opportunities for nurses working in LTC and upgrade their skills.

The flip side of the coin is that by "professionalising" a still relatively easy-to-enter sector, it may raise entry barriers in the future, increasing rigidity in a sector that is regarded by workers as being highly flexible. These measures require investment of resources, too. Countries which have in place relatively good benefit packages for LTC workers, such as Denmark and Belgium, have relative high public spending on LTC. But attaching importance to LTC jobs as a "profession" brings tangible payoffs. The Netherlands and Japan, which have put emphasis on creating a "LTC profession", have been successful at creating a large LTC workforce. Public awareness initiatives to raise public perception on the image of LTC work could contribute to better recognition for the workforce, and, ultimately, better retention.

But there is still a dearth of evidence on successful productivity-enhancement measures

Unlike other service industries, evidence on productivity improvements in LTC labour markets remains sparse. A first issue regards the difficulties in defining productivity in the sector, and, particularly, the appropriate measure of outputs or outcomes with which to compare labour input indicators. Concerns about potential trade-offs between productivity and quality have delayed or hampered initiatives to substitute capital for labour or optimise the intensity of labour supply in the sector. The main avenue for improving care workers' productivity has been from reorganisation of work processes, the use of ICT to reduce bureaucracy and indirect workload, and the delegation to nursing assistants of tasks that were previously the responsibility of nurses.

5. Moving towards universal LTC benefits is desirable irrespective of financing model

There are equity and efficiency rationales for moving towards universal LTC benefits

On fairness and efficiency grounds, a majority of OECD governments have set up collectively financed schemes for personal and nursing-care costs. Many are also moving towards universal entitlement to coverage of long-term care costs.

Only a few low-income OECD countries rely entirely on family or informal arrangements for coverage of LTC costs. In the others, public LTC coverage can be grouped into three models, largely reflecting the eligibility criteria they apply. One third of the countries have *universal coverage within a single programme*, either as part of a tax-funded social-care system, as in Nordic countries (LTC spending between 2 and 3.6% of GDP), or through dedicated social insurance schemes, as in Germany, Japan, Korea, Netherlands and Luxembourg (LTC spending ranging from 0.3% of GDP in Korea to 3.5% in the Netherlands), or by arranging for LTC coverage mostly within the health system (Belgium). While not having a dedicated "LTC system", a large number of countries have *universal personal-care* benefits, whether in cash (*e.g.*, Austria, France, Italy) or in kind (*e.g.*, Australia, New Zealand). Financing of personal care in the second group of countries is fragmented across different schemes and mechanisms. In some of these cases, only a component of the care cost is provided universally, or else care is supported only if it is received in certain settings. In most such countries, benefit levels are closely linked to ability to pay. Finally, two countries have *safety-net, means-tested schemes* for long-term care costs, namely the United Kingdom (excluding Scotland) and the United States.

Uncertainly about whether, when, and for how long an individual might need long-term care services suggests that pooling the financial risk associated with long-term care is a more efficient solution than relying solely on private out-of-pocket payments. Otherwise, the cost of long-term care services and support can rapidly become unaffordable, and not only for low-income seniors. Average LTC expenditure can represent as much as 60% of disposable income for all but those in the upper quintile of the income distribution. The oldest old and those with severest care needs are especially at risk. Hence, universal LTC benefits are better able to ensure high and equitable access to care than means-tested entitlements or social-assistance type programmes – though at a cost. Over the years, there has indeed been a convergence towards providing such a "basic universal floor" in many OECD countries (though how broad and comprehensive is the "basic floor" depends on the financial position and priorities of each country).

Even in universal systems, it is desirable to target
care benefits where needs are the highest

LTC costs can be impoverishing for moderately and severely disabled LTC users, even for those who were not poor before the onset of disability. However, many low-need recipients face relatively affordable long-term care expenses, and some LTC users are income and/or asset rich. This means that universality of entitlement to LTC coverage does not exclude targeting of personal-care benefits to those with highest needs. In fact, in light of the expected growth in age-related spending, *targeted universalism* has the potential to provide fair protection in a fiscally sustainable manner. Such an approach involves some sort of collective provision of support for those with high needs, combined with support for those with low needs which reflects the individual's ability to pay.

A number of countries seem to be moving towards such "targeted universalism", albeit at very different rates and from different starting points. Such an approach requires countries to carefully balance three features of LTC coverage schemes:

⦿ setting the need-level triggering entitlement to coverage;

⦿ the breadth of coverage, that is, setting the extent of user cost-sharing on LTC benefits; and

⦿ the depth of coverage, that is, setting the types of services included into the coverage.

Even within universal LTC schemes, stringent assessment criteria can be in place, as is the case in Korea and Germany, for example, relative to Japan. Some countries target LTC coverage only to the oldest segment of the population. Over the years, there have been efforts to target benefits to those with highest care needs in Sweden or the Netherlands, while Japan moved low-need users to a prevention system in 2006.

Universality of entitlements does *not* mean that all LTC should be free. In fact, all countries have user cost-sharing for LTC, although the extent varies significantly across the OECD. For example, in France a LTC cash benefit pays up to EUR 1 235 per month for a high-need/low-income user, down to EUR 27 for higher-income users, while in Sweden there is a cap for cost-sharing on home-help services of EUR 180 per month. While administratively more burdensome, paying higher benefits to low-income dependents as in France, Austria and Australia is a possible way of ensuring access to care for those who need it without excessive public expenditures. (As discussed below, there is also a strong rationale for charging care recipients for the cost of board and lodging in nursing homes.)

Targeting of the benefit package or setting a basic basket of services that all LTC users need can be trickier. On cost-control grounds, it could be argued that support for domestic care and help with so-called instrumental activities of daily living (IADL) such as shopping, cleaning or administrative tasks should not be included in a basic package. And indeed, in-kind benefits in Korea and New Zealand focus on support for daily living activities (ADL), while the Netherlands moved IADL services for people with small limitations out of LTC insurance into a separate budgeted system in 2009. In practice, however, the distinction between personal and domestic help can be difficult to make, especially where services are jointly provided to high-care-need users. Furthermore, restricting coverage to ADL services gives people an incentive to argue that they have greater needs than they actually do, so as to get access to the higher levels of support. Coverage of support for some IADL activities, as in Sweden, Denmark, Germany and Luxembourg, is reported to have helped to prevent dependent people with relatively high care needs from moving to even more expensive care settings.

Maintaining flexibility to adjust benefit coverage to changing care needs is desirable on both adequacy and quality grounds. For example, Germany and some other OECD countries extended their basket of services to include an extra benefit for those with cognitive diseases. The use of cash benefits provides users with flexibility and can recognise each individual's unique circumstances. An increasing number of OECD countries – the Netherlands, Austria, Germany, France, Italy and the United Kingdom as well as many central and eastern European countries – provide cash entitlements for care.

It is unrealistic for governments to shoulder
all hotel costs of institutional care, but they can
help mobilisation of cash to pay for such costs

Board and lodging (B&L) can be very expensive – twice or three times as large as personal-care and nursing costs taken together. In some Nordic countries, payments to cover B&L costs are income or asset-related, while assistance in United States, United Kingdom, Belgium, France, and Germany is targeted to low-income people through welfare or housing-subsidy programmes. Japan has flat-rate payments for this cost component, which are nevertheless lowered for low-income people.

Reasons for asking individuals to contribute towards their B&L costs go beyond governments' affordability considerations. All individuals should be required to pay at least for a minimum for their food and shelter-related expenses, regardless of their dwelling, and it can be expected that some food and shelter expenses are met by running down accumulated savings and personal wealth, regardless of where a LTC user lives. Moreover, full coverage of B&L could give incentives for LTC users to prefer institutionalisation over receiving care at home.

Including assets in the means-test used to determine individual cost-sharing (or entitlement to public support) for B&L costs better reflects the distribution of economic welfare among individuals. But it can be more cumbersome to administer and act as a disincentive to individual savings. No matter the level of B&L fees, transparency in the way fees are calculated is necessary for fairness and user acceptability.

Home ownership can provide avenues to help users mobilise cash to pay for the cost of food and shelter associated with residing in nursing homes. Possible mechanisms already used in some OECD countries are:

- Bonds/equity release and similar interest-free loan schemes (e.g., Australia). They can foster a sense of ownership towards the LTC residence.

- Public measures to defer payment of nursing-home costs (e.g., Ireland, some local councils in the United Kingdom), or exclude the value of houses from asset-tests (e.g., United States).

- Private-sector products, such reverse-mortgage schemes and combination of life and LTC insurance policies. These facilitate decisions about having to sell the house.

Different approaches to raise finances for long-term care are possible, but to address future cost pressures, a forward-looking set of policies and innovation in financing models are desirable

---

OECD countries rely on different approaches to raise funds to pay for LTC coverage. These often reflect differences in how health care is financed – countries with tax-funded or social-insurance-based health coverage follow similar arrangements for financing LTC costs.

Regardless of the preferred financing model, LTC financing schemes often have too-short a time frame. Benefits or co-payments are adjusted to reflect current resource constraints, rather than making a strategic decision on the appropriate balance between collective and private responsibilities.

Issues that countries need to be considering to prepare for the increased demands for help with LTC costs in the future include:

- *Tax-broadening*, which means financing beyond revenues earned by the working-age population. Japan, the Netherlands, Belgium and Luxembourg complement payroll contributions with alternative revenues sources.

- *Better pooling across generations*, which implies avoiding unduly charging (dwindling) young population cohorts to pay for LTC costs of a growing cohort of old people. For example, in Japan LTC premia are levied on those aged 40 years and over. In Germany, not only the working-age population but also retirees are required to contribute premia to social LTC insurance, based on their pension.

- *Pre-funding elements*, which implies setting aside some funds to pay for future obligations. All social LTC insurances are financed on a pay-as-you-go basis. While a fully-funded system may not be justifiable given the uncertainty surrounding future LTC needs, demographic forecasts indicate a possible role for some pre-funding. Private compulsory LTC insurance in Germany includes some pre-funding elements. The Singapore Eldercare Programme is, in principle, fully-funded. In tax-funded LTC schemes, this would mean building a favourable fiscal position through lower debt-to-GDP ratios.

● *Innovative approaches.* New innovative schemes involving public-private partnership or voluntary funding schemes based on automatic enrolment with opting-out options are being implemented in the United States (the so-called Class Act) and have been established in Singapore. These initiatives borrow features of both public and private insurance, although the voluntary nature of enrolment remains a challenge to manage.

Private LTC insurance has a potential role to play in some countries but unless made compulsory will likely remain a niche market

The market for private long-term care insurance is small in most OECD countries. Even in the United States and France, where coverage is the broadest, less than 10% of the population aged 40 years and over holds private LTC insurance. With the exception of the United States and Germany, in most OECD countries less than 2% of total LTC expenditure is financed through private LTC insurance. The group market is large in France where it represents nearly half of the market; it is 30% of the total in the United States.

Even in countries with a relatively high share of private LTC financing, insurance market failures and consumers' lack of forward planning limit the role of private insurance in the LTC sector, regardless of whether it plays a primary or complementary role. Public initiatives to broaden access to voluntary private LTC insurance, such as preferential tax treatment, targeted regulation or public-private partnerships have met with limited success, as shown by the experience of the United States.

To broaden access, private providers have simplified insurance products (*e.g.,* move towards policies providing a fixed cash benefits) and introduced hybrid financial products such the combination of life and LTC insurance coverage. In France, for example, some 150 000 individuals (about 5% of the market) hold a long-term care insurance coverage as part of their life insurance policies.

6. With growing cost pressure, seeking better value for money in long-term care is a priority

Growth in demand for more and better care will put pressure on governments to improve value for money in long-term care

While long-term care still accounts for a relatively small share of GDP compared with other ageing-related expenditures such as pensions and health, it is projected to experience a faster relative increase over the next decades.

Efficiency discussions in long-term care have received relatively little attention compared with, for example, health care. Yet, in a context where the other large age-related spending items (pensions and health) are also expected to grow, it will be difficult to sustain expansion in long-term care services without proof that high value for money is delivered. Evidence on what works best remains scarse. There is a therefore strong need for focusing policy attention on the efficiency gaps in the sector. International research and collaboration on value for money and the development of measures or indicators of efficiency in LTC deserve much priority.

Encouraging home care is desirable for users but in certain conditions institutional care is more cost-effective

How to balance home and institutional care settings is at the core of long-term care policy initiatives in nearly all OECD countries. In 2008, institutional care accounted for 62% of total LTC costs across OECD countries, while on average only 33% of LTC users received care in institutions. Both utilisation and cost of institutional care are set to rise with growth in cases and the average severity of disability of institutional care recipients. Meanwhile, in many cases, LTC users prefer home-based solutions.

Developing alternatives to institutional care can partly compensate for cost growth, and respond to users' wishes to remain in their home. To do so, several approaches have been followed – ranging from direct expansion of home-care supply (*e.g.*, Canada, Ireland, Japan, New Zealand, Sweden, and Poland); to new legislative frameworks encouraging home care (*e.g.*, Australia, Sweden) and regulation controlling admissions to institutional care (*e.g.*, Finland and the Czech Republic); or the establishment of additional payments, cash benefits or financial incentives to encourage home care (*e.g.*, Austria, Germany, Japan, the Netherlands, Sweden, the United Kingdom and the United States).

The share of over 65-year-old LTC users receiving care at home has increased in many countries in the past few years, but several challenges remain. A market for home care providers may be missing or the supply of home care inadequate. Care organisation and co-ordination can be endangered where different home-care providers visit the same user. Information-support systems to support the choice of home-care providers by users are well-developed in, for example, Nordic countries, but less so in some other countries.

Questions about the appropriateness or cost-effectiveness of home care for high-need users requiring round-the-clock care and supervision remain, and for users residing in remote areas with limited home-care support. There is scope for government to monitor and evaluate alternative services, including incentives for use of alternative settings. LTC users can be supported to make appropriate choices and assessment of individual needs linked to available care-provider options.

Few countries have looked for ways to improve productivity in the LTC sector

Despite hopes to improve productivity in long-term care – that is producing more and better care for a given cost – the evidence gap on what works and under what conditions is still large. According to OECD projections, productivity gains could bring a decrease of about 10% in projected public LTC expenditure, relative to the pure demographic scenario. In practice, however, there is hardly any measurement of productivity in long-term care, partly becomes of difficulties in measuring outcomes. Initiatives to measure and enhance LTC productivity are still in their infancy.

Provider payments for LTC are often on the basis of salary, with fee-for-service used to pay LTC workers in home-care settings in some countries and capitation payments used in some managed-care schemes in the United States. These mechanisms are well known for rewarding *volume* instead of *outcomes* of care. Public LTC systems typically reimburse providers on a *per diem* basis, sometimes adjusted by prospective user's risk. But where budgets are negotiated ex-ante or based on a pre-fixed share of high-need users, providers have complained about risks of budget overruns because public budgets are not adjusted over time to reflect the changes in the disability status of institutional LTC users.

There is a new emphasis in health care policy on changing incentives faced by providers to reward outcomes and performance in lieu of outputs and volumes. But pay-for-performance initiatives in long-term care are limited to a few examples in the US Medicaid Programme. Evaluations from such programmes in some US states show promising outcomes relating to resident satisfaction and employee retention rates, for example. Yet changing provider payment mechanisms is difficult, not least because there is still little assessment, comparative analysis and reporting of quality provided by home care and residential care facilities.

Encouraging competition across LTC providers can be a way to stimulate productivity enhancements. However, it can also hamper the co-ordination of care across different providers unless this is specifically encouraged. The introduction of social LTC insurance in Japan in 2000 led to the market entry of several competing LTC providers, with positive outcomes for user choice and increased incentives for cost-management. Some Nordic countries (Sweden, Denmark, and Finland) have vouchers, enabling LTC users to choose freely among accredited competing providers. Generally, LTC user satisfaction is high, although there is little evaluation of the impact on either quality or cost-effectiveness.

Increased capital intensity in the provision of LTC could improve labour productivity. Assistive devices, for example, facilitate self-care, patient centeredness, and co-ordination between health and care services. ICT can be an important source of information and emotional support to carers, carees and their families. While evidence is still sparse, some research results have shown a positive correlation between technology introduction, job satisfaction and productivity, for example in Australia and Finland. However, rather than being a substitute for labour, technology works well as a complement which enables caregivers to dedicate more time to LTC users needing further assistance. The majority of the studies remain pilot programmes, though, with need for further systematic assessment, particularly about which users could benefit the most from the use of technology.

Healthy ageing and prevention could bring high benefit, but the knowledge gap regarding the cost-effectiveness of interventions must be closed

---

Healthy ageing and preventing physical and mental deterioration of people with chronic care needs are potentially effective at promoting health outcomes and lowering costs. According to OECD projections, healthy ageing and productivity gains could partly compensate for future increase in LTC costs, and reduce the projected increase by about 5 to 10% by 2050.

Prevention and health-promotion efforts can influence lifestyle, help to identify risk groups and detect morbidity patterns earlier. Supporting self-management programmes encourages user centredness and is consistent with attitudes of the elderly to live active and independent lives in their homes and communities. In 2006, the Japanese government introduced in the LTC insurance system a community-based, prevention-oriented LTC benefit targeted at low-care-needs seniors. In 2008, Germany introduced carrot-and-stick financial incentives based on sickness funds success with rehabilitation and management of users' transition from institutions to lower-care settings. However, such innovations are rare and there is still much uncertainty regarding which interventions lead to better payoffs or are cost-effective at managing LTC utilisation and preventing dependency. Filling in the evidence base would prove of significant value.

Addressing value for money in long-term care requires optimising the interface between health and care

The links between health and long-term care are significant. There is potentially scope for efficiency gains by managing the interactions. For example, in several OECD countries, LTC users are admitted or treated in acute-care facilities or settings, which are more costly and less appropriate for LTC care needs. Policy options to facilitate appropriate utilisation across health and long-term care settings can include:

- arranging for adequate *supply of services and support* outside hospitals *(e.g.*, Australia, Hungary, the United Kingdom and Sweden);
- changing *payment systems and financial incentives* to discourage acute care use for LTC *(e.g.*, pay-for-performance in Medicaid in the United States);
- creating better *rules, improving (and securing) safe care pathways and information* delivered to chronically-ill people or circulated through the system, to steer LTC users towards appropriate settings *(e.g.*, Sweden, Finland).

Another important area is better co-ordination of care pathways and along the care continuum. In several OECD countries, long-term care is fragmented across care episodes, providers, settings and services. Many OECD countries have set up co-ordination tasks or assigned responsibilities to guide users through the care process. These range from:

- *single point of access to information (e.g.*, Canada);
- the allocation of *care co-ordination responsibilities* to providers *(e.g.*, Australia, France, Sweden) or to care managers *(e.g.*, Japan, Germany, Denmark, the United Kingdom);
- dedicated *governance structures* for care co-ordination *(e.g.*, Belgium, the French *Caisse nationale de solidarité pour l'autonomie*, Japan);
- the *integration* of health and care to facilitate care co-ordination *(e.g.*, examples in the United States, Canada and Sweden).

Despite these mechanisms, problems of care co-ordination remain. The co-ordination of care *within* LTC systems and *across* health and long-term care deserves considerable policy attention in the future. An overall vision of health and long-term care could lead to gains in management.

Governance of long-term care is often complex

As the discussion on care co-ordination suggested, LTC services and settings are difficult to manage. Long-term care policies interact with other social policy issues such as health, housing, pensions and social infrastructure. The administrative and institutional-efficiency challenges are large. Possible useful approaches that have emerged from the assessment of country practices include:

- establishing good information platforms for LTC users and providers;

- setting guidelines to steer decision-making at local level or by practising providers;

- using care planning processes, based on individualised need assessments, involving health and care providers and linking need assessment to resource allocation;

- sharing data within government administrations to facilitate the management of potential interactions between LTC financing, targeted personal-income tax measures and transfers (e.g. pensions), and existing social-assistance or housing subsidy programmes;

- dealing with cost-shifting incentives across health and care.

Chapter 1

Long-term Care:
Growing Sector, Multifaceted Systems

Long-term care (LTC) is a growing, but relatively small sector in the economy. People older than 65 years of age, especially those aged over 80 years, have the highest probability of receiving LTC services, while women are the main recipients of services. LTC is a labour intensive sector, which is mostly publicly funded. On average, LTC expenditure accounts for 1.5% of GDP across the OECD. Most care is provided by family carers. The LTC workforce (mostly women working part-time in a majority of countries) is about 1.3% of the total OECD workforce. Over the last ten years, new long-term care programmes have been implemented in a number of countries, including cash-for-care programmes in European countries and the United States, aiming at providing consumers with more choice and control over LTC services. Due to the variety in target groups, governance, provision and workforce, LTC services are often fragmented. The connection with health systems is sometimes poor. The size, benefits, target groups, use, provision, governance and financing of long-term care differ markedly across countries. This chapter provides an overview of the sector in OECD countries. It begins by defining long-term care. In the following sections, it offers a snapshot of who uses, provides, and pays for long-term care services. Another section describes available services, with a focus on cash-for-care programmes, while the final section offers a short overview of recent policy developments in the sector.

The statistical data for Israel are supplied by and under the responsibility of the relevant Israeli authorities. The use of such data by the OECD is without prejudice to the status of the Golan Heights, East Jerusalem and Israeli settlements in the West Bank under the terms of international law.

1.1. Scope of this report: How do OECD societies address the growing need for long-term care?

How societies address the issue of long-term care (LTC) – that is care for people needing daily living support over a prolonged period of time – is linked to social, moral and ethical norms, government policy and other country-specific circumstances (Ngai and Pissarides, 2009). For some, LTC is part of the private sphere, where family and friends are mainly responsible for providing unpaid care, while others consider long-term care as a collective responsibility. Furthermore, societies interpret the concept of collective – often state – responsibility for long-term care differently, in terms for example of financing, provision, and regulatory roles of governments.

These differences have implications for the development of formal long-term care systems, which can differ significantly even in societies with similar demographic profiles, or with a similar share of the population needing care. Yet formal LTC systems are just the tip of a largely submerged iceberg. In all countries, the major share of long-term care remains "hidden", in the shape of informal – mainly family and friends – care.

In the future, pressures on long-term care are expected to grow, for at least four reasons. *First*, although the speed at which populations are ageing varies considerably across countries, and despite uncertainties about future trends in disability among the population, demographic transformations will increase demand for LTC services in all societies. *Second*, changing societal models – such as declining family size, changes in residential patterns of people with disabilities and rising female participation in the formal labour market – are likely to contribute to a decline in the availability of informal caregivers, leading to an increase in the need for paid care. *Third*, as societies become wealthier, individuals demand better quality and more responsive social-care systems. People want care systems that are patient-oriented and that can supply well co-ordinated care services. *Fourth*, technological change enhances possibilities for long-term care services at home but may require different organisation of care. This raises pressures for improving the provision of care services, their performance, and, therefore, will drive cost up.

These changes will create upward pressure on the demand for long-term care services and, as a consequence, the human and financial resources necessary to provide LTC services. This report discusses such future demands on long-term care services and systems, in terms of human resources and financial sustainability. While both elderly and younger disabled people, including those with physical and cognitive handicaps, may need LTC, the report focuses mainly on older population groups. Financing appears especially at the top of policy priorities towards long-term care in OECD countries (Figure 1.1).

Figure 1.1. **Financial sustainability is the most important policy priority for LTC systems in the OECD, 2009-10**

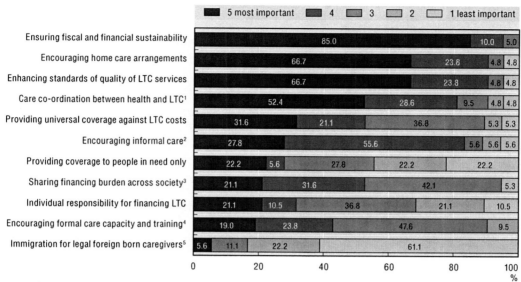

Note: Includes responses from 28 OECD countries. Four countries identified other policies and reforms than the ones listed above, including: improving functional needs assessments and international co-operation.
1. Harmonising LTC and health systems, support care co-ordination.
2. Encouraging informal care and support for informal carers (including family members).
3. Sharing the burden of LTC financing across society as a whole, including seniors or retired high-income individuals.
4. Encouraging formal care capacity and training to caregivers, for example in order to reduce the burden on informal caregivers.
5. Encouraging or facilitating the immigration of legal foreign-born caregivers.

Source: OECD 2009-10 Questionnaire on Long-term Care Workforce and Financing.

StatLink ⟨⟩ http://dx.doi.org/10.1787/888932400589

1.2. What is long-term care?

Long-term care is the care for people needing support in many facets of living over a prolonged period of time. Typically, this refers to help with so-called activities of daily living (ADL), such as bathing, dressing, and getting in and out of bed, which are often performed by family, friends and lower-skilled caregivers or nurses.

As the costs of formal LTC may quickly become high for those in need of care, many countries have set in place public risk-coverage systems. Coverage may be restricted to specific low-income target groups or be universal. Benefits may imply services in kind or in cash and services can be provided in different settings, usually depending on the status of the care recipient. Care workers may have different qualifications depending on the care recipient's status and a country institutional arrangements, as does the intensity of care provision. Long-term care can be provided in home, institutional or day-care settings, from public, not-for-profit or for-profit providers, with services varying from alarm systems to 24h/7 days personal care. Service users may be required to pay a share of the cost for the use of such provisions.

Responsibilities for – and expenditure on – formal long-term systems care can be centralised at one ministry or agency, typically the Health Ministry or the Social Affairs Ministry, or be a shared responsibility, although often lower-level authorities have authority over the provision of services and, in some cases, over funding. Almost a third of

OECD countries have decentralised governance of LTC to state, regional or local level (*e.g.* Canada, Finland, Korea, Mexico, Slovenia, Sweden, Switzerland, the United Kingdom and the United States).

1.3. Who uses formal LTC services?

The use of formal LTC services – measured in terms of LTC recipients – is low in Poland (0.2%), and the United States and Ireland (0.5%) (institutional recipients only), while high use is seen in Austria (5.1%, all in the form of cash benefits), Sweden (4.2%), Norway and Switzerland (3.9%), and the Netherlands (3.8%). On average, 2.3% of the population uses formal LTC services across OECD countries (2008) (Figure 1.2). For the 23 countries for which data are available, around 70% of all LTC users receive services at home, ranging from 55% in Belgium to over 80% in the Czech Republic.

Figure 1.2. **More LTC users receive care at home than in institutions**

LTC users as share of the population in OECD countries, 2008

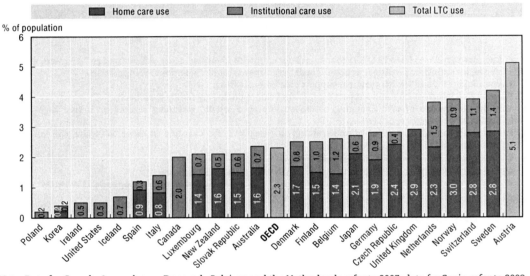

Note: Data for Canada, Luxembourg, Denmark, Belgium and the Netherlands refer to 2007; data for Spain refer to 2009. Data for Japan refer to 2006. Data for Japan underestimate the number of recipients in institutions because many elderly people receive long-term care in hospitals. According to Campbell *et al.* (2009), Japan provides public benefits to 13.5% of its population aged over 65 years. Czech home-care users include 300 000 recipients of the attendance allowance. Polish data underestimate total LTC users. Austrian data represent recipients of cash allowances.

Source: OECD Health Data 2010, the Korean computerised administrative network and additional Australian and Swedish data.

StatLink http://dx.doi.org/10.1787/888932400608

Demand for LTC is highly age-related (Figure 1.3), even though elderly people are not the only target group. Less than 1% of those younger than 65 years use LTC, while after the age of 65 years, the probability of LTC use increases fast. Between 2% (Poland) and 46% (Norway) of the women aged 80 years old or over use LTC services, while the correspondent male proportion ranges from 2.6% in Poland to 32% in Norway. These data reflect higher female life expectancy and survival rates. Still, in most countries, one in five LTC users is younger than 65 years, while around half of all users are aged over 80 years (Figure 1.4).

Figure 1.3. **Most LTC users are women aged over 80 years**

LTC users by age and gender, as a share of respective population group, 2008

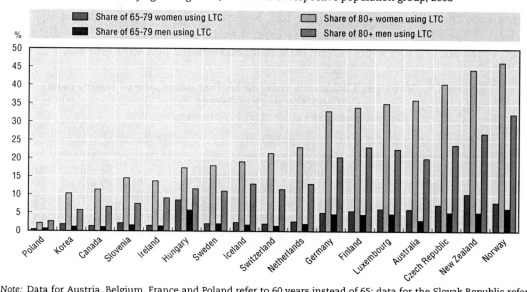

Note: Data for Austria, Belgium, France and Poland refer to 60 years instead of 65; data for the Slovak Republic refer to 62 years; for Norway, data refer to 67 years and over. For home-care users in Poland, the age breakdown refers to 60-74 years and those aged over 75, instead of 65-79 and those over 80. Data for Sweden refer to institutional care only. Data for Canada, the Netherlands, Australia and Luxembourg refer to 2007. Austrian data represent recipients of cash allowances.

Source: OECD Health Data 2010 and additional Australian and Swedish data.

StatLink http://dx.doi.org/10.1787/888932400627

Figure 1.4. **Approximately half of all LTC users are aged over 80 years**

Share of LTC users by age, 2008

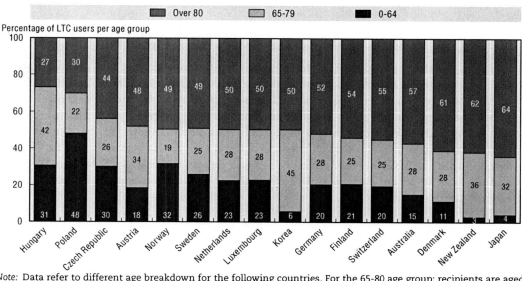

Note: Data refer to different age breakdown for the following countries. For the 65-80 age group: recipients are aged over 60 in Austria, Belgium and Poland; LTC users are over 62 in the Slovak Republic; home-care recipients are aged over 60 and institution recipients are aged over 65 in France; recipients are aged over 67 in Norway). The age breakdown for home-care users in Poland refers to 60-74 and those aged over 75 instead of 65-79 and those aged over 80; Polish data underestimate LTC use. Data for Canada, the Netherlands, Australia and Luxembourg refer to 2007. Data for Japan are for 2006. Austrian data represent recipients of cash allowances.

Source: OECD Health Data 2010 and additional Australian and Swedish data.

StatLink http://dx.doi.org/10.1787/888932400646

In nearly all OECD countries, between half and three quarters of all formal LTC is provided in home-care settings. In all countries, very old users are less likely to receive home care than younger ones (Figure 1.5). Nevertheless, more than half of the care recipients aged 80 years or over receives care at home in most countries. A substantial share of the old LTC recipients suffers from dementia-related problems (see Box 1.1).

Figure 1.5. **Younger LTC users receive higher amounts of home care than the very old ones**

Home-care users as a share of total LTC users by age, 2008

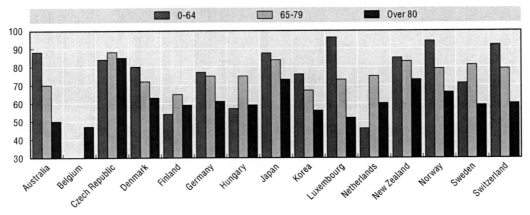

Note: Data for the following countries refer to different age breakdowns. For the 65-80 age group: recipients aged 60 years and over (Belgium); recipients aged 62 years and over (Slovak Republic); recipients aged 67 years and over (Norway). For Poland, the age breakdown for home-care users is 65-74 instead of 65-79 and over 75 instead of over 80. For Norway, the over 80 years age group may be underestimated. Czech home-care users include 300 000 recipients of attendance allowance. Polish data underestimate total LTC users. Data for Japan refer to 2006.

Source: OECD Health Data 2010, additional Australian, Japan and Swedish data.

StatLink 🔗 http://dx.doi.org/10.1787/888932400665

Box 1.1. **Dementia, Alzheimer's disease and LTC**

Psycho-geriatric conditions lead to reduced cognitive functioning and (increasingly) require other people not only to support the care recipient in performing ADL and/or IADL, but also to take over other aspects of the life, including day-to-day supervision, decision making and legal guardianship. For many carers, this is a long-term, physically, mentally and emotionally intense task, which becomes more burdensome, the further the illness progresses. Furthermore, although medical options supporting prevention of vascular dementia are available, for other types of dementia preventive measures are still unknown and medical treatment can, when in early stages, only ameliorate some effects of the disease (Groth *et al.*, 2009).

Recent analysis linked the prevalence of dementia to age groups (Ferri *et al.*, 2005, as reported in Alzheimer Europe, 2006). According to these calculations, some 12% of those aged between 80 and 84 years, and almost one in four of those aged over 85 years, suffer from dementia. With ageing populations, strong increases in the prevalence of dementia may be expected across the world (Brookmeyera *et al.*, 2007), while current global expenditure on dementia-related costs already amounts to 1% of GDP worldwide and 1.24% of GDP in high-income countries (Wimo and Prince, 2010).

> **Box 1.1. Dementia, Alzheimer's disease and LTC** (*cont.*)
>
> Improved diagnostics may lead to earlier recognition, which, if not accompanied by better preventive and treatment options, suggests that a higher than proportional growth of those in need of LTC will have a recognised form of dementia. Earlier detection may lead to increased quality of life, but will possibly be associated with higher treatment costs. The expected drop in the availability of family care and the increase in dementia-related problems – in many cases combined with other health problems – could pose financial and human-resource challenges to LTC systems. Pressures due to increasing dementia prevalence will be especially high in rural areas and for (mainly elderly) family carers, as younger and better educated people tend to move away from these areas, while access to health and care services is often poorer in rural areas.
>
> Several countries pay special attention to dementia-related problems in long-term care, for instance by developing an integral Alzheimer Plan (France, the United Kingdom), or by improving or creating special benefits for dementia-related care needs, which may fall outside the realm of ADL and IADL (Germany, Australia, Austria, Finland).
>
> *Source:* OECD 2009-10 Questionnaire on Long-term Care Workforce and Financing.

Between 1998 and 2008, the share of the population aged 65 years or older increased by 12% across the OECD, while the share of those aged 80 years and over increased by 32%. In most countries this also led to an increase in LTC use except in the Netherlands (2004-07) and in Switzerland (1998-2008) where the share of the population using LTC decreased somewhat. For the OECD countries for which data are available, only in Norway (2001-07), Switzerland (2000-07) and the United States (2000-08), institutional care use remained stable, at the level of the earliest year. In Sweden, institutional care use as share of the population decreased by 19% (1998-2008) accompanied by a steady increase of the share of home-care users, while in 12 other countries the share of the population using institutional care increased over the past five to ten years. The share of the population using home care saw a 15% decrease in the Netherlands (2004-07), was stable in Switzerland (2000-08) and grew in most other countries. The share of the population using home care increased by more than 70% in Hungary, and by around 50% in Japan, Luxembourg, and the Slovak Republic, with smaller increase in Sweden. Japan show sharp increases in total LTC use.

1.4. Who provides long-term care?

Family carers

Definitions of family carers vary, from wide to narrow, depending on variables such as the minimum number of hours per week spent caring, the minimum period spent caring, or wider or narrower inclusion of caring tasks. There can be limitations in the share of the population investigated (people in working age, adults or people of a certain age), and the pre-existing relationship of the care recipient with the family carer (spouse, a parent).

Chapter 3 analyses family carers considering the population aged over 50 years providing personal care support. However, different definitions lead to major differentiations in calculations. For instance, a wide definition led to the count of 100 million carers in the EU25 (Alber and Kohler, 2005), whereas a stricter definition (at least 20 hours care per week) counted 19 million (Grammenos, 2005), of which 9.6 million caring at least 35 hours care per week. According to *OECD Health Data 2010*, in the United Kingdom, only 0.7% of the population and in Luxembourg and the Slovak Republic around 1% of the population are family carers (2006), whereas in the United States 15% (2004) and in the Netherlands 21% of the population between 18-65 years of age (2008) are family carers.[1] These figures may suggest differences in the provision of family care across countries, reflecting different cultures, but data limitations and uneven definitions are a factor explaining these differences.

Crucially, however, even in estimates using narrow definitions, the size of the family care "workforce" is at least double that of the formal care workforce (*e.g.*, in Denmark), and in some cases it is estimated to be more than ten times the size of the formal-care workforce (*e.g.*, Canada, New Zealand, United States, the Netherlands). On average, around 70 to 90% of those who provide care are family carers (Fujisawa and Colombo, 2009).

Family carers are mostly women, especially spouses or adult daughters or daughter in-law. The more intense the care becomes, the more likely it is that women are the family carers, except in a spousal care situation (Glendinning *et al.*, 2009; NAC and AARP, 2005; ABS, 2008). On average, a family carer of frail adults is above 45 years of age. The most intense care is usually provided within a household.

Estimates for the United States suggest that family carers delivered care for an economic value[2] of USD 375 billion in 2007 (Houser and Gibson, 2008), higher than the estimated cost of USD 230 billion of paid LTC services in 2007 (Gleckman, 2009). For Europe, it has recently been calculated that the economic contribution of (unpaid) family work ranges – depending on the method used – between 20.1 and 36.8% of European GDP (Gianelli *et al.*, 2010). These and other studies point to the high economic value of family care.

However, providing care as a family member can lead to costs, for instance related to lost working days and foregone career opportunities. An Australia study estimates the opportunity cost of income forgone as a result of unpaid family caring at AUD 4.9 billion – equivalent to nearly 10% of the total expenditure on formal health care in Australia (Manaaki, 2009). Other costs may be related to the (mental) health of the carer (see Chapter 3). In some countries, family members may be legally required to contribute to the cost of formal care when care recipients are poor (Germany, Slovak Republic, France), while the family caring process may also lead to increased household expenditures, such as heating, medication, telephone costs, medical aids, and transport. This picture led many governments to support family carers (see Chapter 4).

Paid care workers

LTC workers (nurses and personal carers) account – in headcount – for 1.5% of the working-age population in selected OECD countries (Figure 1.6).[3] The lowest shares are found in countries where the formal LTC sector is still small, for example the Czech Republic and the Slovak Republic (0.3%). The highest share (3.6%) is found in Sweden, followed by Norway (2.9%) and Denmark (2.9%).

The size of the LTC workforce does not necessarily relate to the number of those in need. A proxy is the density per 100 people aged over 80 years, which varies from about five in the Slovak Republic to more than forty in Sweden and Norway (Figure 1.7). With a demand for care that may outgrow the size of the LTC workforce (Martin and King, 2008), some countries report shortages of workers in the sector, for example Spain, Austria,

Figure 1.6. **LTC workers represent a small share of the working-age population, 2008**

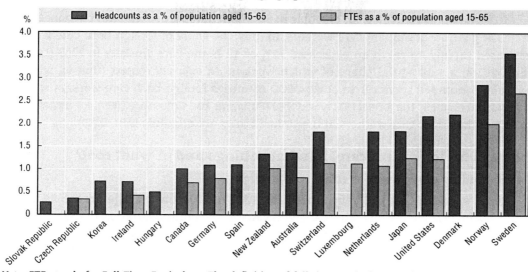

Note: FTE stands for Full Time Equivalent. The definition of full-time equivalents varies across countries. LTC workers include both nurses and personal caregivers. Data for Hungary, Canada, New Zealand, Luxembourg and the United States refer to 2006. Data for the Slovak Republic, Germany, Australia and Denmark refer 2007. Data for the Netherlands, Spain and Sweden refer to 2009. Data for Korea refer to 2010 (National Statistical Office). Data for Germany exclude 170 000 elderly care nurses (2007). Data for the Netherlands refer to ADL workers and nurses in employment only.

Source: OECD Health Data 2010 and Korea National Statistical Office.

StatLink ⬛ *http://dx.doi.org/10.1787/888932400684*

Figure 1.7. **The size of the LTC workforce is limited compared to the number of those in need**

LTC-worker density per 100 persons over 80 years across OECD countries, 2008 or latest available year

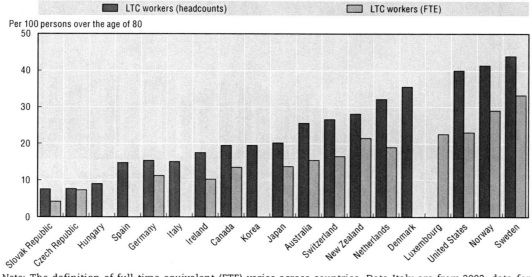

Note: The definition of full-time equivalent (FTE) varies across countries. Data Italy are from 2003; data for New Zealand and the United States are from 2006; data for the Slovak Republic, Germany, Australia, Denmark, Canada, Hungary and Luxembourg are from 2007; data for Spain, Korea, the Netherlands and Sweden are from 2009. Data from Germany exclude elderly care nurses (*circa* 170 000, 2007); data for the Netherlands are limited to nurses and ADL assistants in employment.

Source: OECD Health Data 2010 and Korea National Statistical Office.

StatLink ⬛ *http://dx.doi.org/10.1787/888932400703*

Canada, Finland and Italy (Fujisawa and Colombo, 2009; OECD, 2008), while almost all countries struggle with recruitment and retention (Chapter 6).

In some OECD countries, for example in Southern Europe, demand has been met by an increasing inflow of migrant care workers. In Italy, the share of foreign-born care workers increased rapidly, to reach an estimated 72% of all home-care workers in 2005 (Lamura et al., 2010), a substantial share of which work in an *informal context* (that is, without formally contracted services). In other OECD countries foreign-born care workers shape a substantial share of the *formal* LTC workforce (Fujisawa and Colombo, 2009), for instance up to 23% of the direct-care workers in the United States are migrants (PHI, 2010).

1.5. Who pays for long-term care, in what settings and at what cost?

Public funding plays a major role

Total spending on LTC[4] accounted for 1.5% of GDP on average across 25 OECD countries in 2008 (Figure 1.8). There is significant cross-country variation in the resources allocated to LTC, in line with observed differences in utilisation. This variation reflects differences in care needs, in the structure, and comprehensiveness, of formal LTC systems, as well as in family roles and caring cultures. There is also variation in the extent to which countries report both the health (so-called "nursing") and the social-care spending components of long-term care (Box 1.2).

Figure 1.8. **The share of public LTC expenditure is higher than that of private LTC expenditure in OECD countries**

Percentage of GDP, 2008

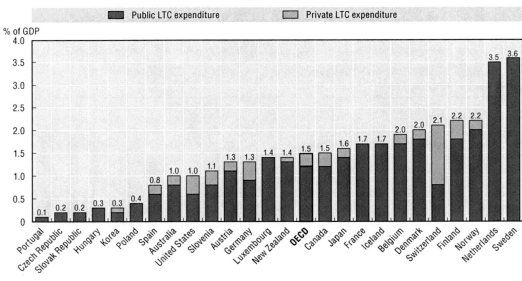

Note: Data for Austria, Belgium, Canada, the Czech Republic, Denmark, Hungary, Iceland, Norway, Portugal, Switzerland and the United States refer only to health-related long-term care expenditure. In other cases, expenditure relates to both health-related (nursing) and social long-term care expenditure. Social expenditures on LTC in the Czech Republic are estimated at 1% of GDP (*Source:* Czech Ministry of Health, 2009). Data for Iceland and the United States refer only to nursing long-term care in institutions. Data for the United States underestimate expenditure on fully private LTC arrangements. Data for Poland exclude infrastructure expenditure, amounting to about 0.25% of GDP in 2007. Data for the Netherlands do not reflect user co-payments, estimated at 8% of total AWBZ expenditure in 2007. Data for Australia refer to 2005; data for the Slovak Republic and Portugal refer to 2006; data for Denmark, Japan and Switzerland refer to 2007.

Source: OECD Health Data 2010.

StatLink ⟱ http://dx.doi.org/10.1787/888932400722

> ## Box 1.2. **Is LTC health or social spending?**
>
> Long-term care includes both health and social-care services. Clear definitions and harmonisation of the boundaries between health spending and social LTC spending help to ensure comprehensive and internationally comparable data on total expenditure on health. However, it is not always straightforward to separate the two components of LTC. Different countries may report the same spending item under health or under social services, sometimes following country practices or the division of responsibilities for long-term care across government authorities. Such variation in the treatment of long-term care spending reduces the comparability of some key indicators, such as the share of health expenditure to GDP.
>
> Total long-term care spending is calculated as the sum of *services of long-term health care* and *social services of long-term care*. The former, which represent health-related long-term care spending, include palliative care, long-term nursing care, personal care services, and health services in support of family care. The second, social services of LTC, include home help (*e.g.,* domestic services) and care assistance, residential care services, and other social services. In other words, the health component of LTC spending includes episodes of care where the main need is either medical or personal care services (ADL support), while services whose dominant feature is help with IADL are considered outside the health-spending boundaries. The WHO, OECD and Eurostat are reviewing definitions of these spending items and providing more guidance to countries on how to separate them; this is part of the process of revision of the System of Health Accounts manual.
>
> *Source:* Long-term care Guidelines under the Joint Eurostat, OECD and WHO Health Accounts data collection.

Sweden and the Netherlands allocate the highest share of their GDP to LTC, around 3.5%. Other Nordic countries (Norway, Finland, and Denmark), as well as Switzerland, similarly spend more than 2% of their GDP on LTC. France, Iceland and Japan allocate about 1.6-1.7%, while Canada is around the OECD average. At the opposite end of the spectrum, southern and eastern European countries, together with lower-income OECD members such as Mexico and Korea, spend relatively little on long-term care. In the case of Korea, which implemented a universal LTC insurance system in 2008 and whose population is rapidly ageing, spending is low but expected to grow in the future.

Long-term care is predominantly funded from public sources – even when taking underreporting of private expenditures into account.[5] The only exception is Switzerland, where the private share of LTC expenditure is over 60% of total spending, although some public social-care spending items are not reported. In aggregate, public and private LTC spending in Switzerland reaches the level of Nordic countries, but public LTC spending represents 0.8% of GDP, a figure comparable to public LTC spending in Germany and Australia. Private spending is also relatively high in the United States (40%), Germany (31%), Slovenia (27%) and Spain (25%). On average, the private share of total LTC spending is equivalent to about 15%, and is a lower fraction than the private share of total health spending (25%). Data on private LTC spending however may not include the high cost of board and lodging in nursing homes which, as explained in Chapters 7 and 9, account for the lion share of the cost borne by residential LTC users.

No place like home, yet spending on institutions remains high

People's preferences for receiving care in their homes do not translate into higher expenditures on home care. Most of the cost of long-term care still originates in the institutional sector (Figure 1.9), due, amongst others, to high worker density and high-cost infrastructure. Only in Denmark, Austria, New Zealand and Poland, does expenditure on home care exceed that of spending in institutional care.

Figure 1.9. **Spending on LTC in institutions is higher than spending at home in OECD countries**

Percentage of GDP, 2008

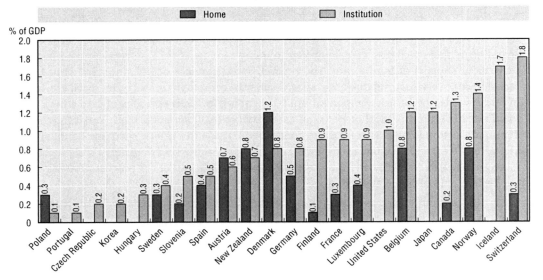

Note: Home care includes day-care expenditure. Data for Denmark, Japan and Switzerland refer to 2007; data for Portugal refer to 2006; and data for Luxembourg refer to 2005. Data for Poland exclude infrastructure expenditure, amounting to 0.25% GDP (2007). Data from the Czech Republic refer to health-related LTC expenditure only. Social expenditures on LTC are estimated at 1% of GDP (*Source:* Czech Ministry of Health, 2009).

Source: OECD Health Data 2010.

StatLink ᘔᓮᓬ *http://dx.doi.org/10.1787/888932400741*

Expenditure on LTC per capita varies widely across the OECD, from USD 42 (international dollar) in the Slovak Republic to USD 1 431 in the Netherlands. Average per capita expenditure across the OECD is USD 543 (Figure 1.10).

LTC is a labour intensive sector

Total LTC spending is associated with the density of workers per 1 000 people aged over 80 years (Figure 1.11). The Netherlands, Sweden and Norway, spend relatively high on LTC and have a high LTC-worker density. The Czech Republic, the Slovak Republic, Hungary and Korea have both low expenditure and low LTC-worker density.

Figure 1.10. **Significant variation in LTC expenditure among OECD countries**

Per capita spending in USD PPPs, 2008 or latest available year

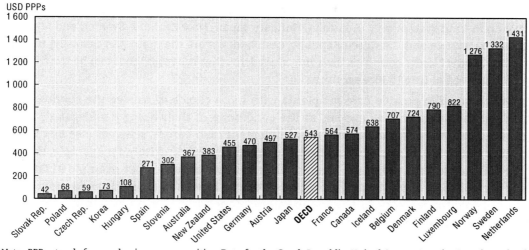

Note: PPPs stands for purchasing power parities. Data for the Czech Republic, United States, Austria, Canada, Iceland, Belgium, Denmark and Luxembourg refer to nursing long-term care only. Social expenditure on LTC in the Czech Republic is estimated at 1% of GDP (*Source:* Czech Ministry of Health, 2009). Data for Australia and Luxembourg refer to 2005; data for the Slovak Republic and Hungary refer to 2006; data for Denmark and Japan refer to 2007.
Source: OECD Health Data 2010.

StatLink http://dx.doi.org/10.1787/888932400760

Figure 1.11. **High LTC expenditure is associated with high LTC-worker density**

2008 or nearest year

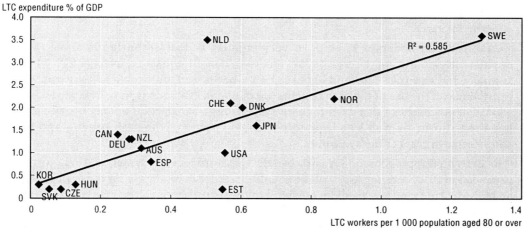

Note: Data for Canada, the Czech Republic, Denmark, Estonia, Hungary, New Zealand, Norway, Switzerland and the United States refer to long-term care nursing expenditure only. Social expenditure on LTC in the Czech Republic is estimated at 1% of GDP (*Source:* Czech Ministry of Health, 2009).
Source: OECD Health Data 2010.

StatLink http://dx.doi.org/10.1787/888932400779

1.6. What services are provided?

Long-term care services can be provided in-kind (with the care recipient solely in the position of care receiver), as an allowance paid to the family carer (see Chapter 4), or as a cash benefit for the care recipient to hire the required services as they see fit. In-kind services can be nursing or ADL services provided at home, can consist of services which can also have a respite function for the carer, such as day care, and furthermore can include institutional care provision such as in a nursing home and palliative care. Both in-kind service and cash benefits may require users to share a part of the cost and typically require an eligibility test. Most OECD countries provide both in-kind services and cash benefits, while a few countries have an in-kind system only (Australia, Hungary, Japan, New Zealand, Sweden and Mexico). In Austria, France and the Czech Republic, cash benefits are the main (but not only) form of benefits. Some Nordic countries have introduced voucher schemes[6] that can be used by the person in need of care to hire services.

Cash benefits provide care recipients with more choice to receive the services they need, by the provider they choose, at the conditions of their liking (Lundsgaard, 2005). However, countries vary in the way they implement cash-benefit schemes (see Box 1.3 for country examples). In Germany, Austria, the Czech Republic and Italy, for example, there is little control over the use of the benefit, while in other countries (for example in France), only accredited or approved service providers can be hired and expenditure is supervised. Similarly, countries vary in the requirements concerning hiring of family members. Table 1.1 offers an overview of cash-for-care schemes.

Box 1.3. **Cash-benefit schemes in selected OECD countries**

In the **United Kingdom**, direct cash payments have been offered as an alternative to pay personal carers since 1997. In 2010, a pilot programme of personal budgets in LTC was implemented. The direct payments take-up has been relatively low, showing significant local and user-group variations. Evaluations of the personal budgets scheme have shown evidence of cost-effectiveness in relation to social care outcomes, but weaker cost-effectiveness evidence in respect to psychosocial well-being. With regards to caregiving, preliminary evidence is promising, showing that personal budgets may be cost effective for carers.

Cash-for-care schemes have been very popular in **the Netherlands** since their implementation during the mid-1990s. The cash benefit equals on average EUR 14 500 annually, but can vary substantially based on a needs and an income assessment. The restrictions on the use of the cash benefits are minimal. Evaluations have indicated a high allocative efficiency of this cash-for-care system. High satisfaction among beneficiaries has been shown, as well as adequate purchasing power of the cash benefit, and low administrative costs of the system.

In 2008, a pilot programme for cash benefit was introduced in **Israel**, and was further expanded in 2010, covering 14.5% of the country. In order to be eligible for the cash benefit, an individual must receive medium or high-intensity care by a caregiver, who is not a family member. The amount of the cash benefit is 80% of the value of the in-kind benefit. Uptake of this scheme is still low, with varying take-up rates, depending on aspects such as age, income and benefit level. Beneficiaries in the cash-for-care scheme have shown greater satisfaction but decreased well-being, compared to individuals receiving in-kind benefits.

In **France**, the *Chèque emploi services universel* (CESU), allows the beneficiaries to pay for LTC services, or directly hire a caregiver. They can then seek reimbursement from the bank or an accredited national organisation. Among the advantages of this scheme are the optimisation of public expenditure and readability of public action. It is a policy priority, therefore, to promote the CESU through the National Solidarity Fund for Autonomy.

Source: OECD Expert Meeting on Long-term Care, November 2010.

Table 1.1. Cash-for-care schemes

Choice between in-kind and cash? Other information? / Y/N: if Y: Do the different benefits vary in value?	Programmes / National/subnational?	Eligibility / Target groups: Age/disability, remote areas	Income-tested?	Asset-tested?	Tax free?	Benefit levels (monthly amounts)	Use restrictions?
Austria[1,2] No	All programmes are national / Pflegegeld	Needs	×			EUR 148.30 to EUR 1 562.10 (2007)	
	24-hour care benefit	At least level 3 Pflegegeld			×	EUR 550 for an employee, EUR 275 for an independent worker	
Belgium[1,2] No	Dementia care benefit	Needs			×	EUR 1 200 to EUR 2 400	
	Programmes national except two: Flemish region and Brussels area						
	Allowance for assistance of the elderly	Income, needs, aged over 65 or veteran	×		× (subnational)	Per annum EUR 925.06-EUR 6 209.71 (2010)	
	Zorgverzekering/Flemish Care Insurance	Needs			× (subnational)	EUR 130 flat allowance	
Czech Republic[2] In-kind benefits not available	Care Allowance Appr. 10% of all persons aged over 65 receive care allowance	At least one year "dependent on care"				CZK 3 000 for I level); CZK 12 000 for IV (total dependency) (2009)	Benefits for services or care received from relatives
Denmark[1,2,3] No	Availability varies according to municipality. BPA (Citizen Controlled Personal Assistance)	Minumum 20 hours help per week needed				Calculated by type and duration of assistance by local council; no minimum or maximum	Not for nursing care
Estonia[1,2] According to local governments, in-kind and cash benefits are available depending on needs and income. From EUR 13 to EUR 41 for individuals of pensionable age and EUR 17 to EUR 54 for persons below pensionable age (2010)							
Finland[1,2,3] No	Care Allowance for Pensioners	Aged over 16, at least one year disabled, receiving disability or retirement pension. Per 2010 extended to carees in institutional care			×	Three monthly rates depending on needs and cost of care: EUR 57.32 to EUR 387.26 (2010)	
	Disability Allowance	Aged over 16, requiring care for more than six months			×	EUR 199.71 to EUR 387.26	
France[1,2] Cash and in-kind benefits are separate	All programmes operate at a national level; APA: by public health insurance, administered regionally						
	Allocation personnalisée d'autonomie (APA)	Aged over 60, six dependency levels	×		×	EUR 529.56-EUR 1 235.65 (2009)	For assistance costs
	Allocation d'éducation d'enfant handicapé (AEEH)	80% disability for a child, at least 50% disability for special care. Supplement to APA			×	EUR 93.41 to EUR 1 029.10. Single parents gets more (2010)	Education and care costs of disabled child
	The PCH, intended to help fund certain expenses related to disability	Additional to AEEH: annual resources less than EUR 23 571, problems with more than two established activities	×		×	Regional disparities Techical aids: Max. EUR 3 960 (three years) Housing modification: Max. EUR 10 000 (ten years) Transport aid: Max. EUR 5 000 (five years)	For various social care and support

Table 1.1. Cash-for-care schemes (cont.)

Choice between in-kind and cash? Other information? Y/N: if Y: Do the different benefits vary in value?	Programmes National/subnational?	Eligibility Target groups: Age/disability, remote areas	Income-tested?	Asset-tested?	Tax free?	Benefit levels (monthly amounts)	Use restrictions?
Germany[1,2,3] Yes. Cash benefits are lower in value than in-kind	LTC insurance. 52% of carees use cash (2008)	Be insured (two years), needs test, no prior legal or accident compensation insurance claims			✗	EUR 225-EUR 685 (2010)	
Italy[1,2] Cash and in-kind benefits are separate	*Indennità di accompagnamento* (Companionship Indemnity); Supplementary care allowances	Universal benefit, no age restrictions; Locally decided, needs test			✗	Flat rate: EUR 472 to EUR 457.66 (2009); Varying rates according to local authority	
Ireland[1,2] Cash benefits depend on resource availability	Home Care Package (Home Care Grant)	Aged over 65, in need of assistance to remain in the community			✗		
Korea[1,2] Yes. Cash benefits are lower in value than in-kind benefits	National Programme: Care Allowance	At least one of three criteria: 1. Live remote with few facilities 2. Unable to use LTC facilites due to disasters 3. Needing care but unsuitable for institutional LTC due to physical or mental condition			✗	Flat rate of WON 150 000 (*circa* EUR 84)	
Luxembourg[1,2] Yes. Cash benefits are lower in value than in-kind benefits	National Programme: Cash allowance for care/*Prestations en espèces*	Eligibility: Severely disabled, requiring ≤ 14 hours of assistance weekly			✗ (up to EUR 3 600 a year)	EUR 267 to EUR 1 100	Cash for the first 10.5 hours of care per week
Mexico[1] No	*National Programa 70 y más*	Eligibility: Aged over 70, living in a locality of up to 30 000 inhabitants; not receiving aid from *Oportunidades*; attending bi-monthly medical consultations			✗	MXN 500 bimonthly	
	Oportunidades Program	Aged over 70			✗	MXN 295	
Netherlands[1,2] Yes. Cash benefits 15% lower than value of benefits in kind	Personal Care Budgets (*Persoonsgebonden budget*, PGB) 12% of carees use PGB (2008)	Eligibility: No age criteria. Needs assessment based on duration and care by family				Average annual budget EUR 15 000-EUR 18 000	All expenses except for 1.5% must be justified. Unspent funds are returned. PGB is stopped after fraud
New Zealand[1,2] Cash and in-kind benefits are complementary	Disability allowances	Eligibility: Disability test, suffering from disability for six months	✗		✗	Maximum NZD 56.98 per week (April 2010)	
Slovenia[1,2] Attendance allowance given to those aged over 65 suffering from chronic disorders or at least 70% reduced mobility. Not income tested but cannot be chosen in lieu of in-kind benefits by the care recipient							

Table 1.1. Cash-for-care schemes (cont.)

Choice between in-kind and cash? Other information? Y/N: if Y: Do the different benefits vary in value?	Programmes National/subnational?	Eligibility Target groups: Age/disability, remote areas	Income-tested?	Asset-tested?	Tax free?	Benefit levels (monthly amounts)	Use restrictions?
Spain[1,2] Yes. Cash benefits varies with programme (el Programa Individual de Atención)	National, implemented at regional level	Assessment of the degree of dependency by the Scale of Dependency test				Calculation of cost and hours of care	
	Allowance for caree to hire services	Dependency grade	✗		✗	EUR 400 to EUR 831.47 (2009)	Hiring through accredited centers
	Allowance for caree receiving informal care	Carer must be a relative of caree; in rural areas a neighbour is eligible	✗		✗	EUR 300 to EUR 519.13 (2009)	To compensate informal carer
	Allowance for personal assistance	High dependency	✗		✗	EUR 609 to EUR 812 (2009)	Expenses justified; carer must have professional qualifications
Sweden[1,2,3] Cash and in-kind benefit are complementary	National, implemented locally	Differences across municipalities. Minimum need of 17 hours/week					
	Attendance allowance				✗	Estimated SEK 3 000 per month	
	Assistance allowance	Aged over 65, ADL, requiring over 20 hours of help a week			✗	Amount according to estimated hours of required assistance	
Switzerland[1,2] No. Cash and in-kind benefit are complementary	"Helplessness" Allowance (Allocation pour impotent/API) of AVS/AI	Moderate or severe impairment, not eligible for Disability Allowance from Accident Insurance			✗	CHF 456-CHF 1 824. When at home, cash benefit is half	
United Kingdom[1,2] No. Cash benefits and in-kind benefits are complementary	National, implemented locally						
	Attendance Allowance (AA)	Age 65+, requires ≥ six months assistance	✗	✗	✗	GBP 47.80-GBP 71.40 a week	
	Independent Living Fund (ILF)	Age 16-65, receiving highest rate of Disability Living Allowance; the higher rate of AA or at least the financially equivalent rate of Constant AA		✗		Maximum of GBP 475 weekly	Restricted for support and IADL. Not to hire a relative, but exceptions
	Disability Allowance	For children and adults under age 65 who need help with personal care or have walking difficulties, because they are physically or mentally disabled			✗	Care component: Three rates depending on level of care needed: GBP 18.95, GBP 47.80 or GBP 71.40 a week. Mobility component: Two rates depending on level of mobility needs: GBP 8.95 or GBP 49.85 a week	
	Direct payments	Local Community Care Assessment	✗		✗	Varies according to needs assessment	For LTC services/equipment. Not to hire a relative, but exceptions
United States[1,2]	There are federal incentives for states and some "experiments" with cash-for-care schemes. The CLASS Act, which promotes a voluntary insurance programme, will offer cash benefits for use on LTC nursing home or home care costs. Until now, several states, including California, Colorado, Kansas, Maine, Michigan, Oregon, Washington, Florida and New Jersey have tested cash benefits for ADL/IADL assistance. As of 2010, a national cash benefits programme for LTC does not exist						

1. Benefits in kind.
2. Benefits in cash.
3. Vouchers.
Source: OECD 2009-10 Questionnaire on Long-term Care Workforces and Financing.

In some cases, cash benefits are provided when no or few formal (public) services are available *(e.g.,* Spain, some central European countries). The Korean LTC insurance system provides cash benefits only for those living in remote areas, having difficulties utilising LTC facilities due to natural disasters or similar reasons or to those unsuitable for admission in an institutional setting.

A cash-for-care programme aims to *contribute* to the costs of care, but does not necessarily provide sufficient payment to buy all the needed care. In Germany, the value of cash benefits is set at a lower level than the cost of equivalent in-kind services. In some countries, cash benefits can offer income support *(e.g.,* Disability Living Allowance in the United Kingdom, Slovenia and the Slovak Republic). The Finnish care allowance for pensioners shows characteristics of both: it is provided as income support and eligibility depends on the duration of disability, but the title refers to care. This also applies to the Belgian APA/THAB[7] (an income-support measure for those unable to cover LTC costs, based on an income and needs' assessment. New Zealand's disability allowance and the invalid's benefit are income-support measures, similar to the invalid benefit, which are described in terms of a share of wages. The Irish disability allowance, aimed at those at least one year disabled, and of working age (aged 16-66 years), too, aims to provide an income.

Countries differ in the way the benefit amount is calculated. In some cases *(e.g.,* Austria, the Czech Republic) it is a flat rate, which depends on the need for care; in others *(e.g.,* France, the United Kingdom and Spain) income or asset testing is also required, which may lead to substantial reduction of the available amounts. In Spain, for instance, those eligible but above a certain income ceiling may receive only 40% of the allowance.

Countries vary also in the tax treatment of the cash benefit. Whereas most care recipients will receive the benefit tax free (the Netherlands, the Czech Republic, Germany), in Luxembourg benefits above EUR 3 600 annually are taxed.

The Netherlands is the only known country where unspent budget needs to be returned, and, as in Luxembourg, the cash scheme can be cancelled in case of fraud (then the user will have no option but to receive care in kind).

1.7. How did countries get here? Where are they going?

Table 1.2 summarises recent policy development in LTC schemes and systems across the OECD. Some countries have implemented changes or reforms affecting only specific aspects of the system, without however changing the main features. For instance, Mexico, a "young" OECD country, installed its first National Gerontology Plan. The Belgian region Flanders introduced a mandatory LTC insurance which supplements the main public LTC coverage. The Swiss cantons started a human resource planning exercise for health and long-term care. Other countries – Germany and France being an example – face a more or less continuous stream of policy adjustments and changes to their system. France is discussing reforms and, potentially, the creation of a fifth social security pillar (early 2011). The United Kingdom (England) has produced in recent years a number of strategic plans on specific issues and target groups, for instance on Independent Living (2006), a Carers Strategy (UK HM Government, 2008), a strategy aimed at older workers that includes the issue of combining work and other commitments such as care (2006) and a vision for adult social care (2010). France has developed a targeted Alzheimer Plan (2008-12), as the United Kingdom did in 2009, while other countries have developed broad strategy

Table 1.2. **Selected LTC policy changes over the past ten years in OECD countries at a glance**

	Title of policy or reform	Coverage			Use		Carer support	Provision	
		Financing	Cost sharing	Access (eligibility) and changes in services	Benefits	Choice		Workforce	Quality
Australia			♦	♦	♦	♦		♦	♦
Austria					♦		♦	♦	
Belgium	Care insurance (Flanders) (2003)								
	3rd protocol: Conversion of rest home beds in nursing home beds (2005-11)	♦							
Canada					♦		♦	♦	
Czech Republic		♦		♦	♦	♦			♦
Denmark	Quality reform (2007)							♦	♦
Finland	National Framework for High-quality Services for Older People (2008)			♦	♦				♦
France	Old Age Solidarity Strategy (2007-10)	♦	♦	♦		♦	♦	♦	♦
	Alzheimer Plan (2008-12)								
Germany	LTC insurance reform (2008)	♦	♦	♦	♦	♦	♦	♦	♦
Ireland	Fair deal (2009)	♦	♦	♦					
Iceland	A new strategy plan for elderly care (2008)		♦	♦		♦		♦	♦
Japan	Partial Revision LTC Insurance Act (2005-06)	♦	♦		♦			♦	
	Revision of LTC Insurance Act (2009)								
Korea	National LTC insurance (2008)	♦	♦	♦	♦			♦	♦
Luxembourg			♦		♦	♦			♦
Mexico	Institutional Gerontology Plan (2006)								
Netherlands	Social Support Act (2007)	♦		♦	♦			♦	
	Care Innovation Platform (2007)								
New Zealand			♦	♦			♦	♦	♦
Portugal	National Network for Integrated Continuous Care (RNCCI) fully implemented in 2016 (2006)	♦		♦	♦				
Slovakia					♦	♦	♦		
Spain	Long-term care law (2006)	♦	♦	♦		♦	♦	♦	
Switzerland								♦	
United Kingdom	Supporting people with long-term conditions (2005)								
	Carers Strategy (2008, refreshed 2010)			♦			♦		
	Working to put people first (2008)								
	Dementia strategy (2009)								
United States	Increasing grants to States for Money Follows Person Programme (2005)								
	More "waivers' assisting states" home-based care programmes (2005)								
	Private LTC insurees can protect more assets if ending up spending down for Medicaid (2005)	♦	♦		♦	♦		♦	
	New opportunities (with increased federal co-funding) for States to offer home-based care services (2010)								
	Class Act (2010, to be implemented 2012)								

Note: Policy developments may refer to more than one cell. For instance the introduction of a (mandatory) LTC system may relate amongst others to access, benefits, co-payments, financing and choice. Coverage issues will be discussed more in depth in Chapters 7 to 9, carers issues in Chapters 3 and 4, workforce issues in Chapters 5 and 6.
Source: OECD 2009-10 Questionnaire on Long-term Care Workforce and Financing, and additional documentation (such as National Strategy reports for Social Protection and Inclusion 2008-10).

documents which still need to be operationalised such as the Icelandic New Strategy for Elderly Care or the Finnish National Framework for High Quality Services for Older People.

Coverage reforms

Coverage reforms relate to *financing* (including *cost sharing*), and *access to services* (including the number and type of). Over the last ten years, a growing number of OECD countries have implemented or expanded policies aimed at increasing LTC coverage and services, while also aiming to improve service provision to specific groups such as those with severe disability or suffering from dementia.

Seven countries made changes to their *financing for LTC*. Two new financing LTC systems were installed, one tax-based (in Spain, 2006), and one based on a national compulsory insurance (Korea, 2008). Both have consequences for access (defining eligibility), benefits (what is covered, what not), payments for (what do citizens pay under what circumstances) and have workforce repercussions (because both countries implemented rules about who can provide services).

Germany, which had introduced LTC insurance in 1994, implemented several ongoing reforms to the system. For instance, in 2004 Germany required retirees to contribute to LTC insurance, while, since 2005, those without children have to pay higher contributions. In 2008, portability across insurers was improved, while market incentives were introduced in 2007 and LTC insurance was made compulsory also for high-income people in 2008. Japan reviews its LTC insurance every three years and has adjusted premia and providers' fees three times, while, in 2006, community and preventive services where strengthened. The Irish *A Fair Deal* (2009) changes the way co-payments and income and asset testing are adjusted to prevent extreme poverty and make access to private providers easier. New Zealand, too, is phasing out asset testing for admission to nursing homes. The Netherlands is perhaps the only country that cut back its system. In 2007, IADL support was transferred out of LTC insurance to municipalities' responsibilities. Per 2012, the CLASS Act is planned to be introduced in the United States, as part of its 2010 Affordable Care Act.[8] CLASS is a privately financed, government provided, voluntary insurance scheme that aims to provide a daily cash allowance to people in need for care after five years enrolment.

Cost-sharing reforms take different shapes. For example, Korea requires a 20% cost sharing on institutional care and a 15% user co-payment for home care, which includes ADL support, as well as for services such as transport, day/night care, short-term respite care and equipment such as wheelchairs and orthopaedic mattresses. In Australia, several changes in cost sharing were implemented over the years to bring more equity between pensioners and self-employed retirees, and reduce co-payments for those with few assets. As mentioned, the Irish *Fair Deal* (2009) substantially changed asset-testing rules, by capping cost sharing at 15% of the asset value over a maximum period of three years.

Access-related reforms involve changes in eligibility procedures or changes in scope and types of services available in the system. Several countries, find that a "one-size-fits-all" assessment and service provision requires adjustment over time as new considerations and target groups may come into play, or as the current model does not fit needs. Thus, some countries have improved benefits for those with severe disabilities and/or those suffering from dementia. Australia simplified its eligibility procedures, while expanding residential support in remote areas as well as increasing residential capacity from 100 places per 1 000 people aged over 70 years in 1985 to 113 in 2011. Finland aimed for integrated assessment of an individual's need in its 2008 National Framework for high-quality services for older people. Both Ireland and France, the latter in the context of the 2007-10 Old Age Solidarity Strategy and the 2008-12 National Alzheimer Plan, have set targets for increasing services in the community, where Finland aims to reduce residential care use from 6.5 to 3% of the population by 2012 and encourage community care. New Zealand implemented in 2008 a national assessment tool.

Use-related reforms

Use-related reforms refer to *benefits and choice.* Most OECD countries expanded LTC-related benefits, including tailored specifics for those living in rural areas and suffering from dementia. The use of cash benefits, information dissemination via for example the internet, and competition between providers are among the options used to improve consumer choice of provider and benefits.

Several countries improved their *benefit package.* For example, Australia, Austria, Finland, Luxembourg (for home and palliative care) and Germany included benefits for special target groups, such as those with severe disabilities or those suffering from dementia. In 2009, Luxembourg started dedicated targeted training for LTC workers. Germany expanded benefits by the (2009) introduction of disease-specific activity measures in the LTC insurance. In 2004, Canada developed a ten-year plan to strengthen health care which provides some short-term home-care services free of charge. Finland aims to improve care provision at home and reduce institutional care. Australia increased benefits for those suffering from severe disability or dementia, and expanded public funding for transitional care services between the health and LTC system.

User choice is increasingly relevant. Cash benefits are one main vehicle being introduced in ever more countries (see Table 1.1). Other options have included providing additional information for users to navigate through the system, for example via easy-to-use websites (Australia). The United States has increased federal co-funding for *money follow the person* programmes, started in 2005. These programmes stimulate service provision at the place where the person in need of care wants it delivered, for instance in his own home, and increased funding for the states to assist states' home-based care programmes in 2010. Some Nordic European countries introduced or expanded market incentives to stimulate private providers into the market.

Supporting carers

Increasingly OECD countries implement policies to support carers, for example through improved options for care leave, either paid (Canada) or unpaid (Germany), or the introduction of targeted carer allowances. Germany, Austria, and the Slovak Republic pay pension contributions to carers or have introduced special pension rights for carers (Spain), while Austria also pays health-insurance contributions and Germany provides low-rate unemployment insurance. Similarly, the Slovak Republic introduced a carer allowance for those below a certain income threshold in 2009. The United Kingdom published a Carers Strategy (UK HM Government, 2008), announcing several measures to support family carers such as expansion of respite services, measures to support carers to (re-)enter the job market, actions to improve support for young carers, General Practitioners and other professionals training to recognise and support carers. Pilot projects have been started on annual health checks for carers, while the right to request flexible working time for carers was extended.

Provision of service reforms

Provision of service reforms relate to the LTC *workforce* and to *quality of care*. Many countries report *workforce* related measures. Some measures include a wage increase, as in Japan (2009), funding of human resource development initiatives and supporting efforts to increase retention. Canada supports initiatives to allow nurses to devote 20% of their working time to professional development (Newfoundland/Labrador). The German federal government, in 2005, took over the cost of adult re-education in the third year of retraining, thus stimulating supply, while Luxembourg implemented a major training programme on palliative care to combine with its new palliative care benefit. Austria (2007) and Italy (2002, 2009) took measures to regulate the foreign-born care workers working in home care, while France aims to increase the worker density per resident in an LTC facility and set in place a recruitment and job-creation programme (2008). New Zealand developed workforce funding initiatives (2007), while England aims for further professionalisation of the social care workforce through a variety of means (2009). Austria has developed means for lower-level care workers to perform nursing or medical tasks, under supervision. Other measures include the implementation of legal qualification requirements (Spain, Austria, Germany), improving benefit packages for LTC workers (Belgium) or increasing worker density in certain specific care settings (France, Germany).

Issues relating to *quality* have become increasingly important. Australia set up a new quality system, including a review of accreditation procedures for providers, improved monitoring and dealing with complaints. The Czech Republic and the Slovak Republic implemented oversight policies, authorisation and compliance of providers' quality, while Germany enhanced quality supervision and aims at enhancing quality *management* of providers, together with improved consumer voice. Ireland published in 2009 the National Quality Standards for Residential Care Settings for older people, while Austria produced a handbook on dementia and Luxembourg has installed a Committee on quality of care.

Other measures include:

- stimulating the volunteering services (Switzerland, Germany);
- the installation of an Office for Older People within the government structure in Ireland (2008);
- conditional adjustment payments in Australia, aimed to strengthen management and governance for provider organisations that are willing to enrol into the scheme, as well as support for remote facilities;
- measures that aim to cross the borders between health care and long-term care, for instance by dedicated staff (United Kingdom), by the introduction of more transfer facilities (Australia) or by policies that enable continuity of worker across these borders, by introducing more options for co-operation and stimulating integrated care (Germany).

Workforce policies aim both at increasing the supply and the quality of care workers. This led to professionalisation initiatives and targeted training. Quality oversight – especially related to institutional care – and incentives to improve quality are the most common. In 2007, the Netherlands installed a Care Innovation Platform, aimed at the development, structural dissemination and implementation of innovations in (long-term) care provision.

1.8. Conclusions

LTC is a growing sector of the economy, serving predominantly people aged 65 years and over, who need assistance with the activities of daily living (ADL). Even though the older population is not the only target group, demand for LTC is highly age-related. LTC is a labour intensive sector comprised of formal workforce, but mostly of family carers, and in particular women. Despite that, the size of LTC workforce does not necessarily reflect the number of those in need, resulting often in shortages.

The structure and financing of LTC systems vary markedly between countries. The majority of LTC cost originates from the institutional sector, despite people's preferences to receive care in their homes. These costs are mostly funded from public sources. As far as benefits are concerned, these can either be in-kind or cash allowances. Cash benefits may either be granted to the family carer, or to the care recipient, allowing more choice regarding the services needed. All these methods have advantages and drawbacks.

Over the last decade, an increasing number of OECD countries has implemented or expanded policies targeted at the increase of LTC coverage and services, while at the same time aiming at improving service provision to those who are most in need. Some countries, such as Germany and Canada, have implemented policies to support carers, while others, such as New Zealand and Japan, have introduced system reforms related to the LTC formal workforce and quality. Many have introduced or are discussing reforms in financing and coverage of LTC.

Notes

1. Of these Dutch working-age family carers, 40% cares more than eight hours per week, 66% cares more than three months, 74% cares more than eight hours per week and/or more than three months, and 31% cares both more than eight hours per week *and* more than three months (SCP, 2010).

2. These place a monetary value to the work of unpaid carers, by multiplying the estimated number of hours of informal care by an estimated hourly value, based on the minimum wage and/or the average wage for formal LTC workers.

3. National data collections can underestimate private care provision and self-employed workers.

4. Total formal spending excludes the economic value and costs of family caring and other informal care. Spending data underestimate the private share.

5. Data tend to be limited to financial flows monitored by governments (*e.g.* mandatory co-payments), and there is therefore underreporting of direct out-of-pocket payments. Private LTC spending data do not cover informal payments.

6. The voucher represents a monetary value to be used for buying services such as care provided at home (or from home), in institutional settings, or through other services, such as night or day care, and palliative services. See Chapter 10 for a discussion on the impact of using vouchers on efficiency.

7. APA/THAB: *Allocation pour personnes âgées/Tegemoetkoming Hulp aan Bejaarden.*

8. CLASS stands for Community Living Services and Support.

References

Alber, J. and U. Köhler (2005), *Health and Care in an Enlarged Europe,* European Foundation for the Improvement of Living and Working Conditions, Dublin.

Alzheimer Europe (2006), *Dementia in Europe Yearbook 2006,* Luxembourg.

ABS – Australian Bureau of Statistics (2008), *A Profile of Caregivers in Australia,* Canberra.

Brookmeyera, R., E. Johnsona, K. Ziegler-Grahamb and H. Michael Arrighic (2007), "Forecasting the Global Burden of Alzheimer's Disease", *Alzheimer's & Dementia,* Vol. 3, pp. 186-191.

Ferri, C.P., M. Prince, C. Brayne, H. Brodaty, L. Fratiglioni, M. Ganguli, K. Hall, K. Hasegawa, H. Hendrie, Y. Huang, A. Jorm, C. Mathers, P.R. Menezes, E. Rimmer and M. Scazufca (2005), "Alzheimer's Disease International Global Prevalence of Dementia: A Delphi Consensus Study", *The Lancet*, Vol. 366, pp. 2112-2117.

Fujisawa, R. and F. Colombo (2009), "The Long-term Care Workforce: Overview and Strategies to Adapt Supply to a Growing Demand", *OECD Health Working Paper*, No. 44, OECD Publishing, Paris.

Giannelli, G.C., L. Mangiavacchi and L. Piccoli (2010), "GDP and the Value of Family Caretaking: How Much Does Europe Care?", *IZA Discussion Paper*, No. 5046, Bonn.

Gleckman, H. (2009), *The Future of Long-term Care: What Is Its Place in the Health Reform Debate?*, Urban-Brookings Tax Policy Centre, accessible at *www.taxpolicycenter.org/UploadedPDF/ 411908_longterm_care.pdf*.

Glendinning, C., F. Tjadens, H. Arksey, M. Moree, N. Moran and H. Nies (2009), "Care Provision Within Families and its Socio-Economic Impact on Care Providers", *Report for the European Commission DG EMPL. Negotiated Procedure VT/2007/114*, Social Policy Research Unit, University of York/Vilans, York/Utrecht.

Government of France (2008), *National Plan for Alzheimer and Related Diseases 2008-2012*.

Government of Portugal (2008), *National Strategy for Social Protection and Social Inclusion 2008-2010*.

Grammenos, S. (2005), *Implications of Demographic Ageing in the Enlarged EU in the Domains of Quality of Life, Health Promotion and Health Care. Studies on the Policy Implications of Demographic Changes in National and Community Policies*, Lot 5 Contract VC/2004/0076, No. S12.396079, Brussels.

Groth, H., R. Kingholz and M. Wehling (2009), "Future Demographic Challenges in Europe: the Urgency to Improve the Management of Dementia", *WDA-HSG Discussion Paper Series on Demographic Issues*, No. 2009/4.

Houser, A. and M. Gibson (2008), "Valuing the Unvaluable. The Economic Value of Family Caregiving. 2008 Update", *Insight on the Issues*, Vol. 13, November, accessible at *http://assets.aarp.org/rgcenter/il/ i13_caregiving.pdf*.

Lamura, G., C. Chiatti, M. Di Rosa, M.G. Mechiorre, F. Barbabella, C. Greco, A. Principi and S. Santin (2010), "Migrant Workers in the Long-term Care Sector : Lessons from Italy", *Health and Ageing Newsletter*, No. 22, Geneva Association, April.

Lundsgaard, J. (2005), "Consumer Direction and Choice in Long-term Care for Older Persons, Including Payments for Informal Care. How Can it Help Improve Care Outcomes, Employment and Fiscal Sustainability?", *OECD Health Working Paper*, No. 20, OECD Publishing, Paris.

Manaaki, T. (2009), "How Should We Care for the Carers, Now and into the Future?", National Health Committee of New Zealand, accessed on 5 February 2010 at *www.nhc.health.govt.nz/moh.nsf/ pagescm/7661/$File/caring-for-the-carers-nhc-2010.pdf*.

Martin, B. and D. King (2008), *Who Cares for Older Australians? A Picture of the Residential and Community-based Aged Care workforce, 2007*, Australian Government, Department of Health and Ageing/National Institute of Labour Studies, Flinders University and Commonwealth of Australia.

Ministerie van VWS (2007), *Arbeidsmarktbrief: Werken aan zorg*, MEVA/ABA/2807123, Netherlands.

NAC and AARP (2005), "Caregiving in the US", National Alliance for Caregiving and American Association of Retired Persons, accessible at *www.caregiving.org/data/04execsumm.pdf*.

Ngai, L.R. and C.A. Pissarides (2009), "Welfare Policy and the Distribution of Hours of Work", *CEP Discussion Paper*, No. 962, December 2009.

OECD (2008), *International Migration Outlook*, OECD Publishing, Paris.

PHI (2010), "Who Are the Direct Care Workers?", *Facts*, No. 3, February 2010 update, PHI, New York.

SCP (2010), *Mantelzorg uit de doeken*, Sociaal en Cultureel Planbureau, Den Haag.

UK Department of Health (2005), "Supporting People with Long-term Conditions. An NHS and Social Care Model to Support Local Innovation and Integration", Department of Health, Leeds.

UK HM Government (2008), "Carers at the Heart of 21st-century Families and Communities. A Caring System on Your Side. A Life of Your Own", accessible at *http://image.guardian.co.uk/sys-files/ Society/documents/2008/06/10/carers_strategy.pdf*.

Wimo, A. and M. Prince (2010), *World Alzheimer Report 2010. The Global Economic Impact of Dementia*, Alzheimer's Disease International, accessible at *www.alz.co.uk/research./files/worlalzheimer report2010.pdf*.

Chapter 2

Sizing Up the Challenge Ahead: Future Demographic Trends and Long-term Care Costs

Pressures on long-term care (LTC) systems are expected to grow in the future, for at least four reasons. First, although the speed at which populations are ageing varies considerably across countries, and despite uncertainties about future trends in disability among the population, demographic transformations will increase demand for LTC services in all societies. Second, changing societal models – such as declining family size, changes in residential patterns of people with disabilities and rising female participation in the formal labour market – are likely to contribute to a decline in the availability of family carers, leading to an increase in the need for paid care. Third, as societies become wealthier, individuals demand better quality and more responsive social-care systems. People want care systems that are patient-oriented and that can supply well co-ordinated care services. Fourth, technological change enhances possibilities for long-term care services at home but may require a different organisation of care. These factors will create upward pressure on the demand for long-term care services. They will raise pressure for improving the provision of care services and their performance, and, therefore, their cost. This chapter presents demographic forecasts for OECD countries, and projections on family carers in selected OECD countries and long-term care costs.

The statistical data for Israel are supplied by and under the responsibility of the relevant Israeli authorities. The use of such data by the OECD is without prejudice to the status of the Golan Heights, East Jerusalem and Israeli settlements in the West Bank under the terms of international law.

2.1. Future demographic trends: Growing LTC demand

Over the next decades, OECD countries will continue to age, leading to unprecedented shares of their population being 80 years and over. In 1950, less than 1% of the global population was aged over 80 years old. By 2050, this share is expected to reach 4%. The most important increase is expected for the OECD countries, where, by 2050, almost 10% of the total population will be very old (compared to 1% in 1950) (Figure 2.1).

Figure 2.1. **The share of the population aged over 80 years old will increase rapidly**

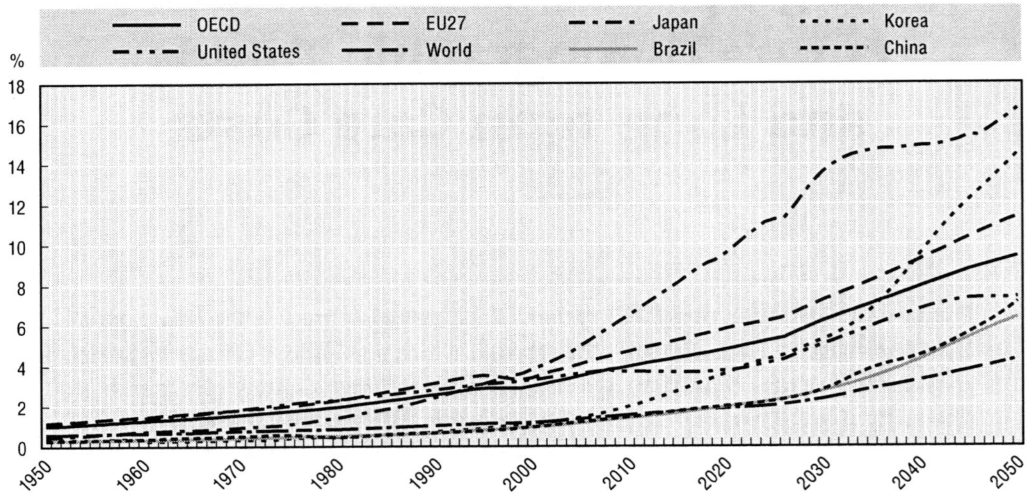

Source: OECD Labour Force and Demographic Database, 2010.

StatLink 🔗 http://dx.doi.org/10.1787/888932400874

As shown in Figure 2.2, in the OECD, the share of those aged 80 years and over is expected to increase from 4% in 2010 to 9.4% in 2050 (OECD Demographic and Labour Market Database, 2010). In Japan, but also in Germany, Korea and Italy, the projected shares of those aged 80 years and over will be the highest: around 15%. South Korea stands out as it will experience the largest absolute change in its share of the very old people, increasing from about 2% in 2010 to about 15% in 2050. For some countries the increase will be more gradual and reach relatively lower levels. These include Australia, Iceland, Ireland, Luxembourg, Norway and Sweden, where the share of the oldest old is expected to increase by less than 5 percentage points between 2010 and 2050, and reach levels under 9%.

The growth of the share of the very old will affect the future demand for long-term care. Although theories differ about the expected relationships between the ageing of societies and the need for care, all suggest that this will increase. The major differences relate to expectations about the amount and intensity of the increase, as well as to the moment at which the need for care will set in (Box 2.1).

Figure 2.2. **The shares of the population aged over 65 and 80 years in the OECD will increase significantly by 2050**

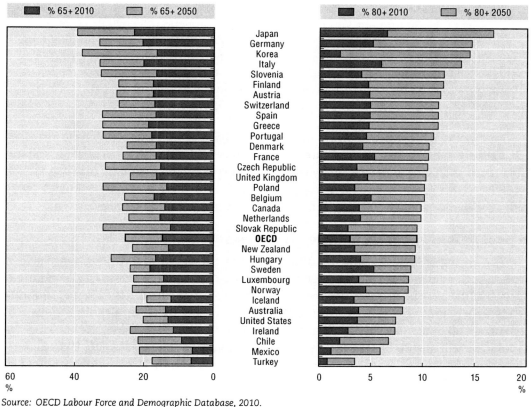

Source: OECD Labour Force and Demographic Database, 2010.

StatLink http://dx.doi.org/10.1787/888932400893

Box 2.1. Trends in severe disability among elderly people

Although theories suggest different relationships between ageing societies and the expected need for long-term care, evidence does not show consistent trends of declining disability in all OECD countries (Lafortune et al., 2007; Bernd et al., 2009).

In 2007, the OECD assessed the most recent evidence on trends in disability among the population aged 65 and over in 12 OECD countries: Australia, Belgium, Canada, Denmark, Finland, France, Italy, Japan, the Netherlands, Sweden, the United Kingdom and the United States (Lafortune et al., 2007). The main findings of this review are that even though, in recent years, disability prevalence rates have declined to some extent in some countries, the ageing of the population and the greater longevity of individuals can be expected to lead to increasing numbers of people at older ages with a severe disability. During the last five to ten years, disability among elderly people declined in Denmark, Finland, Italy, the Netherlands and the United States, remained stable in Australia and Canada and increased in Belgium, Japan and Sweden. No conclusion could be reached for France and the United Kingdom because of data limitations. Similarly, while the reduction in certain health risk factors (such as smoking) might have contributed to reducing some functional limitations in old age, the rising prevalence of obesity among adults of all ages over the past two decades in OECD countries might have the opposite effect (Sturm et al., 2004). There are also some uncertainties pertaining to future trends in neurological and cognitive diseases (such as dementia) as there is greater effort and success in diagnosing these diseases.

> **Box 2.1. Trends in severe disability among elderly people** (*cont.*)
>
> Similarly, recent evidence on disability-free life expectancy at age 65 suggests different processes occur in different European countries (in the period 1995-2001; Jagger *et al.*, 2009). Specific data on Germany (AOK, 2009) suggest that those with a need for long-term care live longer and thus need (more) care for a longer period than in the past (AOK, 2009). This would be in line with the expansion of morbidity theory. However, other German data seem to suggest a compression of disability (Scholz and Schulz, 2010).

Furthermore, life expectancies of those (born and) living with a disability have increased substantially due to better medical care and assistance to those with functional limitations. Those born and living with a disability will increasingly combine a need for care due to their disability with a potential need due to ageing (NDA/NCAOP, 2006; AIHW, 2008; EASPD, 2006). Both developments taken together point to increased needs for LTC services.

2.2. The pool of family carers is likely to decrease

The ageing of societies will also affect the potential supply of individuals available to provide both paid and unpaid long-term care services. On average across OECD countries, the size of the *working-age population* as a share of the total population is expected to shrink by about 9 percentage points, from 67% in 2010 to 58% by 2050, although points of departure and outcomes vary (Figure 2.3). As a share of total population, the working-age population will shrink by less than 6 percentage points in Turkey, Mexico, Luxembourg, Australia, the United States and Sweden, and by more than 15 percentage points in Slovakia, Poland, Czech Republic, Slovenia and Korea.

Figure 2.3. **The share of the working-age populations is expected to decrease by 2050**

Population aged 15-64

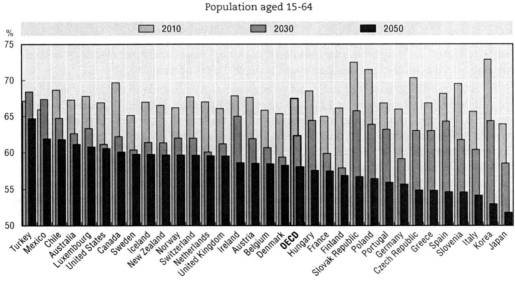

Source: OECD Labour Force and Demographic Database, 2010.

StatLink ⟐⟐ http://dx.doi.org/10.1787/888932400912

In addition, by 2050 the *potential pool of old family carers* will shrink, too. While the average share of the OECD population aged 65 to 79 years is expected to increase from about 10% in 2010 to about 15% in 2050 (Figure 2.4, upper graph), this increase is not sufficient to compensate for the expected relative reduction in the size of the working age population. As a result, for OECD countries, the number of persons over 80 years old per 100 population aged 15 to 80 will triple and increase from about 4 in 2010 to about 12 in 2050 (Figure 2.4, lower graph). Direct human support to those in need and social contributions from working population will reduce as a consequence.

Figure 2.4. **The very old-age dependency ratio is increasing rapidly**

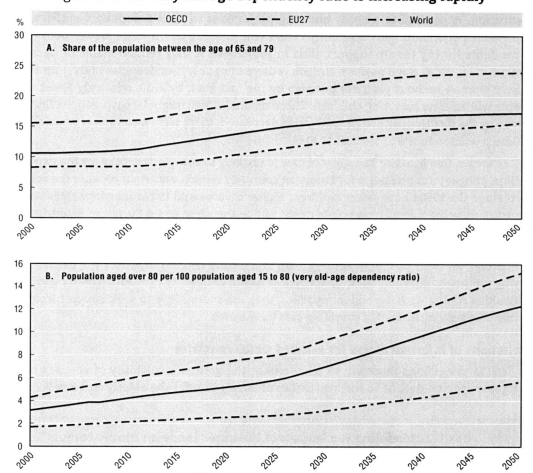

Source: OECD Labour Force and Demographic Database, 2010. World population projection estimates based on UN World Population Prospects, 1950-2050 (2006 Revision).

StatLink ᄤ훼 http://dx.doi.org/10.1787/888932400931

Other societal changes – such as declining family size, rising childlessness, changing living arrangements, with decreased co-residence of elderly with their children and families – are likely to reduce the available pool of family carers, especially working-age children providing intensive care to older parents. Higher divorce rates, rising female participation in the formal labour market and a decline in willingness to care are also likely to contribute to a decline in the availability of family carers (Jenkins et al., 2003).

UK projections estimate that changes in marital status and demographics will increase the numbers of people providing care to older parents by 27.5% by 2041, but to keep the pool of carers constant in relative terms, the number of informal carers of working age would have to nearly double[1] (Pickard, 2008). This indicates that the number of potential informal carers could increase at a slower pace than the number of elderly dependent, leading to a reduction of potential available family carers per dependent person.

The reduction in the number of family carers will be partly compensated by other factors. Longer co-survival of spouses – especially men – makes the elderly more likely to live with a partner in the future thereby increasing the availability of family support.[2] In addition, frail elderly living in couple are less likely to rely on formal care or move to an institution. According to a study showing projections in nine European countries, the dependent population with no family carers will increase much more slowly than other dependents having family support; thus in proportion it may remain stable or decrease (Gaymu et al., 2008). Such positive outlook is driven not only by a decrease in the number of elderly women without partners but also by the fact that, by 2030, relatively fewer older people will have no surviving children. These results, which might be surprising at first, are driven by the fact that, although family size decreased, there were fewer never married and childless women in the 1930s and 1940s.

However, this increase in supply of care is unlikely to compensate fully for the expected decline. Longer-term prospects for European countries remain uncertain because the cohorts born since the 1950s have fewer children, higher divorce and lower marriage rates. While Canada's demographic turning points might not be the same as for European countries, the situation is likely to worsen between 2021 and 2050 mainly because the proportion of women aged 85 and over with no surviving children is expected to rise significantly (Keefe et al., 2007). In addition, an older pool of available carers and elderly couples increases the likelihood of having more couples with both spouses in poor health or needing care. When men experience difficulties coping with dependent spouses, they are more likely to seek support from the formal care system, instead of providing care themselves.

Projections of informal carers for selected OECD countries

OECD projections illustrate to what extent the greater availability of spouses could mitigate expected decline in the availability of family care for the elderly (see Box 2.2).

Box 2.2. **Modeling the impact of life expectancy on family care among older spouses**

OECD projections are based on a "rough" macro approach, essentially using current proportions of the population being married by age group and gender and their corresponding forecasts in life expectancy. Given uncertainties about future rates of marital formation and dissolution, fertility and labour force participation, the projections do not attempt to cover the supply of family carers among prime-age workers. Instead, the projections for a selected number of European and non-European countries examine how changes in mortality will affect the availability of carers aged 50 and over, taking into account ADL restrictions. The projections exploit the likely gains in life expectancy and assume, for each age-group, similar proportion of the elderly population living together, instead of using projected changes in fertility or divorce rates.

> **Box 2.2. Modeling the impact of life expectancy on family care among older spouses** (*cont.*)
>
> In addition, to determine the current population with disability by gender, age and marital status, SHARE (European Survey of Healthy Ageing and Retirement) and the HRS (US Health and Retirement Study) are used. To forecast marriage prevalence, it is assumed that it will increase in line with gains in total life expectancy. This implies that for women, the proportions of married individuals are shifted along the age axis by the equivalent gains in life expectancy of men between 2007 and 2050. The same shift was assumed to take place for men but by the equivalent gains in life expectancy of women over the same period. This borrows from the approach used to estimate potential gains arising from "healthy ageing". Such an estimation method differs from other approaches but it does provide comparable results to other studies. For instance, compared to work undertake by FELICIE (*www.felicie.org/index.asp*), this approach provides for somewhat lower projected estimates for women and higher for men.
>
> An alternative macro approach would be to look at past trends in the provision of informal care and in living arrangements by age group and gender and to extrapolate from there (taking into account other possible changes affecting the demographic structure). This latter approach has been used by the Australian Institute of Health and Welfare in 2003 in a study using data from the Disability, Ageing and Caring Survey from 1993 and 1998 projecting both demand and supply of care for different age groups. The projections are based on general household characteristics such as age, sex and the availability of a co-resident spouse or partner, but also incorporate a 20% linear decrease in the propensity to care for a family member over the projected period.
>
> Some authors also used a cohort approach (similar to the approach used to estimate future participation rates of men and women), combined with multinomial ordered and standard logistic regressions, to both predict the probability of developing certain levels of disability and need assistance at the micro-level for those aged 65 and over. The regression results were used in a micro-simulation model in order to project the availability of family care depending on different scenarios (Carriere *et al.*, 2008). The advantage of such a micro study is to control for household level characteristics, such as the number of living children, employment history or educational attainment. Nonetheless, while this approach could have been used, it would be difficult to take into account marriage dissolution arising because of ageing.
>
> Projections should be taken with caution as many societal changes, combined with demographic shifts, are likely to affect the provision of caring and are difficult to model and quantify. Additional factors such as changes in future trends in living arrangements among the elderly and healthy ageing could decrease or increase the availability of family carers among those aged 50 and over. Changes in willingness to care, social networks and distance to family may also influence the forecasts. All in all, this is likely to change the magnitude of the expected decline in the availability of carers but not the underlying changes in the composition of carers driven by demographic factors. Projections still provide insightful elements to the understanding of the evolution of the caring situation.

Gains in life expectancy, particularly for men, will lead to a reduction in the share of single women. Figure 2.5 shows that, with more surviving men over time, the ratio of men/women aged 70 years and over will improve by more than 15 percentage points from 65 to 80% (0.8 men for every woman). Additionally, the proportion of elderly married women (aged 70+) will increase by around 10 percentage points across selected OECD countries (Figure 2.6).

Figure 2.5. **More surviving old men for each woman by 2050**

Ratio of men/women over the age of 70

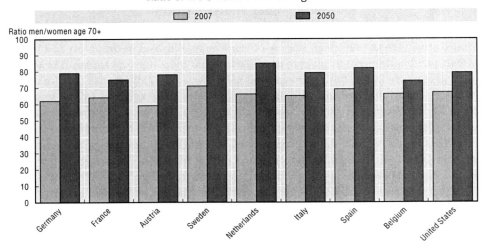

Source: OECD calculations based on population projections.

StatLink 📊 http://dx.doi.org/10.1787/888932400950

Figure 2.6. **Increase in the proportion of old people living in couples, by 2050**

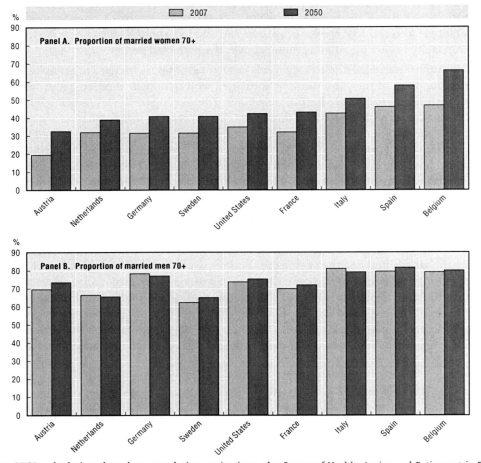

Source: OECD calculations based on population projections, the *Survey of Health, Ageing and Retirement in Europe* (SHARE) and the *US Health and Retirement Study* (HRS).

StatLink 📊 http://dx.doi.org/10.1787/888932400969

Despite this positive outlook, a greater proportion of individuals living together will *both* have ADL restrictions. Given current disability rates, from the total population of dependents aged 70 and over, the proportion of vulnerable dependents, that is those who are not married or who are married but also have a partner with ADL restrictions, will decrease in most OECD countries or remain stable (Spain) (Figure 2.7, Panel A). However, the composition of the vulnerable dependents is expected to change. More specifically, the biggest share of these "vulnerable dependents" concerns those not married: this group will still increase in numbers but will decrease in relative terms. In turn, among the vulnerable dependents, there will be a large increase in the proportion of couples where both are dependent (Figure 2.7, Panel B).

Figure 2.7. **The proportion of frail elderly either living alone or with a frail partner will decrease, but the share of both-frail couples will increase by 2050**

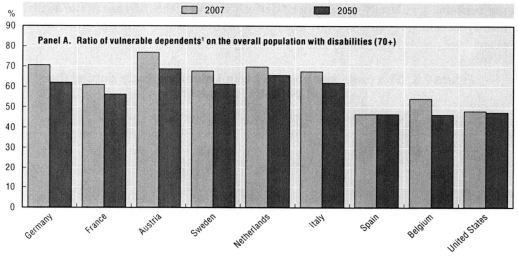

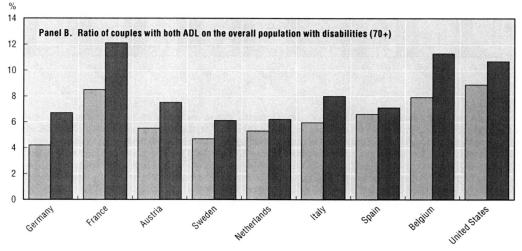

1. Vulnerable dependents are defined as individuals with activity of daily living (ADL) restrictions who are not married or who are married but also have a partner with ADL restrictions.

Source: OECD calculations based on population projections, the *Survey of Health, Ageing and Retirement in Europe* (SHARE) and the *US Health and Retirement Study* (HRS).

StatLink ᵃᵍᵖ http://dx.doi.org/10.1787/888932400988

Using current country-specific proportions of the population providing family care by age group and gender, rough projections on the availability of family carers in the population can be elaborated and compared relative to the expected number of dependent individuals. For the population age 50 years and over, there are important variations across countries in the current ratio of carers to care recipient – ranging from about two carers per care recipient in the United States and the Netherlands to less than 1 carer per care recipient in Austria and Germany. Rough estimates suggest that to maintain the current ratio of family carers to the number of individuals with ADL restrictions, the total number of family carers would need to increase by about 20 to 30% in the selected countries reviewed, except in Germany and the Netherlands where a 40% increase would be needed, and in Italy, where an increase of over 50% would be necessary (Figure 2.8, dark blue bars). By assuming that all "new" expected married dependents would receive care from their non-dependent spouse, a rough upper bound estimate of the impact of males living longer on the availability of family carers can be derived. At most, the increase in the availability of family carers (Figure 2.8, light blue bars) could reduce this shortfall by about 12 percentage points in Germany and 2 percentage points in the Netherlands.

Figure 2.8. **The projected growth in frail elderly greatly outweighs that of potential caregivers**

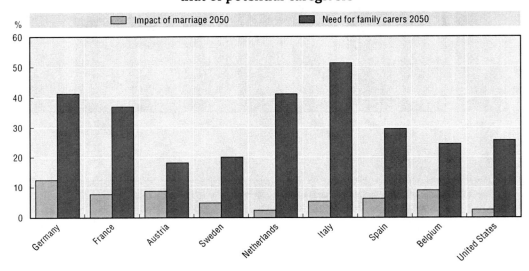

Note: "Need for family carers" indicates the change in family carers necessary by 2050 in order to maintain the existing carer/care recipient ratio. This depends on demographic trends, the existing proportions of individuals with restrictions in daily living activities (ADL) and of those providing unpaid care. A relatively high need for family carers can reflect an existing low proportion of family carers among the oldest old (*e.g.*, Germany and Netherlands) or a high proportion of the oldest old having ADL restrictions (*e.g.*, Italy). *Impact of marriage* indicates expected change in the availability of potential carers (spouses), by 2050. The difference between the two indicates the size of the potential care gap.

Source: OECD calculations based on population projections, the *Survey of Health, Ageing and Retirement in Europe* (SHARE) and the *US Health and Retirement Study* (HRS).

StatLink http://dx.doi.org/10.1787/888932401007

This shortfall does not take into account the existing contribution of prime-age individuals (younger than 50 years of age) in supplying family care. This is important since the availability of prime-age family carers – particularly working women – is also expected to decline, thereby potentially exacerbating the size of the shortfall, although the impact of female labour supply on caregiving might depend on current labour force participation. In countries where current female labour force participation is low, the number of women available for family care could diminish significantly as female labour force participation grows, while in other countries where female participation is already close to the level of males, the impact might be fairly small. For instance, Australian projections show that the number of carers will continue to increase among the working-age population, even with increasing female labour force participation (Jenkins et al., 2003).[3]

2.3. How much will long-term care cost?[4]

Most OECD countries currently allocate between about 1 and 1.5% of their GDP to LTC. Some countries allocate more than 2% of their GDP (e.g. the Netherlands, Sweden and Norway) while some others allocate less than 0.5% (e.g., Portugal, Hungary). In addition, even among countries with similar share of their GDP allocated to LTC, there can be significant variation in the way LTC systems target resources among beneficiaries.

While still relatively small, there is concern across OECD countries that the demographic and societal changes described earlier will lead to higher ageing-related cost in the future. Projections on such cost as a share of GDP provide an indication on the magnitude (size) or urgency (timing) of the challenge ahead and offer a mean to analyse the main drivers affecting programme use. They typically serve to demonstrate where an existing set of policies or programmes is likely to lead, and are therefore sensitive to the initial level of resources allocated to the LTC sector.

Consistent with the results of a number of other international and country-specific projections on long-term care use and expenditures, the projections presented below point to a significant increase in LTC expenditure. These projections reflect the European Commission 2009 Ageing Report (European Commission, 2009) for European-OECD countries, complemented by estimation for a selection of non-European OECD countries, namely, Australia, Canada, Japan, United States and New Zealand. Box 2.3 provides explanations on methodology, as well as a summary of an earlier OECD analysis (OECD, 2006) and other country-specific studies.

Box 2.3. **Recent OECD, EU and country-specific cost projections**

OECD and EU cost projections

OECD and EU projections rely on a macro-simulation approach. Projection models are typically built in two stages. The first stage consists of estimating the future demand of long-term care (volume of care provided) and the second stage consists of estimating the cost associated with providing that future level of care.

Under the *2006 OECD projections* (OECD, 2006; Oliveira Martins and de la Maisonneuve, 2006), the future demand for LTC is estimated by splitting the population into dependants and non-dependants according to a *uniform* rate of dependency (disability) by age group. The rates of disability by age group are derived according to dependency figures for Germany, Italy, Spain, and the United Kingdom (Comas-Herrera et al., 2003). Second, *long-term care cost per dependant* across countries are derived according to a simple econometric model controlling for age and the participation ratio of the population aged 50-64 (proxy for availability of family care), using a panel of eleven EU countries. Total LTC cost equals the product of the estimated number of dependants by age-group and the estimated country-specific LTC-cost curve per dependant by age group.

Box 2.3. **Recent OECD, EU and country-specific cost projections** *(cont.)*

Under the *2009 EU projections*, future demand for LTC is estimated by splitting the population aged 55 years and older into dependants and non-dependants according to the *country-specific* rate of dependency (disability) by age group and gender. The dependant population is then further split according to the probability to receive formal care at home, formal care in an institution or unpaid/informal care only (as a residual) by age and gender. Second, the *average "user-cost"* of providing formal care at home and in an institution, by age, is used to estimate total LTC cost. As for *in-cash disability-related benefits*, total expenditure is estimated by multiplying the dependant population by the proportion of that population receiving the benefits.

For the purpose of *the analysis presented in this chapter*, the methodology used for the 2009 EU projections has been applied to selected non-European countries. This methodology allows for a more refined examination of the organisation of LTC services across care settings. It also allows direct examination of the impact of a shift from family to formal care. In addition, the 5-country projections examine the private component of LTC spending and provide an indication of the expected impact of those projections on future demand for LTC workers. For the purposes of the analysis, projected GDP and employment estimates are based on an OECD report (Duval and de la Maisonneuve, 2009).

Other country studies

Recent studies in selected OECD countries generally use similar methodological approaches as the ones used by the OECD and the European Union. Nevertheless, country specific reports often benefit from a richer set of information on LTC use and cost.

Australia. As part of Australian Government Intergenerational Report 2010 entitled *Australia to 2050: Future Challenges*, projections of aged care expenditure are presented. Spending on aged care is projected to grow from 0.8% of GDP in 2009-10 to 1.8% of GDP in 2049-50. Two-thirds of the growth is accounted for by population ageing alone. Projections assumed that the prevalence of dependency/disability remains constant at the reference year level (pure demographic scenario). The projections allow for estimating the impact of factors influencing the participation rate into the programme. The model also reduces cost to government by increasing private contributions in line with the growing real income of aged-care services users.

Austria. In March 2008, the Austrian Institute of Economic Research published a report entitled *Medium and Long-term Financing of Long-term Care Provision*. The report was commissioned by the Federal Ministry of Social Affairs and Consumer Protection. It provides a range of projection scenarios examining changes in disability across the population, shifts from family/informal to formal nursing care reflecting higher labour market participation of women, as well as pressures to increase the value of the LTC cash allowance in line with the expected rise in the real costs of services. According to these scenarios, total spending in Austria on long-term care would fall in the range of 1.25 to 2.31% of GPD in 2030 relative to 1.13% in 2006.

Czech Republic. The governmental project Roundtable for the future path of healthcare financing in the Czech Republic published a report – *Financial Sustainability of the Czech Healthcare System Until 2050* – which offers detailed information about possibilities and limits of forecasting and predicting revenues and expenditures of the public health sector. The projected public expenditures on long-term care as to 2050 are going to increase by up to 190%, depending on the scenario.

Box 2.3. **Recent OECD, EU and country-specific cost projections** *(cont.)*

Japan. In 2006, the Ministry of Health, Labour and Welfare elaborated projections on the cost and benefits of Japan's long-term-care insurance. At the time, it was expected that total long-term care benefits would increase from 1.3% of GDP in 2006 to about 2.3% in 2025. The projections reflect the expected impact of recently introduced health prevention initiatives to foster healthy ageing, as well as the promotion of community-care settings. By 2025, these reforms are expected to reduce total long-term care insurance benefits by about 15%, relative to the increase that would occur in the absence of reform.

Norway. A recent report of the Norwegian Ministry of Health and Care Services entitled *Long-term Care – Future Challenges* presented information on the projected cost of the nursing and care sector up to 2050. Projections undertaken by Statistics Norway show that the salary costs in the nursing and care sector will increase from 3.1% of GDP in 2005 to 6.1% in 2050. The projection is based on a healthy ageing scenario, under which increase in lifespan are considered to be years with lower dependency.

Sweden. A recent report of the Ministry of Health and Social Affairs entitled *The Future Need for Care, Results from the LEV Project* projects the total costs of elderly care in relation to GDP to fall in the range of 4.2 to 4.5% of GDP in 2050 relative to 3.2% in 2010. The projected increase in costs is demographically driven and varies according to different ageing and technological development scenarios.

Switzerland. In a recent study prepared by the Swiss Health Observatory entitled *Les coûts des soins de longue durée d'ici à 2030 en Suisse*, total (public and private) LTC expenditure is expected to fall in the range of 2.4 to 3.1% of GPD in 2030, relative to 1.6% in 2005. Two-thirds of the growth in aged care spending is accounted for by population ageing alone. The baseline scenario, is a healthy ageing scenario, under which increases in lifespan are considered to be years with lower dependency.

United Kingdom – England. The Personal Social Services Research Unit (PSSRU) elaborated projections of demand for social care and disability benefits for older people (aged 65 and over) in England to 2041. Under the baseline scenario, projected public expenditure on social care and disability benefits would grow from 1.2% of GDP in 2005 to 2.0% in 2041. Under this scenario, it is assumed that the prevalence of dependency/disability remains constant at the reference year level (pure demographic scenario).

Public LTC expenditure expected to at least double and possibly triple by 2050

According to the 2009 European Commission projection scenarios, public LTC spending of OECD-EU member states, as a share of GDP, is expected to at least double by 2050. LTC expenditure are expected to fall in the range of 2.2 to 2.9% of GPD in 2050, relative to about 1.2% in 2007 (European Commission, 2009). Complementary OECD projections for a selected number of non-European OECD countries are consistent with those findings (Table 2.1).

Future trends in LTC expenditure can be affected by a number of factors, such as the prevalence of dependency by age-group, the cost of delivering care, and the availability of family care (see Section 2.2). Given uncertainties as to how these factors will evolve overtime, Table 2.1 presents public LTC projections according to six scenarios. Taken together, these scenarios provide a potential range within which a country's public LTC expenditure may fall in the future. The following section takes a closer look at those three factors and the key assumptions underpinning the projections.

Table 2.1. **Public LTC expenditure expected to rise significantly by 2050**

Percentage of GDP, in base year prices

	Base year	2050					
		Prevalence of dependency		Changes to the LTC cost structure		Decline in the availability of family care	
		Pure ageing	Healthy ageing	−1% of GDP per worker	+1% of GDP per worker	All home care	All residential care
		(1 – Baseline)	(2)	(3)	(4)	(5)	(6)
EU 2009[1]	**2007**						
Austria	1.3	2.5	2.4	2.3	2.7	2.6	2.6
Belgium	1.5	2.9	2.8	2.6	3.2	3.1	3.5
Czech Republic[2]	0.2	0.6	0.5	0.6	0.6	0.6	0.7
Denmark	1.7	3.4	3.2	3.1	3.7	3.7	3.4
Finland	1.8	4.2	4.2	3.8	4.7	4.5	5.3
France	1.4	2.2	2.1	1.9	2.5	2.3	2.6
Germany[3]	0.9	2.3	2.2	2.1	2.5	2.4	2.7
Greece	1.4	3.3	3.2	2.9	3.7	3.5	3.9
Hungary	0.3	0.5	0.5	0.4	0.6	0.7	0.9
Ireland	0.8	1.8	1.8	1.6	2.0	1.9	2.2
Italy	1.7	2.9	2.8	2.6	3.2	3.3	3.9
Luxembourg	1.4	3.1	3.0	2.8	3.4	3.3	3.8
Netherlands	3.4	8.2	7.7	7.5	9.0	8.4	9.2
Norway	2.2	4.5	4.3	4.1	4.9	4.6	5.3
Poland	0.4	0.9	0.9	0.8	1.0	1.1	0.9
Portugal	0.1	0.2	0.2	0.2	0.2	0.2	0.2
Slovak Republic	0.2	0.5	0.5	0.5	0.5	0.6	0.5
Spain	0.5	1.4	1.3	1.3	1.5	1.4	3.0
Sweden	3.5	5.5	5.3	5.0	6.1	5.8	6.3
United Kingdom	0.8	1.3	1.2	1.2	1.4	1.3	1.3
OECD-EU average	**1.3**	**2.4**	**2.3**	**2.2**	**2.7**	**2.5**	**2.9**
Case study	**2006**						
Australia	0.8	1.8	1.6	1.7	2.0	2.0	2.4
Canada	1.2	2.7	2.4	2.4	2.9	2.7	3.4
Japan	1.4	4.0	3.5	3.6	4.4	4.0	4.4
New Zealand	1.4	3.9	3.6	3.5	4.3	4.6	6.2
United States	1.0	1.9	1.7	1.7	2.1	2.2	2.6
Case study – average	**1.2**	**2.9**	**2.6**	**2.6**	**3.2**	**3.1**	**3.8**
OECD 2006 projections	**2006 (actual)**						
Iceland	1.9	2.8	2.5	–	–	–	–
Korea (2007)	0.2	–	–	–	–	–	–
Mexico	–	–	–	–	–	–	–
Switzerland	0.8	1.6	1.3	–	–	–	–
Turkey	–	–	–	–	–	–	–

1. Public LTC expenditure as presented in the European Commission 2009 *Ageing Report*. For 2007, figures may differ from those found in *OECD Health Data*, as information from the Eurostat was used to complement available data. Public LTC expenditure may reflect a broader range of expenditures, including in-cash support or in-kind for instrumental activities of daily living (IADL) services.
2. Data for the Czech Republic only reflect expenditures of the public health insurance funds and do not include expenditures on the attendance allowances.
3. For the projection, unit costs are indexed to GDP per worker and do not reflect the current German legislation under which all long-term care benefits are indexed to prices.

Source: OECD calculations based on European Commission (2009), *Ageing Report*, Statistical Annex; OECD (2006), "Projecting OECD Health and Long-term Care Expenditure: What are the main Drivers"; and Duval and de la Maisonneuve (2009).

StatLink ⬛🖳 http://dx.doi.org/10.1787/888932401862

Pure ageing scenario: LTC spending doubles

Under the *first baseline scenario* – often referred to the pure demographic or pure ageing scenario – the future demand for long-term care is projected according to the prevalence of disability in the reference year. This is equivalent to assuming that the number of years with disability will increase in line with future gains in life expectancy. LTC spending is projected to double from around 1.2 to 2.4% for OECD-EU member countries and to about 2.9% of GPD for the selected number of non-European OECD countries in 2050.

It should be noted that – because of different demographic structures – the period over which LTC cost pressures are expected to peak varies across countries. In addition, the relative intensity of factors driving cost growth – such as the age structure or wage levels – varies across country and over time, as explained in Box 2.4).

Box 2.4. **Some countries face more immediate long-term care costs**

For cross-country comparison purposes, LTC expenditure projections are typically presented as a ratio of projected gross domestic product (GDP). Projections can also examine the composition of the underlying rate of growth of key LTC components, relative to GDP growth.

As shown in Figure 2.9, while real public LTC expenditure is expected to grow consistently at a faster rate than real GDP, for some countries cost pressures associated with LTC are going to be more immediate compared to others.

Figure 2.9. **The average annual growth of LTC expenditure will be significantly higher than real projected GDP growth**

Pure ageing scenario

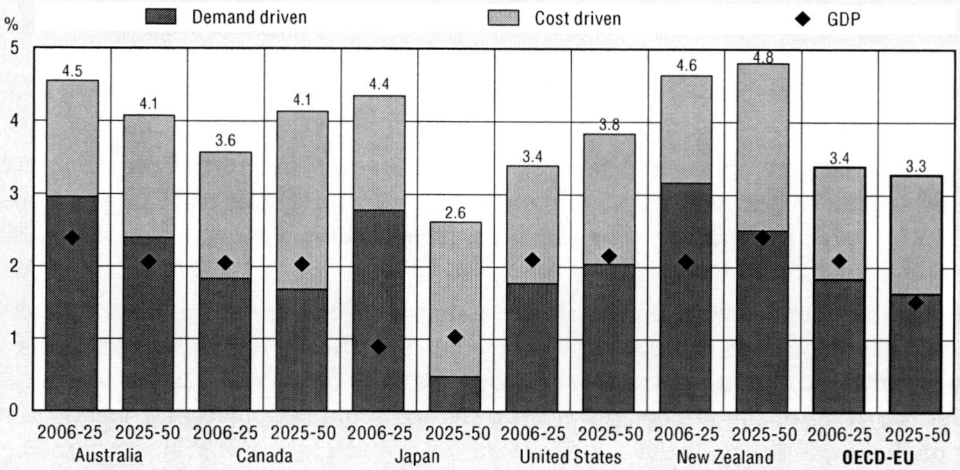

Source: OECD calculations based on *OECD Health Data 2010*; European Commission (2009), *Ageing Report*; OECD *Labour Force and Demographic Database, 2010*; and Duval and de la Maisonneuve (2009).

StatLink ⟲ http://dx.doi.org/10.1787/888932401026

For instance, over the 2006 and 2025 period, Japan's real public LTC spending is expected to grow at an average annual growth rate of 4.4%, compared to 2.6% over the period of 2025 and 2050. On the other hand, LTC spending in the United States is expected to grow at an average annual growth rate of 3.4% before 2025, and 3.9% between 2025 and 2050, while the growth in total LTC spending in OECD-EU countries is expected to remain fairly stable over the whole projection period at just below 3.5% per year.

> ### Box 2.4. **Some countries face more immediate long-term care costs** (cont.)
>
> Generally, at least half of the increase in public LTC expenditure stems from the expected rise in the demand (volume) of care due to population ageing. The only exception is Japan for the period from 2025 to 2050, during which most of the growth is expected to come from the expected rise in the cost of care (*e.g.* wage pressures due to a shrinking workforce).

Healthy ageing mitigates some of the rise in LTC spending

The *second scenario* is a variant of the first one, often referred to as the healthy ageing scenario. It assumes that gains in life expectancy will lead to a delay in the onset of disability, with half of the increase in lifespan considered to be years with lower dependency.

According to this scenario, total public LTC cost could decrease by about 5 to 10% by 2050, relative to the baseline scenario. The projected change in the size and distribution of the population is at the heart of any LTC projections (Wiener *et al.*, 2007). That being said, demand, and hence expenditure, on long-term care ultimately depends on the functional status of the population and especially of the elderly people. The prevalence of dependency (disability) by age is therefore often used as a proxy to project the number of individuals that will likely require long-term care services. Most of the benefits of healthy ageing arise as a result of the oldest of the old (those aged over 80 years) getting healthier and thereby lowering their likelihood of requiring LTC services (Lafortune *et al.*, 2007).

Productivity gains could compensate for future increases in LTC cost

The *third and the fourth scenarios* examine the sensitivity of expected public LTC expenditure to a change to the LTC cost structure. LTC cost structures encompass a number of factors such as the range of services available, the intensity of care provided, the set of eligibility criteria, the existing formal care setting (institutional *versus* home care) as well as the quality of care.

For both the pure ageing and healthy ageing scenarios, the cost of providing LTC is assumed to grow in line with wages in the rest of the economy (*i.e.*, real GDP per worker). Since LTC is a labour-intensive sector, this is a reasonable assumption, to ensure the ability of the sector to retain its workers.

Under the third scenario, on the other hand, it is assumed that the cost of providing LTC grows at a slower rate than real GDP per worker. Specifically, it is assumed that the real cost of providing LTC grows at a rate of 1 percentage point below real GDP per worker, over the first ten years of the projection.[5] Such a change could take place, for instance, as a result of the implementation of a new reform or the introduction of new technologies allowing for more care being provided for the same cost. This would bring a decrease of about 10% in projected public LTC expenditure, relative to the pure demographic scenario.

But increasing demand for LTC and declining labour supply may put pressures on wages in the LTC sector

On the other hand, Scenario 4 examines the impact of LTC cost growing at a faster pace than the average wage level in the economy as a result, for example, of a revaluation of levels of pay in the sector. The real cost of providing LTC is assumed to be growing at a rate of 1 percentage point above real GDP per worker over the first ten years of the projection period (see endnote 5). This scenario results in an increase of about 10% in projected public LTC expenditure, relative to the baseline scenario.

This scenario is very relevant if one considers that meeting the expected demand for LTC services by increasing the supply of workers may be difficult, given that it will take place in the context of a shrinking workforce. As discussed earlier, even though in some countries the *overall* size of the working-age population may still be expected to grow in the coming years, projections until 2050 show a significant reduction in the *share* of the working-age population in most OECD countries. This reduction is, in some countries, coupled with an absolute reduction in population size. Recruiting and retaining LTC workers in the future may be a challenge and could exacerbate pressures on wages in the sector. The data below exemplify these pressures.

Figure 2.10. **The demand for LTC workers is expected to at least double by 2050**

Percentage of FTE nurses and personal carers to total projected working population

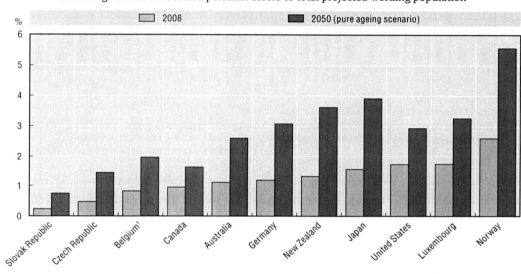

Note: For the purposes of the analysis, the number of LTC workers includes nurses and personal carers working in an institution or at home, express on a full-time equivalent (FTE) basis. The analysis is limited to employed LTC workers and generally does not include other LTC workers under different working arrangements, such as self-employed individuals. The range of occupations considered as nurses and personal carers, as well as the definition of full-time equivalent may vary across countries. Data for Australia, New Zealand and the United States refer to 2007. Data for Canada and Luxembourg refer to 2006.
1. Refers to institutions only.

Source: OECD calculations based on *OECD Health Data 2010*; European Commission (2009), *Ageing Report*; *OECD Labour Force and Demographic Database, 2010*; and Duval and de la Maisonneuve (2009).

StatLink ⟨⟨⟨ http://dx.doi.org/10.1787/888932401045

First of all, the share of the workforce employed in the LTC sector is relatively small and is set to increase significantly. For the eleven OECD countries for which information is available, the total number of full-time equivalent nurses and personal carers working in the LTC sector currently ranges between 1 and 2% of the total workforce, on average. For many countries, this share could more than double by 2050, assuming no changes in the current ratio of LTC workers per recipient (Figure 2.10). This reflects the expected rise in the number of dependents requiring formal care (demand for care).

Second, the growth in the demand for LTC workers, and the expected stagnation – or even decline – of the total workforce, will result in a significant increase in the share of the total workforce employed in the LTC sector, as shown in Figure 2.11. The demand for LTC

Figure 2.11. **Change in demand for LTC workers and working-age population by 2050**

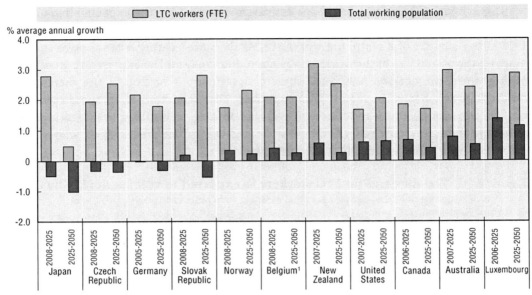

FTE: Full time equivalent.
1. Refer to FTE nurses and personal carers in institutions only.
Source: OECD calculations based on *OECD Health Data 2010;* European Commission (2009), *Ageing Report; OECD Labour Force and Demographic Database, 2010* (pure ageing scenario); and Duval and de la Maisonneuve (2009).

StatLink ⌸⌸ *http://dx.doi.org/10.1787/888932401064*

workers is expected to grow at an average rate ranging between 2 to 3% per year, over the projected period – with the exception of Japan, for which the projected demand for LTC workers is expected to slow down between 2025 and 2050. In absolute terms, by 2050, the demand for LTC workers (on a full-time equivalent basis) is expected to about double in Japan, the United-States and Canada and about triple in Australia, New-Zealand, Luxembourg and Slovak Republic. As to the *total workforce* in the economy, this is projected to grow at less than 1% per year for most of these countries, over the projection period. It is projected to stagnate in Finland, and it is set to decline in Germany, Czech Republic, Japan and Slovak Republic (after 2025).

Declining availability of family care is expected to exacerbate the rise in LTC spending

Under all the projection scenarios examined above, it is assumed that the availability of informal care would remain stable over time. However, as discussed earlier in the section entitled "The pool of family carers is likely to decrease", there is a great deal of uncertainty with respect to the future availability of family care and the consequences this will have on increased demand for formal care.

The *fifth and sixth scenarios* shown in Table 2.1 examine the impact of a shift from family to formal care occurring, for example, because of a decline in the availability of informal care or as a result of a change in policy. These scenarios assume that the number of dependants relying on family or no care will decline at an annual rate of 1% during the first ten years of the projection period (see endnote 5). Under the fifth scenario, all "new" beneficiaries would receive care at home and under the sixth scenario, all "new" beneficiaries would receive care in an institution.

Relative to the projected impact of healthy ageing or slower cost-growth scenarios, the impact of a shift from family to formal care on projected public LTC expenditure varies significantly more across OECD countries. Variations mainly reflect differences in the share of the country's dependent population relying on family or no care, as well as their respective average cost of providing care at home or in an institution.

On average, for the OECD-EU countries, the projected decline in the dependant population relying on family or no care is expected to increase public LTC cost in the range of about 5 to 20%, compared to a range of about 10 to 35% for the other five non-EU OECD countries.

Changing the mix of public/private financing of LTC services has large implications for users' budgets

While most international studies tend to focus solely on the public share of LTC expenditure due to data limitation and concerns regarding the fiscal sustainability of governments in a context of population ageing, the mix of public and private financing determines how much individuals have to pay for LTC services (Kaye *et al.*, 2010). It has major implications for individual's ability to pay for LTC services.

Many OECD countries have introduced in recent years policies that might alter the mix of public and private coverage of LTC cost. Public coverage pools the risk of dependency over a large share of a country's population, thereby significantly reducing the cost incurred by LTC users. On the other hand, universal public schemes inevitably reduce cost incurred by some users who could afford to fully or partially pay for care on their own. Over the years, public coverage has increased in some countries (*e.g.* France, Japan, Spain, Korea) while in others the share of LTC spending financed publicly has gone down or has been further targeted (*e.g.* Germany, Sweden, Netherlands).

The projections presented above are elaborated so that the share of public financing of LTC services unchanged over the projection period. As a result, the private portion of LTC expenditure as a share of GDP can be expected to move in line with the public portion of LTC expenditure, *i.e.*, to at least double and possibly triple by 2050. For those countries which report some information on private LTC spending in *OECD Health Data*, the private share of LTC expenditure generally falls between 0.1 and 0.4% of GDP in 2006 (with the exception of Switzerland with a share above 1% of GDP).

However, policies might also change the public-private mix (*e.g.* higher/lower co-payments), with significant repercussions on the overall share of the cost born by LTC users. As the share of LTC spending which is born privately is relatively low, the private share of LTC would be more sensitive to increases or decreases in the level of public LTC spending (see Box 2.5). The distributional impact of such a change has to be examined carefully in order to mitigate unintended outcomes such as the risk for catastrophic LTC expenditures.

Box 2.5. **Potential shifts between public and private financing of LTC expenditure**

Table 2.2 shows the potential impact of a shift in the public/private share of LTC expenditure resulting from a policy changing the comprehensiveness of public coverage. Two scenarios are examined. Under the first scenario, the public share of total LTC cost increases by 5 percentage points, while under the second scenario the share is reduced by 5 percentage points. Under both scenarios, total LTC (public and private) expenditures remain unchanged.

Table 2.2. **Potential impact of changing the mix of public/private financing of LTC**

Percentage of GDP, in 2006 prices

Case study	Base year	2050		
		Baseline scenario	Shifts in public/private mix	
	2006	Pure ageing	Lower public coverage (−5 percentage points)	Higher public coverage (+5 percentage points)
Australia	Public LTC: 78%			
Public	0.8	1.8	1.7	1.95
Private	0.2	0.6	0.7	0.45
Canada	Public LTC: 83%			
Public	1.2	2.7	2.55	2.85
Private	0.2	0.55	0.7	0.4
Japan	Public LTC: 89%			
Public	1.4	4	3.8	4.2
Private	0.2	0.5	0.7	0.3
New Zealand	Public LTC: 92%			
Public	1.4	3.9	3.7	4.1
Private	0.1	0.3	0.5	0.1
United States	Public LTC: 69%			
Public	1	1.9	1.8	2.1
Private	0.4	0.9	1	0.7

Source: OECD calculations based on OECD Health Data 2010; OECD Labour Force and Demographic Database, 2010; and Duval and de la Maisonneuve (2009). Totals may not add due to rounding.

StatLink ᴬᴵ⬛ http://dx.doi.org/10.1787/888932401881

As shown in Table 2.2, among the five selected OECD countries, the relative importance of the public share of total LTC expenditure varies from about 70% in the United States to about 90% in Japan and New Zealand.

An increase/decrease of 5 percentage points in the public share of LTC would result in an increase/decrease of about 5% in the level of public LTC spending. However, because of its relatively smaller size, the level of private LTC spending would be more sensitive to such a change. For instance, the impact of an increase/decrease of 5 percentage points in the public share of LTC on private LTC spending could range between an increase/decrease of more than 15% in the United States to about 65% in New Zealand.

This analysis is a simplification of reality, as the elasticity of public and private spending may not be the same, resulting in different total LTC spending, depending on whether a measure increases public or private spending. Nevertheless, the analysis suggests that a change in the financing mix could have significant repercussions on the level of private LTC expenditure incurred by LTC users and their household, which could have a disproportional impact on those living on low and moderate income and those with relatively high care needs.

2.4. Conclusions: Policies to address future pressures on long-term care systems

OECD countries will experience a high need for long-term care due to increase of the share of those aged over 80 years in the populations. While the demographic transition is likely to have different outcomes across countries, the increased shares of those in need for care will likely add pressures on family members to become family carers, the more so as the pool of those potentially able to provide care will likely shrink and become older.

Family care projections suggest that, given the existing rate of caregiving and population ageing, the availability of family carers is expected to decline, even when taking into account the impact of men living longer. To palliate this, *i)* either a higher proportion of the population will need to be involved in unpaid care over time; or *ii)* those involved in unpaid care will be pressured to increase their care effort; or *iii)* pressure will increase to shift some care to the formal sector. An increase in the proportion of the population involved in caregiving, particularly with increasingly older and frail spouses becoming more important as the primary source of family care, may have additional implications in terms of health for such population (see Chapter 3). Chapter 4 assesses to what extent counselling and respite care and other policies support carers. Such policies are likely to help both elderly spouses to remain as long as possible in the community and better recognise and encourage the availability of family carers.

The analysis also points to a significant rise in formal LTC use and expenditure by 2050. *Ceteris paribus*, this would translate in higher demand for LTC workers, raising the question of how many LTC workers supply care across OECD, and in what working conditions (Chapter 6). Initiatives directed at the formal LTC workforce, with a view to improve recruitment, retention and productivity will be needed. It also raises the question of how cost will be shared within and across generations, and between the public and private sectors (Chapters 7 to 9).

The expected growth in need and expected decline in both the working-age and the caregiver's populations suggest that addressing future LTC challenges will require a multi-pronged approach focussing on both formal and family care arrangements, as well as their co-ordination. For instance, increasing the supply of LTC workers may be difficult to achieve in a context of a shrinking workforce. Recruiting and retaining LTC workers in the future will be a greater challenge and will likely exacerbate future pressures on wages. Productivity gains could increase the supply of care at a given cost. This is a promising area for government intervention. Healthy ageing policies would help mitigating growth in health or long-term care spending, but also increase the potential size of the labour force and the supply of family carers. In addition, care recipients themselves could take increasing responsibilities towards their own care (*i.e.*, self-caring), through better prevention as well as with the support new technologies (Chapter 10). Policies discussed in the next chapters of this report will offer a menu of possible interventions.

Notes

1. The UK projections are based on the probabilities to provide informal care by gender, age and marital status in 2000 and use projections of changes in marital status and the number of people by age and gender.

2. Changes in mortality are better explanatory factors of the probability to live with a partner than pair formation or dissolution and suggest that the number of elderly living with a partner will increase faster than the total number of elderly (Keilman and Christiansen, 2009).

3. The researchers examine the impact of a 20% reduction in the number of women becoming carers between 1998 and 2013 using information on full-time and part-time labour force participation and on the number of hours of work while providing care and prior to providing care. Compared with the baseline scenario, the reduction in female carers is likely to lead to 1% fewer carers aged 25-59.

4. This section refers to expenditure for *formal* LTC services.

5. Consistent with the methodology used in the European Commission 2009 *Ageing Report*. This is a reasonable assumption since such a change to the LTC cost structure would not be expected to apply over the whole projection period.

References

ABS – Australian Bureau of Statistics (2003), "Disability, Ageing and Carers, Australia: Summary of Findings, 2003", Canberra.

AIHW – Australian Institute of Health and Welfare (2008), "Health Expenditure Australia 2006-07", *Health and Welfare Expenditure Series*, No. 35, Canberra.

AOK (2009), *Trendbericht Pflege II*, University of Hambourg.

Australian Government (2008), "Report on the Operation of the Age Care Act 1997, 1 July 2007-30 June 2008", Department of Health and Ageing, Commonwealth of Australia 2009.

Bernd, B., Y. Doyle, E. Grundy and M. McKee (2009), "How Can Health Systems Respond to Population Ageing?", *Policy Brief*, No. 10, European Observatory on Health Systems and Policies, WHO Regional Office for Europe, Copenhagen.

Brault, M.W. (2008), "Americans with Disabilities: 2005", *Household Economic Studies*, US Census Bureau, Washington DC, December.

Canadian Institute on Health Information (2007), "Public-Sector Expenditure and Utilization of Home Care Services in Canada: Exploring the Data", Ottawa.

Carrière, Y., J. Keefe, J. Légaré, X. Lin, G. Rowe, L. Martel and S. Rajbhandary (2008), *Projecting the Future Availability of the Informal Support Network of the Elderly Population and Assessing its Impact on Home Care Services*, Statistics Canada, Minister of Industry.

Chung, R.Y. *et al.* (2009), "Long-term Care Cost Drivers and Expenditure Projection to 2036 in Hong Kong", BioMed Central Health Services Ltd.

Comas-Herrera, A. *et al.* (2003), "European Study of Long-term Care Expenditure: Investigating the Sensitivity of Projections of Future Long-term Care Expenditure in Germany, Spain, Italy and the United Kingdom to Changes in Assumptions about Demography, Dependency, Informal Care, Formal Care and Unit Costs", PSSRU, LSE Health and Social Care, London School of Economics, London.

Commonwealth of Australia (2007), "Intergenerational Report 2007", Attorney's General Department, Canberra.

Commonwealth of Australia (2010), "Intergenerational Report 2010", Attorney's General Department, Canberra.

Department of Health and Human Services' Office of the Assistant Secretary for Planning and Evaluation *et al.* (2003), "The Future Supply of Long-term Care Workers in Relation to the Aging Baby Boom Generation", Report to Congress, 14 May.

Duval, R. and C. de la Maisonneuve (2009), "Long-Run GDP Growth Scenarios for the World Economy", *OECD Economics Department Working Papers*, No. 663, OECD Publishing, Paris.

EASPD (2006), "The Graz Declaration on Disability and Ageing", accessible at *www.dielebenshilfe.at/fileadmin/inhalte/pdfs/GRAZDECLARATION_final.pdf*.

European Commission and the Economic Policy Committee (2009) (provisional version), "The 2009 Ageing Report: Economic and Budgetary Projections for the EU27 Member States (2008-2060)", *European Economy No. 2/2009*.

Gaymu, J., P. Ekamper and G. Beets (2008), "Future Trends in Health and Marital Status: Effects on the Structure of Living Arrangements of Older Europeans in 2030", *European Journal of Ageing*, Vol. 5, No. 1, pp. 5-17.

Häkkinen, U. *et al.* (2007), "Aging, Health Expenditure, Proximity of Death and Income in Finland", *Discussion Papers*, STAKES, Helsinki.

Hancock, R., A. Comas-Herrera, R. Wittenberg and L. Pickard (2003), "Who Will Pay for Long-term Care in the UK? Projections Linking Macro- and Micro-Simulation Models", *Fiscal Studies*, Vol. 24, pp. 387-426.

IMF (2007), "Manual on Fiscal Transparency", *Glossary*, International Monetary Fund, Washington DC.

Jagger, C., C. Gillies, E. Cambois, H. van Oyen and W. Nusselder (2009), "Trends in Disability-Free Life Expectancy at Age 65 in the European Union, 1995-2001: A Comparison of 13 EU Countries", *EHEMU Technical Report*, No. 2009-5/1, European Health Expectancy Monitoring Unit, accessible at *www.ehemu.eu/pdf/Reports_2009/2009TR5_1_Trends_13EUMS.pdf.*

Japan's Ministry of Health and Welfare (2006), "Projection of Benefits and Costs of Social Security", accessible at *www.mhlw.go.jp/houdou/2006/05/h0526-3.html.*

Jenkins, A., F. Rowland, P. Angus and C. Hales (2003), *The Future Supply of Informal Care 2003 to 2013: Alternative Scenarios*, AIHW Cat. No. AGE 32, Australian Institute of Health and Welfare, Canberra, October.

Jones, A.L., L.L. Dwyer, A.R. Bercovitz and G.W. Strahan (2009), "The National Nursing Home Survey: 2004 Overview", US Department of Health and Human Resources, *Vital and Health Statistics Series*, Vol. 13, No. 167.

Kaye, S., C. Harrington and M.P. La Plante (2010), "Long-term Care: Who Gets It, Who provides It, Who Pays and How Much", *Health Affairs*, Vol. 29, No. 1, January.

Keefe, J., J. Légaré and Y. Carrière (2007), "Developing New Strategies to Support Future Caregivers of the Aged in Canada: Projections of Need and their Policy Implications", *Canadian Public Policy*, Vol. 33, pp. S65-S80.

Keilman, N. and S. Christiansen (2009), "Norwegian Elderly Less Likely to Live Alone in the Future", *European Journal of Population*.

Lafortune, G. *et al.* (2007), "Trends in Severe Disability Among Elderly People: Assessing the Evidence in 12 OECD Countries and the Future Implications", *OECD Health Working Paper*, No. 26, OECD Publishing, Paris.

Martin, B. and D. King (2008), "Who Cares for Older Australians? A Picture of the Residential and Community Based Aged Care Workforce, 2007", Commonwealth of Australia.

Mercer Ltd. (2002), "Study to Examine the Future Financing of Long-term Care in Ireland", on behalf of the Department of Social & Family Affairs, Government of Ireland.

Mühlberger, U. *et al.* (2008), "Medium- and Long-term Financing of Long-term Care Provision", Austrian Institute of Economic Research, Vienna.

National Disability Authority (NDA)/National Council on Ageing and Older People (NCAOP) (2006), *Ageing & Disability: A Discussion Paper*, Dublin: NDA/NCAOP, February.

New Zealand Ministry of Health (2006), "Older People's Health Chart Book 2006", Ministry of Health, Wellington.

Norwegian Ministry of Health and Care Services (2007), "Long-term Care – Future Challenges. Care Plan 2015", *Report*, No. 25 (2005-2006) to the Storting, Chapters 1, 2 and 3, Oslo.

OECD (2006), "Projecting OECD Health and Long-term Care Expenditures: What are the Main Drivers?", *OECD Economics Department Working Paper*, No. 477, OECD Publishing, Paris.

Office for Disability Issues and Statistics New Zealand (2009), "Disability and Informal Care in Zealand in 2006: Results from New Zealand Disability Survey", *Statistics New Zealand*, Wellington.

Official Statistics of Finland (2007), "Care and Services for Older People 2005", Social Protection, Helsinki.

Oliveira Martins, J. and C. de la Maisonneuve (2006), "The Drivers of Public Expenditure on Health and Long-term Care: An Integrated Approach", *OECD Economic Studies*, Vol. 2006/2, No. 43, OECD Publishing, Paris.

Oxley, H. (2009), "Policies for Healthy Ageing: An Overview", *OECD Health Working Paper*, No. 42, OECD Publishing, Paris.

Pickard, L. (2008), "Informal Care for Older People Provided by their Adult Children: Projections of Supply and Demand to 2041 in England", *GRRSU Discussion Paper*, No. 2515, March.

Ruggeri, J. (2006), "Fiscal Sustainability, and Public Investment", *Public Policy Paper*, No. 42, Saskatchewan Institute of Public Policy.

Scholz, R. and A. Schulz (2010), "Assessing Old-Age Long-term Care Using the Concepts of Healthy Life Expectancy and Care Duration: The New Parameter 'Long-term Care-Free Life-Expectancy (LTCF)'", *MPIDR Working Paper*, No. 2010-001, Max Planck-Institut für demografische Forschung, Rostock, January.

Simizutani, S. and N. Inakura (2007), "Japan's Public Long-term Care Insurance and the Financial Condition of Insurers: Evidence from Municipality-Level Data", *Government Auditing Review*, Vol. 14, March.

Statistics and Information Department (2004), "Comprehensive Survey of Living Conditions of the People on Health and Welfare 2004", Japan.

Statistics Canada (2008), "Residential Care Facilities – 2006/2007", Health Statistics Division, *Catalog* No. 83-237-X, Ottawa.

Statistics Canada (2009), "Participation and Limitation Survey 2006: Disability in Canada", Health Statistics Division, *Catalog* No. 89-628-XWE, Ottawa.

Sturm, R., J. Ringel and T. Andryeva (2004), "Increasing Obesity Rates and Disability Trends", *Health Affairs*, Vol. 23, No. 2, pp. 199-205.

Swedish Ministry of Health and Social Affairs (2010), "The Future Need for Care. Results from the LEV Project", Government Offices of Sweden, September.

Weaver, F. *et al.* (2008), "Les coûts des soins de longue durée d'ici à 2030 en Suisse", *Document de travail*, No. 34, Swiss Health Observatory, Neuchâtel.

Wiener, J.M. *et al.* (2007), "The NIC Compendium Project: A Guide to Long-term Care Projections and Simulation Models, December 2007", Prepared for the National Investment Center for the Seniors Housing and Care Industry, Annapolis.

Wittenberd, R. *et al.* (2008), "Future Demand for Social Care, 2005 to 2041: Projections of Demand for Social Care for Older People in England", Report to the Strategy Unit (Cabinet Office) and the Department of Health, Personal Social Services Research Unit, *Discussion Paper*, No. 2514, London.

Chapter 3

The Impact of Caring on Family Carers

Supporting the role of informal carers (family and friends providing mostly unpaid care to frail seniors) is important to provide an adequate continuum of care between informal and formal care. While caregiving can be beneficial for carers in terms of their self-esteem, it can be difficult for working-age carers to combine paid work with caring duties and carers may choose to quit paid works or reduce the work hours. This may compromise their future employability and lead to permanent drop-out from the labour market. Caring may also cause burnout and stress, potentially leading to worsening physical and mental health. This chapter offers an overview of the characteristics of family carers and the impact of caring for frail seniors on labour market and health outcomes of carers. This will provide insights in how to shape policy reforms with the objectives of 1) helping carers to combine caring responsibilities with paid work; and 2) improving carers' physical and mental wellbeing by reducing mental health problems. Countries which want to maintain or increase reliance on family carers will need to alleviate the burden of family carers and reduce the economic costs associated with caring responsibilities.

The statistical data for Israel are supplied by and under the responsibility of the relevant Israeli authorities. The use of such data by the OECD is without prejudice to the status of the Golan Heights, East Jerusalem and Israeli settlements in the West Bank under the terms of international law.

3.1. Addressing caring responsibilities: The impact on informal carers

Using household surveys from Australia and United Kingdom, a household survey for individuals aged over 45 years in South Korea (KLoSA) and two surveys for individuals aged over 50, the *European Survey on Health and Ageing* (SHARE) and the United States Health and Retirement Survey, this chapter provides a snapshot of who are the carers, and analyses the impact of caring on people providing personal care within and outside the household.

The analysis shows that caregiving is associated with a significant reduction in employment and hours of work. Wages of carers do not appear to be lower than those of non-carers, however, once other characteristics are taken into account. On the other hand, there is an increased risk of poverty for carers. Finally, caregiving leads to worsening mental health, even after controlling for pre-existing mental health problems.

3.2. Most carers are women, care for close relatives and provide limited hours of care

Across the OECD, more than one in ten adults (family and friends) is involved in informal,[1] typically unpaid, caregiving, defined as providing help with personal care or basic activities of daily living (ADL) to people with functional limitations. There are significant variations in the percentage of the population involved in this type of caregiving across OECD countries. As can be seen in Panel A of Figure 3.1, the percentage of the population reporting to be informal carers across OECD countries for which data are available ranges from 8% to just over 16%. There is no clear geographic distribution in the rate of caregiving: certain southern European countries have among the highest percentages (Italy, Spain) but Greece ranks among the lowest rates together with Denmark and Sweden. Some of the country differences are due to slightly different definitions and interpretations of caring for dependents across countries (Box 3.1).

A larger number of carers provide help with instrumental activities of daily living (IADL, that is help with shopping or paperwork for instance), even in countries with comprehensive public long-term care coverage. When informal caring is defined with such a broader focus, close to one in three adults aged over 50 provide unpaid care (Figure 3.1, Panel B). Except in southern European countries, a greater proportion of adults provide help with IADL compared to help with ADL. Northern European countries, despite having a comprehensive public coverage for formal care, have the highest share of individuals providing help with IADL.

Carers are more likely to be female but more males become carers at older ages (Figure 3.2). Across the 16 OECD countries reviewed in this study, close to two-thirds of informal carers aged over 50 years are women. Caregiving tends to decrease at older ages with a smaller percentage of carers being present at age 75 and above, probably being related to health limitations. At the same time, the gender distribution of carers changes with age.

Box 3.1. **Defining carers: Complexity and focus of this study**

There is a lack of comprehensive or comparable international evidence on carers. The definition and measurement of unpaid care presents significant challenges, especially in a study which attempts to make international comparisons. Many carers do not see themselves as such and, even if questioned, would not declare that they were carers. Society's attitudes towards family responsibilities and the availability of services to support both carers and people with health limitations vary widely across countries, influencing the pattern and declaration of informal caring. Studies use different definitions of carers which differ depending on the caring activities included and who is the care recipient, leading to the inclusion or exclusion of so-called instrumental activities of daily living, and the inclusion or exclusion of young care recipients and people with ill health. Glendinning et al. (2009) draw attention to how differences in definitions and complex causal relationships make generalisations about international experience difficult.

To assess the characteristics of carers and the impact of informal caring, different national and cross-country surveys are used in this chapter. No threshold is used in the general definition of carers and all individuals with caring responsibilities of at least one hour per week are included. All definitions focus on personal care (ADL) inside or outside the household but there are differences in the scope of the definition. In particular, the question in Australia specifies that the type of activities included in care and that they are performed towards someone who has a long-term health condition, who is elderly or who has a disability. In contrast, the definition in the United Kingdom is broader and includes looking after or providing special help to someone who is sick, disabled or elderly. The results might be sensitive to variable definitions and measurement error.

The descriptive analysis on the characteristics of carers is limited to the sample of individuals aged 50 years and above. The choice is partly driven by data limitations and partly by the fact that this group is more likely to be involved in caring responsibilities and more at risk of labour market exit. Data from Australia and the United Kingdom reveal that 75 to 80% of carers are aged 45 and above. Older workers aged between 50 to 64 years and also more prone to early retirement, particularly in the case of family responsibilities.

Relatively more males are carers among the 75-years-old and above: in two-thirds of the countries a similar or higher percentage of male carers than female carers is observed.

On average, unpaid carers are more likely to devote time to close relatives, such as their parents or their spouse. Yet, there is a non-negligible proportion of carers who also report helping a friend or neighbour (18%) or taking care of other relatives such as brothers/sisters or aunts/uncles (18%). Male carers are more likely to be taking care of their spouse rather than other relatives (Table 3.1).

Most informal carers provide limited hours of care but there is wide variation in hours provided across countries (Figure 3.3). Generally, just over 50% of carers are involved in caring activities of less than ten hours per week on average. This low intensity of caring is particularly prevalent in northern countries and Switzerland. In such countries, less than 20% of carers provide an intensive level of caring of more than 20 hours per week. This may reflect the fact that, in these countries, a relatively greater proportion of elderly receives formal care either at home or in institutions. In contrast, in southern Europe, the Czech Republic and Poland more than 30% of carers are providing intensive caring, reaching even slightly over 50% in Spain. The case of Korea is also striking: over 60% of informal carers

Figure 3.1. **Caregiving varies by country and type of help provided**

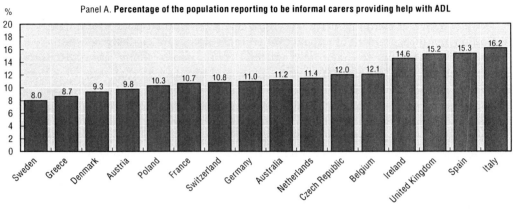

Panel A. **Percentage of the population reporting to be informal carers providing help with ADL**

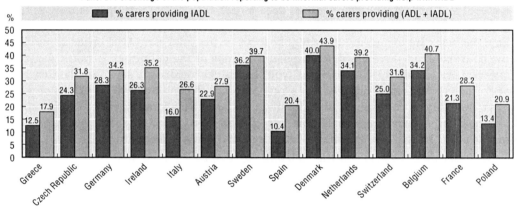

Panel B. **Percentage of the population reporting to be informal carers providing help with IADL**

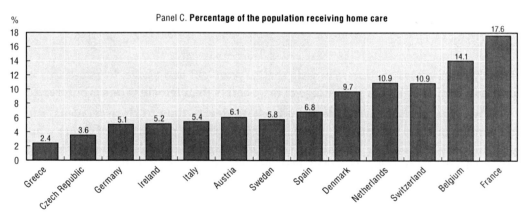

Panel C. **Percentage of the population receiving home care**

Note: Samples include persons aged 50 and above. The United States includes care provided to parents only. The following years are considered for each country: 2005-07 for Australia; 1991-2007 for the United Kingdom; 2004-06 for other European countries; and 1996-2006 for the United States. ADL: Activities of daily living; IADL: Instrumental activities of daily living.

Source: OECD estimates based on HILDA for Australia, BHPS for the United Kingdom, *Survey of Health, Ageing and Retirement in Europe* (SHARE) for other European countries, and HRS for the United States.

StatLink ⬛⬛⬛ http://dx.doi.org/10.1787/888932401083

are providing more than 20 hours a week. The distribution of hours across countries may however be influenced by the definitions of caring, by recall and reporting problems.[2]

Figure 3.2. **Informal carers are predominantly women**

Percentage of informal carers who are female by age group (left axis)
Percentage of the population reporting to be carers by gender and age group (right axis)

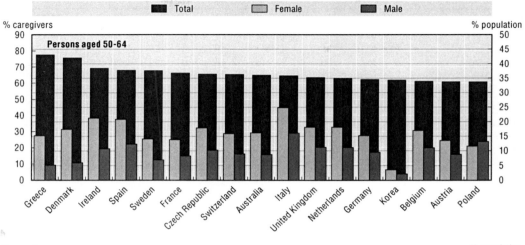

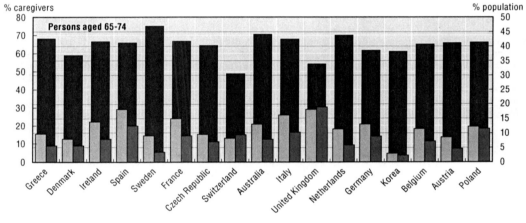

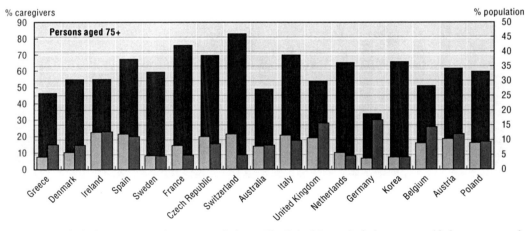

Note: Samples include persons aged 50 years and above. The United States includes care provided to parents only. The following years are considered for each country: 2005-07 for Australia; 1991-2007 for the United Kingdom; 2004-06 for other European countries; 2006 for Korea and 1996-2006 for the United States.

Source: OECD estimates based on HILDA for Australia, BHPS for the United Kingdom, *Survey of Health, Ageing and Retirement in Europe* (SHARE) for other European countries, KLoSA for Korea and HRS for the United States.

StatLink ⟨≡⟩ http://dx.doi.org/10.1787//888932401102

Table 3.1. **Unpaid care is mostly directed towards parents and spouses**

Percentage of carers by relation to the care recipient by country

	Spouse	Parent	Relative	Friend
Australia	26.3	41.0	9.7	8.8
Austria	36.3	34.7	14.7	16.8
Belgium	33.7	40.4	16.6	23.4
Czech Republic	27.5	11.2	33.0	16.2
Denmark	39.7	41.3	15.9	20.9
France	31.8	40.5	19.6	13.7
Germany	34.9	44.2	13.0	21.5
Greece	33.2	35.2	14.9	14.7
Ireland	28.5	35.2	22.4	18.8
Italy	23.1	36.2	22.6	24.1
Korea	43.2	33.5	9.6	–
Netherlands	27.4	46.9	17.2	24.7
Poland	33.8	10.6	27.9	8.0
Spain	28.0	39.9	20.6	10.9
Sweden	26.5	48.5	19.0	18.1
Switzerland	30.1	42.8	17.2	24.1
United Kingdom	34.1	32.2	5.4	27.4
OECD (16)	**31.6**	**36.1**	**17.6**	**18.2**

Note: Samples include persons aged 50 years and above (with the exception of Korea including 45 and above). The following years are considered for each country: 2005-07 for Australia; 1991-2007 for the United Kingdom; 2004-06 for other European countries; 2005 for Korea and 1996-2006 for the United States. Percentage sum is different from 100% as people may care for more than one person and care for children is excluded to avoid confusion between child care and care for dependent children.

Source: OECD estimates based on HILDA for Australia, BHPS for the United Kingdom, *Survey of Health, Ageing and Retirement in Europe* (SHARE) for other European countries, KLoSA for Korea and HRS for the United States.

StatLink ᴀ᭴ᴤᴾ http://dx.doi.org/10.1787/888932401900

Figure 3.3. **Carers tend to provide limited hours of care**

Percentage of carers by category of weekly hours of care

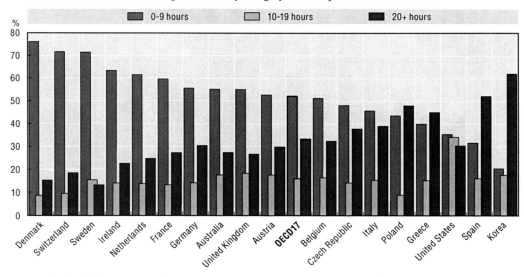

Note: Samples include persons aged 50 years and above (with the exception of Korea including 45 and above). The following years are considered for each country: 2005-07 for Australia; 1991-2007 for the United Kingdom; 2004-06 for other European countries; 2005 for Korea and 1996-2006 for the United States.

Source: OECD estimates based on HILDA for Australia, BHPS for the United Kingdom, *Survey of Health, Ageing and Retirement in Europe* (SHARE) for other European countries, KLoSA for Korea and HRS for the United States.

StatLink ᴀ᭴ᴤᴾ http://dx.doi.org/10.1787/888932401121

Caring responsibilities are largely influenced by the health status of care recipients (Figure 3.4). While 25% of adults aged 50 and above suffering from one limitation of daily activities receive care from family and friends, this proportion doubles in the case of two or more limitations. In half of the countries, the proportion of those receiving informal care does not vary greatly with two or more activity limitations, while in the other half it increases progressively. Individuals with ADL limitations are more likely to receive unpaid care in the Czech Republic, Ireland and southern Europe, irrespective of the number of limitations. This result is consistent with other studies on geographic patterns of caring in Europe (Lamura et al., 2008).

Figure 3.4. **Persons with more ADL limitations require more care**

Percentage of the population receiving informal care by number of ADL limitations

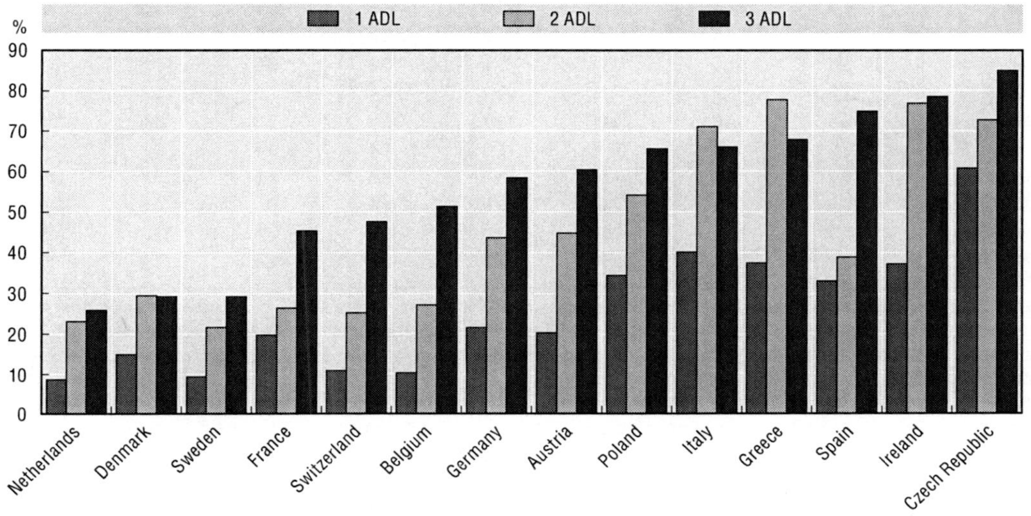

Note: ADL: Activities of daily living. Samples include persons aged 50 and above. The following years are considered for each country: 2004-06.
Source: OECD estimates based on the Survey of Health, Ageing and Retirement in Europe (SHARE).

StatLink http://dx.doi.org/10.1787/888932401140

3.3. High-intensity caring can lead to reduced rates of employment and hours of work

One of the economic costs of caring is related to formal labour force participation. Carers are less likely to be employed and are 50% more likely than non-carers to be home makers (Table 3.2). Country differences in employment rates between carers and non-carers could be linked to overall labour force participation rates and opportunities for part-time work. For instance, the employment gap is small in Nordic countries and tends to be higher in Greece, Spain and Poland. At the same time, in both Greece and Spain, large shares of informal carers are home makers (more than 40%). In other countries, such as Austria and Italy, a large proportion of carers is found among retirees. On the other hand, no clear pattern is found between the number of informal carers and the type of occupation.

Limited labour force participation does not only translate into lower employment rates but also into less time in full-time employment. Indeed, when they are at work, carers work on average two hours less per week than non-carers and they tend to be over-represented in part-time work (Figure 3.5). Furthermore, caring activities could have an impact on career continuity and job choices. This could explain why carers are more likely to hold a

Table 3.2. **Carers are more likely to be home makers, less likely to be employed**

Percentage of carers and non-carers by labour force status

	Retired		Employed		Unemployed		Homemaker	
	Carer	Non-carer	Carer	Non-carer	Carer	Non-carer	Carer	Non-carer
Australia	16.8	16.2	53.1	66.2	1.6	1.8	21.7	6.9
Austria	48.9	44.0	31.8	38.9	3.3	4.0	11.6	9.8
Belgium	22.3	25.6	39.0	42.7	10.5	6.0	16.5	13.0
Czech Republic	34.7	43.4	44.7	48.1	11.2	5.6	0.3	0.0
Denmark	19.1	22.2	59.0	60.6	7.0	5.9	1.3	1.7
France	24.0	25.5	51.6	52.7	4.3	6.1	13.8	9.3
Germany	23.5	20.5	48.2	53.8	9.7	11.2	11.9	8.9
Greece	18.7	23.3	31.4	47.2	2.4	2.8	46.0	25.1
Ireland	11.1	17.0	55.6	51.9	1.7	4.0	24.7	17.8
Italy	36.2	35.5	33.5	35.8	3.2	4.0	24.5	22.3
Korea	7.0	10.6	45.0	48.9	3.8	3.0	36.9	33.2
Netherlands	6.5	11.0	52.4	5.1	2.9	3.0	27.0	17.6
Poland	37.6	36.2	33.6	60.3	3.4	7.9	9.8	5.3
Spain	10.0	13.8	33.0	45.1	5.9	7.5	43.9	25.7
Sweden	12.9	16.3	75.4	73.9	1.4	3.5	0.8	1.1
Switzerland	7.3	10.2	67.0	69.5	3.5	2.8	15.7	10.0
United Kingdom	10.6	7.3	77.9	80.9	1.4	0.9	5.3	5.0
United States	17.7	15.5	58.5	62.0	2.3	1.8	10.7	9.1
OECD (17)	**20.3**	**21.9**	**49.5**	**52.4**	**4.4**	**4.5**	**17.9**	**12.3**

Note: Samples include persons aged 50 to 65 years (except for Korea where 45-65 years-old are considered). The United States includes care provided to parents only. The following years are considered for each country: 2005-07 for Australia; 1991-2007 for the United Kingdom; 2004-06 for other European countries; 2005 for Korea and 1996-2006 for the United States.

Source: OECD estimates based on HILDA for Australia, BHPS for the United Kingdom, *Survey of Health, Ageing and Retirement in Europe* (SHARE) for other European countries, KLoSA for Korea and HRS for the United States.

StatLink ◼◼◼ http://dx.doi.org/10.1787/888932401919

Figure 3.5. **Carers work fewer hours**

Percentage of carers and non-carers working part-time and relative prevalence

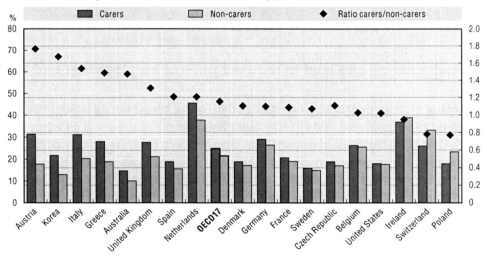

Note: Samples include persons aged 50 to 65 years (except for Korea where 45-65 years-old are considered). The United States includes care provided to parents only. The following years are considered for each country: 2005-07 for Australia; 1991-2007 for the United Kingdom; 2004-06 for other European countries; 2006 for Korea and 1996-2006 for the United States. Part-time refers to less than 30 hours/week.

Source: OECD estimates based on HILDA for Australia, BHPS for the United Kingdom, *Survey of Health, Ageing and Retirement in Europe* (SHARE) for other European countries, KLoSA for Korea and HRS for the United States.

StatLink ◼◼◼ http://dx.doi.org/10.1787/888932401159

temporary work contract. Indeed, in Australia and the United Kingdom where data on the type of contract are available, carers are 30% more likely to hold a temporary job. Data from Australia also indicate that carers have on average nearly three years shorter working career than non-carers.

Providing personal care can be a demanding task that is incompatible with a full-time job or with any type of paid employment, explaining the previous findings. Available jobs might not be flexible enough in terms of working hours or leave options to accommodate caring responsibilities. Caring duties might be unpredictable in terms of their intensity, leading to absences from work.

At the same time, carers have different socio-demographic characteristics and human capital levels which might influence participation choices. Decisions within families as to who will be a carer or whether to use formal care instead might be related to different labour market opportunities and earnings potential, as carers tend to be older and have lower education levels. Labour force participation choices might be influenced by other observed and unobserved characteristics of carers and it is important to control for such factors when researching the impact of caring responsibilities on the labour force status of carers. Surveys following individuals over time provide the opportunity to distinguish whether the correlation between labour force participation (or hours of work) and caring is caused by the negative effect of caring on availability for work, or whether individuals with poor job prospects are more likely to engage in caring activities. This section will consider the effects of caregiving on employment, controlling for other characteristics of carers, followed by the impact on working hours for those working. It will then look at the decision whether to work or reduce working hours simultaneously (see Annex 3.A3 for a description of the methods).

Carers are less likely to be in paid employment, even after controlling for employment status in the previous year and other individual observed and unobserved characteristics (Figure 3.6).[3] The estimation controls for other socio-demographic factors that might affect employment status such as education, house ownership (as a proxy for non-labour income) and marital status. Socio-economic status, for instance, affects both caregiving and labour market outcomes because socially disadvantaged families may be more likely to engage in caregiving and have fewer labour market opportunities. A negative coefficient reflects a lower probability to be in employment. The results show a differential impact depending on intensity of care: the greater the hours of care provided, carers are proportionally more likely to give up paid employment. Increasing hours of care by 1% results in carers being more likely to stop working by 10%. The impact of caring on employment is less important than other factors: low education or the presence of a disability have a much larger effect on reducing employment rates.

The impact of care on labour force participation appears only when individuals provide a high intensity of care: at least 20 hours per week (Figure 3.A2.1). Similarly, the impact is significant only in the case of care towards co-residents. Co-residential living arrangements might reflect the high needs of the person being cared for and/or low availability of formal care services. Conversely, caring does not lead to reduced formal labour force participation when caring responsibilities occupy just a few hours. When only a few hours per week are spent caring, it is easier to combine work and care. Such carers may also be providing care to more autonomous individuals or as a complement to a primary caregiver, giving them more flexibility. Staying at work can also help carers to cope with increase expenditures and a reduction in their disposable income.

Figure 3.6. **Informal caring results in a lower probability of employment**
Coefficients from a dynamic probit

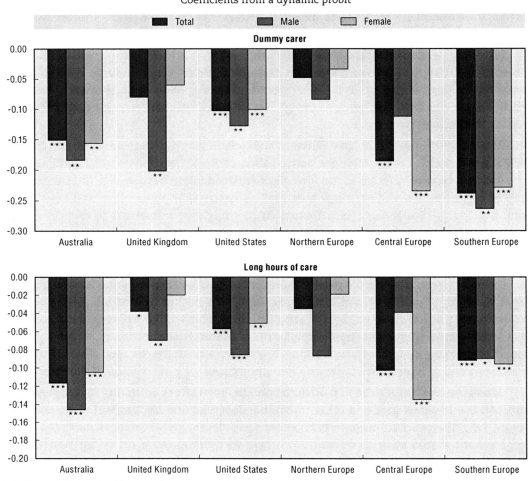

*, **, ***: Statistically significant at the 10%, 5% and 1% level, respectively.

Note: Samples include persons below age 65 in Australia and the United Kingdom, aged 50 to 65 in other European countries and the United States. The following years are considered for each country: 2005-07 for Australia; 1991-2007 for the United Kingdom; 2004-06 for other European countries; and 1996-2006 for the United States. The sample includes individuals present in at least three consecutive waves in Australia, the United Kingdom and the United States. All regressions include the following controls: Age, number of children, marital status, education, house ownership and other non-labour income if available, health status and regions (in Australia and the United Kingdom). The United States includes care provided to parents only. Lagged employment and initial employment status are included in all except for European countries (except the United Kingdom).

Source: OECD estimates based on HILDA for Australia, BHPS for the United Kingdom, *Survey of Health, Ageing and Retirement in Europe* (SHARE) for other European countries, and HRS for the United States.

StatLink ᴴᴵᴸᴾ http://dx.doi.org/10.1787/888932401178

While different definitions of informal carers (see Box 3.1) limit the significance of cross-country comparisons on the impact of caring across countries, certain rough patterns emerge. In particular, being an informal carer is not associated with a significant reduction in employment in northern European countries. At the other extreme, southern European countries exhibit a greater decrease in employment for informal carers. This geographic variation could be explained by the higher labour force attachment in northern countries and different policies which might encourage a better combination of work and family responsibilities. Another explanation of the association between caring and labour force participation can be found in the already observed differences in the intensity and location of care across countries.

Caregiving also leads to reduced working hours across all countries except in northern Europe (Figure 3.7). It leads to a greater reduction in working hours in southern Europe than in central Europe. Hours of work are sensitive to a change in hours of care: a 1% increase in hours of care translates, on average, into slightly more than 1% decrease in hours of work. Other socio-demographic factors, such as education and marital status, are important predictors of working hours.

The impact of caring does not lead to reduced work hours in case of low caring responsibilities and can be attenuated by flexibility of working hours. In Australia and the United Kingdom, all types of care intensity (below 10 hours, 10-19 and 20 or more hours/week) are associated with a reduction in working hours but the reduction associated with low care intensity (below 10 hours) is rarely significant (Figure 3.A2.2). The effect in

Figure 3.7. **Informal carers reduce their working hours when at work**

Coefficients from a random effect tobit

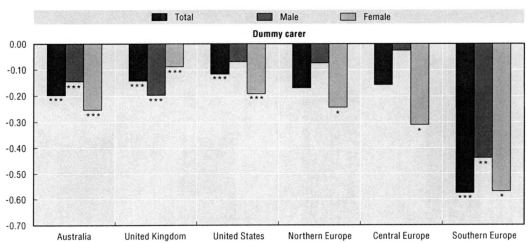

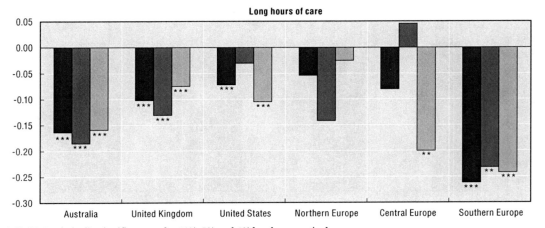

*, **, ***: Statistically significant at the 10%, 5% and 1% level, respectively.

Note: Samples include persons below age 65 in Australia and the United Kingdom, aged 50 to 65 in other European countries and the United States. The following years are considered for each country: 2005-07 for Australia; 1991-2007 for the United Kingdom; 2004-06 for other European countries; and 1996-2006 for the United States. The sample includes individuals present in at least three consecutive waves in Australia, the United Kingdom and the United States. All regressions include the same controls as in Figure 3.6. The United States includes care provided to parents only.

Source: OECD estimates based on HILDA for Australia, BHPS for the United Kingdom, *Survey of Health, Ageing and Retirement in Europe* (SHARE) for other European countries, and HRS for the United States.

StatLink ⚙ *http://dx.doi.org/10.1787/888932401197*

working hours is twice as high for high intensity of caring in comparison with a medium intensity (10-19 hours/week). In the United States and other European countries, a significant impact is observed only when caregiving obligations represent 20 or more hours per week. In Korea, at high levels of caregiving, women tend to decrease their worked hours (Do, 2008). When carers benefit from flexible working hours or the possibility of a leave of absence from work, this tends to increase their working hours.

Previous analysis has shown how unpaid caring is associated with a lower probability of employment and reduced working hours for workers (Carmichael and Charles, 2003; Heitmueller, 2007; Johnson and Lo Sasso, 2000; Viitanen, 2005). At the same time, most workers will face a decision-making process where both options are considered simultaneously, i.e. whether to stop working or whether to work shorter hours. Such decision

Figure 3.8. **Carers are more likely to stop working rather than work part-time**

Relative risk ratios from a multinomial logit

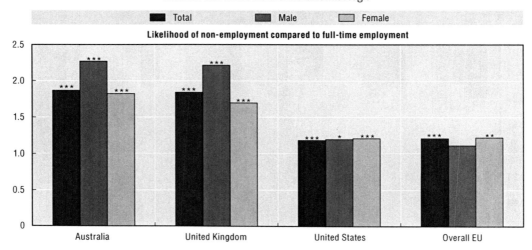

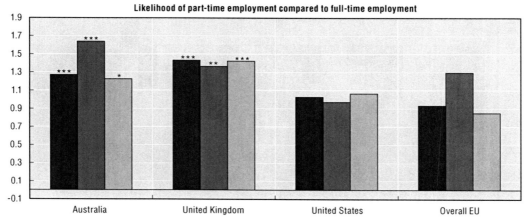

*, **, ***: Statistically significant at the 10%, 5% and 1% level, respectively.

Note: Samples include persons below age 65 in Australia and the United Kingdom, aged 50 to 65 in other European countries and the United States. The following years are considered for each country: 2005-07 for Australia; 1991-2007 for the United Kingdom; 2004-06 for other European countries; and 1996-2006 for the United States. The sample includes individuals present in at least three consecutive waves in Australia, the United Kingdom and the United States. All regressions include the same controls as in Figure 3.6. The United States includes care provided to parents only.

Source: OECD estimates based on HILDA for Australia, BHPS for the United Kingdom, Survey of Health, Ageing and Retirement in Europe (SHARE) for other European countries, and HRS for the United States.

StatLink 🔢 http://dx.doi.org/10.1787/888932401216

depends on multiple factors, in particular the socio-economic situation of the carer as well as on the possibilities to reduce working time. A simplified estimation procedure is presented here where a full-time worker chooses between non-employment and part-time work. The coefficients represent the probability for a carer to move into non-employment or part-time work, as opposed to the option of staying in full-time employment.

Carers are much more likely to stop working than to reduce work hours (Figure 3.8). In Australia and the United Kingdom, informal caring is associated with a higher probability of both stopping working and switching to part-time work. The relative risk ratios on the probability of non-employment are however much higher than for part-time work. In the United States, being a carer leads to a transition to non-employment but has no significant impact on moving into part-time work. This result is also found for women in other European countries while males tend to work part-time.

3.4. For those of working age, caring is associated with a higher risk of poverty

Another possible economic cost associated with unpaid care is lower wages. For instance, informal carers might experience a wage penalty as a result of career interruptions, which lead to a deterioration of human capital or skills depreciation, or the loss of opportunities for career advancement. The wage penalty might also be the result of signalling low career commitment towards employment. However, lower wages for carers might not necessarily reflect a wage penalty as they could also be the result of self-selection into lower-paid jobs or occupations which provide a better balance between work and family obligations. As in the case of employment, it is therefore important to control for different characteristics and preferences of carers to assess the impact on wages (see Annex 3.A4).

After controlling for individual characteristics and the decision to participate in the labour market, there is little evidence that caregiving leads to lower wages (Figure 3.9, Panel A). Wages of carers are 5 to 7% lower than non-carers in the United Kingdom only and the difference is not significant for men. If job characteristics are taken into account, the difference in wages between carers and non-carers is even more limited (amounting to 3-4%)

That said, working-age carers are at a higher risk of poverty (Figure 3.9, Panel B). For this group, caregiving is associated with a higher probability of experiencing poverty across all countries, except in southern Europe. Women carer appear to be especially vulnerable to poverty risks. Since poverty is measured at the household level and includes income from different sources (equivalised by household size and composition), several reasons could explain such findings. Higher poverty may be linked to lower employment rates and lower working hours for carers, which lead to reduced total annual income. Another possible explanation is that the household composition of carers is different, with fewer household members having earnings from work. The results could also partly reflect the higher risk of dependency and health problems associated with lower socio-economic status.

3.5. Intensive caring has a negative impact on mental health

While unpaid carers provide a valuable service to society and looking after family members or friends brings great rewards, there is growing concern about increased psychological distress, strain and overall health deterioration endured by family carers. Isolation and lack of support might prove a high burden and result in distress or mental health problems. Using the same data sources as in previous sections, this section

Figure 3.9. **Unpaid caring leads to lower income but not necessarily lower wages**

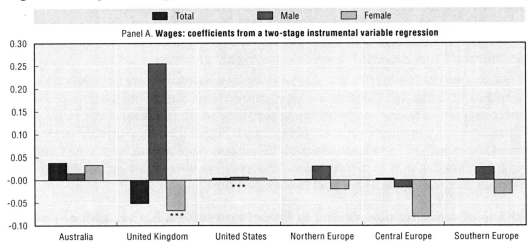

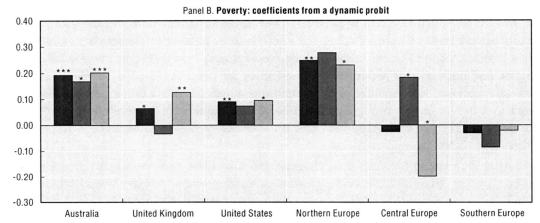

*, **, ***: Statistically significant at the 10%, 5% and 1% level, respectively.

Note: Samples include persons below age 65 in Australia and the United Kingdom, aged 50 to 65 in other European countries and the United States. The following years are considered for each country: 2005-07 for Australia; 1991-2007 for the United Kingdom; 2004-06 for other European countries; and 1996-2006 for the United States. The sample includes individuals present in at least three consecutive waves in Australia, the United Kingdom and the United States. All regressions in Panel A include the following controls: Duration in employment since full-time education and its square (or age as a proxy if unavailable), number of children, education and regions (in Australia and the United Kingdom). The United States includes care provided to parents only. All regressions in Panel B include the following controls: Age, number of children, marital status, education, health status and regions (in Australia and the United Kingdom). The United States includes care provided to parents only.

Source: OECD estimates based on HILDA for Australia, BHPS for the United Kingdom, *Survey of Health, Ageing and Retirement in Europe* (SHARE) for other European countries, and HRS for the United States.

StatLink ⟨⟩ http://dx.doi.org/10.1787/888932401235

considers the mental health of carers and non-carers. Prevalence of mental health problems is calculated using indicators of psychological distress based on a series of checklists. Since each dataset uses a different indicator (see Annex 3.A1), emphasis should be on the comparability within datasets between carers and non-carers rather than on the comparability of prevalence across data sources.

Carers exhibit a higher prevalence of mental health problems across OECD countries for which data are available. Overall, the prevalence of mental health problems among carers is 20% higher than among non-carers. There is no clear geographic pattern in prevalence with the difference in prevalence being highest in Greece and lowest in Switzerland (Figure 3.10). Women tend to have more mental health problems than men but

Figure 3.10. **More mental health problems among carers**

Percentage of mental health problems among carers and non-carers and ratios

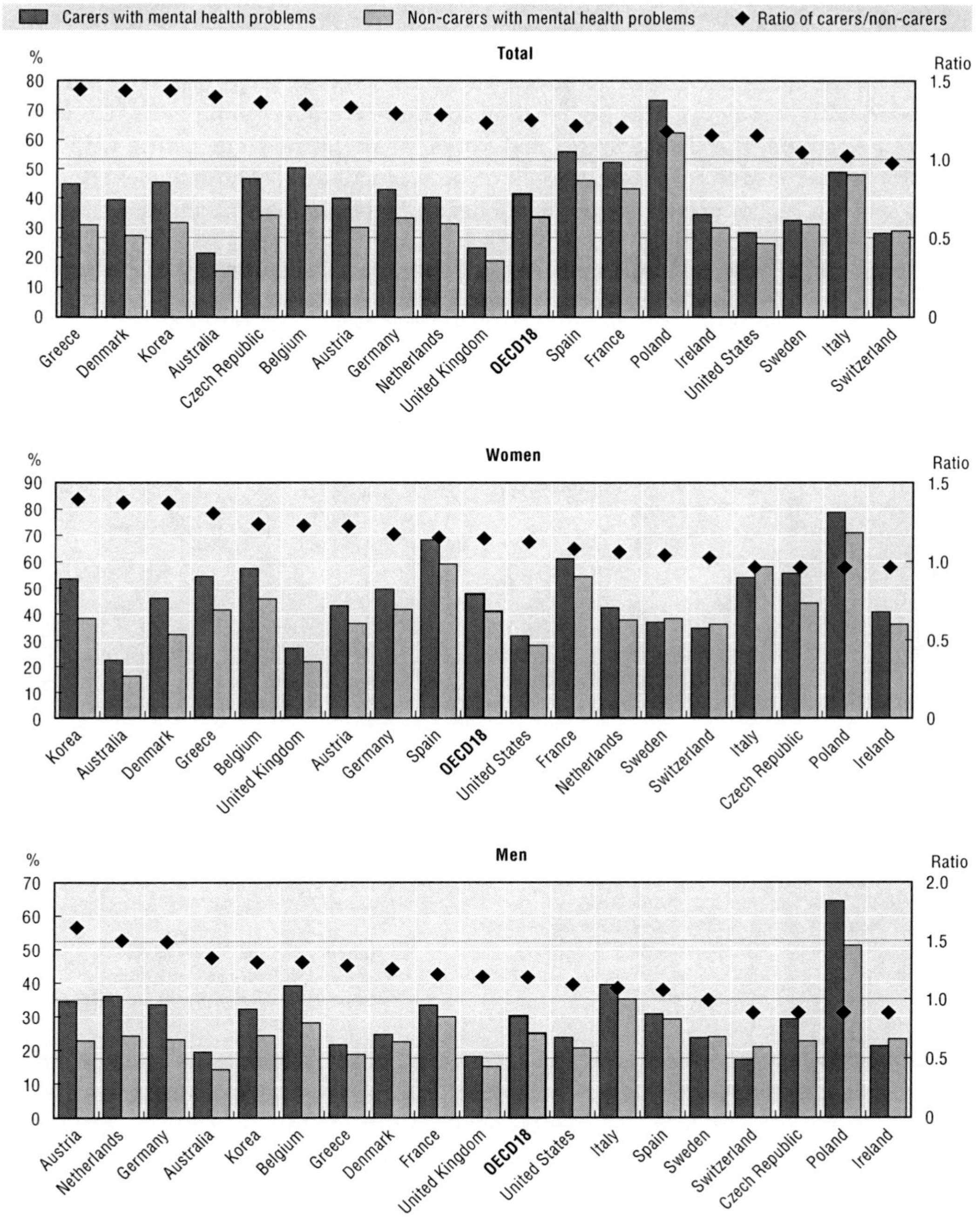

Note: Ratios correspond to the relative prevalence of mental health problems among carers and non-carers. Samples include persons aged 50 years and above (with the exception of Korea where 45 and older are considered). The United States includes care provide to parents only. The following years are considered for each country: 2005-07 for Australia; 1991-2007 for the United Kingdom; 2004-06 for other European countries; 2005 for Korea and 1996-2006 for the United States.

Source: OECD estimates based on HILDA for Australia, BHPS for the United Kingdom, *Survey of Health, Ageing and Retirement in Europe* (SHARE) for other European countries, KLoSA for Korea and HRS for the United States.

StatLink ᴴᴵˢᴾᴸ http://dx.doi.org/10.1787/888932401254

the ratio in prevalence between carers and non-carers is higher for males. The gap also differs by countries among males and females.

Mental health problems might be influenced by the intensity of caring. Figure 3.11 shows that in most countries there is a clear difference in mental health prevalence for very intensive care (more than 20 hours/week). On average, high intensive caring is associated with prevalence 20% higher than for non-carers, reaching even 70% or 80% higher in Australia, the United States and Korea. At the same time, caring with lower intensity (either less than 10 hours/week or between 10 and 20 hours/week) does not always lead to a higher prevalence of mental health problems than among non-carers.

Figure 3.11. **Mental health problems depend on the intensity of caring**

Relative prevalence (1 corresponds to non-carers)

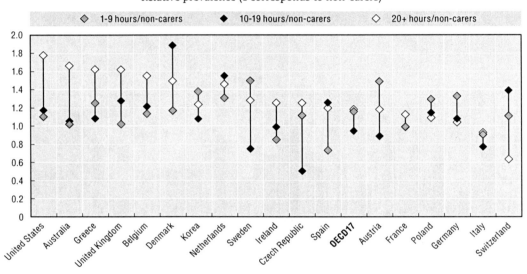

Note: Numbers presented correspond to the relative prevalence of mental health problems among carers by intensity of caring with respect to non-carers. Samples include persons aged 50 years and above (with the exception of Korea where 45 and older are considered). The United States includes care provided to parents only. The following years are considered for each country: 2005-07 for Australia; 1991-2007 for the United Kingdom; 2004-06 for other European countries; 2005 for Korea and 1996-2006 for the United States.

Source: OECD estimates based on HILDA for Australia, BHPS for the United Kingdom, *Survey of Health, Ageing and Retirement in Europe* (SHARE) for other European countries, KLoSA for Korea and HRS for the United States.

StatLink http://dx.doi.org/10.1787/888932401273

Other differences between carers and non-carers might influence their mental health. For instance, carers might be older or have other socio-demographic characteristics which make them more prone to worse mental health. Current mental health problems also depend to a high extent on previous mental health status. There are however relatively few studies which explore this topic, and those that do rarely rely on nationally representative or longitudinal data sources. The few studies available point to a small or non-existent relationship between caregiving and depression (Amirkhanyan and Wolf, 2006; Cameron *et al.*, 2008; Coe and Van Houtven, 2009; Leigh, 2010). Using the same data sources as were used for the econometric analysis of labour force participation, it is also possible to analyse the impact of caring on mental health. A regression analysis which controls for other observed and unobserved characteristics, as well as for mental health status in the previous year, helps to disentangle the effect of unpaid care from other characteristics. The estimation method is the same as for the probability of employment.

Box 3.2. **Intensive carers are older and experience greater social disadvantage than non-intensive carers**

"Intensive carers" (defined as those who provide more than 20 hours of care per week) are more likely to stop working and to have worse mental health outcomes as a result of the caregiving responsibilities. For the government to target support policies at this vulnerable group, it is important to understand who these carers are and how they differ from the rest of the population of carers. Descriptive analysis shows that intensive carers are generally older, less educated and poorer than non-intensive carers.

Most of the intensive carers are found in the 50-64 years old age group, but tend to be much older, compared to non-intensive carers (except in the United States). Across the sample of countries, there are on average twice as many intensive carers aged 75 years and above than non-intensive carers (Figure 3.A2.4).

Intensive care is predominately directed to the spouse of the carer. In the case of the United Kingdom, more than 70% of intensive carers provide help to the spouse, with only 17% to parents. In central Europe, 42.3% of intensive care is targeted to the spouse, against only 3.4% of non-intensive care. Note that in southern Europe, intensive care provided to the spouse is not as high as in the rest of the OECD countries (33% in southern Europe, against 50% on average in the rest of the European sample).There, much of intensive care is directed to parents and other relatives (respectively 14 and 25.5%).

Intensive carers seem to also experience greater social disadvantage compared to non-intensive carers. They tend to have lower income compared to non-intensive carers: 60% of them belong to the first and second income quintile compared to 40% for non-intensive carers. They are also more often below the poverty line: the poverty rate of intensive carers is twice as high as for non-intensive carers. This pattern is particularly clear in Anglo-Saxon countries and in southern Europe, where close to 40% of intensive carers fall below the poverty line. In contrast, in northern Europe less than 10% are classified as poor and poverty rates are comparable for both groups. This situation could be partly explained by lower educational attainment among intensive carers in many of the countries considered. The difference of education level between intensive carers and non-intensive carers is large: The proportion of low-educated intensive carers is almost 30% higher compared to non-intensive carers.

Results from regression analysis confirm that being an informal carer leads to a higher probability of mental health problems. Caring has a large effect and has a higher impact on mental troubles than other socio-demographic variables, with the exception of other indicators of health status, such as the presence of a longstanding illness. A higher probability is observed in all countries for both males and females except for men in Australia[4] (Figure 3.12). The impact of caring is more detrimental for women, with the exception of those living in southern European countries. An important result is that being the recipient of a carers' allowance does not significantly alter the negative impact on mental health in Australia and the United Kingdom (where information on allowances exists).

The detrimental impact of caring on mental health is stronger in the case of intensive and co-residential care. In Australia and in most European countries, significantly worse mental health is only found when care activity is at least 20 hours per week (Figure 3.A2.3 in Annex 3.A2). Intensive carers appear to accumulate disadvantages since they tend to be older, less educated and poorer than non-intensive carers (see Box 3.2). In the United Kingdom, poor mental health is already happening at a medium level of caring intensity (10-19 hours/week)

Figure 3.12. **Caregiving leads to higher chances of mental health problems**
Coefficients from a dynamic probit

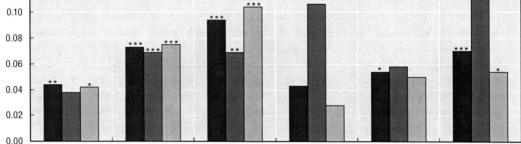

*, **, ***: Statistically significant at the 10%, 5% and 1% level, respectively.

Note: A positive coefficient indicates a higher probability of mental health problems. Samples include persons aged 50 years and above European countries other than the United Kingdom and the United States. The following years are considered for each country: 2005-07 for Australia; 1991-2007 for the United Kingdom; 2004-06 for other European countries; and 1996-2006 for the United States. The sample includes individuals present in at least three consecutive waves in Australia, the United Kingdom and the United States. All regressions include the same controls as in Figure 3.6. Lagged mental health is also included. The United States includes care provided to parents only.

Source: OECD estimates based on HILDA for Australia, BHPS for the United Kingdom, *Survey of Health, Ageing and Retirement in Europe* (SHARE) for other European countries, and HRS for the United States.

StatLink ⟦ms⟧ http://dx.doi.org/10.1787/888932401292

but the impact is smaller. The United States shows a clear gradient on worsening mental health by care intensity for women. Similarly, co-residential care increases the probability of occurrence of mental health problems across all countries.

3.6. Conclusions

Caring can have a major impact on work effort and health, especially for individuals providing a high intensity of care. Since caring does not seem to affect work decisions at low care intensity (below ten hours/week) and for extra-residential caring, intensive caregiving and co-residential carers should be the primary targets of policy interventions. Extra-residential care and less intensive caregiving show some modest effects in terms of mental health outcomes, too. Caregiving is also associated with a higher probability of experiencing poverty across all countries except in southern Europe, and especially for women.

The analysis has shown that many individuals provide low levels of care, although some might underreport hours. This suggests that there may be some scope for an increase in the availability of informal care, as low intensity caregivers could increase their hours of care with only a limited impact on work effort and mental health status. However, with population ageing, it is likely that a greater share of carers will be involved in high intensity care. Without adequate support, informal caregiving might exacerbate employment and health inequalities for these groups of carers. It may also reduce the chances of working-age carers to re-enter the labour market during or at the end of the caring spell.

Policies for carers should be designed bearing in mind these negative outcomes of caregiving. For those combining work and care, the analysis suggests that flexible working arrangements could mitigate reductions in working hours for carers, and should be promoted. For those who opt for temporarily leaving the workforce for caring purposes, training and employment support programmes might facilitate their transition back into the workforce. Payments to caregivers and care recipients (such as cash allowances) should also take into account the possible economic incentives for certain groups to leave the labour market. As to the impact of caring on mental health, this could be alleviated by policies or programmes, ranging from respite care to physiological support and practical help for carers (see Chapter 4 for a discussion of policies to support family carers). Existing studies suggest that combinations of such interventions, and targeting support to specific categories of carers, might work best in supporting carers (Glendenning et al., 2009). Chapter 4 will take a closer look at policies put in place by countries to support carers of frail elderly and, where it exists, evidence of their effectiveness in reconciling caring with work and in reducing the burden on carers.

Finally, while promoting options to combine care and work and provide support to carers are crucial, the availability of formal care is also important. Differences in access to formal care services are likely to influence the possibility of carers to chose the amount and intensity of caregiving provided. As examined in the next chapters, most OECD countries have formal LTC coverage arrangements complementing informal care, although approaches vary across countries.

Notes

1. Most of the statistical analyses that have examined the role of family caring use the terminology of "informal caregiving". This is also used in the rest of the chapter. However, in policy discussion, carers are often referred to as "family and friends", rather than "informal" carers.

2. Chapter 1 ("Cooking and Caring, Building and Repairing: Unpaid Work around the World") in OECD (2011), *Society At a Glance*, use time-use surveys to analyse unpaid work devoted by families, including activities such as cooking, cleaning and caring. Figures from time use surveys report an average of up 0.2 to 6 minutes per day on adult care (OECD, 2011), however these data do not distinguish personal care from domestic care. Most time-use surveys also do not have separate categories for caring for parents, spouse and other family members and other tasks. Women devote on average more time to adult caring than men irrespective of the classification used.

3. Measurement errors of caregiving, which are not controlled for in the analysis, may bias the estimations. First, the variable fails to measure the quality of care. Second, reporting of caring commitment or hours of care may be influenced by employment status *i.e.* to justify not working or fewer hours. Finally, informal caring might be correlated with unobserved factors which influence ability to work. All of these factors may lead to an overstatement of the impact of caring

on employment. At the same time, other studies controlling for endogeneity of care have found that treating care as exogenous leads to an understate of the effects (Watts, 2008).

4. The coefficients for the impact of informal caring on the probability of mental health problems are significant for the overall sample in northern European countries but not for the regressions disaggregated by gender. The absence of significant results by gender might be related to the small sample size.

References

Amirkhanyan, A.A. and D.A. Wolf (2006), "Parent Care and the Stress Process: Findings from Panel Data", *Journal of Gerontology Series B, Psychological Sciences and Social Sciences*, Vol. 61, No. 5, pp. S248-S255.

Camreon, J.I., D.E. Stewart, G.A. Tomlinson, R.L. Franche, I. Hyman and A.M. Cheung (2008), "Emotional Distress among Family Caregivers in Canada: Longitudinal Analysis of the National Population Health Survey", *Archives of Public Health*, Vol. 66, pp. 35-45.

Carmichael, F. and S. Charles (2003),"The Opportunity Costs of Informal Care: Does Gender Matter?", *Journal of Health Economics*, Vol. 22, No. 5, pp. 781-803.

Coe, N.B. and C.H. Van Houtven (2009), "Caring for Mom and Neglecting Yourself? The Health effects of Caring for an Elderly Parent", *Health Economics*, Vol. 18, No. 9, pp. 991-1010.

Do, Y.K. (2008), "Informal Care for the Elderly in South Korea and the Impact on Caregivers' Labor Force Participation", Asia Health Policy Program, *Working Paper*, No. 1.

Glendinning, C., H. Arksey, F. Tjadens, M. Moree, N. Moran and H. Nies (2009), "Care Provision within Families and its Socio-Economic Impact on Care Providers Across the European Union", *Research Works*, No. 2009-05, Social Policy Research Unit.

Heitmueller, A. (2007), "The Chicken or the Egg? Endogeneity in Labour Market Participation of Informal Carers in England", *Journal of Health Economics*, Vol. 26, No. 3, Elsevier, pp. 536-559, May.

Johnson, R.W. and A.T. Lo Sasso (2000), *The Trade-Off between Hours of Paid Employment and Time Assistance to Elderly Parents at Mid-Life*, The Urban Institute, Washington DC.

Lamura, G., H. Döhner and C. Kofahl, on behalf of the EUROFAMCARE Consortium (2008), *Services for Supporting Family Carers of Older People in Europe: Characteristics, Coverage and Usage. A Six-Country Comparative Study*, Lit Verlag, Hamburg.

Lamura, G. *et al.* (2008), "Les travailleurs immigrés dans le secteur de l'aide aux personnes âgées : L'exemple de l'Italie", *Retraite et société*, Vol. 3, No. 55, pp. 71-97.

Leigh, A. (2010), "Informal Care and Labour Market Participation", *Labour Economics*, Vol. 17, pp. 140-149.

Lo Sasso, A.T. and R.W. Johnson (2002), "Does Informal Care from Adult Children Reduce Nursing Home Admissions for the Elderly?", *Inquiry*, Vol. 39, No. 3, pp. 279-297.

Norma, B., C. Coea, H. Courtney and C. Van Houtven (2009), "Caring for Mom and Neglecting Yourself? The Health Effects of Caring for an Elderly Parent", *Health Economics*, Vol. 18, pp. 991-1010.

OECD (2011), *Society at a Glance*, OECD Publishing, Paris.

Viitanen, T.K. (2005), "Informal Elderly Care and Women's Labour Force Participation Across Europe", *ENEPRI Research Reports*, No. 13, 1 July.

Watts, M.J. (2008), "The Impact of the Provision of Informal Care on Labour Force Participation", *CREPP Working Paper*, No. 2008/08, Center of Research in Public Economics and Population Economics, Liège.

Wooldridge, M. (2002), "Econometric Analysis of Cross Section and Panel Data", *MIT Press*, Cambridge MA.

ANNEX 3.A1

Data Sources

The following longitudinal household surveys are used for the analysis in the first section of the chapter. All longitudinal datasets cover a wide range of subjects including personality traits, occupational and family biographies, employment, participation and professional, mobility, earnings and health.

British Household Panel Survey (BHPS) – United Kingdom

The British Household Panel Survey* (BHPS) is a nationally representative household-based yearly survey which began in 1991, interviewing every adult member of sampled households. The wave 1 of the Panel consists of some 5 500 households and 10 300 individuals. Additional samples of 1 500 households in both Scotland and Wales were added to the main sample in 1999, and in 2001 a sample of 2 000 households was added in Northern Ireland. These same individuals are re-interviewed each successive year and, if they split-off from original households to form new households, they are followed and all adult members of these households are also interviewed.

Korean Longitudinal Study of Ageing (KLoSA) – Korea

The Korean Longitudinal Study of Ageing was led by the Korean Labor Institute. The first wave available dates back to 2005 but another wave has been performed since then. The 2005 version (published in 2006) is representative of the 45+ population (excluding those in institutions and residents of Jeju Island) and contains information on more than 10 000 individuals. The questionnaire covers a wide range of topics related to ageing, including take up of formal and informal care, along with other personal and socio-demographic characteristics. KLoSA is also the only large study available in Korea on financial situation of elderly. A follow-up is to be set every other year, organised on the model of the *Household Retirement Survey* in the United States.

Health and Retirement Study (HRS) – United States

The University of Michigan Health and Retirement Study (HRS) surveys more than 22 000 Americans over the age of 50 every two years since its launch in 1992. Supported by the National Institute on Aging and the Social Security Administration, the study collects information on physical and mental health, insurance coverage, financial status, family

---

* The British Household Panel Survey (BHPS) was obtained through the UK data archive (*www.data-archive.ac.uk*).

support systems, labor market status, and retirement planning. The target population for the HRS cohort includes all adults in the contiguous United States born during the years 1931-41 who reside in households. New cohorts are added every six years; therefore, in 1998 the target population was defined as those born in 1947 or before. In 2004, a supplementary sample was added to make the total sample representative of those born in 1953 or before.

Household, Income, Labour Dynamics in Australia (HILDA) – Australia

Household, Income, Labour Dynamics in Australia (HILDA) is an ongoing household-based Panel survey funded by the Department of Families, Community Services and Indigenous Affairs. The survey started in 2001 and contains at the moment seven waves. The wave 1 of the Panel consisted of 7 682 households and 19 914 individuals.

Survey of Health, Ageing and Retirement in Europe (SHARE) – Europe

The *Survey of Health, Ageing and Retirement in Europe* (SHARE) is a multidisciplinary and cross-national Panel database of micro data on health, socio-economic status and social and family networks of more than 45 000 individuals aged 50 or over. Eleven countries contributed data to the 2004 SHARE baseline study ranging from Scandinavia (Denmark and Sweden) through central Europe (Austria, France, Germany, Switzerland, Belgium, and the Netherlands) to the Mediterranean (Spain, Italy and Greece). Information is collected on a bi-annual basis. The sample represents the non-institutionalised population aged 50 and older and the selection is based on probability samples in all participating countries.

Mental health variables

CES-D Scale

The CES-D is a symptom scale measuring depression. It is a composite index of 20 items covering the following domains: Depressed mood, fatigue, pessimism, sleep, enjoyment, interest. The index is constructed by summing binary items. A binary indicator is constructed which takes the value of one if the CES-D scale is three or above and zero otherwise, which has been demonstrated to indicate a clinically significant level of depression.

EURO-D Depression Scale

The EURO-D is a symptom scale measuring depression. It is a composite index of 12 items covering the following domains: Depressed mood, pessimism, suicidality, guilt, sleep, interest, irritability, appetite, fatigue, concentration, enjoyment and tearfulness. The index is constructed by summing binary items. A binary indicator is constructed which takes the value of one if the EURO-D scale is three or above and zero otherwise, which has been demonstrated to indicated a clinically significant level of depression.

General Health Questionnaire (GHQ)

The GHQ is a multidimensional, self-reported screening instrument to detect current, diagnosable psychiatric disorder. It focuses on the inability to carry out normal activities and measures the appearance of psychological distress through four elements: Depression, anxiety, social impairment, and hypochondriasis. It has 60-, 30-, 28-, 20- and 12-item versions. All items of the shorter versions are included in the longer versions. Items ask whether a particular symptom or behaviour has been recently experienced. Responses are indicated using one of the two 4-point scales depending on the nature of the question: Either "Better than usual; Same as usual; Worse than usual; Much worse than usual", or "Not at all; Not more than usual; Rather more than usual; Much more than usual".

The Short-Form Health Survey (SF-36, Sf-20, SF-12)

The Short-Form Health Survey index is a multi-purpose health survey that can be self-administered or used in interviews and covers both physical and mental health. The most frequently used version consists of 36 questions and is the SF-36. SF-36 covers eight main health domains as well as the summary measures of physical and mental health. The eight domains are divided into four physical health scales (physical functioning, role-physical, bodily pain, and general health) and four mental health scales (vitality, social functioning, role-emotional, and mental health). The range of scores possible on each of the eight scales is from 0 to 100, with 100 representing optimal functioning as measured by the SF-36. Norm-based scoring algorithms were introduced for all eight scales in 1998, making it possible to compare meaningfully scores for the eight-scale profile and the physical and mental summary measures in the same graph. SF-12 is a part of the SF-36 that reproduces the physical and mental health summary measures with fewer items.

ANNEX 3.A2

Additional Figures

Figure 3.A2.1. **Higher care intensity and co-residential care have a stronger negative impact on employment**

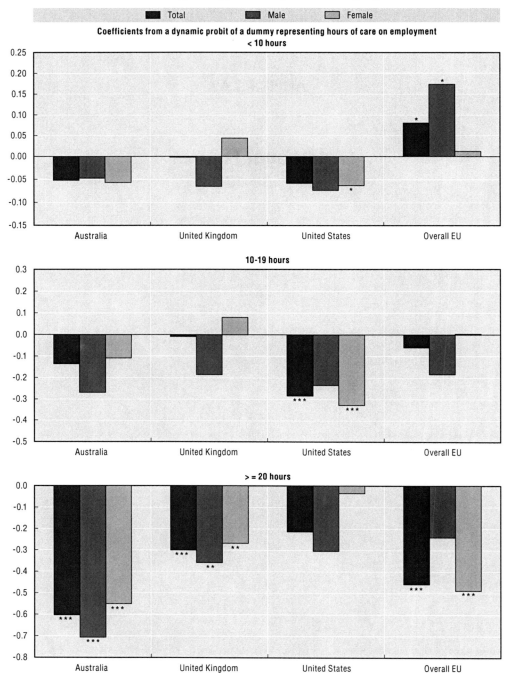

*, **, ***: Statistically significant at the 10%, 5% and 1% level, respectively.

Note: Samples include persons below age 65 in Australia and the United Kingdom, aged 50 to 65 in other European countries and the United States. The following years are considered for each country: 2005-07 or Australia; 1991-2007 for the United Kingdom; 2004-06 for other European countries; and 1996-2006 for the United States. The sample includes individuals present in at least three consecutive waves in Australia, the United Kingdom and the United States. All regressions include the same controls as in Figure 3.6. The United States includes care provided to parents only. Lagged employment and initial employment status are included in all except for European countries (except the United Kingdom).

Source: OECD estimates based on HILDA for Australia, BHPS for the United Kingdom, *Survey of Health, Ageing and Retirement in Europe* (SHARE) for other European countries, and HRS for the United States.

StatLink http://dx.doi.org/10.1787/888932401311

Figure 3.A2.1. **Higher care intensity and co-residential care have a stronger negative impact on employment** (cont.)

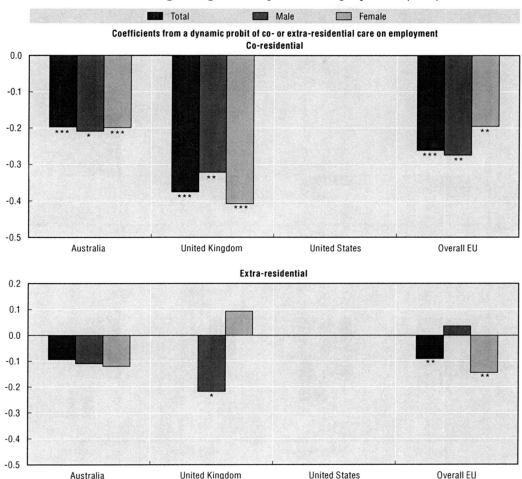

*, **, ***: Statistically significant at the 10%, 5% and 1% level, respectively.

Note: Samples include persons below age 65 in Australia and the United Kingdom, aged 50 to 65 in other European countries and the United States. The following years are considered for each country: 2005-07 for Australia; 1991-2007 for the United Kingdom; 2004-06 for other European countries; and 1996-2006 for the United States. The sample includes individuals present in at least three consecutive waves in Australia, the United Kingdom and the United States. All regressions include the same controls as in Figure 3.6. The United States includes care provided to parents only. Lagged employment and initial employment status are included in all except for European countries (except the United Kingdom).

Source: OECD estimates based on HILDA for Australia, BHPS for the United Kingdom, *Survey of Health, Ageing and Retirement in Europe* (SHARE) for other European countries, and HRS for the United States.

StatLink ⟶ http://dx.doi.org/10.1787/888932401311

Figure 3.A2.2. **Higher care intensity and co-residential care have a stronger negative impact on hours of work**

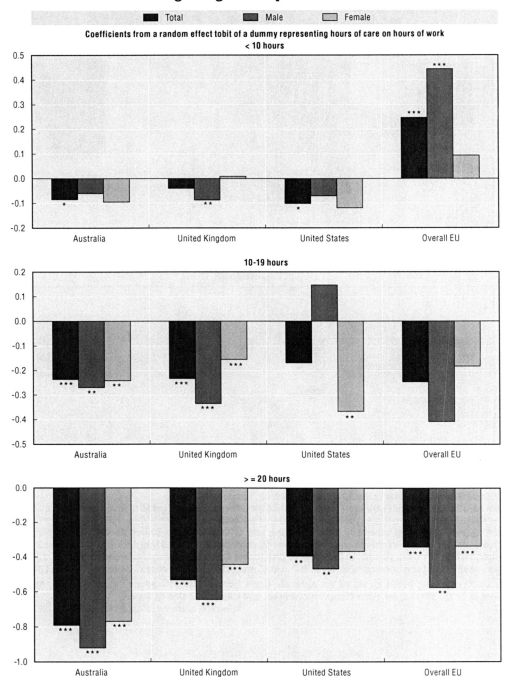

*, **, ***: Statistically significant at the 10%, 5% and 1% level, respectively.

Note: Samples include persons below age 65 in Australia and the United Kingdom, aged 50 to 65 in other European countries and the United States. The following years are considered for each country: 2005-07 for Australia; 1991-2007 for the United Kingdom; 2004-06 for other European countries; and 1996-2006 for the United States. The sample includes individuals present in at least three consecutive waves in Australia, the United Kingdom and the United States. All regressions include the same controls as in Figure 3.6. The United States includes care provided to parents only.

Source: OECD estimates based on HILDA for Australia, BHPS for the United Kingdom, *Survey of Health, Ageing and Retirement in Europe* (SHARE) for other European countries, and HRS for the United States.

StatLink 🔗 http://dx.doi.org/10.1787/888932401330

Figure 3.A2.2. **Higher care intensity and co-residential care have a stronger negative impact on hours of work** (cont.)

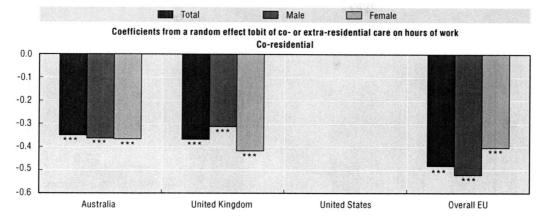

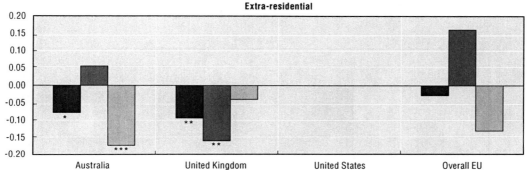

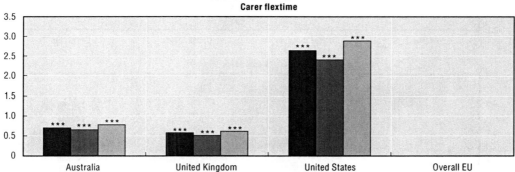

*, **, ***: Statistically significant at the 10%, 5% and 1% level, respectively.

Note: Samples include persons below age 65 in Australia and the United Kingdom, aged 50 to 65 in other European countries and the United States. The following years are considered for each country: 2005-07 for Australia; 1991-2007 for the United Kingdom; 2004-06 for other European countries; and 1996-2006 for the United States. The sample includes individuals present in at least three consecutive waves in Australia, the United Kingdom and the United States. All regressions include the same controls as in Figure 3.6. The United States includes care provided to parents only.

Source: OECD estimates based on HILDA for Australia, BHPS for the United Kingdom, Survey of Health, Ageing and Retirement in Europe (SHARE) for other European countries, and HRS for the United States.

StatLink ⟦ms⟧ http://dx.doi.org/10.1787/888932401330

Figure 3.A2.3. **Higher care intensity and co-residential care have a stronger negative impact on mental health problems**

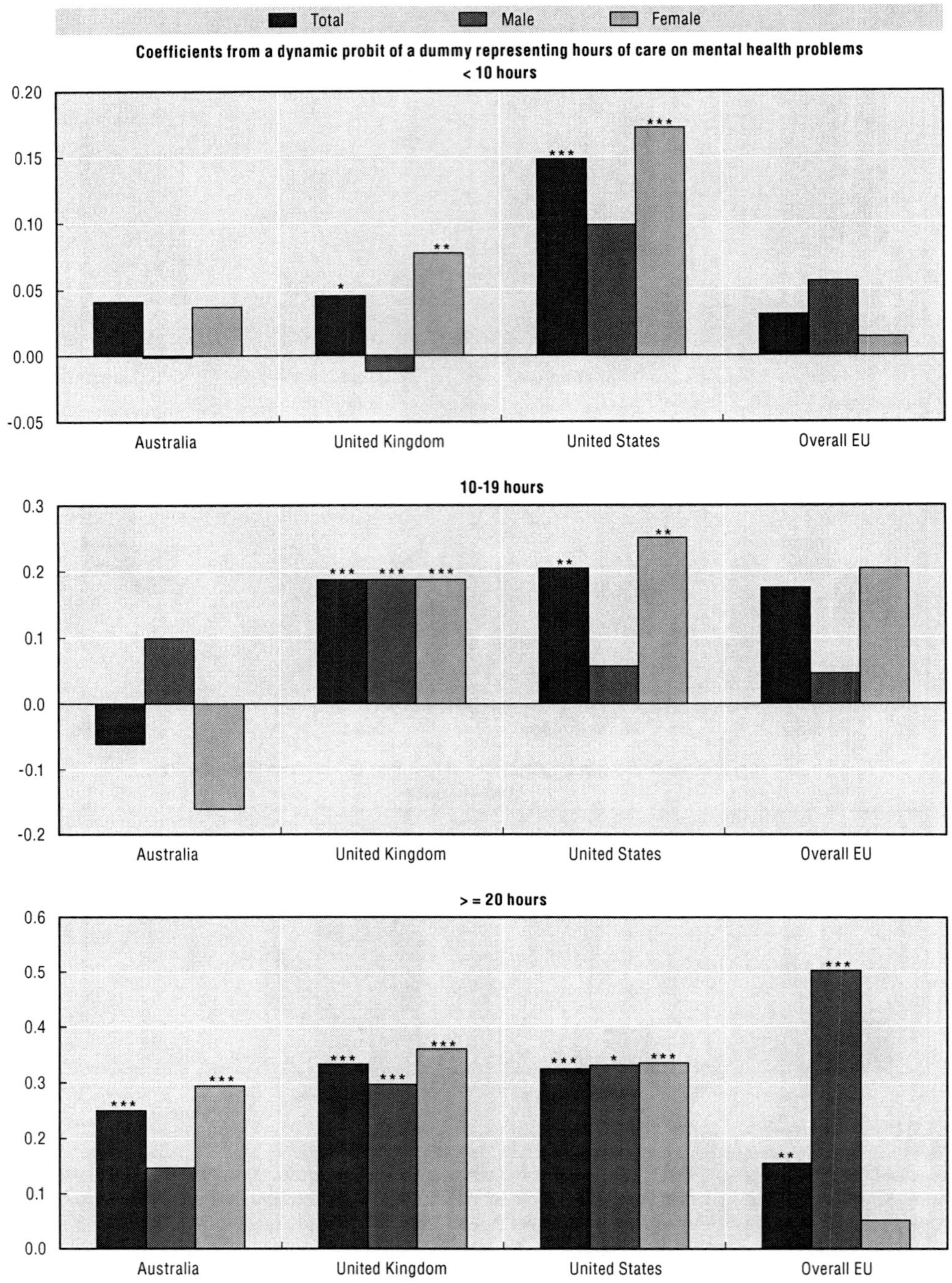

*, **, ***: Statistically significant at the 10%, 5% and 1% level, respectively.

Note: A positive coefficient indicates a higher probability of mental health problems. Samples include persons aged 50 and above European countries other than the United Kingdom and the United States. The following years are considered for each country: 2005-07 for Australia; 1991-2007 for the United Kingdom; 2004-06 for other European countries; and 1996-2006 for the United States. The sample includes individuals present in at least three consecutive waves in Australia, the United Kingdom and the United States. All regressions include the same controls as in Figure 3.6. Lagged mental health is also included. The United States includes care provided to parents only.

Source: OECD estimates based on HILDA for Australia, BHPS for the United Kingdom, *Survey of Health, Ageing and Retirement in Europe* (SHARE) for other European countries, and HRS for the United States.

StatLink ⟐⟐ http://dx.doi.org/10.1787/888932401349

Figure 3.A2.3. **Higher care intensity and co-residential care have a stronger negative impact on mental health problems** (*cont.*)

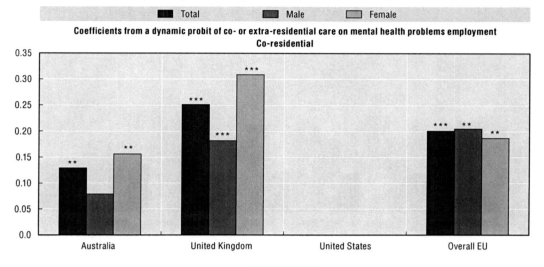

Coefficients from a dynamic probit of co- or extra-residential care on mental health problems employment
Co-residential

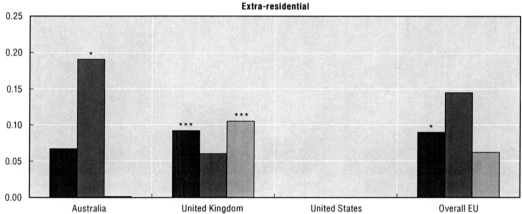

Extra-residential

*, **, ***: Statistically significant at the 10%, 5% and 1% level, respectively.

Note: A positive coefficient indicates a higher probability of mental health problems. Samples include persons aged 50 and above European countries other than the United Kingdom and the United States. The following years are considered for each country: 2005-07 for Australia; 1991-2007 for the United Kingdom; 2004-06 for other European countries; and 1996-2006 for the United States. The sample includes individuals present in at least three consecutive waves in Australia, the United Kingdom and the United States. All regressions include the same controls as in Figure 3.6. Lagged mental health is also included. The United States includes care provided to parents only.

Source: OECD estimates based on HILDA for Australia, BHPS for the United Kingdom, *Survey of Health, Ageing and Retirement in Europe* (SHARE) for other European countries, and HRS for the United States.

StatLink 🔗 *http://dx.doi.org/10.1787/888932401349*

Figure 3.A2.4. **Intensive carers more likely to be older and more disadvantaged**

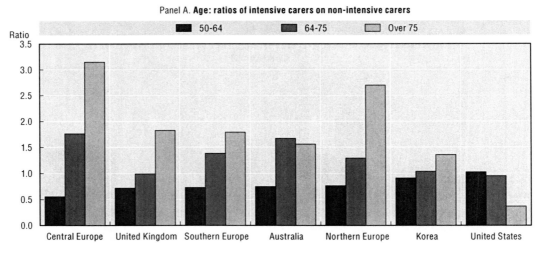

Panel A. **Age: ratios of intensive carers on non-intensive carers**

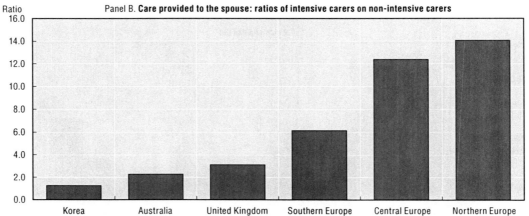

Panel B. **Care provided to the spouse: ratios of intensive carers on non-intensive carers**

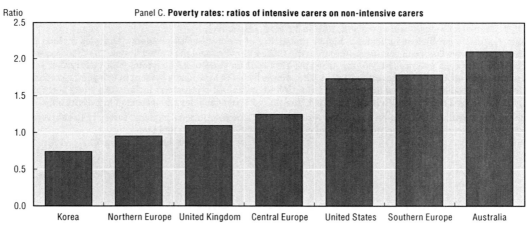

Panel C. **Poverty rates: ratios of intensive carers on non-intensive carers**

Note: Samples include persons aged 50 and above (with the exception of Korea where 45 and older are considered). The United States includes care provided to parents only. The following years are considered for each country: 2005-07 for Australia; 1991-2007 for the United Kingdom; 2004-06 for other European countries; 2005 for Korea and 1996-2006 for the United States.

Source: OECD estimates based on HILDA for Australia, BHPS for the United Kingdom, *Survey of Health, Ageing and Retirement in Europe* (SHARE) for other European countries, and HRS for the United States.

StatLink ᵃˢᴾ *http://dx.doi.org/10.1787/888932401368*

Figure 3.A2.4. **Intensive carers more likely to be older and more disadvantaged** *(cont.)*

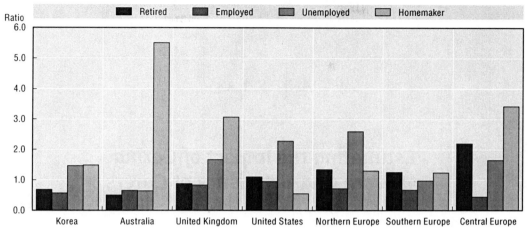

Panel D. **Labour force status: ratios of intensive carers on non-intensive carers**

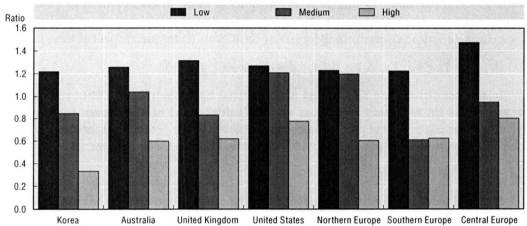

Panel E. **Educational attainment: ratios of intensive carers on non-intensive carers**

Note: Samples include persons aged 50 and above (with the exception of Korea where 45 and older are considered). The United States includes care provided to parents only. The following years are considered for each country: 2005-07 for Australia; 1991-2007 for the United Kingdom; 2004-06 for other European countries; 2005 for Korea and 1996-2006 for the United States.

Source: OECD estimates based on HILDA for Australia, BHPS for the United Kingdom, *Survey of Health, Ageing and Retirement in Europe* (SHARE) for other European countries, and HRS for the United States.

StatLink ⟶ http://dx.doi.org/10.1787/888932401368

ANNEX 3.A3

Estimating the Impact of Caring on Work Characteristics of Carers

Probability of being in employment

A lagged dependent variable model is used for the analysis of employment: a dynamic probit model. This model estimates the probability of being in employment as a function of previous employment status (d), Caring (C) and demographic characteristics as well as work characteristics (X), controlling for initial conditions (δ) for individual i at time t:

$$\Pr(d_{it} = 1 \mid d_{it-1}, X_{it}, \delta_i) = \Phi(d'_{it-1}\phi + X'_{it}\beta + C'_{it}\gamma + \delta_i)$$

Initial conditions are specificied as suggested by Wooldridge (2002) by including means of the time-varying regressors and the initial value of the dependent variable. Because the random effects probit estimates are biased in the presence of feedback effects, the pooled estimator is used as it provides consistent but inefficient estimates.

Hours of work

Hours of work is a continuous variable but the range is constrained because it is zero for a substantial part of the population (the non-workers) but positive for the rest, that is:

$$y_{it} = z'_{it}\theta + \alpha_i + \varepsilon_{it}$$

while $y_{it} = y^*_{it}$ if $y^*_{it} \geq 0$

$y_{it} = 0$ if $y^*_{it} \leq 0$

where y represents hours of work, z are a set of individual characteristics, ε is an idiosyncratic error term and α are individual effects.

A random effects tobit model is used where the likelihood function of hours of work is:

$$f(y_{it} \mid x_{it}, \alpha_i, \theta) = 1 - \Phi(\frac{z'_{it}\theta + \alpha_i}{\sigma_\varepsilon})$$

Multinomial logit

To model the individual choice between not working, working part-time and working full-time, a multinomial model is used. For the purpose of this analysis, the multinomial logit looks at the impact of caring and other individual characteristics on the probability of being in part-time work or non-employment, where probabilities of each alternative are:

$$P\{l_i = j\} = \frac{\exp\{\omega'_{ij}\upsilon\}}{1 + \exp\{\varpi'_{i2}\upsilon\} + ... + \exp\{\varpi'_{iM}\nu\}} \quad j = 1, 2, ..., M$$

For individual I and alternative j where $M = 3$. M refers to the three possible labour force status mentioned above.

Sensitivity analysis was performed for all estimations as follows: 1) using continuous hours of care per week (in log) instead of a dummy variable to model caring status; 2) using three categories for the hours of care per week to capture the care intensity (less than 10 hours per week, 10 to 20 hours and above 20 hours of care). In addition, the analysis was also performed separately for outside/inside household care.

ANNEX 3.A4

How to Measure the Impact of Caring on Wages

This annex assesses the wage penalty of informal caring using hourly wages in several longitudinal datasets. Since wages can only be observed for people in work, observed wages may suffer from a sample selection problem if the unobserved determinants of wages also affect individuals' labour force participation decisions.

In cross-sectional analysis, Heckman's two-step estimation is used. Within a longitudinal analysis, Wooldridge's correction procedure is used. This consists of calculating the inverse Mills ratio from a probit model for the selection equation. The inverse Mills ratio is then included in a pooled two-stage least squares estimator where the first stage includes a participation equation.

$$w_{it} = x_{it}' \beta + \gamma_i + \hat{\lambda}_{it} + \mu_{it}$$

$$p_{it}^* = z_{it}' v + \alpha_i + \varepsilon_{it}$$

$$p_{it} = 1[p_{it}^* \geq 0]$$

where in the wage equation w is the log hourly wage for individual i at time t, as a function of several socio-demographic variables, including the decision and the inverse mills ratio. In the participation equation, p is a dummy variable which takes 1 if the individual participates in the labour market and 0 if s/he does not. The decision to participate depends on a number of explanatory variables z, and individual time-invariant effects as well as a time-varying error. The explanatory variables in the participation equation include additional variables which affect selection but not wages.

Wage equations suffer from possible heterogeneity and endogeneity problems. Sensitivity analysis was performed for the United Kingdom and the United States (where sufficient time lags are present) to correct for such problems. Semykina and Wooldridge (2005) suggest using averages of the strictly exogenous variables as instruments.

Chapter 4

Policies to Support Family Carers

In most countries, family carers and friends supply the bulk of caring, and the estimated economic value exceeds by far expenditure on formal care. A continuation of caring roles will be essential given future demographic and cost pressures facing long-term care (LTC) systems across the OECD. This is also what care recipients themselves prefer. Continuing to seek ways to support and maintain the supply of family care appears therefore a potentially win-win-win approach: For the care recipient; for the carers; and for public systems. This chapter provides an overview and an assessment of the current set of policies targeted to family carers, in relation to three main aspects: Caring and the labour market, carers' wellbeing, and financial recognition to carers. The effectiveness of policies in helping carers combine care with paid work, in reducing burnout and stress of carers, and in recognising the additional costs associated with caring will then be discussed.

The statistical data for Israel are supplied by and under the responsibility of the relevant Israeli authorities. The use of such data by the OECD is without prejudice to the status of the Golan Heights, East Jerusalem and Israeli settlements in the West Bank under the terms of international law.

4.1. Improving carers' role and wellbeing

Countries have implemented a number of policies that directly or indirectly target family carers.[1] Yet, some carers still struggle to combine their caring role with work and often suffer from mental health problems, suggesting that policies to support carers could be improved. OECD countries differ in the extent to which they do so, and in the set of measures targeted to carers, for example in terms of cash and in-kind services (*e.g.* respite care), as well as initiatives to reconcile work and care (*e.g.* flexible work arrangements).

4.2. Helping carers combine caring responsibilities with paid work

Caregiving is associated with a significant reduction in employment and hours of work, especially for individuals providing a high intensity of care (Chapter 3). Other studies have confirmed that, in addition to lower labour force participation, informal caring leads to absenteeism, irregular attendance (coming late and having to leave work) and lack of concentration at work (Gautun and Hagen, 2007). Policies which reduce the dual pressure from work and care for employed caregivers might improve their employability, making caring a viable option for more potential carers. The following section discusses current policies to facilitate the employment of carers and how they could be improved.

Leave from work

While many OECD countries recognise the important role of family carers and incorporate the principles of helping them balance work and caring, this is not always translated into services in practice. Two-thirds of the OECD countries for which information is available have leave for carers, although conditions for leave tend to be limited and paid leave is restricted to slightly less than half of the countries (see Annex 4.A1 and Annex 4.A2 for a detailed description of care leave for each country). In contrast, parental leave to care for children – albeit different in nature and content – is widely available and is paid in three-quarters of OECD countries, although often at low rates (OECD, 2007). Studies on the use of parental leave found positive effects on working hours and the labour force participation of women for short-term leave (Spiess and Wrohlich, 2006). While the literature on care leave is less extensive, some longitudinal studies have found that family leave and access to flexible hours has a positive effect on the likelihood of employment retention for women, although the overall effect on employment is uncertain as it might reduce job possibilities for those caring but not at work (Pavalko and Henderson, 2006).

In three-quarters of the countries where it is available, paid care leave is limited to less than one month or to terminal illness. Belgium provides the longest publicly paid leave, for a maximum of 12 months, which employers may refuse only on serious business grounds. In Japan, paid leave is also fairly long, since carers can take leaves up to 93 days with 40% of wage paid through the employment insurance if the company does not compensate during the leave. In terms of remuneration, Scandinavian countries tend to pay the most. For instance, in Norway and Sweden paid leave is equivalent to 100% and 80% of the wage respectively. In Denmark, in exchange for employers continuing to pay full wages during care leave, municipalities reimburse a minimum equivalent to 82% of the sick benefit ceiling.

In the case of unpaid leave, there is a geographical divide. A group of countries provides long leave of one or more years (e.g. Belgium, France, Spain and Ireland). While being relatively long, unpaid leave is not a statutory right for workers in Ireland and Spain and may be refused by employers on business grounds. In the case of France, while employers may not oppose the leave, eligibility criteria remain strict: leave is only available to care for a relative with an 80% autonomy loss. A second group provides relatively short leave of up to three months[2] (e.g. English-speaking countries and the Netherlands), with a couple of countries providing medium-term leave of six months (Austria, Germany). In Austria the availability of unpaid leave is limited to care for terminally ill relatives.

The use of leave for long-term care might be even more limited in practice because employees fear that it will have an impact on career and household income. In this respect, the use of statutory rights to care leave might be influenced by the intensity of caring obligations and the generosity of leave compensation. Caregivers with less intensive obligations might prefer to use holidays or sick leave, particularly if workers fear that a request for care leave might endanger career opportunities. It is to be expected that the lower the compensation rate, the lower the take up for such care leave will be. Loss of income during care leave is often cited as a reason for preferring to use annual paid leave or sick leave since workers receive full salary during holidays and many countries have generous replacement rates during sickness (Ikeda et al., 2006). On the other hand, for those caring for their partner, providing more hours of care might be more prone to ask for statutory care leave, even if it is unpaid.

Data on leave use are difficult to obtain but a representative survey of companies in European countries contains information on companies providing leave for long-term care purposes (Establishment Survey on Working Time and Work-Life Balance) (Figure 4.1). Roughly 37% of European companies declare that long-term leave is available for employees to care for an ill family member, whereas nearly all establishments offer

Figure 4.1. **Care leave is less frequent than parental leave**

Share of establishments offering leave to employees

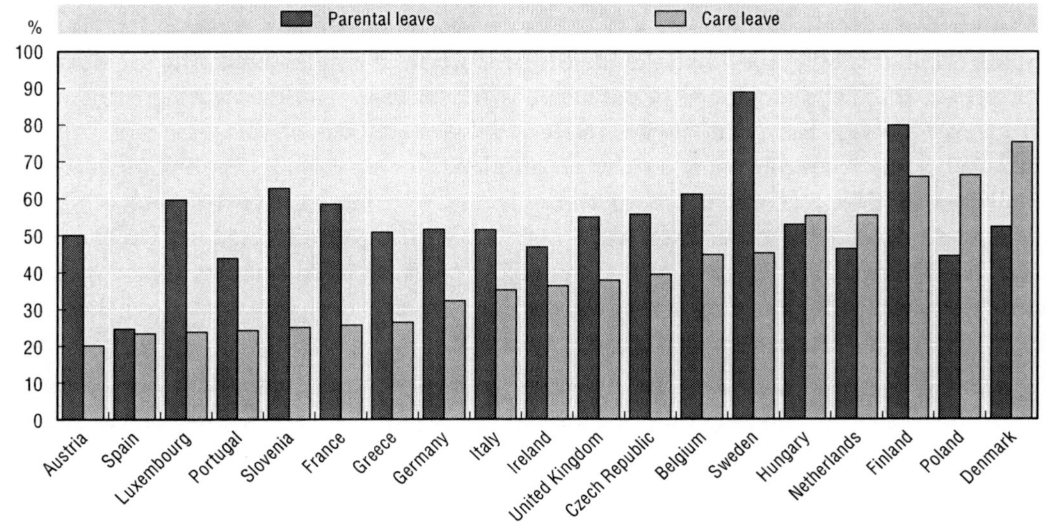

Source: European Establishment Survey on Working Time and Work-Life Balance, 2004.

StatLink ᵃᵐˢ᷀ http://dx.doi.org/10.1787/888932401387

parental leave and in 51% of the establishments employees have taken parental leave in the previous three years. A greater portion of companies offer care leave to their employees in Scandinavian countries and in Poland (60% on average) and a much smaller fraction is found in Southern Europe (around 25%). Similar data from Canada (from the Federal Jurisdiction Workplace Survey 2008) show that approximately 20% of all companies under federal jurisdiction provide annual paid family-related and/or personal leave. This is comparable to data from Japan (Tokyo prefecture only) showing that 10.7% of the companies have one or more persons who took long-term care leave while in contrasts 90.9% of women who gave birth took parental leave (Tokyo Metropolitan Government Bureau of Industrial and Labour Affairs, 2008).

Use of care leave depends heavily on the sector of work and disparities among workers are likely in the absence of statutory rights. Long-term leave to care for an elder or sick relative is most often found in the public sector and/or in larger companies.[3] In terms of firm characteristics, more establishments grant care leave in companies with a higher proportion of female employees, where there are more skilled workers, and care leave is more likely in the service sector than in manufacture. All of these categories of workplaces are most likely to provide child-related provisions, too (OECD, 2007).

Flexible work schedule

In addition to leave from work, flexible working hours may help carers to remain in the labour force and accommodate care needs. Chapter 3 confirmed that flexible working hours lowered the chances of reduced hours of work for carers in Australia and the United Kingdom. A similar study from the United States showed that women with caring responsibilities who worked in companies with flexible hours had 50% greater odds of still being employed two years later than those who did not (Pavalko and Henderson, 2006). Flexible work schemes may offer good solutions to balance care obligations and work by providing carers sufficient income and a social network through work.

While almost two-thirds of firms report some use of part-time work,[4] its use to facilitate care for the elderly or sick remains limited. As it was the case with leave provisions, part-time is less often used for long-term care than for taking care of children. About two thirds of the sample of European establishments has female employees using part-time work for children (Figure 4.2). While the use of part-time work by fathers is more limited (21%), it is still more than double the proportion of employees caring for elderly or sick people (9%). The incidence of part-time work for care reasons varies greatly across European countries and is not always related to the overall use of part-time work. On the one hand, some countries show a relation: only 1% of companies report having part-time employees for care reasons in Greece and only 16% of firms have part-timers, while the respective proportions are as high as 18 and 76% in the United Kingdom. On the other hand, the Netherlands has one of the greatest proportion of companies reporting some part-time work (89%) but only a modest use for care of elderly/disabled (less than 5%). There are also differences across sectors (Figure 4.3).

More widespread provisions for full-time parents to request part-time work than for carers of frail elderly help to explain the limited use of part-time for care reasons relative to childcare. While in eight out of ten OECD countries for which information is available, parents are entitled to part-time work, statutory rights to work part-time for non-parents exist in half of the these countries (two-thirds if collective or sectoral agreements are taken

Figure 4.2. **More mothers than family carers among part-time workers**

Share of establishments reporting mothers and family cares among part-timers

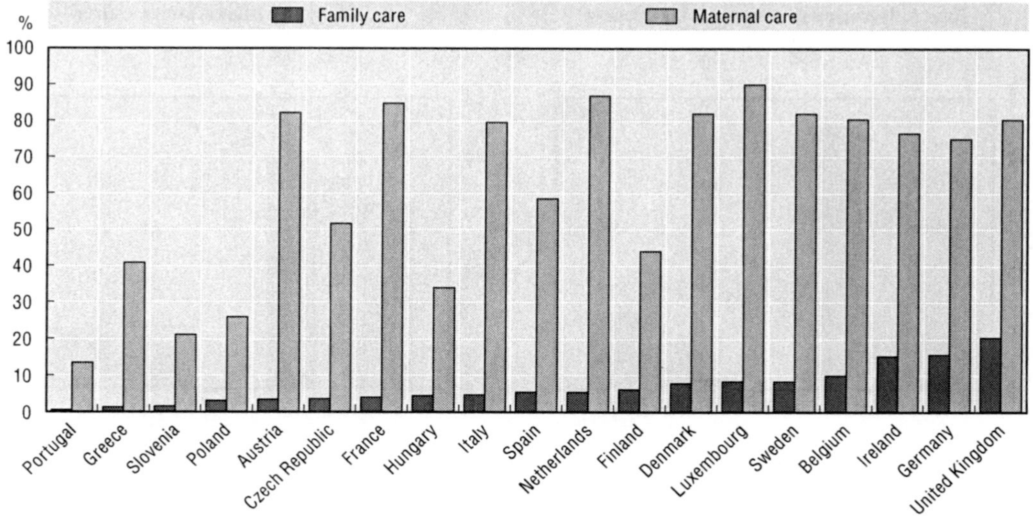

Source: European Establishment Survey on Working Time and Work-Life Balance, 2004.

StatLink ⟨⟨⟨ http://dx.doi.org/10.1787/888932401406

into account). In addition, conditions for employers to refuse the request are often stricter for parental leave than for care leave. These provisions need to be interpreted in light of evidence that part-time work promotes higher labour force participation (OECD, 2010).

Significant variation is also found in the length of part-time work which may be requested for care reasons and the possibility to revert to full-time hours. Slightly less than half of the 14 countries where the right to part-time work for care reasons exists have also an automatic right to revert to full-time hours. In practice, according to the European Working Time Survey, there is virtually no chance for a part-timer to move to a comparable full-time job in the same establishment in eastern European countries and Portugal. In many countries, no limit is mentioned on the duration of the part-time, while in Japan the total of reduced working hours and days of family care leave is 93 days or over, and in the United States it is set at 12 weeks. Germany provides a slightly longer duration (six months) and New Zealand limits the amount of the reduction in hours per week.

Which care leave for the future?

As in the case of parental leave, it is difficult to define the appropriate duration for care leave since a long leave may damage labour market position while a short leave might not be enough and force workers to resign from their job. However, unlike the care of young children which requires more intensive care at a younger age, care for ill or disabled relatives is unpredictable in duration and intensity over time. Workers might benefit from flexibility in the possibility of fractioning leave over several occurrences. Ideally, care leave should take into account the episodic nature of illnesses, deterioration or improvement in health condition or changes in the availability of formal care. Using leave on a part-time basis or returning to work part-time might also be helpful to accommodate the changing needs of carers and frail or disabled people. Other forms of flexible work might be more suitable for carers who need to vary their hours week-by-week or who do not want to cut down on their working hours but want to work flexibly.

Figure 4.3. **Care leave and part-time work is more likely in certain sectors**

Share of establishments reporting offering care leave or part-time work for care

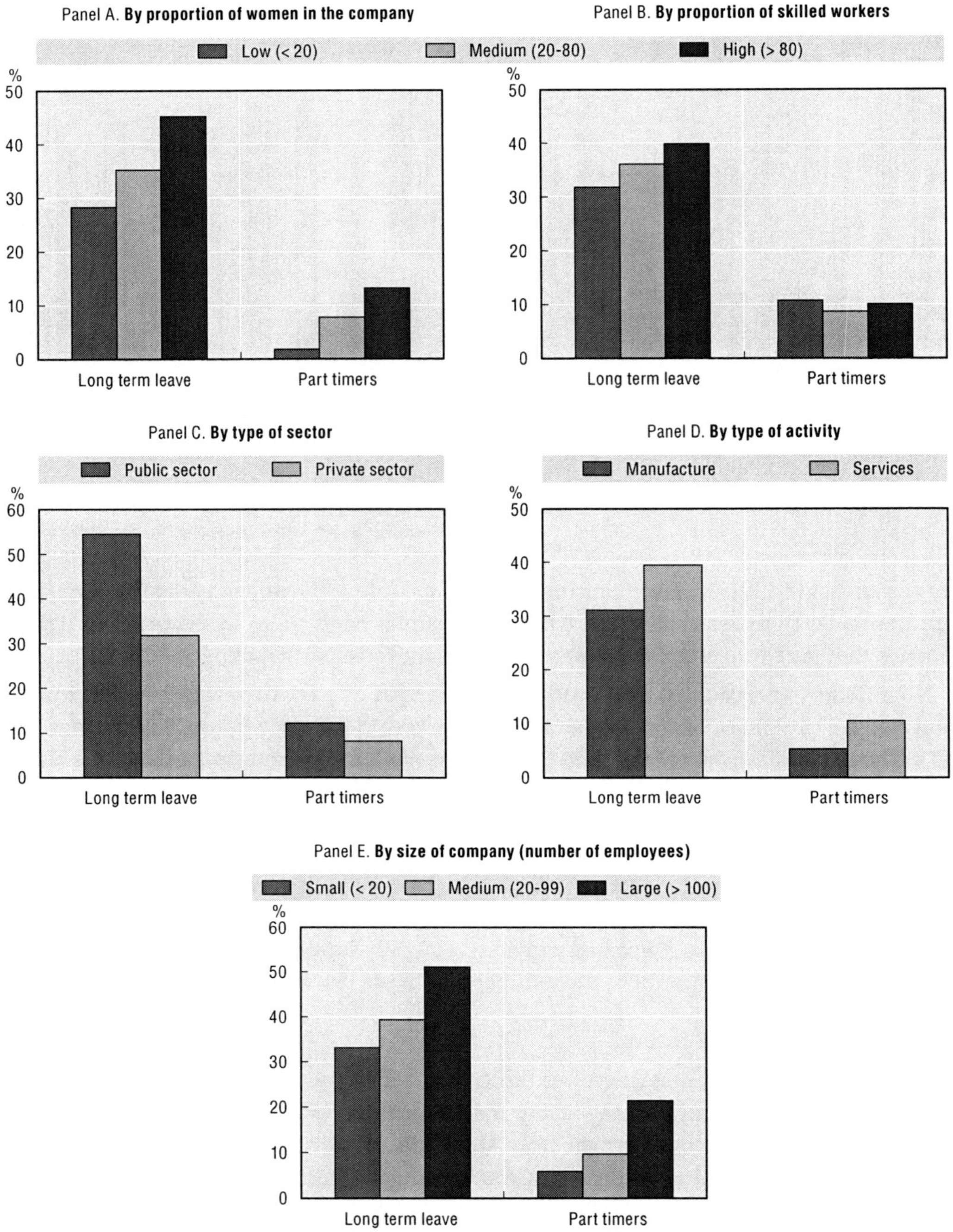

Panel A. **By proportion of women in the company**   Panel B. **By proportion of skilled workers**

Low (< 20)   Medium (20-80)   High (> 80)

Panel C. **By type of sector**   Panel D. **By type of activity**

Public sector   Private sector   Manufacture   Services

Panel E. **By size of company (number of employees)**

Small (< 20)   Medium (20-99)   Large (> 100)

Source: European Establishment Survey on Working Time and Work-Life Balance, 2004.

StatLink ⟶ http://dx.doi.org/10.1787/888932401425

At the same time, care leave, particularly paid leave, could become a pre-retirement option. While parents take parental leave at the beginning or through mid-career, most carers tend to be older than 45 or 50 years. Long paid care leaves, particularly if they offer high replacement rates and if workers are guaranteed pension and unemployment contributions, create a risk of early retirement. This has occurred with the "*Crédit temps*" or

"Time Credit" in Belgium, which can be taken as a full or partial reduction in working time up to a maximum of one to five years.

Care leave is sometimes limited to caring for those with a terminal illness. Obviously, much care is needed also for people with non-terminal diseases. A wider definition of care leave may be desirable but moral hazard could emerge. First, while a parent-child relation and the needs for child care are relatively clear-cut, it remains difficult for policy makers to identify who are the long-term carers and which level of caring commitment should trigger an entitlement to care leave. To prevent such problems, entitlements are defined in terms of the relationship to the dependent person, but since a person might have several carers, the problem of how many carers per person should benefit from leave arrangements emerge. Such provisions are already present in the case of care allowances (*e.g.,* in Ireland). Belgium is considering the introduction of a tax and social statute for carers as a way to identify carers and to provide them with legal rights (Box 4.1). Second, additional difficulties arise with respect to decisions about what care needs justify a care leave and the setting of eligibility conditions that are neither too restrictive (*e.g.* terminal illness, 80% dependency as in France) nor too loose so that any relative may claim to be a full-time carer. Given the fact that most carers are involved in low-intensity caregiving (Chapter 3), this raises the issue of what care efforts justify entitlements to a care leave. The use of care assessment systems already in place to determine eligibility to publicly funded LTC benefits may need to be extended also to dependent people that rely on care by family and friends.

Box 4.1. A statute for informal family carer: The case of Belgium?

Since 2008, Belgium has been researching the possibility of a legal recognition of informal carers. Such legal recognition implies a legal definition of carers, as well as a certificate for a limited duration together with rights and obligations for carers. Goals of the legal recognition include measures to maintain the social entitlement of carers, the creation of mechanisms in labour law for increased flexibility, the granting of tax advantages and to solve problems of civil and criminal liability. Through the statute, time spend in caring for family members will be considered as time at work and carers will be entitled to social security rights and their acquired skills will be more easily recognised. The identification of carers will help in targeting support measures towards them. On the other hand, the legal recognition stumbles upon the difficulty of identifying what should be in the procedure. In particular, criteria need to be set in terms of the dependency level of the care-recipient and on the identification of carers in terms of the charge of care and its duration.

4.3. Improving carers' physical and mental wellbeing

Chapter 3 has shown that caregivers are more likely to experience worse mental health because of their strenuous duties. Policies relieving stress from carers are thus of prime importance, particularly in the context of carers themselves becoming older and possibly frailer. This section discusses the advantages and challenges of three types of policies supporting carers' well-being: Respite care, counselling services and co-ordination of help.

Respite care

Respite care is often perceived as the most important and common form of support to alleviate caregiving burden and stress. Respite care can provide carers a break from normal caring duties for a short period or a longer time (see Box 4.2). Without respite, caregivers

---

Box 4.2. What is meant by respite care?

Respite care may refer to very different types of interventions providing temporary ease from the burden of care. Often, the objective of such breaks is to increase or restore the caregiver's ability to bear this load (Van Exel *et al.*, 2006). The most common forms of respite care include:

- day-care services;
- in-home respite;
- institutional respite.

An important element of respite care definition is the length of respite. Some of the services offer short stays (such as day-care services) and others consider longer periods of time (vacation breaks for carers, emergency care etc.). Both duration and frequency of respite breaks (everyday or every week) are relevant when assessing the importance for the carer and the care recipient. Some countries offer more diversified "packages" of support (combining both short and long-term breaks) in order to better meet the needs of the caregiver. The provision of respite breaks can be provided in various settings, such as community care or institutions, and by various actors, such as family and friends, and nurses.

---

may face serious health and social risks due to the stress associated with continuous caregiving, and may also enjoy little time for leisure or feel isolated. Carers are often reluctant to take such breaks because of uncertainties about the quality of respite care and financial difficulties. Policies ensuring ease of access to respite, for example via financial support to pay for such breaks, geographical proximity and sufficient availability of respite services, are thus important.

Policies for carers in almost all OECD countries include respite care, although legal entitlement to respite services varies widely. In Ireland, an annual grant for respite care can be used throughout the year, while in Austria a specific allowance is available to pay for respite care for up to four weeks. In Germany, the insurance system includes provisions for financing respite care of up to four weeks. In Luxembourg, the long-term care insurance includes additional funding for a three-week respite care. The new Act on Family Caregiving 2006 in Finland grants at least three days respite a month for carers who care on a continuous basis. (The Finnish Ministry of Health and Social Affairs is currently preparing a National Development Plan on Informal Care Support). In many other countries, respite care is seen as a service but there is no specific right to carers to receive such services, or no direct reference to the number of days carers are entitled to.

Direct public provision and financing of respite care is uneven across countries and respite care remains scarce. In most OECD countries, short-term respite care is financed directly by families, although some subsidies exist for those with limited resources. In Austria, Finland and Hungary, in-home respite care is not publicly financed and users need to pay full costs. In certain countries such as Canada, for instance, financial incentives in the form of tax credits for families paying for respite care services are available.[5] On the other hand, in Denmark the municipal council is obliged to offer substitute or respite care services to those caring for a relative and respite services are fully publicly funded. There is also an under-supply of respite services in some OECD countries. For instance, residential respite care services in France and Switzerland have waiting lists as respite is offered only when LTC beds are unoccupied. In addition, charges for respite care in France often exceed the value of the universal cash benefit allowance. In many countries, such as Japan, northern European countries, Spain or the United Kingdom, municipalities are in charge of organising respite care particularly in the case of day-care and in-home respite, which leads to large local disparities in access and availability.

Respite care results in satisfactory outcomes for carers but it is not cost-effective for all forms of service provision. Assessment of the effectiveness of respite is complex because of the multiple dimensions of impact on informal caregiving (mental and physical health, satisfaction or admission in institutions), but recent evaluations show that carers highly value such services (Pickard, 2004; Zank and Schacke, 2002; Van Exel, 2007). Unfortunately, this does not systematically translate into better mental health outcomes for carers. In particular, the evidence on the effectiveness of *day care* in improving the psychological health of carers is mixed, and there is little evidence to draw a conclusion on the effectiveness of in-home respite care. The impact may be higher for high-intensity carers and day care appears to be more effective for carers in paid-employment and where the person cared for has cognitive problems (Davies and Fernandez, 2000). Overnight respite care has proven to be effective at reducing the subjectively reported burden of carers, but it might hasten the institutionalisation of the dependent person (Pickard, 2004). Mixed forms of respite care, including a combination of the above-mentioned types of respite, also showed contradictory results in the United States but these might be driven by low take-up of services.

Well-planned, flexible respite care services may improve carer's outcomes and alleviate barriers to accessing respite services. Yet evidence on the positive effect of respite care on carers remains scant, limiting possible recommendations on the most appropriate form of delivery of respite. In that respect, a range of services is probably most appropriate, to provide flexibility of respite provision and responsiveness to carer and care recipient characteristics and needs, and also changes in those needs over time. More tailoring of respite to the needs of carers instead of fixed hours and days is cited as a suitable option (Pickard, 2004). Mixed forms which include in-home care on demand and drop-in services combined with more traditional forms of respite also appear to be useful for carers (see Box 4.3). As some users of adult day services spend a considerable amount of time in travelling and preparations, combining respite care with services for planning and transportation of the dependents is likely to alleviate the burden of carers.

Counselling and training services

According to surveys, carers would welcome more psychological counselling and information from health professionals (Van Exel *et al.*, 2002). For instance, carers are not always knowledgeable about the disease of the person they care for or have difficulties dealing with disabilities. Counselling has been found to be effective at relieving carer's stress (Pickard, 2004).

Most social support and training is typically provided through local initiatives and relies heavily on the voluntary sector. Many local community organisations and NGOs offer social support and counselling programmes, making them often more widely available to carers than respite services but are often provided in informal settings or as a crisis response. Informal counselling is often provided through support groups which have developed at the local level to provide a listening ear and a forum to exchange experiences. However, evidence on their effectiveness in terms of mental health outcomes of carers is inconclusive.

Box 4.3. **An integrated respite and support system to carers in Sweden**

Sweden has supported family carers through mixed projects involving public entities (such as medical staff in institutions), private actors, local communities, NGOs and families and friends. These projects encompass counseling, training and also respite care.

Respite care, especially in-home respite care, has become very popular in recent years. Municipalities offer family carers in-home respite care during the day free of charge. Almost all 290 municipalities offer such services across the country. Other forms of respite care are also available, such as "24h instant-relief" (or drop-in services) or weekend breaks. Municipalities offer stays at spa-hotels and arrange for care of the care recipient for one or two days. Mixed strategies combining different forms of respite are complementary to relieve carer's stress.

In addition to respite services, public authorities have encouraged communication between socio-medical staff and carers. Collaboration with carers is prone to create more "carer-friendly institutions". Counseling programmes are also seen as a supportive service offered in the core package for family carers. These programmes are both run by voluntary organisations as well as public services, such as help-line services, and are moving towards further integration.

Source: Johansson (2004).

Some country initiatives are promoting a more comprehensive and integrated counselling system. Sweden has promoted a better space for dialogue between the socio-medical sector and the families and friends of disabled. "Caring for Carers" in Ireland developed a comprehensive network of support institutions for carers, which offer 13 skills training courses called "Caring in the Home". The Netherlands uses a preventive counselling and support approach (the POM-method or *Preventieve Ondersteuning Matelzorgers*). Once enrolled in national care plans, individuals are contacted by trained social workers who carry out house visits. These workers provide carers with information and follow-up phone interviews on a three-month basis to prevent the occurrence of mental health problems among carers, especially at the early stages of caregiving. In the United States, the National Family Caregiver Support Programme includes support groups and individual counselling, workshops and group work.

Information and co-ordination services

Carers may not be fully aware of services available to them and may find it difficult to get help from fragmented services. Eligibility criteria for allowance or tax benefits and credits can be confusing and carers may require help from other family carers or social workers. Internet websites and other discussion boards provide useful information to the carer, though they are often left alone to tackle administrative issues. Daily planning of different tasks and duties may be difficult for carers and can cause burnout. Doctor's appointments, organisation of respite care breaks or social workers appointments may be difficult to co-ordinate, especially when combined with personal or familial duties and employment.

One-stop shops for carers and their families can better inform and help carers. Such information centres help carers be in touch with others having similar experiences and acquire information on sources of help (financial, physical, emotional and social), and on the care recipient's illness or disability. For instance, in France, the Local Centres of Information and Co-ordination (CLIC) provide information and help on all topics related to

4. POLICIES TO SUPPORT FAMILY CARERS

ageing and elderly needs. Help is provided individually and social workers meet with carers on a regular basis. These centres also link carers with medical staff to address questions related to the disability of the care recipient.

Linking the efforts of private, voluntary organisations and community associations with public authorities can also be important to reduce fragmentation and improve co-ordination of services. In Bremen (Germany), Social Services Centres inform and support carers throughout the caregiving spells and also help co-ordinate medical and social sectors. These centres are partly funded by NGOs and communities but also receive grants from the city of Bremen.

Case (or care) managers can help alleviate the administrative burden of carers and help them co-ordinate their needs and those of the person cared for. A case manager playing the role of a co-ordinator between the different health and social services can simplify significantly the follow-up procedures of carers. An example of such case management can be seen in Austria, where local centres evaluate carers' needs and help them find appropriate services. Support services are available in different social service centres – such as the Vienna Health and Social Care Centres and the Tyrolean Integrated Social and Health Care Districts. They provide help with different dimension of planning, organisation and information. Carers who enrol in local support centres are put in contact with a district nurse who assesses the carer's needs and directs the carer towards appropriate entities and services. Administrative and co-operative tasks are the primary focus of these institutions, but the services also act as brokers and contacts between clients and formal service. The aim is to avoid gaps between health and social care provision and empower carers with knowledge and skills to face the difficulties of caring duties.

Carers assessment is a first step to define which services are needed for carers but does not necessarily mean that all carers are identified and receive support services. Several countries including Australia, Sweden and the United Kingdom have developed protocols for appropriate assessment of carers' needs, helping professionals to define caregivers daily tasks and identify stressors. There is often no mandate for caregiver assessment except in the United Kingdom, resulting often in lack of resources to perform systematic assessment. Even where the assessment is mandated, an estimated half of carers are not known to service agencies (Audit Commission, 2004). The reasons, besides lack of awareness and self-identification as carers, include lack of knowledge of entitlement and difficulty asking for help.

Identifying carers through actors that carers see regularly is key because many carers are not forthcoming in asking for help. General Practitioners, nurses, pharmacists and other health professionals are well placed to recognise and advice carers because of their frequent interaction with the care recipient or simply through normal consultations. In Scotland, GPs have been given incentives to identify carers, set up carer registers and refer carers to appropriate local support. A resource pack is distributed in each GP practices and GPs (and other primary health professionals) are connected to carers' centres. While it is unrealistic to expect that GPs and other primary health professionals will be able to provide all necessary information and counselling to carers, they can be well placed to refer carers to more specialised sources of information and advice.

HELP WANTED? PROVIDING AND PAYING FOR LONG-TERM CARE © OECD 2011   **131**

4.4. Compensating and recognising carers

A large number of OECD countries provide financial support to carers through cash benefits either paid directly to carers through a carer allowance or paid to those in need of care, part of which may be used to compensate family carers. Slightly less than half of OECD countries have a direct payment towards the carer and slightly over a half of the countries have cash benefits for the care recipient (Annex 4.A1 and Annex 4.A3). A few countries provide both types of cash benefits (*e.g.* Norway, New Zealand, Slovak Republic, Sweden and the United Kingdom) and one-fifth does not have either type of benefit. This section will discuss the effects of both types of cash benefits on carers and the relative advantages and disadvantages of both. Other financial incentives not in the form of allowances include tax incentives, discussed in Box 4.4.

Box 4.4. **Tax incentives benefiting carers**

Tax relief is an indirect form of financial assistance to the caregiver, aiming to encourage family caregivers. Most countries have no specific tax incentives for carers with the exception of tax exemptions for carer's allowances in a variety of countries (Czech Republic, Ireland, for example). Canada and the United States have tax credit programmes.

In Canada, caregivers may be eligible to financial support through the federal tax system. Non-refundable tax measures that offer assistance to unpaid caregivers include the Caregiver Tax Credit, the Eligible Dependent Tax Credit, the Infirm Dependent Tax Credit, the Spousal or Common-Law Partner Tax Credit, the transfer of the unused amount of the Disability Tax Credit, and the Medical Expenses Tax Credit (METC). Under the METC, caregivers can claim, on behalf of a dependent relative, up to USD 10 000 in medical and disability expenses. The Infirm Dependent Tax Credit provides approximately USD 630/year in tax reduction to those who care for disabled family members with severe impairments. Alternatively, the Caregiver Tax Credit provides co-resident carers with a similar amount of money, if the care receiver's income is low. In addition to the federal tax credits, comparable caregiver tax credits are available in each of Canada's 13 provinces and territories. The provinces of Québec and Manitoba also offer refundable tax credits to eligible caregivers

The United States has a tax credit for working caregivers: The Dependent Care Tax credit. It is a non-refundable credit available to lower income working tax payers who co-reside with the care recipient and provide at least 50% of a dependent's support. Since it is only for tax payers who are employed, those unemployed or out of the labour force, who comprise a large section of caregivers, are not eligible. Tax credits often represent a small fraction of household's income and it can be complex for those most in need to claim tax refunds. Limited evidence shows that the eligibility criteria have resulted in such credits not reaching a large percentage of the carer's population (Keefe and Fancey, 1999).

Carer's allowance

A carers' allowance recognises that providing care involves costs for carers. It may help carers to juggle their responsibilities by having some income to compensate for reduced working hours or for additional expenses incurred as a result of caring. In addition, it also provides a strong signal that carers' play an important social role and should be acknowledged by providing a financial reward for their efforts.

Countries with direct payments to carers have very different compensation and eligibility conditions. Two main approaches, discussed below, emerge: i) countries providing remuneration to family carers who are formally employed; and ii) countries with means-tested allowances. In addition, some countries provide other types of allowances to carers, such flat-rate allowances in the Slovak Republic and in Belgium (three-fourths of the Flemish Municipalities and three Flemish Provinces), and allowances at provincial level in Canada (Nova Scotia's Caregiver Benefit). The amount and the eligibility conditions vary.

In Nordic European countries (Denmark, Finland, Norway, and Sweden), the payment to carers is considered as remuneration. Municipalities, which are responsible for long-term care services, employ family caregivers directly. Salaries vary across municipalities but they include a minimum regulated amount in Finland (EUR 336 per month in 2009), while in the other countries they vary with care needs and are equivalent to the hourly pay received by regular home helpers. Compensation levels are thus fairly generous and offer a fair compensation for carers' efforts, while not providing sufficient disincentives for family members to work because the compensation constitutes a relatively low wage (see Chapter 5 on working conditions in LTC) and is unlikely to compensate the full value of caregiving.

Nordic countries target more intensive care but the entitlement depends on assessments made by local authorities. Municipalities are very restrictive in granting such allowances and they are not obliged by law to provide them, possibly to limit their attractiveness to low-wage earners. Carers' allowances tend to be granted particularly to keep the care recipient at home instead of moving to an institution, and when the care performed is extraordinarily heavy or burdensome. In comparison, many more family carers benefit from payments via the care recipient. Such form of compensation requires appropriate definitions of care intensity, and standardised assessments may be useful to limit local variations in entitlement. While care wages seem a promising avenue to improve targeting and compensate the effort of carers, they remain a relatively costly option and there is a legitimate question as to whether the use of more qualified or experience formal carers should not be used instead.

Means-tested benefits paid directly to carers are found mostly in English-speaking countries (Australia, Ireland, New Zealand, and United Kingdom).[6] Allowances are limited to those most in need, with heavy and regular caring duties that result in forgone earnings. In all cases the definition of carers is linked to a threshold on weekly earnings from work and/or a minimum amount of hours of care per week. In addition, the care recipient must be in receipt of a disability benefit. Such means-tested allowances presuppose that individuals are involved in full-time care. Their stringent eligibility is also linked to low recipiency rates. Just under 1% of the total UK population (or less than one-tenth of carers) received a Carer's Allowance in 2008, while in Australia and Ireland the equivalent figure is around 0.5% – or roughly one-fifth of carers – and there is only a handful of carers receiving Domestic Purposes Benefits in New Zealand (5 246 in 2008).

Means-testing and eligibility conditions may result in disincentives to work. For example, they might discourage carers from working additional hours per week outside the house, particularly those having most difficulties to enter the labour market, such as those with low skills. Indeed, means-tested allowances in Australia and the United Kingdom generate incentives to reduce hours of work for carers (Figure 4.4). The impact depends on the skill level, especially for women, and the availability of formal care. Low-skilled women are more often in receipt of cash transfers and tend to have lower caring responsibilities

Figure 4.4. **Carer's allowances generate incentives to reduce work hours**

Coefficient estimates on hours of work from a random effects tobit

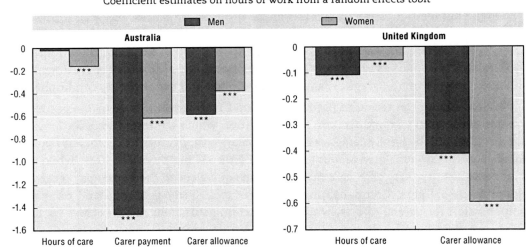

Note: Samples include persons below age 65. The following years are considered for each country: 2005-07 for Australia; 1991-2007 for the United Kingdom. The sample includes individuals present in at least three consecutive waves. All regressions include the same controls as in Figure 3.6. See Chapter 3 for more details on the data and the estimation method.

Source: OECD estimates based on HILDA for Australia and BHPS for the United Kingdom. Negative coefficients indicate a reduction of hours of work.

StatLink ⟨⟩ http://dx.doi.org/10.1787/888932401444

when in-kind benefits are provided instead of cash transfers (Sarasa, 2007). Such allowances seem thus to provide some form of income assistance, while maintaining caring as a low-paid and low-status work.

Targeting cash allowances to carers is a difficult task, involving a number of trade-offs. Typically, such cash allowances involve a number of eligibility requirements with a view to define an eligible carer (*e.g.* primary carer), the level of care effort (*e.g.* number of hours of care per week), the relationship between the carer and the care recipient (*e.g.* certain relatives, co-residency) as well as the care level of an eligible care recipient (*e.g.* high care need). In practice, some of these requirements can be difficult to verify administratively and may be subject to abuse. They may also be viewed as unfair or simply arbitrary. For example, in the United Kingdom only one carer per LTC recipient is entitled to receive the allowance and carers cannot receive more than one allowance even if they are caring for more than one person. In Ireland, "part-time caring" or sharing caring duties among two carers is permitted as long as each carer is providing care from Monday to Sunday but on alternate weeks. Leaving aside issues pertaining to setting legitimate eligibility requirements, the trade-off in designing a carer allowance is generally between providing a token recognition to a broader group of carers, including some involved in low care intensity, and providing more meaningful support to a narrowly targeted subset of carers. Most countries have opted for the latter.

Cash benefits for the care recipient

Cash benefits for dependants are often advocated as a good approach to maximise the independence of the disabled person and have become more prominent in recent years. In more than three-quarters of OECD countries, such cash schemes allow the use of the allowance to support family carers or even to hire family members formally (see Annex 4.A3 for detail on cash benefits which may be used to compensate family carers, and Chapter 1 for an overview of all cash benefits for LTC). Often, the dependent person prefers to hire relatives if they have the choice, as they tend to rate them as more reliable, trustworthy and knowledgeable about their needs (Simon-Rusinowitz *et al.*, 2005). While the primary aim of cash for care schemes is often to expand choice and flexibility for the care recipient, compensating or encouraging family carers can be a secondary aim. In certain countries (Germany, the Netherlands), the cash benefit is set at a lower value than equivalent services in kind.

In all OECD countries with cash benefits, the amount of the benefit for the care recipient depends on care needs. Following an assessment of their care needs, individuals with ADL restrictions are classified according to their degree of autonomy loss into three to four levels and up to seven levels in certain countries. In some countries, the care recipient can chose to receive care services in-kind or through a cash benefit, except in Austria, France and some eastern European countries, where only cash allowances are available. Most countries do not target allowances depending on income, apart from Belgium and Spain, where the allowances are income-tested, and France and the Netherlands, where above a certain level of income the benefit amount is income-tested.

This type of support may present several advantages for carers and policy makers. First, eligibility requirements for carers might be simpler since policy makers avoid the difficulties of defining who are primary carers and interfering with family relations in that way. Many carers do not identify themselves as carers and do not necessarily apply for a specific allowance while carers may be reached via a cash benefit targeting the user. In addition, such cash benefits can be used by elderly carers since they do not constitute wages as in the case of carer's allowances in northern Europe. They can also provide more generous benefits than the means-tested allowances given to carers in English-speaking countries. Finally, a fairer allocation of cash resources is likely to be achieved if allocated to the care recipient since the amount of the allowance depends on needs.

On the other hand, cash benefits given to the dependent person might not always be used to pay family carers and may generate financial dependence of the carer. The allowance might compensate for the additional care expenses and may be used to supplement family income if there is no specific provision to pay for family carer. This leaves carers dependent on the care recipient in terms of the compensation for their efforts or to buy formal care services for breaks. Certain countries (France for relatives other than spouses, the Netherlands) have gone around this problem by having relatives employed through a formal contract if they provide care above a certain number of hours per week. Holidays rights are also included in the conditions of employment. Germany also guarantees holidays and time off during sickness through in-built funding for substitute services (see below). This still leaves carers financially vulnerable if the person needs to receive long-term care in an institution or dies.

Another risk of providing cash benefits to the dependent person is the risk of monetising family relations. Altruism and a sense of duty are often cited as the primary motivations for relatives to provide informal care. Hope of monetary transfers and bequests in particular are another intrinsic motivation. Introducing cash allowances whereby the dependent person may chose among relatives on how to allocate additional resources may increase competition among family members.

The extent to which cash benefits are used by family carers is partly related to restrictions in the use of the allowance and to the degree of monitoring. In Germany, cash benefits are predominantly chosen over home care agency services, in spite of such benefits being 50% lower than direct home care. Cash benefits do not require compliance with a certain use of services and there is no monitoring on the way benefits are spent, nor care management requirements; cash benefits appear thus to have generated incentives for informal care, resulting in an increase in the number of caregivers per care dependent (Glendinning, 2003). Piloting of personal budgets in certain German counties, which were financially more attractive but included closer monitoring by care managers, showed that this resulted in a shift of cash recipients to personal budgets and a substitution of informal care for formal care. Unregulated benefits in Austria were similarly used for family carers but have progressively been used to hire migrant carers. In contrast, in France and the Netherlands, cash benefits or personal budgets come with the definition of a care package, especially in France where service needs are defined by health professionals and not by the dependent person, and are thus rarely used to pay family carers.

Flexibility of the cash benefit, in terms for example of relatives that can be included or not as family carers, also influences the use of such benefits. In France, hiring a relative is permitted with the exception of spouses who are by law providing assistance to their partners. While it is true that partners should care for each other, given the forecasted increase in the number of elderly spouses providing informal care, the question of how best to support the work of frail spouses without providing incentives for inappropriate use of benefits remains open.

Both types of cash benefits could help to expand the supply of workers in the long-term care sector and stimulate home care by tapping on otherwise unpaid carers, but their critics point to important trade-offs for both carers and care recipients. First, cash benefits may discourage the emergence of private providers, as households will continue to rely on family carers. In certain countries, cash benefits have stimulated a grey market, where families use allowances to hire untrained non-family members, often migrants, at the detriment of formal care services. Italy is an example of such developments. A related issue is whether promoting a substitution of formal for informal care has an impact on the quality of care. Second, cash benefits may trap family carers into a low-paid unwanted role. Japan, for instance, decided not to have explicit policies targeting family carers because of a strong tradition of family responsibility and policy focused on decreasing the burden of family carers, although some municipalities do have cash benefits under strict conditions.

The impact of public financial support on the supply of informal care is likely to be influenced by a complex set of factors, including the link between formal and informal care. Several studies have found that formal and informal care may be substitutes or complements depending on the type of care and care needs. Informal care has been found to be a substitute for formal home care (Bolin et al., 2008; Van Houtven and Norton, 2004) but this is only the case for domestic help, while it is a complement to nursing/personal care (Bonsang, 2009). In addition, when the care recipient has a higher degree of disability, the substitution effect for paid domestic help disappears (Bonsang, 2009). Providing financial incentives for carers might be a helpful strategy especially for low-intensity or low-skilled care, but it might be more problematic as care needs increase or require a relatively high allowance to provide sufficient financial incentives. In addition, relying on family carers without adequate support for them and their needs is likely to have detrimental consequences for their health and employment (Chapter 3).

4.5. Conclusions

OECD countries are increasingly concerned about the burden on carers of frail and dependent people and the need to support them. With demographic changes leading to a greater need for care and higher cost for public systems, it is important to recognise the role of carers, whether formal or informal. Carers are more likely to continue caring if they feel valued. Knowledge about good-practice policies remains still fairly limited in this field, however, and especially on the effectiveness of alternative interventions to mitigate the negative impacts of caring on work and mental health.

Cash benefits to carers provide compensation and recognition but they are not the only policy option to support carers. Cash support is a simple way of recognise the important role of carers but can also raise difficult eligibility decisions and policy trade-offs. Cash benefits should therefore be seen in the context of a proper care plan, including basic training for the family member concerned, work reconciliation measures – including flexible work arrangements – and other forms of support to carers, including respite care.

Notes

1. Informal care in the context of this chapter refers to care by family and friends. While disabled groups include both young people with handicaps and frail elderly, this chapter does not provide en encompassing overview of the range of services, labour market and social integration policies directed to young disabled people.

2. In Australia and the United Kingdom, no unpaid leave for care reasons exists; leave consists of a few days only for very short emergency reasons

3. Care vouchers could be used to stimulate the use of leave for the caring of adults. The main idea of care vouchers is that employers provide workers with vouchers, which may be used to buy formal care in lieu of a part of the employee's income. The voucher would be exempt from both national insurance contributions for the employer and from income tax for the employee. While vouchers may provide an alternative half-way to leave for care, their financial implications need to be weighed against other forms of financing long-term care.

4. Flexible work schedule include other forms aside part-time work but no sufficient statistical information was available on flexible hours, and this section focuses therefore mostly on part-time work.

5. In addition, the Veterans Independence Programme provides personal care and housekeeping support for primary caregivers to veterans.

6. Means-tested allowances might be subject to a labour earnings/income limit or to a wealth limit, depending on the country.

References

Bolin, K., B. Lindgren and P. Lundborg (2008), "Informal and Formal Care Among Single-Living Elderly in Europe", *Health Economics*, Vol. 17, No. 3, pp. 393-409.

Bonsang, E. (2009), "Does Informal Care from Children to their Elderly Parents Substitute for Formal Care in Europe?", *Health Economics*, Vol. 28, No. 1, pp. 143-154, January.

Davies, B. and J. Fernandez (with B. Nomer) (2000), *Equity and Efficiency Policy in Community Care: Needs, Service Productivities*, Efficiencies and their Implications, Ashgate.

Gautun, H. and K. Hagen (2007), "A Moral Squeeze? Does the Supply of Public Care Services towards the Very Old Affect Labour Force Participation of their Children?", Paper presented at the 8th Congress of the European Sociological Association, Glasgow, 3-6 September, Research Network Session: Ageing in Europe Session 5a Norms and Values in Ageing.

Gledinning, C. (2003), "Support for Carers of Older People – Some Intranational and National Comparisons", Audit Commission at the National Primary Care Research and Development Centre at the University of Manchester.

Johansson, L. (2004), "Eurofamcare", *National Background Report Sweden*.

Keefe, J. and P. Fancey (1999), "Compensating Family Caregivers: An Analysis of Tax Initiatives and Pension Schemes", *Health Law Journal*, Vol. 7, pp. 193-204.

Mason, A., H. Weatherly, K. Spilsbury, H. Arksey, S. Golder, J. Adamson, M. Drummond and C. Glendinning (2007), "A Systematic Review of the Effectiveness and Cost-Effectiveness of Different Models of Community-Based Respite Care for Frail Older People and their Carers", *Health Technology Assessment*, Vol. 11, No. 15.

Mestheneos, E. and J. Triantafillou (2005), *Supporting Family Carers of Older People in Europe – The Pan-European Background*, Eurofamcare.

OECD (2007), *Babies and Bosses – Reconciling Work and Family Life: A Synthesis of Findings for OECD Countries*, OECD Publishing, Paris.

OECD (2010), *OECD Employment Outlook*, OECD Publishing, Paris.

Pavalko, E.K. and K.A. Henderson (2006), "Combining Care Work and Paid Work: Do Workplace Policies Make a Difference?", *Research on Aging*, Vol. 28, No. 3, pp. 359-374.

Pickard, L. (2004), "The Effectiveness and Cost-Effectiveness of Support and Services to Informal Carers of Older People", Audit Commission PSSRU, University of Kent, London School of Economics and University of Manchester.

Spiess, C.K. and K. Wrohlich (2006), "The Parental Leave Benefit Reform in Germany: Costs and Labour Market Outcomes of Moving towards the Scandinavian Model", *IZA Discussion Paper*, No. 2372, Bonn.

Van Exel, J., G. Graaf and W. Brouwer (2007), "Care for a Break? An Investigation of Informal Caregivers' Attitudes toward Respite Care Using Q-Methodology", *Health Policy*, Vol. 83, No. 2.

Van Exel, J., M. Morée, M. Koopmanschapa, T. Goedheijtb and W. Brouwera (2006), "Respite Care – An Explorative Study of Demand and Use in Dutch Informal Caregivers", *Journal of Health Policy*, Vol. 78, No. 2-3, October.

Van Houtven, C.H. and E.C. Norton (2004), "Informal Care and Health Care Use of Older Adults", *Journal of Health Economics*, Vol. 23, No. 6, pp. 1159-1180, November.

Zank, S. and C. Schacke (2002), "Evaluation of Geriatric Day Care Units: Effects on Patients and Caregivers", *Journal of Gerontology*, Series B, Vol. 57, No. 4.

ANNEX 4.A1

Summary Table: Services for Carers

Table 4.A1.1. **Summary Table: Services for carers**

	Carers allowance	Allowance for the person being care for	Tax credit	Additional benefits	Paid leave	Unpaid leave	Flexible work arrangements	Training/ education	Respite care	Counselling
Australia	Y	N	N	N	Y	N*	N	Y	Y	Y
Austria	N	Y	N	Y	N	Y	Y	Y	Y	Y
Belgium	Y**	Y	N	N	Y	Y	Y	Y	Y	Y
Canada	Y**	N	Y	Y	Y	Y	N**	Y	Y	Y
Czech Republic	N	Y	N	Y	N	N	Y	Y	Y	Y
Denmark	Y	N	N	N	Y	N	N**	Y	Y	
Finland	Y	N	N	N	Y	N	Y			Y
France	N	Y	Y	Y	Y	Y	Y	Y	Y	Y
Germany	N	Y	Y	Y	N	Y	Y	N	Y	
Hungary	Y	N	N	Y	N	Y	Y	N	N	Y
Ireland	Y	N	Y	Y	N	Y	N		Y	Y
Italy	N	Y	N							
Japan	N	N	N	N	Y	N	Y	Y	N	N
Korea	N	N	N	N	N	N	N**	Y	N	N
Luxembourg	N	Y	Y	Y	N	Y	N**	Y	N	Y
Mexico	N	N	N	N	N	N	N	Y	N	N
Netherlands	Y	Y	N	Y	Y	Y	Y	Y	Y	Y
New Zealand	Y	Y	Y	N	N	N	Y	Y	Y	Y
Norway	Y	Y	N	Y	Y	N	Y	N	N	N
Poland	N	Y	N	N	Y	N	N	N	N	N
Slovak Republic	Y	Y	N					Y	Y	Y
Slovenia	N	N	N	N	Y	N	N**	Y	Y	Y
Spain	N	Y	N	Y	Y	Y	N	Y	Y	Y
Sweden	Y	Y	N	Y	Y	N	N	Y	Y	Y
Switzerland	N	N	Y	N	N	N	N**	Y	Y	Y
United Kingdom	Y	Y	N	Y	N	N*	Y	Y	Y	Y
United States	N	Y**	Y	N	N	Y	Y	Y**	Y**	Y**

N*: Leave for only a couple of days for emergency reasons is available.
N**: No nationwide policy is available but collective agreements exist.
Y**: Not at the national/federal level but available in provinces/states/counties.
Source: OECD 2009-10 Questionnaire on Long-term Care Workforce and Financing.

ANNEX 4.A2

Leave and Other Work Arrangements for Carers

Table 4.A2.1. **Leave and other work arrangements for carers**

| | Paid leave | | | Unpaid leave | | | |
	Paid leave	Eligibility criteria	Payment conditions	Unpaid leave	Eligibility criteria	Flexible work arrangements	Additional benefits
Australia	New National Employment Standards (2010): Ten days of personal/care leave	An immediate family member or household resident requires care because of injury. Provide proof of caring needs and reasonable notice	Paid at an hourly rate no less than the employee's basic period rate of pay	New National Employment Standards (2010): two days for each occasion where immediate family requires care or support because of illness, injury or unexpected emergency	The carer should provide relevant document (such as a medical certificate)	May request if have been working for 12 months but employer may refuse on reasonable business ground (only for a sick child)	No
Austria	Paid leave for two weeks per year for sick children and one week per year for other dependents/family members needing care	Care for sick children or dependent relatives	100% of previous earnings	Federal Act Governing Family Hospice Leave in 2002 provides flexible work arrangements or unpaid leave to care for terminally ill relatives (up to six months) and for seriously ill children (up to nine months)	Spouses, registered partners, partners in life, persons directly related to the employee (parents, children, grandparents, grandchildren), adopted and foster children, adoptive or foster parents, parents and children in law, brothers and sisters and children of the spouse, of the registered partner or the partner in life	Employees have a qualified legal claim to a reduction of the ordinary working hours, to a change in the schedule of their ordinary working hours and to leave from work (the so-called "Karenz") for the purpose of caring for a dying person or for a seriously ill child. Family leave can be taken as 24 months of part-time work to care for a seriously ill family member. Employers in companies with <50 employees can refuse on business grounds	Employees acquire compulsory pension insurance contribution periods and they are covered by health insurance during their absence

Table 4.A2.1. **Leave and other work arrangements for carers** (cont.)

| | Paid leave | | | Unpaid leave | | | |
	Paid leave	Eligibility criteria	Payment conditions	Unpaid leave	Eligibility criteria	Flexible work arrangements	Additional benefits
Belgium	Palliative care leave to take care of a parent in terminal illness up to two months (one month extendable). May be granted full-time of part-time	For anyone who needs help (can be friends or neighbors): A doctor should provide evidence that the care needs will be provided by the employee and that the person is in terminal illness	State compensation (Office National de l'Emploi) allocation: EUR 741.40 per month (proportional amount in case of part-time leave)	Emergency leave (Congé pour raison impérieuse) of ten days per year (private sector) or two months/ 45 working days per year (public)	All unforeseen circumstances that require the urgent intervention of the worker. This includes illness, accident or hospitalisation of a person residing in the same house or a first degree family member	Time credit	No
	Medical assistance leave: Up to 12 months which can be taken in several periods, from one month up to three months per disabled. May be granted full-time of part-time	Family member (2nd degree) or co-residential relative needing assistance. Doctors should provide evidence on the need of constant care. If the enterprise has fewer than ten employees, the employer can deny leave on business and organisational grounds. The employee is protected from being fired during the whole period and extended to three months after the end of the leave	State compensation: EUR 741.40 per month				
	Time credit (part-time or full-time career break	One year to up to five years leave full or part-time. Can be taken in periods from three months to one year at a time	State compensation: According to sector and length of service. Public sector: EUR 379.37/month. Private sector: EUR 453.28 or EUR 604.38 per month (Flemish Community). Additional care allowance EUR 110.41				

Table 4.A2.1. Leave and other work arrangements for carers (cont.)

	Paid leave			Unpaid leave		
	Paid leave	Eligibility criteria	Payment conditions	Unpaid leave	Eligibility criteria	Flexible work arrangements	Additional benefits
Canada	Compassionate Care benefit: Up to six weeks of income support. Collective agreements complementary: 15% of companies provide annual paid family-related or personal leave	Care for family member who is gravely ill and at the risk of dying. The caregiver must have accumulated 600 insured hours in the 52 weeks prior to the claim	Income support provided up to maximum CAD 447/week (55% of the average insured earnings) through the Employment Insurance Compassionate Care Benefit for those whose income has been reduced by more than 40%	All territory and province legislation on unpaid leave (exception Alberta) provide up to eight weeks of leave per occurrence	Occurrence to care for family members who are seriously ill and have a significant risk of death within 26 weeks	Flexible work arrangements exist in various collective agreements and are set up by companies and sector ($^1/_3$ contain family leave provisions, $^1/_{20}$ eldercare provisions, $^7/_{10}$ personal leave)	Canada Pension Plan general drop-out provision allows contributors to preserve benefit levels by excluding 15% of the months or years of lowest earnings from the calculation of pension benefits (maximum seven years) for a variety of reasons (including but not limited to caregiving)
Czech Republic				No		Since 2001, employees who care for a bedridden person can request part-time work. The employer can deny the right on serious operational reasons and there is no right to revert to full-time work after the caring period ended	Yes
Denmark	Employees have the statutory right to leave for the care of a someone close dying, according to the Act on Leave from work due to Special Family reasons (March 2006). There is no fixed time limit for the leave	The dependent can be a spouse, cohabitant or parents in terminal illness but no requirements for close/familial relationships. Evidence should be provided to prove that the dependent has two to six months to live	The minimum amount during the care leave is equal to 82% of sick pay ceiling (and up to 1.5 times the sick pay if there is more than one dependent). The municipality can also pay maintenance fees when expenses are very high	Relies on collective agreements		Flexible work arrangements exist through collective agreements	No

Table 4.A2.1. **Leave and other work arrangements for carers** (cont.)

	Paid leave		Unpaid leave			
	Paid leave	Eligibility criteria	Payment conditions	Unpaid leave	Eligibility criteria	Flexible work arrangements	Additional benefits
Finland	Legislated right: job alternation leave is available for 90 up to 359 days but company-specific – or collective agreements may differ. The leave is to be taken as successive 90 days minimum	The carer should have been working for at least 12 months prior to the claim (and have at least ten years of experience)	Compensation of 70% of the daily unemployment allowance (80% if more than 25 years work history) paid by the state through the unemployment funds and the Social Insurance Institution	Relies on collective agreements		Flexible working arrangements have been possible as part of the job alternation leave since 2010. Those who decide to work part-time for caring reasons are eligible to a part-time allowance from the Employment and Economic Development Office (need to be agreed with the employer). The compensation is proportional to the reduction of working hours. Any employee can request part-time work for social or health reasons for 26 weeks maximum at a time. The employer must consider the claim but is not required by law to agree on the arrangement	No
France	Since 2 March 2010 Law, family solidarity leave is eligible to compensation – for three months (renewable once)	Care of a first degree family member or co-residential member terminally ill. The employee should make a claim two weeks prior to the leave and the employer cannot deny the leave	A daily compensation will be paid to the carer up to 21 days	Family support leave (*Congé de soutien familial*) for three months, renewable once, with job guarantee, to take care of a dependent family member	Care of a dependent relative (until fourth degree family member but co-resident) – the employee must have at least two years experience and the person needs to have a permanent disability of 80%	With agreement from the employer, the Family solidarity leave can turn into reduced working hours	Yes

Table 4.A2.1. **Leave and other work arrangements for carers** (cont.)

	Paid leave		Unpaid leave			
	Paid leave	Eligibility criteria	Payment conditions	Unpaid leave	Eligibility criteria	Flexible work arrangements	Additional benefits

	Paid leave	Eligibility criteria	Payment conditions	Unpaid leave	Eligibility criteria	Flexible work arrangements	Additional benefits
Germany				Leave is possible up to six months	A family member (until second degree) needs care for a long period. The employer can refuse on business grounds if employs less than 15 employees	Since 2008, employees in firms with more than 50 employees can request part-time work to care for a disabled co-residential family member – up to six months (renewable once). The employer can deny the leave only on urgent operational reasons. There is a right to revert to full-time hours	Yes
				Emergency leave for medical reasons is also possible up to ten days	Second degree family needs assistance because of severe illness, accident or terminal illness. The employer cannot deny the right to the employee		
Hungary	No			Unpaid leave for a maximum of two years, for the duration of care	Upon the employee's request for care of a dependent relative	Any employee can request part-time work but may be refused on a business case	Yes, nursing fee. As for pension rights, the period of nursing fee payment is counted towards service time. Beneficiaries are entitled to health care service
Ireland	No			Unpaid carer's leave available since 2001. Leave is for a maximum of 104 weeks, can be taken in one period (with 13 weeks minimum each time) or several – employee protected by the Carer's Leave Act of 2001. Employer may refuse "on reasonable grounds"	For employees with at least 12 months of continuous service – proof of full-time care required (only 24 hour care basis). Assessment done by a general medical practitioner and the Department's medical advisor	No	Pension rights/credits: Home-maker's scheme allows for up to 20 years spent caring for children or incapacitated adults be disregarded for pension purposes but still requires a person to contribute 260 contributions and enter insurance ten years before pension rights

Table 4.A2.1. Leave and other work arrangements for carers (cont.)

	Paid leave			Unpaid leave		
	Paid leave	Eligibility criteria	Payment conditions	Unpaid leave	Eligibility criteria	Flexible work arrangements	Additional benefits
Japan	Family care leave benefit: leave of up to 93 days is permitted for each family member

The LTC leave system itself does not set any provision for compensation paid by employers, but when a subscriber of Employment Insurance takes a LTC leave, s/he can receive a LTC leave benefit | Need to be a subscriber to Employment Insurance. A worker (excl. a day worker) that provides LTC to a spouse, parent and child (or grandparent, brother/sister, or grandson/ daughter living with the worker), or parent of the spouse. The care recipients must require regular care for two weeks and over. In addition, in order to receive a LTC leave benefit from the Employment Insurance, a minimum insured period of 12 months in the two years before the start of leave is required | If the insured of the Employment Insurance meets the requirement in the left column, he/she can receive a LTC leave benefit equivalent to 40% of his/her wage before the leave (if the total of his/her wage and benefit exceeds 80% of his/her wage before the leave, the exceeded amount is reduced) for maximum three months | Nursing leave is also possible for five days a year or ten days a year if more than one dependent | A worker that provides long-term care to a person in need of care (excl. a day worker). The person in need of care and the required condition is the same with Family care leave | The employer must provide either of the following for at least 93 days, on request of his/her employee providing care to the qualifying family in need of care:
1) Shortened working hours
2) Flexible working time
3) Staggered working hours
4) Subsidies or other measures to aid the employee's with LTC spending | No |
Korea	No			No		Flexible working arrangements are available depending on the sector/company defined by collective agreements	No
Luxembourg	End-of a life leave (Congé d'accompagnement de fin de vie) for five working days at time and per year (can be taken in several periods or as reduced working hours)	When a first or second degree family member (spouse, parent or children) is terminally ill	The leave days are paid by the sickness fund (Caisse d'Assurance Maladie) in charge of the employee	Unpaid leave for family care for six months at a time. Relies on collective agreements	Should be documented by the employee (proof of need for care with a doctor's certificate). The dependent should be a first degree family (parents or spouse)	Flexible working arrangements based on collective agreements	Pension contributions guaranteed by dependency insurance
Mexico	No			No		No	No

Table 4.A2.1. Leave and other work arrangements for carers (cont.)

	Paid leave			Unpaid leave			
	Paid leave	Eligibility criteria	Payment conditions	Unpaid leave	Eligibility criteria	Flexible work arrangements	Additional benefits
Netherlands	Paid leave up to ten days. Employers can refuse to grant leave on serious business ground	Care of a sick relative	Paid at 70% of the earning by the employer	Legislation at the national level: minimum standard set in the long-term care leave: An employee may take a maximum of half the number of hours that he works as care leave for a period of twelve weeks, in one or several periods	Care of a sick first-degree relative, whose life is threatened in the short term. The employer can deny the leave on serious business grounds	Flexible work hours are possible, depending on collective agreements but an insured minimum is set in legislation	Yes
New Zealand	No			No		Since 2008, employees with six months tenure who work at least ten hours per week and have care responsibilities for children or adults can request part-time work. Employer can deny the claim on operational and business grounds	No
Norway	Nursing care leave for periods up to 20 days, plus Care leave paid up to ten days		Both schemes are paid at full wage			Employees who for health, social or other weighty welfare reasons need to have their normal working hours reduced can request part-time work. Employers may refuse only for serious operational or business reasons	Automatic pension credits for carers who provide more than 22 hours of care per week and during at least six months in a year (three credits a year. Below an average wage)
Poland	Paid leave set at national level. Duration – max. 60 days per year		Paid 80% of salary	No		No	No
Slovenia	Leave for a sick co-resident family member: Up to seven days. For severe illness can be extended to 30 days (up to six months in extreme case)	Co-resident family member should be a child or a spouse. Need to be a subscriber to have compensation	Paid at 80% of average earnings of the preceding 12 months			Flexible working arrangements set at national levels are available, depending on the sector/company	No

Table 4.A2.1. **Leave and other work arrangements for carers** (cont.)

	Paid leave			Unpaid leave			
	Paid leave	Eligibility criteria	Payment conditions	Unpaid leave	Eligibility criteria	Flexible work arrangements	Additional benefits
Spain	Care for a sick child or other serious family reason: Two days for private sector (extended to three if involves traveling) and three for central state public sector (five if traveling)		Paid by the employer	Long-term leave for a dependent: Up to two years (extreme cases: Three years)			Pension credits granted by the state
Sweden	Paid leave set at national levels. Leave for terminal care for 100 days	A relative in terminal care; refers only to persons in working age (up to 67 years). Need to provide evidence such as doctor's certification	On average, paid at 80% of the wage	No		No	Yes
Switzerland	Depending on the sector/company. Set at national levels, by employers or through collective agreements			Depending on the sector/company. Set at national levels, by employers or through collective agreements		Depending on the sector/company. Set at national levels, by employers or through collective agreements	No
United Kingdom	No			Emergency leave can be taken for caring of a family member. The length of the leave should be "reasonable" – *i.e.* two days		Work and Families Act (2006) gives carers the right to request flexible working, can only be refused for clear business reasons. Eligibility: Must have worked for over 26 weeks prior to the claim, must not have requested flexible work the 12 months prior to the claim, dependent must be first-degree family. There is no time limitation as for the flexible work arrangements and should be arranged with the employer	Yes

Table 4.A2.1. **Leave and other work arrangements for carers** (cont.)

	Paid leave			Unpaid leave			
	Paid leave	Eligibility criteria	Payment conditions	Unpaid leave	Eligibility criteria	Flexible work arrangements	Additional benefits
United States				All private companies with 50 or more employees grant them up to 12 weeks' unpaid leave per year. Leave may be taken on an intermittent basis or reduced work schedule	Serious illness of a spouse or a child	Employees with 12 months of service working for employers with more than 50 employees can take 12 weeks of Family and Medical Leave (per year) as a period of part-time work (reduced leave schedule) for the birth or adoption of a child, to care for a spouse, child or parent with a serious health condition or if the employee him/herself has a serious health condition. The employer cannot deny this right. Right to revert to full-time	No

Source: OECD 2009-10 Questionnaire on Long-term Care Workforce and Financing.

ANNEX 4.A3

Financial Support for Carers

Table 4.A3.1. Financial support for carers

	Allowance to the carer			Allowance to the disabled dependent (only allowances that can be used to pay the family carer)			Tax benefits
	Name	Eligibility criteria	Payment conditions	Name	Eligibility criteria	Payment conditions	
Australia	Carer payment system	Must be Australian resident and personally provide constant care in the home income and assets test	Paid at pension rates AUD 671.90/fortnight for single and AUD 506.5 for each eligible member of a couple; possibility of carer supplement				No
	Carer allowance	Not income or assets tested – for only co-residential dependents	A fixed amount of AUD 105/fortnight				
Austria	No, but there is a special allowance in case of dementia	Caring for their relatives who have dementia	Contribution to covering the costs of organising professional or private substitute care if the main caregiver is incapacitated (EUR 1 200 to EUR 2 200)	Austrian long-term care allowance system	Need-tested but not means-tested. Eligible people must require care on a full-time basis (included mental disability/dementia)	The allowance should cover between 26 and 70% of monthly expenses (about 36% of nursing homes); Up to EUR 1 655 a month for more than 180 hours a month	No
Belgium	Carer allowance in Flanders (*mantelzorgpremie*)	Variable	Variable according to municipalities or provinces (average EUR 32/month)	Integration allowance for those with serious ADL restrictions	Income-tested (should not exceed EUR 2 630.82 for the household) and need-tested (should have a doctor visit and ongoing control). The claim should be made before 65 years old	Ranges from EUR 1 061.26 to EUR 9 550.33 per annum depending on the number of restrictions	Tax deductions for households with a co-residential disabled and aged below 65 years old.
				Income replacement allowance	For those aged 21-65 whose handicap prevents them from making enough money to live. Income-tested and depends on familial status	The allocation can reach up to EUR 11 618.44 per annum	

Table 4.A3.1. **Financial support for carers** (cont.)

	Allowance to the carer			Allowance to the disabled dependent (only allowances that can be used to pay the family carer)			Tax benefits
	Name	Eligibility criteria	Payment conditions	Name	Eligibility criteria	Payment conditions	
Canada	Not at the federal level but relying on provincial systems. The Nova Scotia Caregiver Benefit (July 2009) provides caregivers assisting severely impaired low-income care recipients aged over 19 years with a financial benefit of CAD 400 per month in taxable income. Caregivers must provide a minimum of 20 hours of care per week for more than 90 days. From September 2010, the new Legacy of Care Programme, including the Forces Attendant Care Benefit, provides up to CAD 100/day for family and friends who leave their jobs to care for an injured soldier						Federal: Caregiver Tax Credit (provides co-resident carers with CAD 630/year, if the care receiver is low income); Eligible Dependent Tax Credit; Infirm Dependent Tax Credit (CAD 630/year in tax reduction to carers of disabled family members with severe impairments); Spousal or Common-Law Partner Tax Credit; transfer of the unused amount of the Disability Tax Credit; Medical Expenses Tax Credit (METC, claim can be up to CAD 10 000). The Infirm Dependent Tax Credit Provincial/Territorial: Comparable tax credits for caregivers. Quebec and Manitoba also provide refundable tax credits for eligible caregivers
Czech Republic				Care allowance	Dependent on care: > one year of disability and need assessed by a doctor or a social worker. Not income-tested and amount depending on degree of disability. No age limitation	Amount: CZK 2 000 per year for mild disability, to CZK 12 000 for heavy disability	No

Table 4.A3.1. **Financial support for carers** (cont.)

	Allowance to the carer		Allowance to the disabled dependent (only allowances that can be used to pay the family carer)			Tax benefits
Name	Eligibility criteria	Payment conditions	Name	Eligibility criteria	Payment conditions	
Denmark Consolidation Act on Social Services (CASS): The carer shall be employed by the municipality for six months (possible extension for three months)	An employment contract shall be made between the carer and the municipal council, setting the employment terms and conditions, including the identity of carer, the duration of the employment, the duties and responsibilities, notice periods, etc.	The salary will amount to DKK 16 556 per month. 12% will be paid into a pension scheme, 4% of which is withheld from the salary, and 8% of the salary will be contributed by the employer				No
Finland Carer allowance	No income test. Support paid to the carer is considered as income when other social allowances are allowed	EUR 336/month minimum				No
France			Allocation Personnalisée d'Autonomie (APA) is paid to the care recipient for arranging help with ADL restrictions (can be paid to the carer but not his spouse or partner) Compensatory Allocation For Third Person Benefits (ACTP): is directed towards the payment of the family carer	Must be aged over 60 years and have residency in France; amount depending on disability and on income High levels of disability and income-tested. Must be aged below 60 years old	Ranges from EUR 529.56 to EUR 1 235.65 per month (but regional disparities), but a co-payment is required for the care recipient, depending on income Ranges from EUR 415.34 to EUR 830.69 for high levels of needs and low levels of income	Planned support for carers through tax reductions (hiring of formal labour can lead to tax reductions under certain requirements)
Germany Carer allowance under the pension insurance scheme	Directed towards the payment of a carer providing care for at least 14 hours a week – levels of needs assessed by a medical staff determine the payment. The carer will have a contract with the insurance company and salary will be based on the number of hours worked. No specified relationship between carer and care recipient	From EUR 225 to EUR 665 in 2010 for home care and from EUR 1 023 to EUR 1 918 per month for institutional care (depending on partial/full institutional care)				Income tax allowance of EUR 924/year if they do not get payments for care; can declare total costs of care and claim a tax allowance if the person cared for is eligible for nursing care level III

Table 4.A3.1. **Financial support for carers** (cont.)

	Allowance to the carer			Allowance to the disabled dependent (only allowances that can be used to pay the family carer)			Tax benefits
	Name	Eligibility criteria	Payment conditions	Name	Eligibility criteria	Payment conditions	
Hungary	Nursing fee	Monthly financial support to persons who nurse at home a close family member requiring long-term care due to serious disability and long-term illness	From January 2011, the nursing fee will be HUF 29 500, irrespective of the minimum old-age pension in case of severe dependency of family members requiring permanent care. Cannot be cumulated with other benefits except of old age pension (in case of ten years care before retirement)				The nursing fee is not subject of taxation. The period of nursing fee payment is counted as service time
Ireland	Carer allowance	Income and assets tested but means test has eased significantly over the years. An income disregard of EUR 665 per week for a couple and EUR 332.50 for a single person applies. The person receiving care requires full-time or continual supervision and frequent ADL assistance and is likely to require care for at least 12 months	EUR 220.50/week for those aged under 66 and EUR 239/week for those aged over 66. If caring for more than one person, receive the 50% in addition				Home carer tax allowance of EUR 900/year if carers' income does not exceed EUR 5 080. Carers' allowance/benefit not taken into account for the determination of income. Incapacitated child tax credit and dependent relative tax credit when maintaining a relative
	Carer's benefit. Introduced in 2000 for insured persons who leave the workforce to care for someone		Payable for 104 weeks at a rate of EUR 221.20/week				
Italy				Attendance allowance (Indennità di accompagnamento)	For high levels of disability and incapacity to work. Need tested but not means tested, no age limits and within a broad national scheme	Cover max of 65 hours of care per week	No
Japan	No			No			No
Korea	No						No

Table 4.A3.1. Financial support for carers (cont.)

	Allowance to the carer			Allowance to the disabled dependent (only allowances that can be used to pay the family carer)			Tax benefits
	Name	Eligibility criteria	Payment conditions	Name	Eligibility criteria	Payment conditions	
Luxembourg				Cash allowance for care (prestations en espèces). Under the LTC insurance, recipients can choose between care in-kind and this allowance		Payment levels ranges from EUR 267 to EUR 1 100	Tax deductions for LTC services to hire someone up to EUR 3 600/year; the carer hired should be below 65 years old and cannot have own pension allowance contributions for carers
Mexico	No						No
Netherlands	Additional allowance for carers providing care to those eligible for long-term care services	Relative or friend living with the carer	EUR 250 (2009) per month for carers providing support to a recipient needing at least 371 days of care	Personal budget: Following reform in 2003, all home care users can choose in-kind services or cash to pay a relative, including spouses and parents, to provide care. Roughly 40% of budget holders hire family members and neighbors	No age limits or income-test to claim. The maximum hourly rate is EUR 4.70 (EUR 129 a month for a single aged over 65 earning more than EUR 40 718 a year)	Average amount per year: EUR 15 350	No
New Zealand	Domestic purposes benefit	Must provide more than four hours of care to a disabled person who would otherwise require rest home care, residential disability care, extended care provided for severely disabled children and young people, hospital care, or care of a similar kind. Income and asset tested	Can reach up to NZD 202.20 per month if married or in couple	Disability allowance: Received in cash with no restrictions on the use	The disability must last at least six months or in case of terminal illness. Income tested (for married couple, income should be below NZD 807.04 a week)	The maximum disability allowance is of NZD 56.98 per week	No tax incentives but may qualify for tax credit for housekeeping (NZD 310/year)
Norway	Care wage for carer: Only for high levels of caregiving (when home care is considered more suitable than residential care)	Pays relatives or others for caring when this is considered better than agency care. Typically 3-10 hrs/week. Not income tested	The carer is paid for a given number of hours, typically using the hourly wage of a care assistant in the public agency. Usually this amounts to about NOK 4 600 a month	Cash payment to the care recipient. Assistance pension is paid by the National social security board, typically on a long-term basis		Depend on care load. Average NOK 4 600 per month	No

Table 4.A3.1. Financial support for carers (cont.)

	Allowance to the carer			Allowance to the disabled dependent (only allowances that can be used to pay the family carer)			Tax benefits
	Name	Eligibility criteria	Payment conditions	Name	Eligibility criteria	Payment conditions	
Poland				Nursing allowance	For those with a disability who do not receive disability benefits	PLN 153 monthly	No
Slovak Republic	Care allowance	For those taking care of relatives or neighbors with severe disabilities. Income-tested EUR 200-260/month (EUR 83-110 if retired). Cannot be cumulated with other benefits but may be with earnings from employment (with a maximum)		General social benefit-payment in the framework of pensions (paid from state budget) for recipients of pension (invalidity or retirement) who have ADL dependency, benefit is not means tested			No
Slovenia							No
Spain				Carer allowance	If LTC services are not available, the dependent person may receive allowance in order to provide themselves for home care. The allowance is means tested. Requirement: The disabled person should be a third degree relative or a spouse. Do not need to justify the spending	Ranges from EUR 300 to EUR 519.13 depending on the level of need	No
Sweden	Paid kin caregiver	The caregiver needs to be employed by the municipality through a proper contract. Directed towards the care of elderly in constant need of care and attention	Based on the number of hours provided by the carer. Paid as a salary equal to one on the formal market and offering the same social security benefits	Attendance allowance	Minimum level of needs of 17 hours per week. Needs tested but allowance varies across municipalities	According to flat rate: USD 515 (SEK 5 000) per month	No
				Assistance allowance	20 hours a week, several ADL measured (payment of estimated hours needed), only for the disabled aged over 65 years		

Table 4.A3.1. Financial support for carers (cont.)

	Allowance to the carer			Allowance to the disabled dependent (only allowances that can be used to pay the family carer)			Tax benefits
	Name	Eligibility criteria	Payment conditions	Name	Eligibility criteria	Payment conditions	
Switzerland	Bonuses for caregiving	For those caring for disabled family members (e.g., parents, parents-in-law, children, brothers or sisters and spouses). Need to be a caregiver for at least 180 days/year	Bonus for those receiving old-age pension				Tax deductions for fees as a result of illness/disability
United Kingdom	Carer's allowance	For those spending at least 35 hours/week caring. Not eligible if the carer is in full-time education (21 or more hours/week) or earning more than GBP 100/week after deductions	Flat rate: GBP 55.55 per week	Attendance allowance	For those aged over 65 and who need assistance for more than six months	Two rates: GBP 49.30 or GBP 73.60 a week depending on level of disability. Non-means tested and tax free	No
				Disability allowance	For children and adults aged under 65 who need help with personal care or have walking difficulties because they are physically or mentally disabled	Care component – Three rates depending on level of care needed: GBP 19.55, GBP 49.30 or GBP 73.60 a week. Mobility component: Two rates depending on level of mobility needs: GBP 19.55 or GBP 51.40 a week. Non-means tested and tax free	No
				Independent Living Fund	Allowance aimed at encouraging home care instead of institutional care. The Fund is now closed to new applications	Amount based on the cost of care required. Maximum available payment to existing claimants is GBP 475 per week. Non-means tested and tax free	No
United States				Consumer directed home care: Medicaid insures specific services provided by agencies to assist in living with disability: provides a cash-like benefit within the constraints of Medicaid's service delivery model. Cash and Counseling: Evaluation programmes in Arkansas, Florida and New Jersey		Amount of money varies across states: From a low of USD 350 per month in Arkansas to a high of USD 1 400 in New Jersey for elders and adults with disabilities	Medical Expenses Tax Deduction. If the tax payer – either the caregiver or the care-receiver – has medical expenses that exceed 7.5% of their adjusted gross income, medical expenses are deductible

Source: OECD 2009-10 Questionnaire on Long-term Care Workforce and Financing.

Chapter 5

Long-Term Care Workers:
Needed but Often Undervalued

This chapter describes the size and the composition of the long-term care (LTC) workforce, in terms of gender and skill mix, working hours and work pressures. The analysis focuses on the two major parts of the LTC workforce: those working in home care and those working in institutional care. Developments in the mix of qualifications in nursing LTC are considered. The chapter then examines the relative importance of factors behind the difficulties in matching demand for, with the supply of, LTC workers, such as salary levels and working conditions. The analysis seeks to answer the following questions: does the workforce meet current (and potential) demand? How many people work in the different components of LTC sector and what is their background? What are the working conditions in the LTC sector? What can be said about developments over time?

The statistical data for Israel are supplied by and under the responsibility of the relevant Israeli authorities. The use of such data by the OECD is without prejudice to the status of the Golan Heights, East Jerusalem and Israeli settlements in the West Bank under the terms of international law.

5.1. How many long-term care workers are there?

Is there a long-term care (LTC) workforce "crisis"? Reports from the United States suggest so (Stone and Wiener, 2001; Harmuth, 2002; IFAS, 2007). Yet, the answer to this question may be more complex across the OECD. What is the crisis: in the workforce itself, or in the tension between demand and supply? In order to answer this question, it is first of all important to review available statistics on the LTC workforce. Despite data limitations, many OECD countries have stepped up their LTC-workforce data collections.

More care recipients per worker in home care but most care workers are in institutional settings

While in Australia there is one full-time equivalent (FTE) LTC worker for each two LTC care recipients, in many countries a full-time worker serves more clients, with lower ratios in institutional care than in home care (Figure 5.1). Especially in the Czech Republic and in the Slovak Republic, the user/FTE ratio is very high, representing large workloads. The differentiation in workload in institutional care shows less variety than in home care.[1]

Figure 5.1. **Higher ratio of LTC users per full-time equivalent worker in home care than in institutions**

Selected OECD countries, 2008

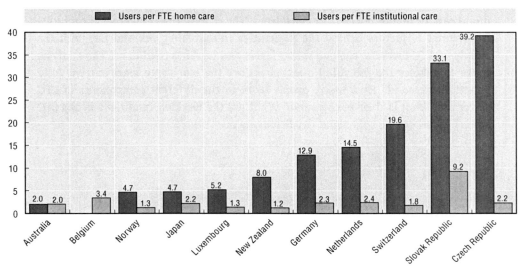

Note: The definition of full-time equivalent (FTE) varies across countries. Available years for home care: Australia and Germany: 2005; Luxembourg, New Zealand and the Netherlands: 2006. Other countries: 2008. Available years for residential care: Luxembourg, New Zealand and the Netherlands: 2006; Australia, Belgium, Germany and the Slovak Republic: 2007. Data for the Netherlands consider nurses and ADL workers in employment only. Australian data exclude allied health workers (home care). German data exclude elderly care nurses (170 000 estimated in 2007).

Source: OECD Health Data 2010.

StatLink http://dx.doi.org/10.1787/888932401463

Even though most care recipients receive care at home, most LTC workers practise in residential care – although Japan and Korea are exceptions (Figure 5.2).

Figure 5.2. **Less than half of LTC workers are in home care in most OECD countries**
Selected OECD countries, 2008

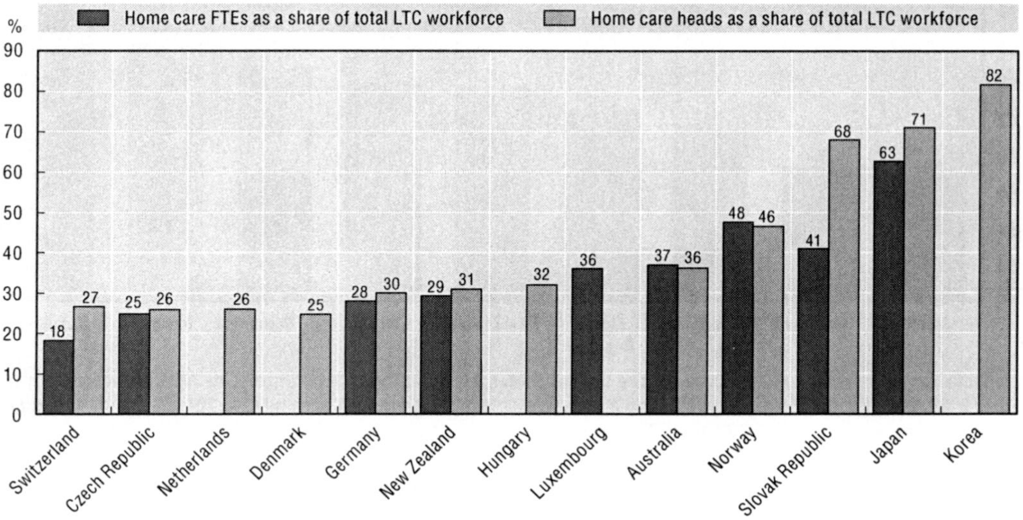

Note: Data for Luxembourg refer to 2005. Data for the United States, Canada, New Zealand refer to 2006. Data for Denmark, Germany, Australia and the Slovak Republic refer to 2007. For Australia, home-care data do not include allied health workers. German data exclude elderly care nurses (170 000 estimated in 2007). Data for the Netherlands reflect nurses and ADL workers in employment only.
Source: OECD Health Data 2010.

StatLink http://dx.doi.org/10.1787/888932401482

The size of the LTC workforce seems to keep up with population developments

In most countries for which data are available, the number of LTC workers is growing in line with the share of the population aged over 80 years, although in Luxembourg, Germany and Japan the size of the LTC workforce outgrew the increasing share of people aged over 80 years. The opposite occurred in the Slovak Republic, where worker density (number of workers per 100 people aged 80 or over) decreased from 1.6 in 2004 to 0.7 in 2008.

5.2. Who are the LTC workers?

Most LTC workers are women and work part-time

The LTC sector is a major source for female employment in many OECD countries (Fujisawa and Colombo, 2009; Figure 5.3). In the Netherlands, one in every seven working women is employed in the care and welfare sector (van der Windt *et al.*, 2009). In most countries there is little change in the gendered character of the LTC workforce. Only in the Slovak Republic, the share of women in the LTC workforce has quickly increased to a level similar to that of other OECD countries, from 61% in 2004 to 90.5% in 2006. Cangiano *et al.* (2009a) report that female employment in care is mostly restricted to direct care work in the United Kingdom, while managerial jobs tend to be held by men.

Based on the number of care workers per full-time equivalent it can be calculated that many LTC workers work part-time, and slightly more so in home-care settings (Figure 5.4). In Japan, for example, 84% of home-care workers work part time. Moreover, five in every six home-care workers face monthly adjustments in their hours and working days per week.

Figure 5.3. **Most LTC workers are women**

Share of women in the LTC workers, selected OECD countries, latest available year

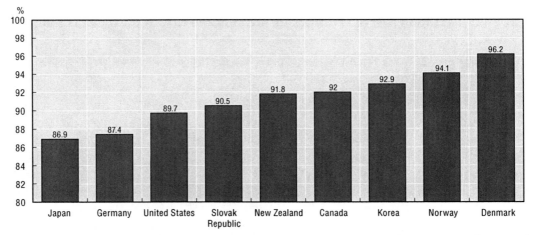

Note: Data for Japan refer to 2003. Data for the United States, New Zealand, Canada refer to 2006. Data for Denmark refer to 2007. Data for the Slovak Republic and Norway refer to 2008. Data for Korea refer to 2009. German data do not include elderly care nurses (170 000 in 2007).

Source: OECD Health Data 2010.

StatLink ᵐˢ⊑ http://dx.doi.org/10.1787/888932401501

Figure 5.4. **Part-time work is more frequent in home-care settings**

Number of LTC workers per full-time equivalent (FTE), selected OECD countries, 2008

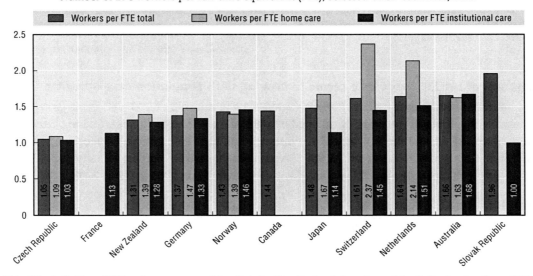

Note: The definition of FTE varies across countries. Data for New Zealand, Canada, and the Netherlands refer to 2006; data for France, Germany. Australia and the Slovak Republic refer to 2007. German data exclude elderly care nurses (170 000 estimated in 2007). Australian data exclude allied health workers. Data for the Netherlands reflect nurses and ADL workers in employment only.

Source: OECD Secretariat calculations based on OECD Health Data 2010.

StatLink ᵐˢ⊑ http://dx.doi.org/10.1787/888932401520

A Japanese survey of institutional care employers suggests that 40% of the institutional care workers work on a part-time basis (Hotta, 2010). On the other hand, part-time working hardly exists in the Czech Republic. The same goes for those working in institutional care in the Slovak Republic (Figure 5.4). In most countries for which data are available,workers in institutional care settings work more paid hours than those in home care. In the United States, 43% of "direct care workers" were employed less than full-time all year round in 2007 (PHI, 2007; PHI, 2010). Over half of personal and home-care aides (54%) worked part-time, or worked full-time only for part of the year (PHI, 2007). Although the LTC workforce in German nursing homes increased by 29% between 1999 and 2007, the share of full-time workers decreased from 46 to 35%. And while the share of *male* full-time workers in nursing homes increased by 92%, the share of *female* full-time workers decreased by 8%, even though the total share of female workers in German nursing homes remained at 87% (see *Drei-Verdi.de* in the list of web pages at the end of the chapter).

For five countries, developments in working time could be analysed through time series – mostly showing reductions in average weekly working hours. Data for Norway suggest that workers increased their working hours between 2003 and 2008, while fewer hours were worked per week in the Czech Republic (2005-08), Germany (2003-07) and the Netherlands (home care, 2004-07). Since 2000, Japanese home-care workers decreased their hours per week, while institutional care workers have increased their working hours (Hotta, 2010). German sources confirm decreased working hours (Oschmiansky, 2010; Rothgang et al., 2009). The Australian institutional care sector shows a 10% reduction in working hours per week since 2002. Generally, a reduction in working hours reflects aggregate trends in OECD labour markets, with an increase in part-time work across the OECD from 12% in 2000 to 16% in 2009,[2] together with an associated 4% decrease in annual hours worked in the same period.[3]

LTC workers, especially the less qualified, sometimes hold multiple jobs. In New Zealand, 17% have multiple jobs – typically LTC-related or IADL-type activities (cleaning, private support work, and cooking) (Ministry of Health/University of Auckland, 2004). Cangiano et al. (2009a) and Martin et al. (2009) report similar results for migrant care workers in the United Kingdom and the United States, while Eborall et al. (2010) report that each social-care worker in England has on average 1.6 jobs.

With populations ageing, so is the workforce in general and the LTC workforce in particular. A major and increasing proportion of LTC workers is middle aged (Table 5.1).

There are different age patterns of entry in the LTC sector for different qualification levels. For example, Australian nurses start working in long-term care at an earlier age than other LTC workers, but still a quarter of the Australian LTC nurses starts their long-term care career at the age of 40 years. More than half of the community care workers start their LTC job when older than 40 years, and one in five when aged at least 50 years (Martin and King, 2008).

Entering the long-term care workforce may follow a period of economic inactivity. Between 16 and 29% of the Dutch low-level LTC workers were economically inactive before entering the current employment (van der Velde et al., 2010). Similarly, about one third of the support workers in New Zealand was economically inactive prior to taking the job, of which 40% were housewives, and 46% were unemployed (Ministry of Health/University of Auckland, 2004).

LTC workers generally have low qualifications but requirements for institutional care are higher

LTC workers typically include nurses and lower-level care workers. The division of labour, the scope and type of activities, and LTC workers' regulation vary markedly across countries. This translates into different qualification mixes and ratios between nurses and lower-skilled workers across the OECD.[4] In most countries for which data exist, less than

Table 5.1. **Evidence on ageing of the LTC workforce**

	Ageing workforce indicator	Type of workers	Trend	Source
Australia	70% of community care workers are over 45 years; and 60% of institutional care workers are over 45 years (female workforce age: 36% is over 45 years)		1997-2005: Average age of nurses moved from 40 to 45 years; the share of workers aged over 55 years increases	Martin and King (2008)
	Average age of employed nurses 44.1 years		Share of nurses aged 50 or over: 1998: 18.9; 2008: 34.9	AIHW (2008b)
Canada	Canadian LTC registered nurses are older than in Canadian health care			O'Brien-Pallas *et al.* (2003)
Germany			1995-2005: Nursing care workers aged 50+ increased from 18 to 23%	BGW (2007)
Japan	60% older than 50 years	Home-visit helpers		Hotta (2010)
Netherlands	2003 and later: > 50% older than 40 years		2002-06: Average age of workers in institutional care moved from 38.9 to 40.2 years. Share of those aged over 45 years: from 31 to 41%	*www.azwinfo.nl*
New Zealand	> 50% are 40-60 years old; 16% is 60 or over	56% provides IADL and ADL; 21% provides IADL only		Ministry of Health/University of Auckland (2004)
United Kingdom	No signs of ageing of the LTC workforce			Cangiano *et al.* (2009a)
United States	Average age: – all direct care workers: 41 years – institutional care workers: 38 years – home-care workers: 45 years (2009). – self-employed or working directly for private households: 49 years		Average age of home-care workers in 2007: 43	PHI (2007; 2010)

Source: OECD Secretariat compilation.

half of the nursing LTC workforce consists of nurses, ranging from 12% in New Zealand to 85% in Hungary (Figure 5.5).

Figure 5.5. **In most OECD countries, less than half of the LTC workforce consists of nurses, mostly employed in institutional settings**

Share of nurses in the LTC workforce (head counts), selected OECD countries, 2008

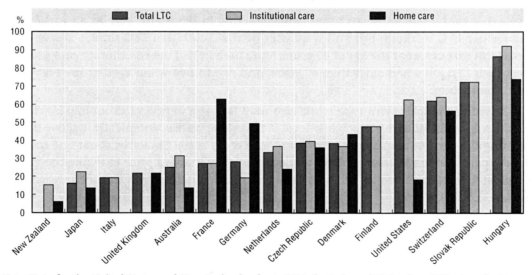

Note: Data for the United States and New Zealand refer to 2006; for Italy and Finland, to 2005; data for France (institutional care and total) refer to 2003, while home-care data refer to 2002; data for Australia, Germany and Denmark refer to 2007. Data for Australia do not include *allied health workers*. Data for Germany exclude elderly care nurses (170 000 estimated in 2007). Data for the Netherlands reflect nurses and ADL workers in employment only.
Source: OECD Health Data 2010.

StatLink 🔊 http://dx.doi.org/10.1787/888932401539

Qualification patterns across care settings tend to follow the overall pattern within a country, but there are exceptions. So, while New Zealand has low shares of nurses in both home as well as in institutional care, and Switzerland has high shares of nurses in the subsectors, patterns are different in France and Germany, with high shares of nurses in home care and fewer in institutional care. The United States shows a different pattern: relatively few nurses in home care and relatively many in institutional care. Nurses, however, may work more hours than other direct care workers, so data based on headcounts can under estimate the actual input by nurses as compared to that of other lower-level care workers. Australian data, for instance, point to lower shares working part-time and higher numbers of weekly working hours, the higher the qualification and working level of nurses (AIHW, 2008a).

National or regional regulations set minimum requirements to qualify as a LTC worker, although other training schemes – often short-term training programmes provided by employers – also play a role, the latter in more on-the-job training programmes. Nurses typically qualify in a targeted – and possibly certified or accredited – vocational education, although there may be different work categories, for instance, registered nurses (RNs) and licensed practice nurses (LPNs) in the United States.[5] Nursing education generally requires at least three years of targeted education, but here, too, a practice component may form a major share of the education. While some countries have no targeted education for LTC workers (such as Hungary and Poland), many countries – especially for lower-level workers – have educational programmes that combine some theory with practice training. Japan is among the countries reporting several training levels for LTC workers. Training is available to enable qualification as a care worker or as home helper. The duration of such (initial) vocational education is highly variable across OECD countries (Table 5.2).

In most countries, initial vocational training for LTC is publicly financed, although in some, there is a mix of public programmes with national certification, and private funding. For instance, in New Zealand, the industry's own training organisation provides for – mostly on site – training. However, although the demand for long-term care services is changing, curricula for the LTC sector show little development. This is especially the case for lower-level care workers. For instance, in the United States, the minimum federal training requirements of 75 hours training for nursing aides/home-health aides (with 12 hours per year of continued education) have not changed in 20 years (IOM, 2008). Many states have, however, installed additional requirements.

For lower-skilled care workers, standardisation of qualification is often lacking and many LTC workers will not have such qualifications. In the Netherlands, between 17 and 60% of the LTC employees do not have relevant LTC-related qualification (van der Velde et al., 2010, p. 15). In Australia 30% of the community care workers have no relevant qualifications, with those in community based care less likely to hold a relevant certificate than their colleagues in institutional care (Martin and King, 2008). Data for the United Kingdom point to an overall low qualification level of social care workers (Cangiano et al., 2009a). In the United States, 59% of the direct care workers have a maximum qualification level of high school or less (PHI, 2010) and in Germany, fewer than half of the workers in home care have a relevant qualification. Across Germany, some 300 different qualifications for "care assistant" existed in 2007 (Oschmiansky, 2010).

But over qualification is also not uncommon: 20% of the Dutch "helpers" have higher care-related qualifications (van der Velde et al., 2010). The Canadian Home Care Resources Study (2003) reports generally high educational levels of Canadian LTC workers, with a

Table 5.2. Initial training levels for the lower-level LTC workforce across the OECD

	Nationwide training programmes available for LTC workers	Job title or category	Training scheme	Training content and duration	National minimum requirements in curriculum?	Remarks
Australia	Yes	Ancillary Worker	Community Service Training CHC20108	430 hours, 5 weeks in practical and theoretical training	Yes	
	Yes	Residential Aged Care Worker	Personal Care Worker Certificate III in Aged Care	555 hours/8 to 16 weeks. Practical and theoretical	Yes	
	No	Specialisation for Care Worker	Home and Community Care CHC40208	730-740 hours/up to 18 weeks. Includes additional work placement training, voluntary	Yes	
Austria	Yes	Home Assistants (*Heimhilfe*)	Basic training	200 hours theoretical course, 120 hours of practical training in ambulatory working stations and 80 hours in stationary departments	Yes	
	Yes	Care Assistants (*Pflegehilfe*)		Minimum 17 years of age, mental and physical fitness. One year/1 600 hours of theoretical and practical instruction	Yes	
Canada	No	Ontario: Personal Support Worker (PSW)	PSW training programme	Two academic years (eight months), 384 hours of in class theory. 386 hours of practical experience. In-service training with employers	Regional	Overseen by the National Association of Career Colleges
	No	Personal Attendants		Similar to PSW programme but shorter in duration	Regional	
	Yes	Worker of Basic Social Care		Basic education + 150 hours expert course. Duty of 24 hours of additional education annually	Yes	
Czech Republic	Yes	Health Assistant / Nurse (assistant)		Four years high school / Three years high school		
Denmark	Yes	Social and Health Care Helper		One year seven months: 20 week basic course, 24 weeks school study, 31 weeks practical training	Yes	Six months relevant work experience, command of Danish
	Yes	Social and Health Care Assistant		One year, eight months, 32 weeks school study, 48 weeks practical training periods	Yes	Nordic/EU citizen
Estonia		Social Care Worker		Training of two years, of which 25% practice		

Table 5.2. Initial training levels for the lower-level LTC workforce across the OECD (cont.)

	Nationwide training programmes available for LTC workers	Job title or category	Training scheme	Training content and duration	National minimum requirements in curriculum?	Remarks
France	No	Home aid (aide à domicile) Household Assistant (aide ménagère) Family and Life Assistant (auxiliaire familiale et de vie)	Qualification for Social Carer (Diplôme d'État d'auxiliaire de vie sociale)	504 hours of technical and methodological training, 560 hours of practical training. Voluntary. Employer based	Yes	Pre-requisites: 3 000 hours of work over the last ten years
Finland		Long-term Care Worker		Vocational education, three years, 120 credits in total, with at least 29 credits of on-the-job training	Yes	
Germany	No	Elderly Carer		In accordance to Geriatric Nursing Act (2004), three years training programme. 200 hours theoretical training and 2 500 hours professional practice teaching	Local (Länder)	
		Additional institutional care workers (Betreuungskräfte)		Five day orientation internship, three modules of at least 160 hours, plus two weeks internships	Yes	
Ireland	Yes	Care Assistant for Elderly	FETAC Level 5 Certificate in Healthcare Support	36 weeks. 16 weeks training with Training and Employment Authority (FAS), 15 weeks integrated training (FAS and host employer), and five weeks on-the-job training with a host employer	Yes	At least 16 years of age
Japan	No	Home Helper		Special academic institutions	No	
	Yes	Certified Care Worker		To be eligible for State Examination for Certified Care Workers: One-year programme at training facility, or two- to four-year programme or three years of experience in personal care-related occupation	Yes	
	Yes	Certified Social Worker		To be eligible for State Examination for Certified Social Workers: Completion of a combination of theoretical and practical training for two to four years or college/university education in care-related subject	Yes	

Table 5.2. **Initial training levels for the lower-level LTC workforce across the OECD** (cont.)

	Nationwide training programmes available for LTC workers	Job title or category	Training scheme	Training content and duration	National minimum requirements in curriculum?	Remarks
Korea	Yes	Skilled Care Worker	2nd degree 1st degree	120 hours dedicated training 240 hours dedicated training		Licensing required before one can work as LTC worker
Norway			Health and Social Care Programme	Completion of lower secondary education. 2-3 years, 50% theory	Yes	
Netherlands	Yes	Care Work Assistant		Level 1: One year of training, no prior requirement. Mainly practice based		Dual trajectories: either a practice based education (BBL) or more theory-based (BOL) (full time)
	Yes	Care Work/Social Care Work Helper	Vocational training Level 2	Level 2: At least age 16, two years full-time assistant vocational education. Theory based	Yes	
	Yes	Individual Carer	Vocational training Level 3	Level 3: Requires preparatory intermediate vocational education (VMBO) or equivalent prior education (incl. diploma level 2); three years	Yes	
Slovak Republic				High school for nurses. 220 hours, emphasis on practical experiences		
Sweden	Yes	Auxiliary Nurse	Upper secondary level education	Three years	Yes	
	No		Private Association Training	Depending on programme: A few days to a month		
United Kingdom	Yes	Care and Support Workers	National Vocational Qualification Level 2 or 3 in Health and Social Care	Level 2: one year – six units, four mandatory and two optional units. Units of study vary according to educational institution Level 3: two years – eight units, four compulsory and four optional. Units of study vary according to educational institution	Yes	Government Target: 50% of all personal care must be provided by NVQ qualified by 2008
United States	Yes	Home Health Aid		Two weeks training	Yes	High school diploma
		Personal Care Assistant		No Federal training requirements	Yes	
		Certified Nursing Aid		75 hours of classroom and practical training (some states require 120 hours). Competency evaluation within four months of work	Yes	Working in a federally certified nursing home

Source: OECD 2009-10 Questionnaire on Long-term Care Workforce and Financing, and additional country documents.

third of the workers feeling underemployed. In Australia, 13% of the community care workers have higher but untargeted qualifications (Martin and King, 2008). Such outcomes are in line with more general outcomes according to which women often work below their qualification level (OECD, 2007a).

While LTC workers, on average, have lower qualifications than health workers (Fujisawa and Colombo, 2009), in many countries those working in institutional care have higher qualifications than those working in home care. In Australia, community care workers are more likely to have post secondary qualifications than institutional care workers, even though unrelated to their aged care work (Martin and King, 2008). Smith and Baughman (2007), and van der Windt *et al.* (2009) provide a similar picture for the United States and the Netherlands.

5.3. What are the working conditions in long-term care?

Benefits and wages are lower in home care

Wages in LTC are generally low (Table 5.3). Fujisawa and Colombo (2009) state that low-skilled LTC workers in most countries earn somewhat more than the average for low-skilled workers. For instance, the median hourly pay for care workers in adult care services in the United Kingdom is GBP 6.56, which is 14% higher than the national minimum wages (Cangiano *et al.*, 2009a; 2009b) and lower than in the health care sector, particularly in home care. Data are scarce, however, and inconclusive.

Furthermore, experience may not translate into remuneration. Direct care workers in the United States often lack annual wage increases, while home-care workers are exempt from minimum wages and overtime protection as they do not fall under the Fair Labour Standards Act. German, US and New Zealand data indicate nurses in long-term care earning lower wages (and working fewer hours) than those in other parts of health care (Rothgang and Igl, 2007; Ministry of Health/Auckland University, 2004). Wages may also differ according to region. Canada, for instance, reports lower wages for LTC workers in rural areas.

As in many other sectors, there are gender differences in pay levels in LTC.[6] In Japan, male nursing care workers earn 11% more than their female colleagues (Health and Welfare Bureau for the Elderly, 2010), irrespective of the number of years of continued employment in the sector, while institutional earnings are higher than in home care (Hotta, 2010).

Besides wages, in some countries, LTC workers lack job benefits, such as health insurance in the United States (PHI, 2007; 2010), or have more limited benefits than most other workers have. Partly, this is because there is an overrepresentation of part-time work in the LTC sector, and, in general, part-time workers have more limited access to such benefits. Low wages combined with part-time work may therefore lead LTC direct care workers to remain dependent on public safety nets. In the United States, many LTC workers are dependent on public support programmes such as food stamps, Medicaid, public housing, child care, energy and transportation assistance.

Care work is demanding and burdensome (Korczyk, 2004; Cangiano *et al.*, 2009a), leading often to early retirement due to stress and burnout (European Foundation for the Improvement of Living and Working Conditions, 2006). The likelihood of poor work-related health, too, is an important reason for discontinuing employment (Ministry of Health/ University of Auckland, 2004). While Dutch care and welfare workers are satisfied with their jobs compared to those in other sectors, they are also less likely to state their willingness to continue working until their 65th birthday (CBS, 2010, p. 145). Similarly,

Table 5.3. **Wages in LTC**

	Wages (monthly gross, unless mentioned otherwise)	Remarks/sources
Australia	Registered nurses (RN) Level 1 top per annum wages: AUD 55 123 (around EUR 40 122) to 61 869 (around EUR 45 038). Personal care worker: AUD 28 079-37 267 (around EUR 20 440-27 128) to AUD 36 131-38 986 (around EUR 26 299-28 377) (levels around 2009)	Wages vary according to function and jurisdiction. Wages for personal care workers at max classification may include managerial positions Wages are 50% more than minimum weekly in 2002 (Fujisawa and Colombo, 2009)
Belgium	Basic annual (gross) wages 2009: EUR 21 997-34 562: Nurse assistant EUR 22 798-37 596: Registered nurse	www.werk.belgie.be/CAO/330/330-2009-000655.pdf Exclude additional payments (inconveniency, annual leave, etc.)
Canada	Home-care workers: CAD 16.1 (around EUR 11.8) per hour. LTC workers: CAD 12.7 (around EUR 9.3) (home-service workers) to CAD 24.4 (around EUR 17.9) hourly (RNs)	Fujisawa and Colombo (2009)
Czech Republic	Nurses: CZK 22 900 (around EUR 944) Nurses auxiliary and ambulatory attendants: CZK 14 400 (around EUR 593) Salaries in social services sectors: Nurses: CZK 24 009 (around EUR 989) Nurses auxiliary: CZK 18 395 (around EUR 758) Ambulance attendants: CZK 16 179 (around EUR 667) per month	2008 data. Average salary: CZK 24 282 in 2008 (according to Czech Statistical Office)
Estonia	Nursing care hospital workers salary (March 2009) EEK 22 809 (around EUR 1 458) (March 2008: EEK 18 550; around EUR 1 185)	
Finland	(end 2009) Average salary licensed practical nurse: EUR 2 370 RN: EUR 2 860	There are no significant differences in salary levels between local government and private sector
France	Monthly wages (2009) at 31 years of age in private not-for profit sector: – *infirmier diplômé d'État* EUR 2 442 – *aide-soignant* (personal carer) EUR 1 852 – *aide médico-psychologique* EUR 1 856 – *auxiliaire de vie sociale* EUR 1 856	LTC workers in private contract earn minimum wage, while those working through agencies earn 50% more (Fujisawa and Colombo, 2009)
Germany	72% of all elder care full-time employees interviewed earn under EUR 2 000; 48% earn less than EUR 1 500	Nölle and Goesmann (2009); Fuchs (without year); reported in: Oschmiansky (2010)
Ireland	Annual Home Help: EUR 29 352-EUR 30 659 (levels: 2008) Nurses aides (Dublin, non-paypath): EUR 29 269-EUR 30 630	
Japan	**Home helper,** age 43.9 years, 4.4 years service, nine overtime hours: JPY 211 700 (around EUR 1 888) monthly; special annual wage: JPY 278 600 (around EUR 2 485) **Nursing care worker of welfare facility,** age 35.8 years, 5.2 years service, four overtime hours: JPY 215 800 (around EUR 1 924) with special annual wage JPY 505 000 (around EUR 4 502) **Home-visit care workers,** average monthly: JPY 207 641 (around EUR 1 844) **Institutional care workers:** JPY 217 415 (around EUR 1 937)	(data reported June 2008) *Heisei Nijyu Jyuhachi Nendo Kaigo Rodo Jittai Chosa* (2008 Fact Finding Survey on Long-term Care Work) Wages appr. 64-47% of average (Fujisawa and Colombo, 2009)
Luxembourg	*Infirmier:* EUR 2 978-EUR 6 071 *Aide-soignant:* EUR 2 373-EUR 4 402	Excl. inconveniences, annual leave, etc.
Netherlands	Example: "*Ziekenverzorgende in de wijk*": Wages: EUR 1 729 to EUR 2 558 (2008), depending on experience	Wages based on collective labour agreements (CAO-VVT-2008-10). Employers receive compensation for "wage sensitive" costs. Wages exclude overtime, inconvenience rostering, annual extras
New Zealand	Median hourly wage for personal and home-care aids (2000): NZD 7.50 (around EUR 4.2)	Health Outcomes International (2007)
Norway	(as of end 2008): NOK 29 000 (around EUR 3 657) per month	
Slovak Republic	2009: EUR 276-EUR 385 gross monthly (both institution and home care)	Overall average salary: EUR 766.41; minimum (2009): EUR 295.5

Table 5.3. **Wages in LTC** *(cont.)*

	Wages (monthly gross, unless mentioned otherwise)	Remarks/sources
Slovenia	Basic monthly wages: Nursing assistant II, 15 wage grade (WG): EUR 817.43 Nurse holding secondary education degree, 21 WG: EUR 1 034.30 The basic wage for a social carer, 13 WG: EUR 755.75	Wages between 50-70% of national average (Fujisawa and Colombo, 2009)
United Kingdom	Median hourly wages for LTC in adult social care: GBP 6.56 (around EUR 7.62)	14% above minimum; lower than in health care, esp. in home care Private sector pays lower than not for profit, lower than public sector (Cangiano *et al.*, 2009a, 2009b)
United States	2007: Direct care workers: Median hourly wages USD 10.48 (around EUR 7.67) (2007). In 2008: 0.5% decrease	Wages are 31% below US median. 2008: US Median increases by 3% (PHI, 2007, 2010) Wages appr. 51% of average wage in 2007 (Fujisawa and Colombo, 2009)

Notes: Country currencies are converted into euros using the 2011 exchange rates. LPN: Licenced professional nurse. RN: Registered nurse.
Source: OECD 2009-10 Questionnaire on Long-term Care Workforce and Financing, unless other sources are mentioned.

Australian data suggest that there may be limits to how long-term care workers remain in the sector (Martin and King, 2008). Even though, in Australia, the United States and New Zealand, some LTC workers continue to work until their 70th birthday, few LTC workers generally remain active in the sector until retirement.

Work-related accidents and injuries are common in LTC. In the United States, nursing aides, orderlies and attendants have the third highest number of injuries and illnesses, second only to truck drivers and labourers (US BLS, reported in Squillace *et al.*, 2009). A third of the certified nursing aides incurred at least one work-related injury, leading almost one in four unable to work for at least one day during the last year. Depression and – due to lifting and carrying of care recipients – lower back problems and being hurt on the job are common (Gleckman, 2010). High psychological pressures, caused by high work pressures and lack of labour satisfaction are also said to contribute to sickness (BGW, 2006). Especially the care for people with dementia can lead to high psychological stress (Schmidt and Hasselhorn, 2007).

High work pressures may also contribute to violence. Half of residential care workers in New Zealand feared violence by clients, as opposed to 25% in home care (Ministry of Health/University of Auckland, 2004), while verbal abuse by especially dementia patients is not uncommon. The *European Nurses Early Exit Study* (NEXT) found that 22% of nurses experience violence by patients or family at least once per month (Estryn-Behar *et al.*, 2008), with nursing aides more often experiencing violence. Frequent work interruption, high workload, longer working-week duration, working in night shifts, all increased the likelihood of experiencing violence. Those working in geriatrics and long-stay departments reported at least monthly violence by patients or family (those in day care and home care experienced least violence). Those experiencing the highest levels of violence have the highest incidence of burn out and are more likely to leave the employer or even the sector. Nearly half of the Canadian institutional care workers experience violence (verbal, sexual, racial) on a daily basis (Banerjee *et al.*, 2008). Such experiences, are likely to be associated with understaffing, lack of communication and collegial support (Banerjee *et al.*, 2008). Similar problems have been signalled by Koshitani (2008) for Japan.

Relationships with management affect how LTC workers deal with experiences of high work pressures and violence. For instance, bureaucratic procedures, a blame culture, the lack of trust between direct care workers and their management, as well as management's focus on residents, all prevent workers in Canada from reporting incidents (Banerjee *et al.*,

2008). Similarly, most Japanese care workers have major concerns about how they are treated and evaluated by management (Hotta, 2010). Work pressures and unskilled or inadequate management, coupled with high turnover including in management, can lead workers to feel inadequate, and take blame where pressures are systemic such as in the case of staffing shortages.

Despite often poor working conditions, LTC workers in many countries consider their work meaningful and rewarding and an option for growth (Kushner et al., 2008; BGW, 2007, for Germany; Hotta, 2010, for Japan). They like their caring responsibility and teamwork in institutions, giving recipients dignity and respect as well as a sense that they are not alone. There is also the family's satisfaction with the job done, and learning from residents' life experiences (Teal, 2002; Cangiano et al., 2009a). Compared to most other sectors, Dutch workers in health and welfare score third among the most satisfied with their work (CBS, 2010, p. 142). They also, however, consider their work more varied. This is despite workers' considering their work heavier in terms of the required use of force and uncomfortable working positions, or psychosocial stress and emotional demands.

Job appreciation seems to have an age-related component. For instance, German care workers aged 50 or over are happier with their job than younger care workers, even though both categories appreciate their work to a similarly positive extent (BGW, 2006; 2007, Box 5.1). Caregivers in Japan also appreciate the flexibility of the work, but younger workers experience a lack of prospects (Hotta, 2010).

Box 5.1. **Working conditions in home care differ from those in institutional care**

The differing location and character of service delivery in home care and institutional care have consequences for working circumstances (van Ewijk et al., 2002; Korczyk, 2004; Rothgang and Igl, 2007; Bourgeault et al., 2009). In both, issues relate to night- and broken shifts and fixed term contracts. In home care more than institutional care, there is a lack of compensation for travel costs, and lack of compensation for team meetings and travel between clients. Working circumstances may be especially difficult in socially less advantaged neighbourhoods and in difficult home situations and often there are no options to work in a safe and healthy way. In institutional care settings, colleagues may act as direct soundboard, while there is super- or inter-vision. In home care, such mechanisms are often lacking and workers act in isolation (Ministry of Health/University of Auckland, 2004). Moreover, in home care, conflicts of interest can arise between the care recipient, the available family members and the worker's knowledge, attitude and allowed responsibilities, while in institutional care colleagues are available, including a hierarchy. In institutional care, however, the share of care recipients with severe cognitive problems tends to be higher than in home care, as well as the share of care recipients without family network.

German workers reflect on work in residential and home care as follows (BGW, 2007):

"Institutional care involves much lifting and carrying, high emotional and quantitative demands, too much engagement during work, much psychic exhaustion (burnout). Younger workers feel the meaning of their work is hardly recognised by others, while older workers experience uncertainty about employment, relative bad health and a very high degree of daily life impairment as a result of spinal disorders. On the positive side workers are happy about the management quality, interhuman relationships and with wages. Both young and (especially older) workers feel high commitment with the facility.

> **Box 5.1. Working conditions in home care differ from those in institutional care** (cont.)
>
> *Home care: Fewer negatives, more positives: Workers experience little influence on work, working conditions and circumstances burdening the family, while family's worries influence the work. Especially younger workers experience high uncertainty about the treatment, involvement in work is 'excessive' (younger but especially older workers). Mental exhaustion (and the risk of burnout) is relative strong, especially for older workers. Positive for workers are: Little lifting, few quantitative labour demands, good developmental possibilities at work (especially older workers), good management and social support by management as well as social support by colleagues (younger workers only), good interhuman relationships (especially older workers), relative high labour satisfaction, high commitment with the facility."*
>
> Regulations concerning home-care delivery are often far less detailed or strict than those in institutional care, and also relate to worker guidance and protection. Given the longer tradition of institutional care *versus* home care in many countries, it is also likely that institutional care workers have a higher unionisation rate, thus having a better voice for their needs.
>
> The subsectors seem also to reflect worker characteristics such as age and education levels. Wages in home care tend to be lower than in institutional care (for the same qualification level), but educational requirements are also lower.

Poor working conditions lead to recruitment problems and high turnover[7]

Poor working conditions can lead to recruitment problems, high turnover, workers leaving the sector and workers limiting the number of years spent working in the sector. For instance, vacancy rates in social care in the United Kingdom are twice as high as in other sectors (Cangiano et al., 2009a). In the United States, between two and three out of five home-health aides leave the job within a year, and over two-thirds leave in the first two years. For Certified Nursing Assistants, the turnover was 71% annually, leading to staffing shortages (IOM, 2008). Similarly, turnover in the Japanese LTC sector (27.5%) is higher than in other industries especially for non-permanent employees in institutional care (Hotta, 2010; Japan Long-term Working-condition Survey, 2008; Japan employment situation survey, 2008). Many of those leaving an LTC job leave the sector altogether.

While turnover may be higher for lower-level workers, vacancy rates for higher-level LTC workers – especially nurses – may have more adverse consequences because they often hold higher responsibilities, and often fulfil middle management tasks. Low staffing levels of registered nurses in nursing homes have led to adverse resident outcomes, such as urinary tract infections, pressure ulcers, catheter use and weight loss (Decker, 2008). Recent US vacancy rates in LTC are higher for registered nurses (16.3%) than for licensed practical nurses/licensed vocational nurses (11.1%) and for certified nurse assistants (9.5%) (American Health Care Association/National Center for Assisted Living, 2009).

The costs of high turnover and recruitment efforts affect the public budget, as in many countries a major share of LTC is publicly funded. For instance, estimated turnover costs for the US public programmes Medicaid and Medicare are USD 2.5 billion, based on a cost per replacement of USD 2 500 (Seavey, 2004).

5.4. Foreign-born workers play a substantial and growing role in some countries

Why care workers migrate?

In a number of OECD countries, foreign-born care workers play a substantial role in the care sector (Table 5.4). They may enter LTC by active recruitment in their home country, but can also, especially when already in the host country, be a target group to fill vacancies. In 17 of 23 European countries that took part in the Eurofamcare study, migrant care workers played a more or less significant a role (Mestheneos and Triantafillou, 2005).

Table 5.4. **Foreign-born care workers in LTC**

	How many foreign-born LTC workers?	Source
Australia	25% of care workers (2007)	Fujisawa and Colombo (2009)
	33% in residential aged care (2007)	Martin and King (2008)
	27% in home-based care (2007)	
	12.5% of nurses are foreign-trained (2005)	OECD (2007b)
Austria	50% of all (formal and family) care providers	Fujisawa and Colombo (2009); Di Santo and Ceruzzi (2010)
	40 000 illegally operating care workers (mid-2006)	European Foundation for the improvement of living conditions (2009)
Belgium	3.3% foreign nurses (2005)	OECD (2007b)
Canada	23% of institutional care workers	Bourgeault et al. (2009)
	7.7% of registered nurses foreign-trained (2005)	OECD (2007b)
Denmark	6.2% of registered nurses foreign-trained (2005)	OECD (2007b)
	11% of all LTC workers have a migration background*	Rostgaard et al. (2010)
France	50/70% of those providing IADL support	Di Santo and Ceruzzi (2010)
	1.6% foreign nurses (2005)	OECD (2007b)
Finland	0.3% of nurses foreign-trained (2005)	OECD (2007b)
Germany	Circa 200 000 migrant care workers (2007)	Di Santo and Ceruzzi (2009)
	3.8% of nurse s foreign trained (2005)	OECD (2007)
Greece	Circa 250 000	Di Santo and Ceruzzi (2009)
	70% of care workers in private households	Fujisawa and Colombo (2009)
Italy	Appr. 1 million, 72% of all care workers	Lamura et al. (2010)
	Circa 700 000 migrant workers in home care	Di Santo and Ceruzzi (2009)
Ireland	14.3% of registered nurses	OECD (2007)
Israel	55 000 migrant LTC workers, about 50% of all LTC workers	OECD (2010b)
Netherlands	8% of LTC workers	Fujisawa and Colombo (2009)
	1.5% of registered nurses foreign-trained (2007)	OECD (2007b)
New Zealand	24.3% of nurses are foreign traineed (2004)	OECD (2007b)
Sweden	20% of 19 000 new employees in health and welfare	Swedish Association of Local Authorities and Regions (2006)
	13% of all employees in care of the elderly and disabled (2005)	
	2.7% of registered nurses foreign-trained	OECD (2007)
United Kingdom	Nurse auxiliaries: 17%	Cangiano et al. (2009a)
	Nurses in home care: 23%	
United States	Of direct care workers: 21% (2007) to 23% (2009)	PHI (2007, 2010)
	33% of home personal and home-care aides	Martin et al. (2009)
	3.5% of registered nurses foreign-trained (2004)	OECD (2007b)

Source: OECD Secretariat compilation.

Pull factors attracting foreign-born care workers to a foreign country include geographical proximity, language, culture, and wealth – and thus options to earn a living – of the host country. Some countries have a history as immigrant countries and are perceived as attractive, while others may be attractive for certain people for certain reasons, amongst which climate, options for education, options for *temporary* migration, or an already existing migrant community. Across countries, all these factors or just a few can be observed. For instance, the attractiveness of LTC work in Greece for Philippine workers seems linked to the opportunity to work while language, culture and geographical proximity and other factors do not play a substantial role. A significant share of the foreign-born LTC workers in the United Kingdom has a student status (Cangiano et al., 2009a). Proximity, as well as language and cultural likeness can be seen in the 15% nurses migrating to Australia from New Zealand, as well as in the 10% Belgium-trained nurses in the Netherlands (OECD, 2007b).

Patterns of migration show similarities for LTC workers and for nurses. Geographical proximity, combined with high cross-border earning differences, seem important, for instance in Southern Europe, Germany and Austria. The enlargement of the European Union in 2004 facilitated such migration patterns. Half of the Italian recognition procedures (2005) referred to Romanian nurses, for example (OECD, 2007b, p. 189).

Profile of migrant care workers

The overall profile of foreign-born LTC workers generally follows that of other LTC workers. Most are middle-aged women (Fujisawa and Colombo, 2009), although recently migrated foreign-born care workers in the United Kingdom are, more often than other care workers, aged between 20 and 35 years (Cangiano et al., 2009a).

Qualifications levels differ, but in many countries a phenomenon of de-skilling can be observed (OECD, 2007b; 2009; Fujisawa and Colombo, 2009; for the United Kingdom: Jennings, 2009). In Canada, 44% of the foreign-born care workers is a registered nurse in the country of origin, but works at a lower level (Bourgeault et al., 2009). Similarly, many foreign-born nursing aides in the United States are university trained in their home country (Redfoot and Houser, 2005). Of the Moldovan family assistants in Italy, 70% have a university degree (Di Santo and Ceruzzi, 2010). For most countries, however, the share of foreign-born LTC workers with a nursing qualification is unknown. Data on foreign-born nurses in Table 5.4 are therefore likely to underestimate the migration of those *qualified* as a nurse in their home-origin country and not – yet – recognised in the host country. Indeed, for some foreign-born nurses, working at lower level in a host country can be a phase while working towards the recognition of qualifications (Bourgeault et al., 2009, p. 62).

Data from around 2000 about foreign-born and/or foreign-trained and recognised nurses, of which an unknown share may work in long-term care, suggest a fourfold categorisation. Countries with both high inflow and high outflow of nurses include Luxembourg, Canada, the United Kingdom, New Zealand and Ireland. Countries with high immigration and low emigration of nurses are the United States, Australia, Austria and the Czech Republic. Finland was the only OECD country with little inflow but high outflow of nurses. Other countries have both little immigration or emigration (OECD, 2008, p. 31). Of the foreign-born nurses in Australia, 48% is from the United Kingdom or Ireland (OECD, 2007b).

Working conditions of migrant care workers

Foreign-born care workers often work with shorter contracts, more irregular hours, broken shifts, for lower pay and in lower classified functions than non-migrant care workers and may have to work with the least favourable care recipients (Bourgault et al., 2009; Fujisawa and Colombo, 2009; Cangiano et al., 2009a). Uncertainty about immigration rules and their rights may lead them to adhere more closely to employers' wishes and stay in the job longer than domestic workforce (Cangiano et al., 2009a). They may be subject to verbal abuse or outright refusal to be cared for by the client, especially at the starting phase of a caring contact

(Walshe and O'Shea, 2009), but they may also experience such behaviour from colleagues and employers (Cangiano *et al.*, 2009a). Those in round-the-clock live-in arrangements are especially vulnerable to personal and financial exploitation (Cangiano *et al.*, 2009a; 2009b; Lamura *et al.*, 2010) due to lack of communication problems, and lack of freedom to move. Opportunities for upward mobility and training may also be more restricted for foreign-born workers, while they can lack trade union support (Cangiano *et al.*, 2009a).

Poorer working conditions than for native-born workers can be observed across the OECD. For example, fewer foreign-born health professionals have a permanent contract, compared to natives (OECD, 2007b, p. 75). In both the EU27 and EU15,[8] higher shares than native nurses and health professionals work longer than 41 hours per week, work at night regularly, and work "usually" on Sundays. However, foreign-born nurses are just as likely as native-born to have a permanent contract (OECD, 2007b, p. 199).

Nearly a third of the foreign-born care workers in the United Kingdom earn wages below the national minimum, as opposed to 22% of UK-born care workers (Jennings, 2009). Higher shares of foreign-born care workers can be found in the private sector in Ireland and the United Kingdom, as opposed to the better paying and more unionised public sector (Walshe and O'Shea, 2009; Cangiano *et al.*, 2009a; Yeates, 2005; Lamura *et al.*, 2010). For the United States, employers are quoted saying that they hire foreign-born workers because they are more willing to accept lower wages and less flexible working conditions relative to native workers. Lower wages for foreign-born workers, are, however, not specific for long-term care. Such differences have been analysed for several countries in the labour market as a whole (OECD, 2010a, pp. 170-172).

In England, foreign-born LTC workers tend to work in institutional facilities, whereas in Southern Europe they are mostly working in home-based settings (Cangiano *et al.*, 2009a; Jennings, 2010). In the United States, substantial shares of foreign-born workers are in institutional LTC but even higher shares work in households.

Are migrant care workers over represented?

Figure 5.6 shows the share of foreign-born in the household sector, and the health and community sector. In Greece, Portugal, Spain and France, migrants are overrepresented in household services, including home care, *i.e.*, the share of foreign-born employment in the sector is larger than the share of foreign-born employment in general. Similarly, in Greece, the Czech Republic, Poland, Austria, Ireland, Switzerland Finland, the United Kingdom, Sweden and Denmark, foreign-born workers are over represented in health and community services. Data may, however, under-represent un-contracted migrant care workers.

While a multi ethnic workforce may reflect the increasing diversity in a country's population and demand for care, overrepresentation of minorities in LTC jobs may point to the sector being unattractive to native-born workers. For instance, more than half of the direct care workers in the United States are from an ethnic minority with a further 23% foreign-born (PHI, 2010). Similar overrepresentation of minorities is reported for Australia, New Zealand, and the United Kingdom (Martin and King, 2008; Ministry of Health/University of Auckland, 2004, Cangiano *et al.*, 2009a). Partly, such patterns may reflect *past* immigration processes. On the other hand, the Dutch health and care professions have substantial underrepresentation of workers with a Turkish or Moroccan background (Ministerie van Volksgezondheid, Welzijn en Sport, 2007).

Figure 5.6. **Employment of foreign-born in health
and other community services and households**

Share of all foreign-born employment, 2005-06 average

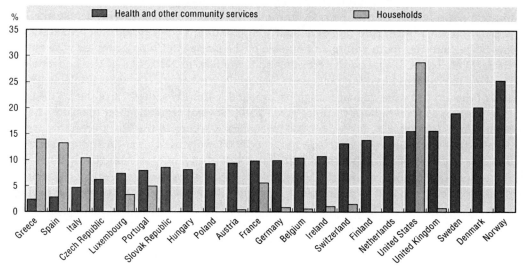

Note: For the United States, "Health and other community services" refer to the wider "Education", and the "Households" to "Other services". Data for Germany refer to 2005 only, for Japan to 2006 only.

Source: European countries: *European Community Labour Force Survey* (data provided by Eurostat); Japan: *Labour Force Survey*; United States: *Current Foreigners Population Survey*, March Supplement, reported in: *OECD International Migration Outlook* (2008).

StatLink http://dx.doi.org/10.1787/888932401558

Migrant care workers follow different channels

Migration processes may differ. Many foreign-born LTC workers in the United States are actively recruited in their home country by specific job agencies (Martin *et al.*, 2009). In several low-income European Union countries, job agencies specialised in sending workers to other EU Member States operate (Di Santo and Ceruzzi, 2009). But most foreign-born care workers in the United Kingdom are recruited domestically (Cangiano *et al.*, 2009a) or have entered the country via non-labour related channels, such as being refugee, in the context of family reunification schemes, working holiday, or as students (Cangiano *et al.*, 2009b). Similarly, a major share of the foreign-born care workers in the United States has been naturalised, an indication of a longer stay in the country.

In some OECD countries, especially southern European countries, several migrant carers work without legal immigration papers or work contracts. This is due to a combination of factors, such as economic incentives for both the migrant carers and the employer, as well as to the lack of formal legal migration possibilities for low-skilled workers (see for example the case of Italy in Box 5.2). Formal legal entry into a country's care workforce may also be difficult as it may require linguistical skills, *a priori* proof of a certain minimum income in the host country, adaptation periods and recognition of professional qualifications (Redfoot and Houser, 2005; Martin *et al.*, 2009). Moreover, while almost all OECD countries stimulate immigration of highly skilled workers, few have programmes that allow for easy access of migrants in relation to lower-level jobs (OECD, 2009, see also Chapter 6).

As options for legal entry for lower skilled jobs are limited in some countries despite high demand, irregular inflows can exceed the regular one, as for example in the United States, Spain and Italy (OECD, 2009, p. 125). In 2009, estimates of the share of illegal

---

Box 5.2. **Italian family assistants**

Home-based care provision in Italy relies mainly on foreign-born care workers. This is almost entirely due to a universal, unregulated cash-benefit system; a fast ageing population with increasing female labour participation; and geographical proximity to low-wage countries (both within and outside of the European Union), coupled with entry via legal channels, illegal border crossing and overstay. In 2010, 13% of the households involved in care had hired migrant carers, especially for heavy care tasks. While, in 1991, 16% of the 181 000 workers had foreign background, currently some 72% of the 1.5 million care workers is foreign-born (Lamura et al., 2010). Several regularisation measures have been taken. In 2002, 22% of the 646 000 foreigners working in the black economy were regularised, while between 2002 and 2008, 300 000 family assistants (including nannies and care workers) were regularised, an estimated 42% of all family assistants. Not only were there more applicants than available visas, but families seeking care workers had immediate needs and could not wait for a visa, while employers did not apply for a visa without having seen the foreign worker. The 2009 regularisation processed 39% out of the 750 000 expected, possibly because migrants had to pay EUR 500 in social insurance contribution. Employers had also to prove the worker's accommodation, have a minimum – declared – income of EUR 20 000 per year, while the contract should be at least 20 hours per week. Moreover employers were to pay social contributions after regularisation. Studies suggest that other migrants than care assistants took advantage of the scheme as well.

For foreign-born workers, working as a family assistant often is the easiest or only job to find. One third lives permanently with the family. House cleaning is part of the job for 80% of them, and more than half goes shopping. Half cares for an older person, and a third provides ADL support, while 29% provides medical assistance. Newly arrived foreign-born care workers, more than those arrived since the mid-1990s, often work on an hourly basis instead of 24 hours/7 days, and focus on shorter periods of work before returning. More than half of the foreign-born family assistants work entirely or partially without a contract, while regular workers, too, increasingly work undeclared.

Recently, some regions implemented registers for family-care assistants, while local councils installed social care helpdesks. Moreover, home-tutoring initiatives and training courses to further educate and train the migrant care workers have been started at local level, but content varies and certification has no wider value. Regions such as Abruzzo and the Veneto Region introduced further incentives for legalisation: up to full compensation for the required social security contributions, in the shape of an additional allowance, under certain conditions, amongst which a contracted or registered status as family assistant.

Italian-born family assistants currently account for 10% of those working in private households.

Source: Bettio et al. (2006); Chaloff (2010); Lamura et al. (2010); Di Santo and Ceruzzi (2010).

---

migrants in OECD populations varied from 0.2% in Japan to 3.9% in the United States, with illegal migrants accounting between 3.7% of all foreign residents in Austria to 63.5% in United States (OECD, 2009). For Canada, it was estimated that some 60 000 migrants were in the country illegally, most of which refugees (Bourgeault et al., 2009).

5.5. Changes in LTC policies affect LTC labour markets

Worsening working conditions for lower-level LTC workers

Most people requiring LTC prefer care at home, and both institutional and home-care settings are increasingly populated by higher-need care recipients (CBS, 2010; Ministry of Health/University of Auckland, 2004). But across the OECD, the number of workers per care recipient and the qualification mix have remained stable over time, possibly leading to heavier workloads and more intense care processes in both subsectors, *ceteris paribus* (such as the mix of technology and labour). Lower-level care workers appear to be especially affected by changes. According to Oschmiansky (2010), the introduction and expansion of market-based incentives for care providers in Germany led to deteriorated working conditions – less job security, smaller contracts and less social security – for lower-level care workers, while at the same time conditions for a new class of highly qualified LTC specialists improved. The LTC insurance law led to job differentiation and professionalisation, while also leading to increased shares of "atypical" workers in the LTC workforce (*e.g.*, workers with small contracts). Since 2003, previously existing traditions of employers providing qualification options in LTC were replaced by short-term training options. These changes took place in a context of labour market policies under the framework of the European internal market. Data for Japan and Germany show a substantial increase in, especially, lower-level care workers, resulting in a reduction of the share of nurses in the sector.

The 2007 Dutch introduction of tendering procedures for the delivery of household care led to risk transfer from central government to local authorities, and subsequently from these to care provider organisations. These then shifted the risk to low-level care workers by deteriorating working conditions and labour contracts (Box 5.3). Toronto

---

Box 5.3. The Dutch transition of IADL support to the Social Support Act

In the Netherlands, IADL care was transferred from the Exceptional Medical Expenses Act (AWBZ) to the new Social Support Act (WMO) in 2007. It included a transfer of EUR 1 billion for the provision of household care from the AWBZ to the municipalities, the executors of the WMO.

As of 2007, home-care providers were to bid for contracts, while previously, IADL care was contracted by regional "care offices" – the executive branches of the AWBZ – under a relative competition-free environment. While IADL previously was provided by so-called "helpers 1" and "helpers 2", in certain ratios (for instance, 35:65), many municipalities reversed this ratio, requiring providers to accept lower tariffs. However, while the composition of the workforce reflected the old ratios, with available tariffs often below cost (for the new ratio), some providers refused to enter a bid, others felt obliged to but either accepted losses or adjusted working conditions, especially for those providing IADL. Layoffs and rehiring for worse conditions occurred. Other workers had to change employer, or accept a worse collective labour agreement, for instance that for cleaning agencies (Roerink and Tjadens, 2009). Van der Windt *et al.* (2008, pp. 76-77) add that some workers were additionally trained, while new employees got only temporary contracts, and for a more limited number of hours. Many workers had to accept the option to work as "alfa worker", a self-employed worker against tariff, who can work for maximum 24 hours per week. The care recipient is to pay part of sickness benefit in case the alfa worker becomes incapacitated to work. Often, the previous employers acted as job agency with the clients sometimes unaware of this change in status, even though, now, they were employer.

Box 5.3. **The Dutch transition of IADL support to the Social Support Act** (*cont.*)

While between 1998 and 2005 the number of alfa workers declined steadily (CBS Statline), 2008 estimates suggest that the number of alfa workers was higher than in 1998 (Torre and Pommer, 2010). For 2009, further increases were expected. This development led to repair laws stimulating employers to rehire workers "transferred" into alfa workers, and forbidding care provider agencies from acting as "employment agency" for alfa workers. Per 2010, a care recipient decides whether to receive care in cash (and hire an alfa worker), or receive "care in kind" (de Klerk *et al.*, 2010). It is estimated that by the end of 2010 some 16 000 alfa workers will be re-employed (Torre and Pommer, 2010).

home-care workers cite heavy provider competition as undermining co-operation and leading to lower wages (Kushner *et al.*, 2008; see also Hunter, 2009). Several reports point at the wage pressure in the LTC sector, often a consequence of cost control measures leading to relative high shares of foreign-born workers in the United States, the United Kingdom and Australia (AAHS/IFAS, 2007; Charlesworth and Marshall, 2010; Cangiano *et al.*, 2009a; Spencer *et al.*, 2010).

The role of self-employed and agency workers

Using "external workers", such as those hired through a job agency, is one way for providers to deal with shortages and high turnover. The use of agencies is becoming increasingly common. For instance, in Japan, almost one in three workers is hired through an agency in facilities providing institutional care services, although high shares can also be seen in other types of facilities (Hotta, 2010). External workers, however, may lack relevant qualifications. Moreover, due to agency fees, external workers may come at a higher cost.

Another type of external worker is the self-employed worker. Estimates for the United States suggest that between 400 000 (PHI, 2010) and 560 000 (PHI, 2007) direct care workers work as independent contractors. A substantial share of those that were forced into self-employment in the Dutch decentralisation of IADL provision does not wish to return to employee status. Self-employment has the attraction of allowing workers to provide the services as they see fit. Some self-employed may focus on the more "endearing" care recipients and circumstances that fit their own requirements, an option often not available for employees. For others, the self-employed status may provide them with an option to get work, without relevant qualifications. However, self employment comes at a cost, as workers will have to arrange for their own social security, and there may be more uncertainty about future work. Issues may finally arise as to quality, responsibilities and the supervision of the self-employed. Without supervision of the way resource (*e.g.*, cash benefits) are spent, grey and black labour markets serviced by self-employed workers may develop (Di Santo and Ceruzzi, 2010).

The impact of cash benefits on LTC labour markets

Cash-benefit schemes may have differential consequences for the labour market, depending on their regulation. Some schemes provide relatively low allowances and expect the care recipient to contribute to the costs of services. In some cases the cash benefit is only provided if no in-kind services are available.

Cash-benefit systems can reinforce a direct connection between worker and care recipient, which is often shown to increase care recipient satisfaction as s/he is empowered to take decisions. The direct connection is also one of the elements that is often favoured by care workers, and which may lead them into self-employment. Such systems introduce an employer-employee relationship into the care situation, with both desirable and undesirable effects for both the care recipient and the care worker, especially if a family member becomes the employed care worker. Furthermore, cash benefits may increase the entry of non-qualified workers in home-care settings, as it is up to the beneficiary to choose and employ workers.

The impact of cash benefits on LTC labour markets is mixed. Unregulated cash benefits led to high use of irregular workers in a number of countries (Fujisawa and Colombo, 2009), in some cases introducing competition between those acting on the black labour market and the formal LTC workforce, such as in Germany.[9] The unregulated Austrian and Italian cash-benefit schemes led to high demands for cheap labour, and to competition with contracted care workers.

Some cash benefits are explicitly aimed at supporting family carers. The Spanish system provides cash benefits when no public services are nearby; and the Korean LTC insurance provides a cash benefit when it is impossible to use formal LTC services, for instance due to natural disasters or related reasons, and when individuals are unsuitable for admission in an institution. In the Netherlands, the budget is lower than the comparable in-kind benefits as the expected co-payments are taken into account in advance. Eligible people are free to hire the services they want and feel is best-equipped to deal with their particular need. Budget holders are, however, required to declare their expenditures. Unspent budget has to be returned, and in case of fraud, people may be restricted from further use of the budget option. In general, people do not spend their full budget while being satisfied with service delivery.

While Germany seems to manage to save money in its LTC scheme due to lower cash benefits and, in the Netherlands, supervision of expenditure takes place, Doty et al. (2010) report higher costs for pilot cash and counselling (C&C) programmes in the United States, as compared to "traditional" programmes. The C&C programmes are consumer directed LTC programmes, giving the care recipient not only "employer authority" but also "budget authority". The higher per-user costs can be explained by the fact that the care recipients using C&C benefits were successful in hiring alternative care workers, where "traditional" providers suffered from recruitment and retention problems. In Arkansas, those in the comparison group received only two thirds of their eligible services, especially in rural areas. The popularity of C&C led, in three years, to major savings on nursing home care, because, even though individual costs were higher than expected, overheads fell to a third of their previous level.

As LTC recipients become employers, other recruitment patterns appear with consequences for required qualifications and quality. Nies and Leichsenring (2010), for continental Europe, Glendinning et al. (2008) and Glendinning (2009) for the United Kingdom, and Galantowitz et al. (2010) for the United States, point to quality-control issues in cash-benefit systems. When family members are hired, the relationship may change into a business agreement, with many hired family workers feeling compelled to work more hours than contracted. This may lead to more stress than previously. Some programmes require users to hire from registered agencies only – or provide other guarantees. The

Dutch Health Care Inspectorate, for instance, recently raised questions about the way personal budgets are currently organised in the Netherlands, and the consequences for vulnerable older people (Mot, 2010). Doty *et al.* (2010) report that overcoming resistance against the empowerment of care recipients from within the system especially by focusing on quality, is important for the success of such programmes. However, others argue that quality in such schemes is guaranteed because care recipients are in the position to hire and fire assistants, which empowers them to such an extent that regulation is then to be considered as paternalistic (Arksey and Kemp, 2008).

5.6. Conclusions

This chapter analysed the size, composition of and some of the complex features of LTC workforces across the OECD. The size of the LTC workforce is increasing along with the share of the population aged over 80 years. The majority of the LTC workers are employed in institutional care, usually with part-time contracts – even though most care recipients receive care at home. A large proportion of the LTC workers are female and middle aged.

Although minimum qualification requirements exist in most OECD countries, variations can be observed in qualification mixes and ratios. Particularly for lower-level care workers, required entry-level qualifications vary widely across the OECD. Wages are generally low, in some cases lacking annual increases or job-related benefits. Even though workers find their job meaningful, they regard it as demanding. This can lead to early retirement and work-related accidents.

Vacancies and turnover rates can be high. Many OECD countries employ external workers, for instance through a job agency. Migrant workers – usually middle-aged women – play a significant role in LTC in some countries. Many are employed as lower-level care workers, but may have more qualifications than native-born care workers. Their working conditions can, however, be harder than those of non-migrant care workers, while their earnings is in many instances lower than for non foreign-born workers. In some OECD countries, illegal migrants participate in the LTC workforce.

Future research in this field is needed, in order to address potential data limitations and to encourage countries to collect reliable information.

Notes

1. Additional Dutch data – using broader workforce indicators – show a further differentiation between subsectors: 5.3 users per FTE in home care; 1.7 users per FTE in residential care homes; and 0.6 users per FTE in nursing homes (*Source:* Eggink *et al.*, 2010; 2005 data).

2. *http://stats.oecd.org/Index.aspx?DatasetCode=FTPTC_I.*

3. *http://stats.oecd.org/Index.aspx?DatasetCode=ANHRS.*

4. Responsibilities, qualifications and competences of LTC workers vary widely, due to differentiation between categories of lower-level workers, while differentiations between "registered" and "licenced" nurses exist, with the latter being lower-grade nurses than the former.

5. Licensed practical nurse: A graduate of a school of practical nursing whose qualifications have been examined by a state board of nursing and who has been legally authorised to practise as a licensed practical or vocational nurse (LPN or LVN), under supervision of a physician or registered nurse. Registered nurse: A graduate nurse who has been legally authorised (registered) to practise after examination by a state board of nurse examiners or similar regulatory authority, and who is legally entitled to use the designation RN. *Source: http://medical-dictionary.thefreedictionary.com.*

6. According to feminist critiques, perceptions about gender roles also play a role in wages for care workers (Browne and Braun, 2008; Charlesworth and Marshall, 2010).

7. Annual replacement rate of workers. A turnover of 75% implies that three out of four workers need to be replaced on an annual basis.

8. EU15: The European Union of 15 Member States, before 1 April 2004. EU27: The European Union after 2007, when in total 12 new states had joined.

9. In Germany, with an estimated gross cost of EUR 1 200 per month for 24 hours/7 days care, hiring *three* family care workers becomes cheaper than one arrangement respecting labour law (EUR 4 000). Expenditure by the care recipient is not supervised, although regular checks exist to assess the care recipients' situation.

References

AIHW – Australian Institute for Health and Welfare (2008a), *Nursing and Midwifery Labour Force 2005*, AIHW, Canberra.

AIHW – Australian Institute for Health and Welfare (2008b), *Nursing and Midwifery Labour Force 2008*, AIHW, Canberra.

American Association of Homes & Services for the Aging and the Institute for the Future of Aging Services (2007), *The Long-term Care Workforce: Can the Crisis be Fixed? Problems, Causes and Options*, Prepared for National Commission for Quality Long-term Care, AAHS/IFAS, Washington DC.

Arksey, H. and P.A. Kemp (2008), "Dimensions of Choice: A Narrative Review of Cash-for-Care Schemes", *Working Paper*, No. DHP 2250, University of York, Department of Social Policy and Social Work, York.

Banerjee, A., T. Daly, H. Armstrong, P. Armstrong, S. Lafrance and M. Szebehely (2008), *"Out of Control": Violence against Personal Support Workers Long-term Care*, York University/Carleton University.

Bettio, F., A. Simonazzi and P. Villa (2006), "Change in Care Regimes and Female Migration: The 'Care Drain' in the Mediterranean", *Journal of European Social Policy*, Vol. 16, No. 271.

BGW (2006), *Aufbruch Pflege. Moderne Prävention für Altenpflegekraft. BGW Pflegerapport*, Erstveröffentlichung 02/2006, Stand 12/2007, Berufsgenossenschaft für Gesundheitsdienst und Wohlfahrtspflege, Hamburg.

BGW (2007), *Sieht die Pflege bald alt aus? BGW-Pflegereport 2007. Stand 08/2007*, Berufsgenossenschaft für Gesundheitsdienst und Wohlfahrtspflege, Hamburg.

Bourgeault, I. *et al.* (2009), "The Role of Immigrant Care Workers in an Aging Society. The Canadian Context and Experience", University of Ottawa.

Browne, C.V. and K.L. Braun (2008), "Globalization, Women's Migration and the Long-term Care Workforce", *The Gerontologist*, Vol. 48, No. 1, pp. 16-24.

Canadian Home Care Human Resources Study (2003), accessible at *www.cha.ca/documents/pa/ Home_Care_HR_Study.pdf*.

Cangiano, A., I. Shutes, S. Spencer and G. Leeson (2009a), "Migrant Care Workers in Ageing Societies", Report on Research Findings in the United Kingdom, Centre on Migration, Policy and Society (COMPAS), University of Oxford.

Cangiano, A., I. Shutes and S. Spencer (2009b), "Memorandum to Social Care Inquiry", ESRC Centre on Migration, Policy and Society (COMPAS), University of Oxford, November.

CBS – Central Bureau of Statistics (2010a). *De Nederlandse samenleving*, CBS, Den Haag.

CBS – Central Bureau of Statistics (2010b), *Gezondheid en zorg in cijfers*, CBS, Den Haag/Heerlen.

CBS – Central Bureau of Statistics (2011), "Werken in de zorg zwaar, maar geeft veel voldoening", *Webmagazine*, Monday 24 January 2011, 9:30, accessible at *www.cbs.nl/nl-NL/menu/themas/ gezondheid-welzijn/publicaties/artikelen/archief/2011/2011-3287-wm.htm*.

Centre de Formation et de Rencontres Internationales, Ile-de-France (2010), "DEAVS, diplôme d'État d'auxiliaire de vie sociale", accessible at *www.cpcvidf.asso.fr/page/deavs.html*.

Chaloff, J. (2008), "Mismatches in the Formal Sector, Expansion of the Informal Sector: Immigration of Health Professionals to Italy", *OECD Health Working Paper*, No. 34, OECD Publishing, Paris.

Charlesworth, S. and H. Marshall (2010), "Chosen Sacrifices? Some Paradoxical Effects of Strategies to Attract and Retain Care Workers", *Working Paper*, No. 8, RMIT University, Centre for Applied Social Research, School of Global Studies, Social Science and Planning, Melbourne.

Commonwealth of Australia (2008), "CHC20108 Certificate II in Community Services", *CHC08 Community Services Training Package*, Vol. 2 of 3, Qualifications Framework, accessible at *www.training.nsw.gov.au/cib_vto/cibs/documents/chc20108.pdf*.

Cort, P. (2002), "Vocational Education and Training in Denmark", Danish Institute for Educational Training of Vocational Teachers, accessible at *www.cedefop.europa.eu/EN/Files/5130_en.pdf*.

Department of Health (2000), "Domiciliary Care national Minimum Standards", London, accessible at *www.dh.gov.uk/prod_consum_dh/groups/dh_digitalassets/@dh/@en/documents/digitalasset/dh_4083671. pdf*.

Department of Health and Human Services (2003), "The Future of Long-term Care Workers in Relation to the Ageing Baby Boom Generation", Washington, accessible at *http://aspe.hhs.gov/daltcp/reports/ltcwork-A.htm*.

Di Santo, P. and F. Ceruzzi (2010), "Migrant Care Workers in Italy. A Case Study", *Interlinks*, European Centre for Social Welfare Policy and Research, Rome/Vienna.

Doty, P., K.J. Mahoney and M. Sciegaj (2010), "New State Strategies to Meet Long-term Care Needs", *Health Affairs*, Vol. 29, No. 1, pp. 49-56.

Eborall, C., W. Fenton and S. Woodrow (2010), "The State of the Adult Social Care Workforce in England, 2010", Fourth report of Skills for Care's Research and Analysis Units, Skills for Care, Leeds, May.

Eggink, E., D. Oudijk and I. Woittiez (2010), "Zorgen voor zorg Ramingen van de vraag naar personeel in de verpleging en verzorging tot 2030", SCP, Den Haag.

Enomoto, Y. (2007), "Population Aging and Support to the Elderly People in Communities in Japan", Japan International Corporation of Welfare Services, accessible at *www.jicwels.or.jp/about_jicwels/ASEAN&JapanHighLevelOfficialsMeeting/5th%20Country%20Report%202007%20-Community%20Services%20for%20the%20Elderly-/Japan.pdf*.

Estryn-Behar, M., B. van der Heijden, D. Camerino, C. Fry, O. Le Nezet, P.M. Conway and H.M. Hasselhorn (2008), "Violence Risks in Nursing. Results from the European 'NEXT' Study", *Occupational Medicine*, Vol. 58, pp. 107-114, published online 21 January 2008, *DOI:10.1093/occmed/kqm142*.

European Foundation for the Improvement of Living and Working Conditions (2006), *Employment in Social Care in Europe*, Office for Official Publications of the European Communities, Luxembourg.

Ewijk, H. van *et al.* (2002), "Care Work in Europe: Current Understandings and Future Directions", in P. Moss (ed.), *Mapping of Care Services and the Care Workforce: Consolidated Report*, Working Paper, No. 3, Thomas Coram Research Unit, Institute of Education, University of London.

Fag og Arbejde Denmark, "Welcome to the Social and Health Sector", accessible at *www.foa-international.dk/art_uk/social_uk*.

Federal Institute for Vocational Education and Training Germany (2004), "Vocational Training for Human Services".

Finnish National Board of Education (2004), "Vocational Education and Training in Finland", accessible at *www.ammatillinenkoulutus.com/upload/images/muut_kuvat/pdf/alakoht/English/Vocational_education_%20and_training in_Finland.pdf*.

Fujisawa, R. and F. Colombo (2009), "The Long-term Care Workforce: Overview and Strategies to Adapt Supply to a Growing Demand", *OECD Health Working Papers*, No. 44, OECD Publishing, Paris.

Galantowitz, S., S. Crisp, N. Karp and H. Accius (2010), *Developing Effective Criminal Background Checks and Other Screening Policies for Home Care Workers*, AARP, Washington.

Gleckman, H. (2010), "The Faces of Home Care. Report from the Field", *Health Affairs*, Vol. 29, No. 1, pp. 125-129.

Glendinning, C. (2009), "Cash for Care: Implications for Carers", *Health and Ageing*, Newsletter, No. 21, The Geneva Association.

Glendinning, C., D. Challis, J. Fernandez, S. Jacobs, K. Jones, M. Knapp, J. Manthorpe, N. Moran, A. Netten, M. Stevens and M. Wilberforce (2008), *Evaluation of the Individual Budgets Pilot Programme: Final Report*, Social Policy Research Unit, University of York, York.

Harmuth, S. (2002), "The Direct Care Workforce Crisis in Long-term Care", *North Carolina Medical Journal*, Vol. 63, No. 2, pp. 87-94, March/April.

Health and Welfare Bureau for the Elderly (2010), *OECD Japan Mission 2010 Basic Information*, Ministry of Health, Labour and Welfare, Japan.

Health Outcomes International (2007), *Health Evaluation of the Home-based Support Service (HBSS) Training Initiative*, Health Outcomes International, St. Peters, South Australia.

Health Professionals Regulatory Advisory Council (Ontario) (2006), "The Regulation of Personal Support Workers", accessible at *www.health.gov.on.ca/english/public/pub/ministry_reports/personal_support_workers/personal_support_workers.pdf*.

Hotta, S. (2010), "Kaigo Jyūjisha Mondai" (Professional Caregiver Issue in Japan), in H. Miyajima, S. Nishimura and T. Kyogoku (eds.), *Shakai Hoshō to Keizai (Social Security and Economy)*, Vol. 3, *Shakai Sabisu to Chiiki (Social Services and Community)*, University of Tokyo Press, pp. 149-172, Tokyo.

Hunter, J. (2009), "Response: The Case Against Choice and Competition", *Health Economics, Policy and Law*, Vol. 4, pp. 489-501.

IFAS (2007), "The Long-term Care Workforce: Can the Crisis be Fixed? Problems, Causes and Options", Prepared for National Commission for Quality Long-term Care, Washington DC, IFAS, January.

IOM – Institute of Medicine (2008), "Retooling for an Aging America: Building the Health Care Workforce", accessible at *www.iom.edu/agingamerica*.

Jennings, C. (2009), "Migrant Workers in Adult Social Care in England", Report for Skills for Care, accessible at *www.skillsforcare.org.uk/nmsruntime/saveasdialog.aspx?lID=4483&sID=444*.

Kirino *et al.* (2006), "Kaigoshokuin ni kiin suru storess ga shisetsukoureisha no seishintekikenkou ni ataeru eikyou", *Kouseinoshyou*, Vol. 53, No. 6.

Klerk, M. (de), R. Gilsing and J. Timmermans (eds.) (2010), *Op weg met de WMO. Evaluatie van de Wet maatschappelijke ondersteuning 2007-2009*, SCP, Den Haag.

Korczyk, S. (2004), "Long-term Workers in Five Countries: Issues and Options", AARP Public Policy Institute, Washington DC.

Koshitani, M. (2008), "Influence on Caregiver's Psychological Health of Patients' Violence against Caregivers in Nursing Homes and Group Homes", *Long-term Care Welfare Journal*, Vol. 15, No. 1, pp. 62-73.

Kubalčíková, K. and J. Havlíková (2010), "Current Strategy of Social Services for the Elderly in the Czech Republic: The Domiciliary Care. Opportunities and Risks", European Population Conference 2010, accessible at *http://epc2010.princeton.edu/download.aspx?submissionId=100178*.

Kushner, C., P. Baranek and M. Dewar (2008), "Home Care: Change We Need", Report on the Ontario Health Coalition's Home Care Hearings, 17 November.

Lamura, G., C. Chiatti, M. Di Rosa, M.H. Mechiorre, F. Barbabella, C. Greco, A. Principi and S. Santini (2010), "Migrant Workers in the Long-term Care Sector: Lessons from Italy", *Health and Ageing Newsletter*, No. 22, The Geneva Association, April.

Mandl, I. and A. Dorr (2009), "Gearing Adult Education towards Occupational Mobility: National Assessment Report Austria", accessible at *www.mobility-training.eu/final/report/austria.pdf*.

Martin, S., B. Lindsay Lowell, E.M. Gzodziak, M. Bump and M.E. Breeding (2009), *The Role of Migrant Care Workers in Aging Societies: Report on Research Findings in the United States*, Institute for the Study of International Migration, Walsh School of Foreign Service, Georgetown University.

Martin, W. and D. King (2008), *Who Cares for Older Australians? A Picture of the Residential and Community Based Aged Care Workforce 2007*, National Institute of Labour Studies for the Department of Health and Ageing, Flinders University, Adelaide.

Maucher, M. (2008), "Modernisation Processes in the Field SSGI: Challenges Related to Employment and Qualification", 2nd Forum on SSIG, Paris, accessible at *http://cms.horus.be/files/99931/MediaArchive/2008-FPEU+DG-EMPL-2nd-Forum-SSGI-28.+29.10.08-Paris-text-MM.pdf*.

Mestheneos, E. and J. Triantafillou (eds.) (2005), "Supporting Family Carers of Older People in Europe – The Pan-European Background Report: Empirical Evidence", *Policy Trends and Future Perspectives*, Lit Verlag, Hamburg.

Ministry of Education and Culture Finland, "Vocational Education and Training in Finland", accessible at *www.minedu.fi/OPM/%20Koulutus/ammatillinen_koulutus/?lang=en*.

Ministry of Health, Labour and Welfare Japan (2006), "Overview of Certified Social Workers and Certified Care Workers", accessible at *www.mhlw.go.jp/english/wp/wp-hw3/dl/8-11.pdf*.

Ministry of Health/University of Auckland. Disability Support Services in New Zealand (2004), *The Workforce Survey, Final Report*, 20 August.

Ministry of Labour and Social Affairs, "Odpovědi na časté dotazy k dalšímu vzdělávání sociálních pracovníků a pracovníků v sociálních službách", accessible at *www.mpsv.cz/files/clanky/8109/Povinne_dalsi_vzdelavani.pdf*.

Ministry of Social Affairs and Health Finland (2005), "Act on Qualification Requirements for Social Welfare Professionals", accessible at *www.finlex.fi/fi/laki/kaannokset/2005/en20050272.pdf*.

Ministerie van Volksgezondheid, Welzijn en Sport (2007), *Arbeidsmarktbrief 2007 Werken aan de zorg*.

Mot, E. (2010), "The Dutch System of Long-term Care", *CPB Document*, No. 204, CPB, Den Haag.

Nies, H. and K. Leichsenring (2010), "Quality Management and Quality Assurance in Long-term Care", *European Overview Paper*, Interlinks, Utrecht/Vienna.

Norwegian Directorate for Education and Training, "Vocational Education and Training in Norway", accessible at *www.udir.no/upload/Fagopplaring/Vocational_Education_and_Training_in_Norway.pdf*.

O'Brien-Pallas, L., C. Alksnis and S. Wang (2003), *Bringing the Future into Focus. Projecting RN Retirement in Canada*, Canadian Institute for Health Information, Ottawa.

OECD (2007a), *Babies and Bosses. Reconciling Work and Family Life, A Synthesis of Findings for OECD Countries*, OECD Publishing, Paris.

OECD (2007b), *International Migration Outlook*, OECD Publishing, Paris.

OECD (2008), *The Looming Crisis in the Health Workforce: How Can Countries Respond?*, OECD Publishing, Paris.

OECD (2009), *International Migration Outlook*, OECD Publishing, Paris.

OECD (2010a), *International Migration Outlook*, OECD Publishing, Paris.

OECD (2010b), *OECD Reviews of Labour Market and Social Policies: Israel*, OECD Publishing, Paris.

Oschmiansky, H. (2010), "The Marketization of Formal Elder Care in Germany and its Consequences for the Labour Market", Paper for the International Conference "Transforming Care: Provision, Quality and Inequalities in Later Life", Copenhagen, 21-23 June.

PHI (2007), *Facts No. 3. Who Are the Direct Care Workers?*, PHI, New York.

PHI (2010), *Facts No. 3. Who Are the Direct Care Workers?*, PHI, New York, February 2010 Update.

Redfoot, D. and A. Houser (2005), *We Shall Travel on Quality of Care "Economic Development, and the International Migration of Long-term Care Workers"*, AARP Public Policy Institute, Washington DC.

Roerink, H. and F. Tjadens (2009), *From Household Care to Household Help in the Dutch Transition from AWBZ to WMO. Consequences for Workers and Clients*, Bureau Secondant/Health and Social Care Associates, Alphen aan den Rijn, October.

Rostgaard, T., C. Chiatt and G. Lamura (in press), "Care Migration – The South North Divide of Long-term Care", in B. Pfau-Effinger and T. Rostgaard (eds.), *Care Between Work and Welfare in Europe*, Palgrace, Houdsmills.

Rothgang, H. and G. Igl (2007), "Long-term Care in Germany", *Japanese Journal of Social Security Policy*, Vol. 6, No. 1, pp. 54-84.

Rothgang, H., D. Kulik, R. Müller and R. Unger (2009), *GEK Pflegereport 2009*, GEK, Schwäbishc Gmünd.

Schmidt, S. and H. Hasselhorn (2007), "Gesundheitsrisiko Altenpflege. Ein Projekt zur Verbesserung der Qualität in Altenpflegeeinrichtungen", *Pflegen: Demenz*, Vol. 5.

Seavey, D. (2004), "The Cost of Frontline Turnover in Long-term Care. Better Jobs, Better Care", IFAS/AAHSA, Washington.

Smith, K. and R. Baughman (2007), "Caring for America's Aging Population: A Profile of the Direct Care Workforce", *Monthly Labor Review*, September, pp. 20-26.

Spencer, S. *et al.* (2010), "The Role of Migrant Care Workers in Ageing Societies: Report on Research Findings in the United Kingdom, Ireland, Canada and the United States", International Organisation for Migration, Geneva.

Squillace, M.R. *et al.* (2009), "The National Nursing Assistant Survey: Improving the Evidence Base for Policy Initiatives to Strengthen the Certified Nursing Assistant Workforce", *The Gerontologist*, Vol. 49, No. 2, pp. 185-197.

Stone, R. and J. Wiener (2001), *Who Will Care for Us? Addressing the Long-term Care Workforce Crisis*, Urban Institute and the American Association of Homes and Services for the Aging, October.

Swedish Association of Local Authorities and Regions (2007), *Care of the Elderly in Sweden Today 2006*, Stockholm, January.

Teal, C. (2002), "Direct Care Workers. Number One Quality Indicator in Long-term Care. A Consumer's Perspective", *North Carolina Medical Journal*, Vol. 63, No. 2, pp. 102-105, March/April.

Theobald, H. (2004), "Care Services for the Elderly in Germany: Infrastructure, Access and Utilisation from the Perspective of Different User Groups", Veröffentlichungsreihe der Arbeitsgruppe Public Health Forschungsschwerpunkt Arbeit, Sozialstruktur und Sozialstaat Wissenschaftszentrum Berlin für Sozialforschung (WZB), accessible at *http://bibliothek.wz-berlin.de/pdf/2004/i04-302.pdf*.

Torre, A. and E. Pommer (2010), *Voorlopig advies over het WMO budget huishoudelijke hulp voor 2011 van het Sociaal en Cultureel Planbureau Uitgebracht aan het bestuurlijk overleg*, SCP, Den Haag, 1 April.

Training and Employment Authority Ireland, "Healthcare Assistant Traineeship", accessible at *www.fas.ie/en/Training/Traineeships/Traineeship+Courses/Personal+Service+Occupations/Care+Assistant +Care+for+the+Elderly+Traineeship.htm*.

Velde, F. (van der), F. Verijdt and E. Arnold (2010), *De arbeidsmarkt voor lagere functies in de zorg: veel vissen in de vijver*, OEZW19, Prismant, Utrecht.

Walshe, K. and E. O'Shea (2009), *The Role of Migrant Care Workers in Ageing Societies: Context and Experiences in Ireland*, Irish Centre for social gerontology, National University Galway.

Windt, W. (van der), R.C.K.H. Smeets and E.J. Arnold (2008), *Regiomarge 2008. De arbeidsmarkt van verpleegkundigen, verzorgenden en sociaal-agogen 2008-2012*, Prismant, Utrecht, June.

Windt, W. (van der), R.C.K.H. Smeets and E.J. Arnold (2009), *Regiomarge 2009. De arbeidsmarkt van verpleegkundigen, verzorgenden en sociaalagogen 2009-2013*, Prismant, Utrech, June.

Winsløw J.H. and V. Borg (2008), "Resources and Quality of Care in Services for the Elderly", *Scandinavian Journal of Public Health*, Vol. 36, pp. 272-278, accessible at *http://sjp.sagepub.com/ content/36/3/272.full.pdf+html*.

Yeates, N. (2005), "Migration and Social Policy in International Context: The Analytical and Policy Uses of a Global Care Chains Perspective", Arusha Conference, "New Frontiers of Social Policy", 12-15 December.

Web pages

www.azwinfo.nl.

www.cbs.nl.

www.werk.belgie.be/CAO/330/330-2009-000655.pdf.

http://medical-dictionary.thefreedictionary.com.

http://stats.oecd.org/Index.aspx?DatasetCode=FTPTC_I.

http://stats.oecd.org/Index.aspx?DatasetCode=ANHRS.

https://drei.verdi.de/2010/ausgabe-36/ausblick/seite-8/zwangsteilzeit-im-altenheim (accessed 10 December 2010).

http://cupe.ca/updir/CUPE-long-term-care-seniors-care-vision.pdf.

Chapter 6

How to Prepare
for the Future Long-term
Care Workforce?

Although the effects of the economic crisis may mitigate shortages of LTC workers in the near future, an integrated approach is required to prepare for the LTC workforce in the longer term. Measures can be targeted at education, recruitment and retention, as well as at job content, productivity and quality. These can cover subsectors (home care, day care, residential care) but could also take the form of integrated sector approaches. Furthermore, for different categories of workers (nurses, lower-level workers), specific policies may be required, as for nurses an LTC career often is not a natural choice, while for lower-level workers LTC jobs are often not perceived as a "profession" but as "dead end job", with few options for progressing other than finding a job elsewhere. This can lead to high turnover and limited job retention, with subsequent high cost for employers, public finances, those in need of care and their families. Potential measures look at valuing LTC work and the workforce and may require substantial change in the organisation and management of care. Moreover, while in some countries foreign-born workers will represent sizable shares of the LTC workforce, there may be questions about the sustainability of such an approach. This chapter explores policies to improve inflows, retention, and productivity of LTC workers.

6.1. The future challenge for the long-term care workforce

The after-effects of the economic crisis are impacting on health and long-term care systems in complex ways. On the supply side, funding levels for health and long-term care services may face pressure (Marin *et al.*, 2009). Demand may increase due to deterioration of health status (SPC, 2009) or as a consequence of unemployment, which may deteriorate people's financial capacities and thus may lead to *increased* demand on public systems (Cangiano *et al.*, 2009b). The crisis after-effects may also affect LTC labour markets. For instance, turnover of LTC workers may be mitigated as people seeking employment may be more inclined to enter the sector. LTC workers may stay longer and retire later than expected.

Vacancy rates dropped in the LTC sector in the United Kingdom, the Netherlands and Japan (Eborall *et al.*, 2010; Eggink *et al.*, 2010; Cangiano *et al.*, 2009a, 2009b; Hotta, 2010a). Indeed, there are signs that LTC could be acting as a safe haven: in the United States, retention of certified nursing aids is higher in areas with high unemployment (Wiener *et al.*, 2009). At the same time, strained public finances can affect the available training opportunities negatively (European Commission, 2010), for instance for nurses (OECD/WHO, 2010), hereby increasing gaps in the availability of global nursing services. The main challenge, however, is for the longer term. While the LTC workforce is currently a relatively small share of the total workforce, its size is set to grow. The challenge will therefore be to develop a sustainable quality LTC workforce that can meet growing demand.

The following section discusses countries' efforts to improve recruitment and retention. The next two sections describe these issues in more detail. Section 6.5 touches upon productivity. Section 6.6 provides final remarks.

6.2. Improving recruitment and retention: Overview of national policies

Many OECD countries already experience or expect recruitment and retention problems in the LTC sector, and most have developed and implemented measures to improve recruitment and retention in the sector (Table 6.1). These widespread problems signal a major overall problem of the LTC sector: its strong relationship with a context of deterioration of human daily capabilities. Moreover, they signal the struggling of OECD countries with the consequences of ageing societies.

Some OECD countries have workforce planning initiatives, such as Canada, Germany, the Netherlands, New Zealand, the United Kingdom and the United States (McHale, 2009; Afentakis and Maier, 2010; Zorginnovatieplatform, 2009; SPC, 2009; Badkar, 2009; Cangiano, 2009 and 2009b; IOM, 2008). Most countries report measures to stimulate entry into LTC through traineeships (United Kingdom), additional job creation (Austria created 2 000 extra jobs; and Norway funded 10 000 new full-time equivalent workers), additional public funding for training (Australia, Belgium), the development of a standardised training course (New Zealand) or new curricula (United States). Ireland and England aim to recruit more LTC workers by offering the option of entering without qualifications under the requirement that relevant qualifications will be gained during employment. New Zealand

Table 6.1. **Workforce policies to increase the supply of LTC services**

	Recruitment measures	Public funded training	Wages and benefits increases	Improvements in working conditions	Raising status/job profile	Management improvement	Career creation	Workforce certification	Workforce planning	Other retention measures
Australia	√	√					√			√
Austria					√		√			
Belgium	√	√	√						√	
Canada	√								√	
Czech Republic		√	√							
Finland		√		√						
France	√	√	√	√	√	√	√			
Germany	√	√	√	√	√	√			√	
Ireland	√				√					
Japan	√		√	√	√			√		
Korea	√		√	√	√			√		
Mexico										
Netherlands	√					√			√	√
New Zealand	√	√	√						√	
Norway	√	√		√	√	√	√	√	√	√
Slovak Republic		√								
Slovenia		√								
Switzerland		√		√					√	
United Kingdom	√	√			√	√	√	√	√	√
United States	√		√	√		√	√	√	√	√

Note: Canada and Switzerland report regional initiatives, Sweden and Finland report local initiatives; United Kingdom refers to England Working to Put People First (Department of Health, 2009).
Source: OECD 2009-10 Questionnaire on Long-term Care Workforce and Financing, and additional documentation.

has developed public-private partnerships, where employers provide mentoring, on-the-job training and help job seekers to obtain a certificate. Some countries offer financial incentives to re-recruit workers (Australia), while other countries specifically aim efforts at specific target groups, such as young people, those re-entering the labour market and under-represented groups or alternative labour pools (Germany, the Netherlands, United Kingdom, United States). Japan has implemented various policies to attract and retain LTC workers (Box 6.1).

Box 6.1. **LTC workforce policy reforms in Japan**

Labour market conditions in Japan changed after 2002 resulting in a tighter labour market, making it necessary to implement better policies in order to retain or attract workers. Fee levels are set centrally and are revised every three years. The 2009 revision enabled many employers to increase wages by around JPY 9 000 per month (EUR 79.6 per month). At the same time, a fund was set up to assist providers in offering higher salaries. The fund was set at the prefecture level and providers submitted applications to obtain the financial aid. This is expected to raise wages by 15 000 yen per month (EUR 132.6 per month). Moreover, providers receive an extra fee if they have a higher number of certified care workers or, since 2009, if they employ more than three care managers.

The fund is not limited to wage subsidies, but is a part of an overall package to improve working conditions in LTC. For example, providers receive subsidies for introducing LTC equipment, such as lifts, that promote welfare and reduce the burden of care workers. Another tool to improve working conditions is the Labour Stability Centre. This is a private

---

Box 6.1. LTC workforce policy reforms in Japan *(cont.)*

certified institution, which provides advice on working conditions after on-site visits. Evidence from evaluations so far is promising, showing a 10% decrease in turnover, observed in the facilities that followed the advice.

Training is another important element for attracting and retaining LTC workers. While there is renewed emphasis on training and career plans, each institution has managerial freedom to set up their own training programmes.

At the governmental level, there are various subsidies available to attract young people in the LTC sector. Such subsidies include training for job leavers or for those who are currently working in other sectors. LTC training is free for job seekers and it is organised through the Public Employment Services ("Hello Work"). It includes commissioned training at specialised private institutions or training schools. Even though LTC trainees constitute around 10% of total trainees, their employment in the LTC sector is quite high. The government also subsidises the cost of hiring replacements, when staff is sent to training.

In addition, training subsidies are granted as part of an increasing capacity-building initiative for care workers. Such subsidies help set up career plans, develop know-how on training for institutions and practical courses. LTC capacity-building advisors and career consultants located at 47 branches of Care Work Foundation (CWF) nationwide provide consulting and support services by visiting homes or institutions, telephoning and e-mailing.

Source: OECD 2009-10 Questionnaire on Long-term Care Workforce and Financing.

Some countries report measures related to wages and benefits, and a fewer focus on working conditions. Among other things, Japan, aims at improving the working conditions in long-term care by enhancing employer compliance to labour law. Where federal structures exist, such as in Canada and the United States, the options available to the federal government to influence recruitment and retention of LTC workers can be limited. Jurisdictions may not have specific powers over employers to improve working conditions. In the United States, the federal government provides financial aid to the states so as to increase wages.

Eight OECD countries report measures related to continued education and training, for instance, for enrolled nurses to up-grade to registered nurses (Australia), or the requirement for all LTC workers to acquire specific targeted skills, such as gerontological skills (Finland). The United States supports specific training on dementia and abuse prevention. Only a few countries invest in measures aimed at career building, for instance by means of scholarships (Australia), or modular educational pathways (Austria). More countries aim at improving the quality and job status in long-term care, either by developing national profiles (Austria) or curricula (Germany), by professionalising the sector (France), or by ensuring more trustworthy care by requiring workers to be certified (Korea). In Germany, in particular, the federal government pays for the whole three years of further LTC education. The United States, the United Kingdom and some other OECD countries are working towards accreditation schemes and public registers of LTC workers. England, for instance, is preparing a *voluntary* register for home-care workers (Department of Health, 2009). In other European countries, this is still far-fetched (European Foundation for the Improvement of Living and Working Conditions, 2006, p. 43). Some Italian regions have taken the initiative to register foreign-born care workers (Di Santo and Ceruzzi, 2010). The United States is also taking steps to require criminal background checks.

Some countries devote efforts to leadership and management improvement or restructure care provision. England is undertaking efforts to remodel the workforce. The Netherlands aims at innovating care processes and stimulates regional co-operation between employers and educators. France aims to modernise services, especially at home. Germany has not only introduced national educational requirements for elderly care nurses, but also, in 2008, a new job category in nursing homes, especially targeted at social and IADL types of work. Workforce prognoses have become important instruments for many countries.

6.3. Ensuring an adequate inflow of long-term care workers

Ensuring adequate inflow requires a continuous effort to secure an enough and adequately trained LTC workforce. This implies both a better use of available recruitment pools of human resources, as well as seeking new recruitment pools.

Using the available workforce pools better

Young people are a natural source for LTC jobs, but competition for youngsters will get fiercer as the share of youngsters in the population is below replacement level in many countries. While new training programmes could be set up to better attract young people to the sector, such programmes are more successful if they provide a realistic image of the sector, for instance by means of internships or a preview when applying. As young people are among the most likely to leave an LTC job early, measures to prevent young workers to quickly depart, for instance by providing career opportunities, are crucial (Hotta, 2010 a). So far, however, there is little evidence of successful efforts to improve entry of young people in vocational education and training for the sector, and subsequent successful bridging of education and enduring LTC employment. Norway has recently adopted initiatives in this direction.

The second major source – especially for lower-level LTC workers – is women re-entering the labour market. Older women are an important segment of the LTC workforce. In the United States, for instance, older workers appear to be evalued by employers. In Germany, older LTC workers seem to have high job satisfaction (BGW, 2007). Targeted approaches may be able to better reach these women. In the United States, tax benefits aim at providing older LTC workers with greater access to education and training, while, for lower-income older adults, additional federal funding is available for training and employment.

As for nurses, current nursing education curricula often give little attention to management of chronic and long-term conditions, or geriatric issues (IOM, 2008), while there are often wage and career differences with the acute-care sector. Without specific LTC knowledge, experience or other incentives, nurses are less likely to see LTC as a sector of interest. Initial education, for instance by conditional loan forgiveness, scholarships and internships, could stimulate nurses to work in the LTC sector, as suggested for the United States (AAHSA and IFAS, 2007). Specific public funding streams could be allocated to employers or to the care workers interested in further qualifying into a nursing profession. Such schemes can be found in Australia.

Similar to delegation to nurses of tasks normally performed by doctors (Buchan and Calman, 2008; Delamaire and Lafortune, 2010), delegation of nursing tasks to lower-level workers could be fruitful to address shortages of nursing staff in LTC. A pilot in the Netherlands, in which lower-level care workers in nursing homes could work more independently with patients with both dementia and depression, based on developed nursing guidelines, proved positive for both the safety and quality of life of patients, as well as for work satisfaction of the staff (Verkaik et al., 2010b). In the United States, several projects aim to achieve such delegation. For instance, in the Nurse Delegation Pilot Program in New Jersey, voluntarily participating registered nurses formally delegate tasks concerning medication for patients to Certified Nurse Assistants (CNAs). As often nursing aids are insufficiently trained in this field (IGZ, 2010), the New Jersey nurses association developed guidelines to decide in which cases delegation would be possible and how. The volunteering registered nurse instructs and supervises the lower-level care worker.

One often-used method to improve recruitment is through media campaigns. Fujisawa and Colombo (2009) report mixed results. Experiences in the United States suggest that such campaigns might lead to "the wrong people at the door" (Box 6.4). England developed a national social-care contest among workers, with media attention for the winner, hoping to improve attractiveness of the sector. Consequences for sector image, attractiveness and possibly higher recruitment rates are unknown as yet.

New employment pools

The largest potential recruitment pool consists of men. In 2005, Germany introduced a new policy (Neue Wege für Jungs, New Avenues for Guys), offering young men, amongst others, the opportunity to participate in caring work for elderly or children.[1] While 70% of the participating young men surveyed were positive about "atypical" professions (amongst which child and elderly care), the available data suggest that numbers may be low relative to forecasted need.

Several countries have programmes to lead the unemployed to the LTC sector. The United Kingdom, for instance, targets young people who have been unemployed for more than a year, while in Japan "Hello Work" employment agencies seek to recruit unemployed people to the LTC sector by providing vocational counselling, employment placement opportunities, seminars on work in the long-term care sector, and guided tours of social welfare facilities. Such schemes typically focus on lower-level care work (see for example, Box 6.2 on Finland).

Box 6.2. Work reactivation and elderly care in Helsinki (Finland)

Orienting unemployed people to LTC work is not an easy task. In Helsinki, long-term unemployed people are encouraged to re-ender the workforce by helping elderly people living at home with their household management and errands. The unemployed are offered the option, supported in taking responsibility for their process, and enticed to work in the caring industry. Work trainers, together with home-care workers, provide guidance. The city activated 60 to 70 long-term unemployed people at a time at the cost of the salaries of seven work trainers (a total of EUR 20 000 per month). Approximately 40% of the home-care support groups moved on to paid work or to study for an occupation. The project aided 14 000 elderly with IADL services as well as with escorts to medical services and outdoor activities. The city saved EUR 300 000 a year, even with those involved received an additional EUR 8 per day. Interviews suggest that the workers required less social and health services and that their mental well being, way of life, and readiness to return to work improved.

Source: OECD 2009-10 Questionnaire on Long-term Care Workforce and Financing.

Other programmes aim to recruit people who may not consider entry into the LTC sector. England, for example, focuses on underrepresented groups. The Netherlands experiences a strong underrepresentation of people from a Turkish and Moroccan background, both in vocational care education and in the LTC workforce. The government also intends to enable more care provision by workers from this background, especially for people from the same ethnic groups (Ministerie van VWS, 2008). Some countries also invest in efforts to re-recruit workers that left the LTC workforce, for example Australia (for nurses), Ireland and Germany.

A relatively new option consists of family members that are hired through cash-benefit programmes. There is some evidence that family members and friends who successfully cared for a loved one as a paid caregiver, can be attracted to the "regular" workforce, although in many other cases, their caring position did not last beyond this one-off process. Family members, who in some cases can be hired and compensated through cash-for-care benefits, offer a partly "hidden" supply that could lead to additional inflow in the "regular" LTC workforce.

Generally speaking, the success of activation programmes and target group-based recruitment in the LTC workforce is not always positive. Many of the targeted people actually use LTC as a first step towards further employment. Long-term evaluations often are lacking and may not focus on their effects for LTC job tenure, but on employment in general.

Foreign-born workers

In several OECD countries, demand for foreign-born LTC workers keeps growing. Between 2008 and 2009, over half of the 6% increase in institutional care employment in the European Union – the third fastest growing sector in numbers of workers – was accounted for by foreign-born workers. In the United States, the fourth largest growth in foreign-born workers can be seen in social assistance (18.2%) (OECD, 2010a, pp. 112-113). Such data suggest that foreign-born LTC workers are likely to continue to play a substantial and possibly increasing role (Cangiano et al., 2009b; McHale, 2009, for Canada).

Many OECD countries have a history of and act as immigration countries. Some of these are targeting LTC workers, for example specific programmes exist in Canada and Israel. Broader LTC migration initiatives and ex post regularisation programmes have been implemented in other countries (Box 6.3). However, given the importance, and expected growth in the migrant care phenomenon, the lack of reference to long-term care in migration programmes of many OECD countries is conspicuous.

While foreign-born care workers in LTC can be a short-term mechanism to address care needs, in some countries they form a structural component of the LTC workforce. However, as options for legal entry for lower-skilled jobs are limited in countries such as the United States, Italy and Spain, the irregular inflow exceeds the regular inflow by far (OECD, 2009, p. 125). In 2009, estimates of the share of irregular migrants in OECD countries ranged from 0.17% in Japan to 3.94% in the United States, with irregular migrants shaping between 3.7% (Austria) and 63.5% (United States) of all foreign residents (OECD, 2009). For Canada, it was estimated that about 60 000 migrants were in the country illegally, most of which refugees (Bourgeault et al., 2009). Unregulated/illegal care workers can undermine a country's stability and social systems.

Box 6.3. **Immigration policies related to LTC workers in selected OECD countries**

The **Canadian** Live-In Caregiver Programme (LCP) enables immigrants to obtain permanent residence after two years of full-time work as "live-in carers". The programme is employer driven, meaning that employers must first offer a job. The arrangement requires the carer to remain with the same employer for two years. There are no formal caps, but the number of LCP work permits issued is determined by the processing capacity of visa offices.

Applicants for the LCP must have an education level equivalent to Canadian grade 12, six months caregiving training or experience, and sufficient English or French language proficiency to provide care in an unsupervised setting. After completing two years of live-in caregiving work, within 3 years of arrival, care workers can apply for permanent residence, which will then require them and their dependent family members (spouse and children) to pass medical, criminal and security examinations. When permitted permanent residence, they can work in any occupation (OECD Questionnaire on Long-term Care Workforce and Financing, 2009; Bourgeault et al., 2009).

In 2008, approximately 13 000 foreign nationals entered Canada on LCP work permits. Most participants are women from developing countries, such as the Philippines (83%). The programme is being further developed, introducing more thorough checks on employers by 2011, as well as, in 2010, assisting the live-in carers to better meet the requirements for permanent residence, as working overtime can speed up the application process, while the application period can also be extended, for instance in the case of illness (Citizenship and Immigration Canada, 2010).

Long-term care is the main route through which foreign workers enter **Israel**. In 2009, the 54 500 migrant workers in the care sector represented about half of total employment in the sector and almost all provide live-in care. Since 1988, an LTC benefit has provided subsidies, enabling elderly people to employ migrant care workers. Although no quotas are imposed, eligibility criteria exist for both migrant candidates (e.g. language skills) and employers (e.g. ADL score, medical records). The criteria for issuing permits to employ foreign caregivers are expected to be restricted, limiting eligibility to individuals who require 24 hours home care (OECD, 2010b; Kemp, 2010).

Migrant caregivers can work in Israel for a maximum of 63 months, but have no option of permanent residence afterwards. The visa may, however, be extended if the caregiver has been working with the same employer for at least one year, and if the employer is dependent on home care. At the same time, migrant carers are not allowed to change employers (Israel Government Portal). Foreign-born care workers must be registered with licensed recruitment agencies, which place them directly with a patient (OECD, 2010b). New legislation requires recruitment agencies to find new jobs for unemployed foreign caregivers, in order to minimise fee-bringing international recruitment. However, this is not enforced, leading to new inflows while other foreign-born workers are unemployed.

If the subsidy pays for part of the care, the worker is jointly employed by the agency and the recipient, in which case care receivers are to pay social contributions to the NII, but they do not have to provide workers with pay slips. More than half of the foreign care workers, however, are employed directly by the receiver without NII subsidy (OECD, 2010b). In Canada, again, the Temporary Foreign Worker Programme allows employers to hire migrant workers on a temporary basis, when Canadians or permanent residents are not readily available.

Box 6.3. Immigration policies related to LTC workers in selected OECD countries (cont.)

Other examples

In some other OECD countries immigration policies that can apply to LTC workers exist. In **Italy**, LTC workforce immigration has been supported through *ex post* legalisations of foreign workers (Box 5.3) (Lamura, 2010). In the **United Kingdom**, LTC caregiving is an occupation with recognised shortages, under Tier 2. This means that applicants are provided easier access and the job is not subject to a resident labour market test, facilitating foreign carers' entry in the country. Entry, however, has been recently limited (OECD Questionnaire on Long-term Care Workforce and Financing, 2009). In **France**, care workers (*aide-soignants*) are on a shortage list for EU citizens, and house workers are on a shortage list targeted at the Senegalese population (Immigration Professionnelle, 2008). Housework may refer to ADL caregiving for the elderly, too. The **Spanish** shortage list of professions included caregivers up until 2008 (Fujisawa and Colombo, 2009). Persons with the skills and experience required to work as a LTC worker may be able to migrate to **Australia** through General Skilled Migration (GSM) and employer nominated visa programmes such as the Employer Nomination Scheme (ENS) and Regional Sponsored Migration Scheme (RSMS). Furthermore, through the Family Stream, an individual can obtain a visa to care for a relative who has a medical condition (OECD Questionnaire on Long-term Care Workforce and Financing, 2009). Finally, **Japanese** bilateral agreements with Indonesia, Vietnam and the Philippines allow immigration of a limited number of care workers in the country. However, the requirements to pass language tests and Japanese national qualifications reduces inflow, even though qualified LTC workers can stay in the country indefinitely (Fujisawa and Colombo, 2009; Cortez, 2009).

Beside *ex post* regularisation initiatives, some countries have developed policies to reduce uncontracted, black labour in LTC. Germany issued special working permits for domestic workers, *Haushaltshilfen*,[2] entering from countries that entered the European Union in or after 2004 (van Hooren, 2008). France developed tax deductions and lighter administrative regimes for those hiring LTC workers formally. Germany, too, introduced a tax benefit, which can save up to 20% of the costs of legally hired care. In 2007, Austria developed a framework to regularise previously illegal care workers, enabling a legal provision for round-the-clock work at home and, per 2008, pardoned those having hired undeclared migrant carers if they registered those workers with the social insurance institutions. Such measures may or may not be accompanied by awareness raising campaigns about the risks and punishment of those employing black labour (Switzerland).

OECD (2009) has developed guidelines for labour immigration policies. They can apply to foreigners working in LTC. The main steps are listed below.

Identify unmet labour needs. Provide work permits in numbers commensurate with the extent of labour needs

Only a few countries, such as Australia, the United Kingdom and Canada, have immigration programmes that can apply to long-term care workers (Box 6.3). Germany's bilateral agreements with Croatia do not include care migrants. Quotas can control inflow but require enforcement. Quotas are considered necessary to adjust available supply to limited employment options in the receiving country. In Israel, 10% of the labour force consists of foreign-born temporary workers, most of which are care workers. While in early 2009 a registry of unemployed foreign-care workers was installed to prevent new entries when unemployment among foreign-born workers became too high, the register has been set on hold because agencies continue to recruit from abroad (OECD, 2010b).

Develop means for matching migrant workers to jobs, either overseas or in the country

For care workers, a job offer often is a prerequisite to enter the country. Intermediary agencies can support such processes. However, in most countries, there are few or no certified intermediaries. Special job-search visas could enable *legal* employment, and thus redirect employment practices. When a job is found, a residence permit and work permit could be provided.

Work towards efficient permit processing and delivery procedures

As the example of Italy showed (Box 5.2), getting a visa may be hampered by formal requirements, while the need to match demand and supply may require speed. Thus, especially in the case of privately hired care workers, adaptations of the process may be desirable.

Develop means for employers to verify the status of potential employees

Specifically for home care – or live-in care work – it may be difficult for both the prospective employer and the potential worker to decide whether the other person is trustworthy. The efforts in some Italian regions (Di Santo and Ceruzzi, 2010) to develop registers of home assistants are a means to achieve this, if only from the employer side.

Effective border control and workplace enforcement procedures

While border control is a logical link in the process, in the European Union this may be difficult to achieve, due to its internal open borders. Workplace enforcement may furthermore be difficult in the case of live-in long-term care. The 2011 changes in the Canadian Live-in Carer Programme suggest, however, new options to protect the care workers by means of more *ex ante* employer checks. Another example of how to deal with this issue can be seen in France where the receipt of targeted subsidies requires reporting on employment status. Another method is to combine inspections with major fines. In the context of those in need and receiving a cash benefit, it could be envisaged withdrawal of the cash benefit, such as can happen in the Netherlands in case of fraud with the personal budgets.

While recruitment may sometimes be easy, hurdles with retention may be as important an issue as for native-born workers. For instance, while Martin *et al.* (2009) report foreign-born nurses in the United States starting their own care agency to provide services for frail elderly from their own cultural background, and while some of the participants in the Canadian Live-In Carer Programme seek work in LTC after fulfilling the requirements of the programme (Bourgeault *et al.*, 2009, p. 63), Chaloff (2008) states that "many immigrants working in the private care sector are not interested in investing in a care career".

Finally, there are some concerns regarding the impact on quality of care. Language and cultural differences can affect the quality of care due to higher error rates associated with barriers in communication, lack of familiarity with equipment, medicines or practices (Dussault *et al.*, 2009, p. 25). There are also some concerns about short job tenures of many migrant LTC workers who are only looking for temporary jobs.

6.4. Improving retention: Valuing work, building careers

A major challenge for the sector is to better value LTC work and the LTC workforce. This may require a mix of general as well as sector-specific measures. For instance, Japan aims to boost LTC workers' compliance with general labour law as a means to improve working conditions in the sector. More specific, sector-based approaches will, however be required, too.

Recruitment and initial training costs associated with high turnover can be saved by improving job quality and workplace conditions, thereby improving retention and the sector image (Seavey, 2004). However, initial investment cost can be high and there is often limited evidence to assess the cost-effectiveness of alternative interventions. In addition, the costs of increasing retention in LTC may be borne by some stakeholders, while benefits may go to other parties. For instance, improved LTC nurses' retention in the United States' may imply higher wages for Medicaid, while savings – reduced hospital stays and re-hospitalisation – accrue to the Medicare programme. Still, measures to improve retention can have a good return on investment, such as lower turnover, higher job satisfaction and better quality of care, as reported for example in Japan (Onodera *et al.*, 2006).

Enabling LTC workers to work more hours

If LTC workers worked more hours per week and for longer periods in their working carriers, this could reduce recruitment needs. For instance, one estimate from the Netherlands suggests that these measures would attenuate the need for new workers by 125 000 FTE LTC workers by 2025 (Zorginnovatieplatform, 2009). A substantial number of LTC workers have more than one job or work part-time, suggesting that they could work more hours in LTC than they do now. Although not specific to LTC jobs, 16% of part-time working women across the OECD signals a willingness to work more hours.[3] Stimulating LTC workers to stay in the sector and delay retirement could also reduce recruitment needs.

Competitive wages and benefits matter, but are not the magic bullet

Increasing wage levels can reduce turnover (Smith and Baughman, 2007; Ministry of Health/University of Auckland; Hotta, 2010a and 2010b). Belgium, Luxembourg, the Slovak Republic, the Czech Republic, France and New Zealand have recently implemented wage increases. New Zealand reports higher wage increases in home care than in residential care. Slovenia plans further wage increases for in 2011, after a 10-15% wage increase in 2008. In 2009, Japan increased the long-term care insurance fees by 3%, after a long period of constant fees, enabling employers to raise workers' remuneration. Germany, which does not have a federal minimum wage, implemented a mechanism whereby LTC workers earn at least the usual *regional* minimum wage. In the United States, additional federal funding has recently been directed to states with the purpose of facilitating wage increases.

However, wage increases are not the sole or only solution. In the period 2003-08, while wage increases in the English social care sector were 4% higher than in other jobs (and 20-30% higher than in other low-paid jobs), turnover remained high (Cangiano *et al.*, 2009b). Even substantial and structural increases may have short-lived effects in terms of recruitment and retention if not accompanied by other measures.

One option is to better recognise experience in wage levels. Collective labour agreements typically differentiate pay scales according to years of experience. In countries where this occurs, such as Belgium, the Netherlands and Sweden, retention is higher. One-off financial incentives, such as bonuses, as tried in the United States did not reduce turnover, vacancies or increase job satisfaction significantly, as amounts were too small and taxed. In Canada, non-financial incentives have been tried, like giving nurses 20% of their time to spend on professional training.

Entitlement to work-related benefits can help job retention and satisfaction. In some OECD countries (e.g., Denmark, Germany, Belgium, the Netherlands), collective labour agreements regulate paid sick leave, health insurance, paid travel to and from work, or between work settings (including travel time, especially in home care), extra pay for inconvenient hours and rosters, and paid work meetings. In others these conditions depend on bilateral agreements between employees and employers.

German and Swedish data (BGW, 2007; Swedish Association of Local Authorities and Regions, 2007) point to high job appreciation and low tendency to leave, where work-related benefits are provided. Turnover in Sweden is 5%. In the Dutch system, benefit packages for LTC workers, such as annual wage increases reflecting work experience, extra compensation for irregular hours and – limited – compensation for travel costs for home-care workers go together with high loyalty to the sector (van der Velde et al., 2010). In the United States, the idea of health coverage provided a clear incentive for workers to stay (Box 6.4). However, recent analyses also showed no significant effect of health insurance coverage on job retention, while a USD 1 increase in hourly wages could increase job tenure by an additional 2.1 months, just as a pension benefit led to increased retention (Wiener et al., 2009).

Implementing worker centred workforce policies

The high job appreciation by many LTC workers contrasts starkly with high turnover. According to a study on nurses in Europe, nurses that feel able to provide the care they think is required are less prone to burnout (Schoot et al., 2003), while good working conditions improve retention (Hasselhorn et al., 2005). Worker-centred policies increase the likelihood that workers feel valued in their work and increase worker control over the job. In the United States, two major demonstration projects showed that a combination of measures can contribute positively to worker satisfaction and retention, as long as the LTC worker feel that care work is valued (Box 6.4). Key aspects relate both to a worker's situation in the life course as well as to the organisation and communication patterns. An example from Germany is illustrated in Box 6.5.

Efforts to retain LTC workers, amongst which nurses, could have most impact if applied at early stages of training and employment and when workers have higher prospect of job tenure. In the United States (Box 6.4) and in Japan (Hotta, 2010), organisations geared towards the worker, for instance by means of coaching supervision, enhancing work-related discussions, and modes of continuous training, succeed in retaining LTC workers longer. According to a repeated survey among home nurses in California, job tenure was the main important predictor of intention to stay (Ellenbecker et al., 2009).

Appropriate human-resource management strategies reduce work-related stress among LTC workers and improve the well-being of LTC recipients. For those working in Japanese nursing homes, mentoring opportunities at provider levels, and merit-based remuneration mechanisms had negative associations with their stress levels. Workers were also less stressed when they had opportunities to learn about provider's management principles, care strategies and LTC-system reforms (Hotta, 2010a and 2010b). Evaluating performance and assignment of responsibilities was associated with a reduction of care-worker burnout, thereby raising worker confidence (Hotta, 2007; 2010a and 2010b). Other studies also indicate that establishing staff-appraisal mechanisms, career ladders,

Box 6.4. **Projects to improve LTC workers recruitment and retention in the United States**

During the early 2000s, the federal Centres for Medicare and Medicaid Services (CMS) funded ten demonstration projects aimed at improving recruitment and retention of direct care workers. The "Better Jobs, Better Care" (BJBC) programme, financed by the Robert Wood Johnson Foundation and Atlantic Philanthropies, aimed to reduce high vacancy and turnover rates among direct care workers in LTC and to contribute to improved workforce quality. The total investment was USD 25 million. Evaluations of results showed the following and, especially, that much of the worth of the initiatives appears to be in demonstrating to the workers that they are valued.

	Effect on:				
	Turnover	Vacancies	Job satisfaction	Intention to stay	Retention
Health care coverage*	Health care coverage critical to retention of workers#				
Wages# (fair compensation and benefits, competitive wages)			+		+
Realistic job previews/targeted recruitment campaigns*	–	–	+	+	
	Increase job satisfaction for workers with long tenure				
Realistic job previews*	–	–			
	Especially when preview matched job content, done prior to hiring and combined with post-hire initiatives. Mass marketing led to inflow of unsuitable candidates				
Coaching and supportive supervision#			+		+
	Supervisors require targeted training				
Peer mentorship*	+	+	+		–
	Probable cause: lack of funding and structure				
Worker recognition*	–	–	+		
Financial recognition*	Rewards were small and temporary especially when a bonus instead of wage increases, moreover taxation reduced amounts				
Merit recognition*		–	+	+	+
	Creating a community larger than the agency gave workers a support system and a sense of pride and job identity				
Training*	+				
	Causes: major participation problems; lack of identification of worker needs				

Older workers#: Were considered more stable, providing better care than younger workers. They seemed to prefer working in home-based setting (more supportive tasks than hands on care), while stereotypes about physical capacity did not apply.
Family and friends as pool#: substantial shares of those providing paid care for a family member were interested in further work in LTC; their motivation to start was often "to make a difference". Those who continue to provide care after this care process stressed the aim to "help others" or "affect people's lives". Paid family and friend caregivers who did not stay in LTC tended to earn "more" than as paid care workers).
Supervision#: coaching (instead of command) supervision and showing respect was critical to job satisfaction and worker retention, suggesting that worker autonomy should be accompanied by good supervision. However, many supervisors felt ill-prepared for the job. Clear recommendations were shaped for targeted education and training for supervisors.
Job satisfaction#: high job satisfaction was associated with low turnover and positive interactions among staff.
Career#: more than half of the direct care workers wanted to leave the work within three years, of which almost half wanted to become licensed practical (or registered) nurse.
Quality of care#: greater job commitment of direct care workers was associated with better care for residents.
Retention efforts#: a "retention specialist"(*e.g.*, trained team, with dedicated time and financial and administrative support) was more favourably perceived by workers in the agency administration.
Initial training#: was often perceived as not enough; it should last longer and focus on hands-on work, communication skills, and dealing with problem behaviours.
(Employer-based) continuing education#: should be fit to suit all workers' circumstances and be flexible, address communication and team work, take place in the context of stable management and require management commitment as well as clear co-ordination.
Cultural competence#: zero tolerance on racism and train staff in cultural diversity and cultural competence in care, including non-verbal communication are important and should include communication with residents and family members. Higher cultural competence is associated with higher job satisfaction.
Sources: *: Engberg *et al.* (2009); #: Livingston (2008).

Box 6.5. **Germany: Initiatives to enhance care work**

The New Quality of Work Initiative (abbreviated to INQA in German) is a joint project by the federal government, the federal states, social insurance institutions, social partners and businesses. The Initiative's members aim to promote a new quality of work, stimulate good working conditions and employee-oriented staffing policies in the service sector, including health and care. INQA stimulates public debate, organises knowledge transfer, supports innovative projects and draws media attention to examples of good practice. Together with the Professional Association of Health and Welfare Services (BGW), INQA organises an annual contest for the best health and care employer. For the BGW – executor of the statutory accident health insurance for more than six million policy holders – the primary purpose is the prevention of occupational accidents, occupational diseases and work-related health hazards.

In 2007, INQA produced a memorandum on *healthy nursing,* defined as oriented to prevent overburden, worker oriented, embedded in a healthy-work and co-operation culture, communication enhancing within the organisation and with those in need and their families, care-recipient oriented, aimed at developing personal competences, taking place in a healthy workplace, and flexible.

The Joint Labour Protection Strategy (*Gemeinsame Deutschen Arbeitsschutzstrategie, GDA)*, a collaboration of federal and state-level stakeholders, also focuses on care, especially to prevent muscular skeleton problems, psychological stress and improve safety. It has online self-assessment tools for preventive measures, trains managers to implement risk assessments and holds regional information meetings to improve the culture of prevention and health literacy of employees.

Source: OECD 2009-10 Questionnaire on Long-term Care Workforce and Financing.

---

promoting work-life balance (Suga, 2007) and involving staff in decision-making (Matsui, 2004) reduce stress levels, although the appropriate approaches seem to differ by type of institutions (Jeong Jang, 2007; Nagami and Kuroda, 2007).

Worker recognition, especially merit recognition (including membership of a professional organisation or a trade union), proved to be advantageous. Countries with well-developed social dialogue and a structured approach to the recognition of worker's needs, such as the Netherlands, Norway, and Sweden, manage better retention than others with a limited development of structural dialogue. In the Netherlands, a new concept of care provision was developed by LTC workers, who started a new type of organisation to provide better care while giving the care worker recognition (*Buurtzorg*) (Box 6.6).

Box 6.6. **More responsibility to the care professional?** *Buurtzorg Nederland* **in the Netherlands**

Buurtzorg Nederland is a care provider organisation offering high-level care and giving as much responsibility as possible to the carer. According to *Buurtzorg Nederland,* nationwide implementation could help save resources while at the same time improving quality. The concept works with self-responsible teams, without management and minimal support services, with overhead reduced to an optimal information process through high quality ICT.

Started in 2007, 260 teams were active as of September 2010, consisting of 1 700 workers with higher vocational education and 1 000 intermediate vocational qualifications. The number of clients is approaching 35 000. Active interest for the concept exists in Belgium, Sweden, Switzerland, Japan and the United States.

Source: Information provided by *Buurtzorg Nederland.*

Implementing life-course and age-related measures

These policies help workers to better juggle life-specific challenges and work. Such measures can be included in general labour-market policies, but also be sector specific, due to the gender composition of the LTC workforce and harsh working circumstances. The difficulties in combining work with caring for a child or an elderly parent are a barrier for 40% of women working part-time to work more hours (OECD, 2004). Although older LTC workers seem to be better valued than younger workers, age-related workforce policies – that is, policies that take the consequences of one's age into account – become increasingly important given the ageing LTC workforce.

Safety at work

A care worker in bad health may not be able to provide the care required and may endanger the care recipients' health. Worker-health measures relate to occupational health and accident prevention. Given the occupational hazards related to LTC, policies to support LTC workers, such as those described for Germany in Box 6.5, are crucial. Supportive measures can be taken by having workers use specific tools or equipment, but more generally, by monitoring the functional, mental and health status of the worker. These health and safety measures are even more important for workers in home care, but also more difficult to implement and monitor without intruding into the care recipient household.

Work organisation and process

Management in long-term care facilities appears to be lacking in quality and efficiency. This has detrimental effects for both the worker and care recipients. Some OECD countries are therefore implementing policies to remedy this situation (Table 6.1). In Sweden, for instance, the government has recently initiated a management and leadership programme for LTC managers.

Many LTC workers also lack a say in planning and responsibility in care provision, even if they are those in closest contact with the care recipient. Several options can be implemented to improve worker voice, amongst which self-steering teams, who plan and share workload based on the needs of the care recipients. Mentorships and coaching may stimulate workers – if properly organised – while also acting as means for informal learning. Work-related measures that have been shown to improve retention of nurses are also applicable to the LTC workforce. These include overtime strategies, flexible work arrangements, family care initiatives, leave and compensation, health and well-being, work environment and safety practices, as well as a supportive organisational culture, and union and management support. A trust relationship between employer and employee and good management modalities are a contributor factor to successful retention (Simoens et al., 2005). Japanese policies to promote stability of the LTC workforce by supporting improvements of the working environment also seem to require managerial change. Instead of management working strictly top-down, LTC management could be motivated to work in different modes, enabling and supporting LTC workers in their professional roles. However, professional management skills are often lacking in LTC settings.

The English National Social Care Skills Academy, established in 2009, provides evidence for and options to improve LTC management. The Academy aims to provide training support to small and medium-sized care providers in particular, in recognition of their limited training budgets. It also provides training programmes for employers and includes an accreditation scheme to encourage consistency in the quality of employer- provided training of care workers. In 2010, the Skills Academy hosted the finals of the Worldskills UK Caring Competition, in an effort to raise the profile of social care, where care workers competed in role-playing scenarios (*www.nsasocialcare.co.uk*). Germany has a contest for the best care employer. Box 6.6 provides a recent Dutch example of successful LTC workers' organisation and practices.

Educating the LTC workforce: Life-long learning and employability

Basic education

Depending on the job level and country, basic training for LTC may be limited (Chapter 5). This lack of targeted (vocational) training implies that many workers, when entering the LTC sector, may not be adequately prepared to do their work. However, the nature of the job, which can be physically, emotionally and psychologically enduring, requires know-how. Furthermore, technological progress and the use of ICT in the sector may change the care process. Not being properly prepared to enter the LTC workforce may therefore imply not being able to respond adequately to the challenges of care provision, which risk hampering quality of care and retention. For instance, in Japan, training and improving caregiving skills has been associated with reduction of care-worker burnout and better co-worker relationships (Hotta, 2007; 2010a and 2010b).

Austria and Germany, together with regional jurisdictions, have national requirements for care workers. The Austrian agreement on social-care professions, which was enacted into regional laws early in 2009, aims to implement a wide system of training in social care and to better integrate medical care professions. To improve job attractiveness, the law creates flexibility and mobility in the labour market. In the case of Germany this applies to elderly care nurses (2004). In 2008, Germany created a new job category in nursing home care, that of IADL assistant. The work is specifically targeted at assisting people suffering from dementia and related illnesses. The United States, as part of the measures to be implemented with the health reform, will devote efforts to develop core competences for LTC workers (Harahan and Stone, 2009).

Continued education and training

Educational innovation can enhance recruitment as well as retention (Dill *et al.*, 2010) but can also, when not targeted at the care-workers' wishes, desires or circumstances, actually lead to increased turnover. Worker education and development is often not part of the strategic management of LTC organisations, while employees' individual needs are not sufficiently taken into account (*Sosiaali Ja Terveysministeriö*, 2004). Even if they are, worker education tends to be aimed at adjusting to changes in direct job requirements, than at efforts to stimulate qualification levels. The low upward mobility in the sector gives some evidence to this notion, even though the differences in initial qualification requirements between two job levels may be limited (one extra year of education for a higher job-level, for instance).

Still, several countries among which Australia, France, New Zealand and Switzerland aim to boost training of the LTC workforce. Germany has recently increased public funding for the third and last year of training of older workers who want to change career into LTC, where it previously only paid for the first two. The United States has several initiatives to assist workers wishing to raise their qualifications. However, it may well be that there is more targeted – continued – training available in health care than in LTC. Especially lower-level care workers in home care receive fairly little continued education and training, as in the Netherlands (Verkaik *et al.*, 2010a).

Differentiated policies may be required to stimulate educational levels among different workers' categories. Other options include flexible worker-based education, including e-learning. In some countries, the relatively high shares of high – but not LTC-targeted – qualified workers in the sector, could be a basis for focused training and education. For instance, Germany and the Netherlands recognise previously gained competences, enabling those with relevant knowledge, skills and experiences, to skip parts of the vocational education. Australia aims to rehire and up-skill associate nurses into LTC and qualifying them as registered nurses. For relatively low-educated workers, additional efforts and measures may be required to increase participation in training as there are indications that these workers are less aware of the positive economic returns of education. For instance, taking away fear of exams and guidance could increase their successful participation in training (Fouarge et al., 2010). This suggests that the low-educated LTC workforce may need different modes of continued education than higher-educated LTC workers.

In some countries LTC work is differentiated depending on complexity of tasks and responsibilities. As turnover tends to be highest in the lowest-level jobs, these workers can be stimulated to perform more complex tasks by targeted education. Workers doing these other tasks can then also be stimulated to be further trained. Constructing such a "ladder of training" has been tried in the United States and proved to be successful. Such a process could, ultimately, assist in reducing shortages.

Careers in LTC

As jobs in LTC in most countries are dead-end jobs, building a career implies further education and training. For this purpose, Austria implemented a modular training system that allows for flexible use and is geared towards smooth transition between occupations. France, too, invests in developing career-like options and the United Kingdom invests in career pathways. As yet, however, there is little known about the results.

Finding the right balance between work requirements and the development of options for professional and personal growth is a challenge. Task integration may be a mode to increase job satisfaction and retention by creating more attractive jobs and minimising job fragmentation (Oschmiansky, 2010). In the United States, the Green House project required workers to provide more integral care by doing hands-on work – both IADL and ADL support. This approach led to reduced job fragmentation and increased continuity in the carer-LTC recipient contacts. The system is cost effective due to reduced turnover, a reduced need for middle management, even though the – better trained – workers earn more than Certified Nurse Assistants. Belgian nurses in LTC also provide ADL support.

Nevertheless, improving career-building options in LTC may well require a change in perspectives. Four blocks to building more professional careers in LTC come into play. First of all, part-time workers – a very common category of worker in LTC – are not the most likely candidates to be stimulated by employers to participate in education or career-building initiatives. Second, a major share of LTC workers is ageing. Ageing workers are not the most likely candidates to whom employers offer targeted (further qualifying) education, nor are these workers the most likely to *desire* such trajectories. Older workers in adult social care in the United Kingdom are often seen as lacking flexibility and up to date knowledge (Hussein, 2010). Moreover, there is little evidence of successful career building in later life. A third issue relates to the fact that women, in many countries, appear less career-oriented than men and thus less likely to enter into targeted education (and are less likely to be *offered* education). Finally, as discussed elsewhere in this chapter, there may be hindrances for lower-level care workers to participate in educational trajectories as they may not see themselves as likely candidates to participate or succeed.

6.5. Increasing productivity among LTC workers?

Clear-cut, widely-accepted options to increase productivity in LTC are scarce, as is the evidence about such options. Only a few countries report approaches to increase LTC workers' productivity. Canada reports some tele home-care initiatives having shown a reduction in hospital admissions, while improving clients' self-management ability and enhancing staff satisfaction. The Dutch health-care innovation platform aims to enhance and stimulate innovation in care, while a "transition programme" aims at better care co-ordination, using screen-to-screen communication, and monitoring through video and sensors. The Czech Republic reports the availability of emergency care for elderly living at home. For other countries, although improving productivity is an important issue, there are still no or little outcomes to report. Individual country efforts, albeit limited to a few, suggest that there are possible options for productivity improvements in long-term care, although uncertainty exists about how this can be achieved.

Increasing the role of technology is often seen as an important option to improve user friendliness and quality of services, care co-ordination and personalisation of care, as well as a means to improve worker productivity and communication. A key issue is whether workers can work smarter. Additional skills and technological tools can help workers better cope with the demands of their work. Administrative handling can be automated, making major reductions of overhead possible, while modern tools such as smart phones can be used especially in home care to reduce the administrative handling and enhance connectivity between users, their families, and care provider. However, technological developments can add to work pressures and workload (Evers *et al.*, 2009), while the desire for slim and flat organisations with little overhead may sometimes be at odds with supervisory and clinical requirements.

A related issue is whether productivity improvements via technology and work reorganisation are compatible with quality enhancement goals. In the Netherlands, for example, productivity developments in elderly care have been associated with quality loss (Van der Windt *et al.*, 2009). However, this is not necessarily a trade-off. Win-win solutions can imply smarter use of technology to improve processes and quality of care. For instance, the implementation of Electronic Medical Records (EMRs) in nursing homes in the New York area led to time savings and reductions in medical errors, as well as to improved recruitment ability, lower level of workplace conflict one year following the adoption of EMRs, and increases in communication levels between employees and supervisors (Lipsky and Avgar, 2009).

Such experiences suggest that LTC may need to undergo some change in *modus operandi*, embracing different modes of thinking and unorthodox options. For example, instead of the nurse going to the patient at home (which takes costly working time), in some cases the provision of a transport service for the care recipient to go to and from a nursing station may be cheaper and result in a higher patient/nurse ratio with the same quality. But change risks being relatively slow. In many countries, LTC is a fragmented sector, which prevents quick entry and wider implementation of technological and process innovations. It is also a traditional sector with limited technological or workforce innovations. In the Netherlands, this line of thinking led to the installation of the "care innovation" platform, aimed at speeding up innovations for better care by stimulating continuous "social innovation" by providers and investment in labour-saving technology, especially ICT and home automation (Ministerie van VWS, 2007).

However, technology is no cure for all. For instance, the use of remote monitoring may not lead to a substitution of labour for dementia-suffering clients and can raises ethical questions, for instance related to privacy (Depla *et al.*, 2010). Telemonitoring proved not to improve heart failure outcomes in a large trial study (Sarwat *et al.*, 2010). More generally, there is a dearth of scientific evidence on the cost-effectiveness of most technologies used in LTC settings, which often do not undergo randomised clinical trials, particularly in home-care settings (Rand Health, 2010).

6.6. Conclusions

As in most OECD countries the share of the LTC workforce is still relatively small, there seems to be growth potential for the sector in these countries. LTC can incorporate a share of the growing female labour-force participation because it offers flexible and part-time work, in line with preferences of many women. However, high turnover reflects the difficulties in retaining workers. Supporting these workers in their endeavours may not only serve the worker's goals but also those of the sector as a whole.

There are options to increase the size of the LTC workforce. Indeed, Germany and Japan, some of the fastest ageing countries in the OECD, managed to quickly expand LTC systems and LTC workforces. At the same time, an "old" country with a large LTC workforce, the Netherlands, prepares to meet shortages with a native-born LTC workforce by 2025.

The LTC sector faces a number of challenges linked to its workforce. In a context of ageing societies and growing demand for care, the LTC sector will compete with other labour market sectors for scarce manpower. Even though an oversupply of low-skilled workers is expected in some countries, for instance in Germany, given the increasing complexity of LTC recipients' statuses, more skills may be required in LTC. All of this may imply increased pressures to improve the sector and its attractiveness, while at the same time its image will be more deeply affected by the increasing prevalence of dementia.

The expected reliance on foreign-born care workers in some OECD countries may have consequences on the quality of care if measures aimed at workforce development do not reach foreign-born care workers, especially those who may aim to work in LTC on a temporary basis with little inclination to invest in an LTC career. Some may lack the language capabilities required to successfully participate in retention and professionalisation initiatives, especially if the complexities in LTC work increase.

Supporting care workers in their work and life and valuing them for what they do have clear and positive relevance for job satisfaction, turnover, and intention to stay. But such measures, as well as measures to address workforce shortages, are likely to increase the cost of LTC. This will put public expenditures which is already under increased fiscal pressure, under even higher strains.

The increasing diversity in modes of employment of the LTC workforce results in several challenges. One challenge is that in unregulated systems, cash benefits offer clear incentives for black labour. Another challenge relates to the question of how to integrate irregular – or black – workers, self-employed workers and family carers that received remuneration out of cash-benefit programmes into LTC workforce programmes aimed at retention, quality enhancement and safety. A further issue relates to the quality of working conditions for these different groups.

Continued education and (on-the-job) training are widely used to support and retain care workers, but are primarily aimed at helping workers do their job better and are mostly not targeted at improving qualification levels or developing career options. On the other hand, cost, content and time required may all be hindrances for LTC workers to participate, while fear of exams is also observed. When educational efforts are not associated with better job prospects, they may have limited impact on participation, including the intent to stay in the sector, even when training is targeted to workers' needs and enables them to do their work better. A clear improvement in many countries could be through accreditation mechanisms, which can also improve the attractiveness of training. Continued education or training may serve both the employer's, and worker's needs. There is, however, no evidence about the actual value of accreditation of continued education related to LTC.

Work organisation and culture may require changes in many countries to better comply with worker's wishes and needs, while also better adjusting to the needs of the populations served. While such changes may be burdensome and sometimes difficult to achieve, there may be significant positive returns on investment in terms of job satisfaction, retention as well as quality of care.

If the current mode of production remains unchanged, many countries are likely to face challenges in meeting the future workforce requirements, especially in light of the reduction in the female "recruitment réservoir". This implies that recruitment efforts need to be improved and diversified, and that the current highly labour intensive mode of care production re-examined via, for example, improved productivity.

Notes

1. *www.neue_wege_fuer_jungs.de/Neue_Wege_fuer_Jungs/Das_Projekt* (German language only).

2. Many of these household workers can provide care.

3. *http://stats.oecd.org/Index.aspx?DatasetCode=INVPT_I*. In 2000, this share was 13%.

References

AAHSA and IFAS (2007), "The Long-term Care Workforce: Can the Crisis be Fixed? Problems, Causes and Options", Prepared by the American Association of Homes and Services for the Aging and the Institute for the Future of Aging Services for National Commission for Quality Long-term Care, Washington DC.

ACTiZ (2010), "Transitie naar toekomstbestendige zorg. Inizchten vanuit de benchmark zorg 2010", ACTiZ, Utrecht.

Afentakis, A. and T. Maier (2010), "Projektionen des Personal-bedarfs und -angebotes in Pflegeberufen bis 2025", *Wirtschaft und Statistik*, Vol. 11/2010, Statistisches Bundesamt, pp. 990-1002.

Aiken, L.H. and R. Cheung (2008), "Nurse Workforce Challenges in the United States: Implications for Policy", *OECD Health Working Paper*, No. 35, OECD Publishing, Paris, accessible at *www.oecd.org/dataoecd/34/9/41431864.pdf*.

Antonopoulos, R., K. Kim, T. Masterson and A. Zacharias (2010), "Investing in Care: A Strategy for Effective and Equitable Job Creation", *Working Paper*, No. 610, Levy Economics Institute of Bard College, Annondale on Hudson, accessible at *www.levyinstitute.org/pubs/wp_610.pdf*.

Badkar, J. (2009), *The Future Demand for Paid Caregivers in a Rapidly Ageing Society*, Department of Labour, Wellington.

BGW (2007), *Sieht die Pflege bald alt aus? BGW-Pflegereport 2007. Stand 08/2007*, Berufsgenossenschaft für Gesundheitsdienst und Wohlfahrtspflege, Hamburg.

Bourgeault, I. et al. (2009), *The Role of Immigrant Care Workers in an Aging Society. The Canadian Context and Experience*, University of Ottawa.

Buchan, J. and L. Calman (2008), "Skill Mix and Policy Change in the Health Workforce: Nurses in Advanced Roles", *OECD Health Working Paper*, No. 17, OECD Publishing, Paris, accessible at *www.oecd.org/dataoecd/30/28/33857785.pdf*.

Canadian Home Care Resources Study (2003), accessible at *www.cdnhomecare.ca/media.php?mid=1030*.

Cangiano, A., I. Shutes and S. Spencer (2009a), "Memorandum to Social Care Inquiry", ESRC Centre on Migration, Policy and Society (COMPAS), University of Oxford, November.

Cangiano, A., I. Shutes, S. Spencer and G. Leeson (2009b), "Migrant Care Workers in Ageing Societies", Report on Research Findings in the United Kingdom, COMPAS, University of Oxford.

Chaloff, J. (2008), "Mismatches in the Formal Sector, Expansion of the Informal Sector: Immigration of Health Professionals to Italy", *OECD Health Working Paper*, No. 34, OECD Publishing, Paris, accessible at *www.oecd.org/dataoecd/34/10/41431698.pdf*.

Citizenship and Immigration Canada (2010), accessed 8 November 2010 at *www.cic.gc.ca/english/department/media/backgrounders/2010/2010-08-18a.asp*.

Cortez, M.A. (2009), "Japan-Philippines Free Trade Agreement: Opportunities for the Movement of Workers", *Ritsumeikan International Affairs*, Vol. 7, pp. 125-144, accessible at *www.ritsumei.ac.jp/acd/re/k-rsc/ras/04_publications/ria_en/7_05.pdf*.

Delamaire, M.L. and G. Lafortune (2010), "Nurses in Advanced Roles: A Description and Evaluation of Experiences in 12 Developed Countries", *OECD Health Working Paper*, No. 54, OECD Publishing, Paris.

Department of Health (2009), "Working to Put People First: The Strategy for the Adult Social Care Workforce in England", Department of Health – Adult Social Care Workforce Development, Leeds, May, accessible at *www.dh.gov.uk/prod_consum_dh/groups/dh_digitalassets/documents/digitalasset/dh_098494.pdf*.

Depla, M., S. Zwijsen, S. te Boekhorst, A. Francke and C. Hertogh (2010), "Van fixaties naar domotica? Op weg naar 'goede' vrijheidsbeperking voor mensen met dementie", EMGO+/Nivel, Amsterdam/Utrecht.

Di Santo, P. and F. Ceruzzi (2010), "Migrant Care Workers in Italy. A Case Study", *Interlinks*, European Centre for Social Welfare policy and Research, Rome/Vienna.

Dill, J.S., J. Craft Morgan and T.R. Konrad (2010), "Strengthening the Long-term Care Workforce. The Influence of the WIN A STEP UP Workplace Intervention on the Turnover of Direct Care Workers", *Journal of Applied Gerontology*, Vol. 29, No. 2, pp. 196-214.

Dussault, G., I. Fronteira and J. Cabral (2009), "Migration of Health Personnel in the WHO European Region", Instituto de Higiene e Medicina Tropical/World Health Organisation, Lisbon/Copenhagen.

Eborall, C., W. Fenton and S. Woodrow (2010), "The State of the Adult Social Care Workforce in England, 2010", Fourth report of Skills for Care's Research and Analysis Units, Skills for Care, Leeds, May.

Eggink, E., D. Oudijk and I. Woittiesz. (2010), "Zorgen voor zorg", SCP, Den Haag.

Ellenbecker, C.H., F.W. Porell, L. Samia, J.J. Byleckie and M. Milburn (2009), "Predictors of Home Healthcare Nurse Retention", *Journal of Nursing Scholarship*, Vol. 40, No. 2, pp. 151-160.

Engberg, J., N.G. Castle, S.B. Hunter, L.A. Steighner and E. Maggio (2009), *National Evaluation of the Demonstration to Improve the Recruitment and Retention of the Direct Service Community Workforce*, Rand Corporation, Pittsburg, Santa Monica, Arlington.

Estryn Behar, M., B. van der Heijden, D. Camerino, C. Fry, O. Le Nezet, M. Conway and H.M. Hasselhorn (2008), "Violence Risks in Nursing. Results from the European 'NEXT' Study", *Occupational Medicine 2008*, Vol. 58, pp. 107-114, published online 21 January 2008, DOI:10.1093/occmed/kqm142.

European Commission (2010), *Joint Report on Social Protection and Social Inclusion 2010*, Brussels.

European Foundation for the Improvement of Living and Working Conditions (2006), *Employment in Social Care in Europe*, Office for Official Publications of the European Communities, Luxembourg.

Evers, H., N. Blijham, C. Willems and L. de Witte (2009), *Zorg op afstand, literatuurstudie naar internationale ontwikkelingen en kennis over effecten. Een analyse van de samenvattingen van recente publicaties over toepassingen voor langdurende zorg op afstand*, Vilans, Utrecht.

Fouarge, D., T. Schils and A. de Grip (2010), "Why Do Low Educated Workers Invest Less in Further Training?", *IZA Discussion Paper*, No. 5180, Bonn, accessible at *http://ftp.iza.org/dp5180.pdf*.

Fujisawa, R. and F. Colombo (2009), "The Long-term Care Workforce: Overview and Strategies to Adapt Supply to a Growing Demand", *OECD Health Working Paper*, No. 44, OECD Publishing, Paris.

Groth, H., R. Kingholz and M. Wehling (2009), "Future Demographic Challenges in Europe: The Urgency to Improve the Management of Dementia", *WDA HSG Discussion Paper Series on Demographic Issues*, No. 2009/4.

Harahan, M. and A.R. Stone (2009), "Defining Core Competencies for the Professional Long-term Care Workforce: A Status Report and Next Steps", AAHSA/IFAS, Washington DC.

Hasselhorn, H.M., B.H. Müller and P. Tackenberg (2005), "NEXT Scientific Report 2005", University of Wuppertal, NEXT Study Coordination, Wuppertal, accessible at *www.next.uni_wuppertal.de/EN/download.php?f=133131f960ff1150b2e0192c51d18f53&target=0*.

Hooren, F. (van) (2008), "Bringing Policies Back In: How Social and Migration Policies Affect the Employment of Immigrants in Domestic Care for the Elderly in the EU-15", Paper prepared for "Transforming Elderly Care at Local, National and Transnational Levels", International Conference at the Danish National Centre for Social Research (SFI), Copenhagen, 26-28 June 2008, and European University Institute, Florence.

Hotta, S. (2007), "Toward Maintaining and Improving the Quality of Long-term Care: The Current State and Issues Regarding Home Helpers in Japan under the Long-term Care Insurance System", *Social Science Japan Journal*, Vol. 10, No. 2, pp. 265–279, DOI: 10.1093/ssjj/jym056.

Hotta, S. (2010a), "Kaigo Jyūjisha Mondai" (Professional Caregiver Issue in Japan), in H. Miyajima, S. Nishimura and T. Kyogoku (eds.), *Shakai Hoshō to Keizai* (Social Security and Economy), Vol. 3, *Shakai Sābisu to Chiiki* (Social Services and Community), University of Tokyo Press, Tokyo, pp. 149-172.

Hotta, S. (2010b), "Kaigohoken jimusho (shisetu kei) ni okeru kaigoshokuin no storess keigen to koyou kanri", *Quarterly of Social Security Research*, Vol. 46, No. 2, National Institute of Population and Social Security Research.

Hussein, S. (2010), "Adult Care Workers at the Upper End of the 'Third Age' (60-75) in England", *Working Paper*, King's College London, Social Care Workforce Research Unit, London, March.

IGZ (2010), "Medicatieveiligheid voor kwetsbare groepen in de langdurige zorg en zorg thuis onvoldoende", IGZ, Den Haag.

Immigration Professionnelle (2008), accessed 9 November 2010 at *www.immigration-professionnelle.gouv.fr/nouveaux-dispositifs/m%C3%A9tiers-en-tension*.

IOM – Institute of Medicine (2008), "Retooling for an Aging America: Building the Health Care Workforce", accessible at *www.iom.edu/agingamerica*.

Israel Government Portal, accessed 10 November 2010 at *www.gov.il/FirstGov/TopNavEng/EngSituations/ESMigrantWorkersGuide/ESMWGRights*.

Jeong Jang, Y. et al. (2007), "Tokubetsu yougo roujin home ni okeru kaigo shokuin no sutoresu ni kansuru kenkyu: shoukibo care gata shisetsu to juuraigata shisetu no hikaku", *Journal of Gerontology*, Vol. 29, No. 3, Japan Socio Gerontological Society, pp. 366-374.

Katseli L.T. et al. (2006), "Effect of Migration on Sending Countries: What Do We Know?", OECD Development Center, *Working Paper*, No. 250, accessed 29 November 2010 at *www.un.org/esa/population/migration/turin/Symposium_Turin_files/P11_Katseli.pdf*.

Kemp, A. (2010), "Reforming Policies on Foreign Workers in Israel", *OECD Social, Employment and Migration Working Papers*, No. 103, OECD Publishing, Paris, accessed 8 November 2010 at *www.oecd-ilibrary.org/social-issues-migration-health/reforming-policies-on-foreign-workers-in-israel_5kmjnr8pbp6f-en*.

Kodama, A. et al. (2002), "The Effects of Environmental Consideration for People with Dementia Upon the Stress Fesponse of Care Staffs of Nursing Homes", *Long-term Care Welfare Studies*, Vol. 9, No. 1, Japanese Association of Research on Care and Welfare, pp. 9-70.

Lamura, G. (2010), "The Role of Migrant Work in the LTC Sector: Opportunities & Challenges", Conference on "Long-term Care in Europe. Discussing Trends and Relevant Issues", Budapest, 22-23 February 2010, accessed 9 November 2010 at *www.euro.centre.org/data/1267541472_78930.pdf*.

Lamura, G., M.G. Melchiorre, C. Chiatti and M. di Rosa (2010a), "Migrant LTC Workers: What Role, What Challenges, What Policies?", OECD Expert Meeting on Long-term Care Workforce and Finances, OECD Conference Centre, 15-16 November, Paris.

Lipsky, D.B. and A.C. Avgar (2009), "Caregivers and Computers: The Effect of Electronical Medical Records on Employment and Labor Relations in Nursing Homes", final report submitted to the quality care oversight committee and 1199SEIU Training and Employment Funds, School of Industrial and Labor Relations, Cornell University, University of Illinois at Urbana-Champaign, School of Labor and Employment Relations.

Livingston, J. (2008), "Solutions You Can Use. Transforming the Long-term Care Workforce", AAHSA/IFAS, Washington DC.

Marin, B., K. Leichsenring, R. Rodrigues and M. Huber (2009), "Who Cares? Care Co-ordination and Co-operation to Enhance Quality in Elderly Care in the European Union", Conference on Healthy and Dignified Ageing, 15-16 September 2009, Stockholm.

Markova, E. (2010), "Effects of Migration on Sending Countries: Lessons from Bulgaria", GreeSE Paper, No. 35, Hellenic Observatory Papers on Greece and Southeast Europe, Hellenic Observatory-European Institute, accessed 29 November 2010 at www.lse.ac.uk/collections/hellenicObservatory/pdf/GreeSE/GreeSE35.pdf.

Martin, S., B. Lindsay Lowell, E. Gzodziak, M. Bump and A.M. Breeding (2009), "The Role of Migrant Care Workers in Aging Societies", Report on Research Findings in the United States, Institute for the Study of International Migration, Walsh School of Foreign Service, Georgetown University, Washington DC.

Matsui, M. (2004), "Chihousei koureisha gurûpu hômu no shokuin ni okeru storesu", Journal of Japanese society for dementia care, Vol. 3, No. 1, pp. 21-29.

McHale, J. (2009), "Projecting Canada's Elder Care Workforce", in I. Bourgeault et al. (eds.), The Role of Immigrant Care Workers in an Aging Society. The Canadian Context & Experience, University of Ottawa.

Ministry of Health/University of Auckland (2004), "Disability Support Services in New Zealand", The Workforce Survey. Final Report, 20 August 2004.

Ministerie van VWS (2007), Arbeidsmarktbrief 2007, Werken aan de zorg, MEVA/ABA/2807123.

Ministerie van VWS (2008), Arbeidsmarktbrief 2008, MEVA/ABA-2900709.

Ministerie van VWS (2009), Arbeidsmarktbrief 2009, MEVA/ABA-2900709, MEVA/ABA-2978507.

Mosthaf, A., C. Schnabel and J. Stephani (2010), "Low Wage Careers: Are There Dead End Firms and Dead End Jobs?", IZA Discussion Paper, No. 4696, Bonn, January.

Nagami, H. and K. Kuroda (2007), "Tokubetsu yougo roujin Hôme ni okeru shoukibo care no jisshi to kaigoshokuin no sutoresu no kankei", Journal of Health and Welfare Statistics, Vol. 54, No. 10, Health and Welfare Statistics Association.

OECD (1995), The OECD Jobs Study: Implementing the Strategy, OECD Publishing, Paris.

OECD (2004), "Female Labour Force Participation: Past Trends and Main Determinants in OECD Countries", OECD Economic Department Working Paper, OECD Publishing, Paris.

OECD (2008), The Looming Crisis in the Health Workforce. How Can OECD Countries Respond?, OECD Publishing, Paris.

OECD (2009), International Migration Outlook, OECD Publishing, Paris.

OECD (2010a), International Migration Outlook, OECD Publishing, Paris.

OECD (2010b), OECD Reviews of Labour Market and Social Policies. Israel, OECD Publishing, Paris.

OECD/WHO (2010), "International Migration of Health Workers. Improving International Co-operation to Address the Global Health Shortage Crisis", Policy Brief, OECD Publishing, Paris, accessible at www.oecd.org/dataoecd/8/1/44783473.pdf.

Office of Disability, Aging and Long Term Care Policy. Assistant Secretary for planning and evaluation. US Department of Health and Human Services (2006), "Ensuring a Qualified Long-term Care Workforce: From Pre-Employment Screens to On-The-Job Monitoring", Washington DC.

Onodera, A. et al. (2006), "Ninchishou kaigo senmontou shokuin ni taisuru shokubanai kenshuu no kokoromi : performance management wo mochiita torikumi no kouka kenshou", Japan Dementia Care Journal, Vol. 5, No. 3, pp. 403-415.

Oschmiansky, H. (2010), "The Marketization of Formal Elder Care in Germany and its Consequences for the Labour Market", Paper for the International Conference "Transforming Care: Provision, Quality and Inequalities in Later Life", Copenhagen, 21-23 June.

Rand Health (2010), *Health and Well-Being in the Home. A Global Analysis of Needs, Expectations and Priorities for Home Health Care Technologies*, Brownse Books and Publications, Rand Health.

Rubin, J. et al. (2008), *Migrant Women in the European Labour Force. Current Situation and Future Prospects*, RAND Europe.

Sarwat, I. et al. (2010), "Telemonitoring in Patients with Heart Failure", *New England Journal of Medicine*, Vol. 363, pp. 2301-2309.

Schoot, E. (van der), H. Ogińska, M. Estryn Behar and the NEXT Study Group (2003), "Burnout in the Nursing Profession in Europe", *Working Conditions and Intent to Leave the Profession Among Nursing Staff in Europe*, NEXT Study, University of Wuppertal.

Seavey, D. (2004), "The Cost of Frontline Turnover in Long-term Care", Better Jobs, Better Care, IFAS/AAHSA, Washington.

Simoens, S., S. Villeneuve and A.J. Hurst (2005), "Tackling Nurse Shortages in OECD Countries", *OECD Health Working Paper*, No. 19, OECD Publishing, Paris.

Smith, K. and R. Baughman (2007), "Caring for America's Aging Population: A Profile of the Direct Care Workforce", *Monthly Labor Review*, September, pp. 20-26.

SPC – Social Protection Committee (2009), "Second Joint Assessment by the SPC and the European Commission of the Social Impact of the Economic Crisis and of Policy Responses", SPC/2009/11/13 final.

Sosiaali Ja Terveysministeriö (2004), "Terveydenhuollon, Täydennyskoulutussuositus", Summary, Helsinki.

Suga, Y. (2007), "Factor Analysis of Work Stress Among Home Help Organizers", *Long-term Care Welfare Studies*, Vol. 14, No. 2, Japanese Association of Research on Care and Welfare, pp. 143-150.

Swedish Association of Local Authorities and Regions (2007), *Care of the Elderly in Sweden Today 2006*, Stockholm, January.

Tanabe, T. et al. (2005), "Tokubetu yougo roujin houme ni okeru yunitto kea kankyou ikou ga kaigo sutaffu no shinshin ni ataeru eikyou: bân auto to sutoresu taisho chousa", *Journal of the Japanese Society for Dementia Care*, Vol. 4, No. 1, Japanese Society for Dementia Care, pp. 17-23.

Velde, F. (Van der), F. Verijdt and E. Arnold (2010), *De arbeidsmarkt voor lagere functies in de zorg: veel vissen in de vijver*, OEZW19, Prismant, Utrecht.

Verkaik, R., A.J. de Veer and A.L. Francke (2010a), "Veel bij- en nascholing in de verpleging en verzorging, Panel V&V", *TVZ tijdschrift voor verpleegkundigen*, No. 4, pp. 24-26.

Verkaik, R., A. Francke, B. Meijel, P.M. van Spreeuwenberg, M.W. Ribbe and J.M. Bensing (2010b), "The Introduction of a Nursing Guideline on Depression at Psychogeriatric Nursing Home Wards: Effects on Certified Nurse Assistants", *International Journal of Nursing Studies*, DOI:10.1016/j.ijnurstu.2010.06.007.

Wiener, J.M., M.R. Squillace, W.L. Anderson and G. Khatutsky (2009), "Why Do They Stay? Job Tenure among Certified Nursing Assistants in Nursing Homes", *The Gerontologist*. Vol. 49, No. 2, pp. 198-210.

Windt, W. (van der), R.H. Smeets and E. Arnold (2009), *Regiomarge 2009. De arbeidsmarkt van verpleegkundigen, verzorgenden en sociaalagogen, 2009-2013*, Prismant, Utrecht, June.

Zorginnovatieplatform (2009), *Zorg voor mensen, mensen voor de zorg; arbeidsmarktbeleid voor de zorgsector richting 2025*, Zorginnvatieplatform, Den Haag.

Chapter 7

Public Long-term Care Financing Arrangements in OECD Countries

> With population ageing and reductions in family care, utilisation of formal long-term care for disabled people is growing in all high-income countries. Higher demand for formal services is emerging also because of people's expectations for high-quality care. These factors are pushing up the cost of formal long-term care across OECD countries and raise questions about who should pay more prominent in policy discussions. This chapter offers an overview of public long-term care (LTC) coverage in OECD countries. For illustrative purposes, countries are clustered into three main groups, ranging from universal and comprehensive to means-tested system or systems with a mix. Over time, coverage systems are evolving towards universal systems or benefits and more user-choice models, with, in many cases, increased targeting of care benefits to those with the highest care needs.

The statistical data for Israel are supplied by and under the responsibility of the relevant Israeli authorities. The use of such data by the OECD is without prejudice to the status of the Golan Heights, East Jerusalem and Israeli settlements in the West Bank under the terms of international law.

7.1. Collective coverage of long-term care costs is desirable on efficiency and access grounds

There are powerful rationales for creating long-term care (LTC) coverage mechanisms to complement family and volunteering care arrangements. First, the cost of care can be high and thereby place a significant burden on users, especially those living on low-income or with high levels of dependency. For example, in the United States, the cost of formal care averages USD 75 000 per year in a skilled nursing facility and USD 20 per hour for home health aides (Gleckman, 2010), nearly three times as much the average disposable income for a person aged 65 years. LTC coverage, especially public systems, provides old-age support, helping seniors face dependency costs. Second, there are significant uncertainties for individuals about the need for long-term care, especially the time the need will develop, as well as its duration and intensity. It is understandable that they will wish to cover this risk but cost can be high and access reduced when covered by actuarial insurance mechanisms (Bar, 2010).

Mechanisms for pre-payment (*i.e.* raising contributions to pay for cost that may arise in the future) and pooling (*i.e.* sharing of the risk and of the cost across a broad "pool" of covered individuals) for LTC costs, such as LTC insurance, allowances and targeted assistance, provide an answer to high uncertainty and high cost. They pool risk and ensure protection against potentially catastrophic long-term care cost. They help to protect disposable income and assets of users, therefore offering a safety net and preventing care-dependent people from falling into poverty. They also enable access to LTC services by offering compensation for the cost of such services, thus helping to prevent deteriorating health and increased dependency and being deprived of necessary care due to lack of financial resources. By sharing costs across individuals within the pool, they can also respond to demand for intergenerational equity.

The formal LTC sector is still relatively small in OECD countries (as a share of GDP), especially when compared to the estimated value of family care and expenditure on health or pension systems. However, it is a sector in evolution. LTC expenditure – particularly public LTC spending – has shown a faster upward trend than health care spending.[1] The expected increases in formal LTC use are pushing ahead discussions about how to improve equity and efficiency in the financing of long-term care. These discussions often concern public schemes because, in most OECD countries, the risk of dependency is mainly pooled through publicly financed mechanisms. Private coverage is, for a number of reasons discussed in Chapter 8, a niche market.

This chapter informs those discussions by offering an overview of public LTC coverage in OECD countries. The next chapter (Chapter 8) discusses private coverage arrangements, their possible role as a complement to public LTC systems, as well as the reasons for limited market development to date. A third chapter (Chapter 9) considers future directions and useful country experiences to address two main policy challenges in LTC financing: providing fair and adequate access to care; and controlling cost growth.

7.2. Public long-term care coverage for personal care can be clustered in three main groups[2]

While LTC coverage comprises a complex mix of services, benefits, and schemes, it is still possible to distinguish clusters of countries with similar approaches.[3] The taxonomy is derived looking at variation in support for personal care – that is help with so-called activities of daily living (ADL) – whether at home or in institutions. This is because ADL support is the type of care for which more variation in public coverage arrangements exists across OECD countries. Reference is however made in the following section of this chapter to how coverage for skilled nursing care, board and lodging cost and other LTC services varies across the OECD. Where a country has multiple benefits for older and younger disabled, the description typically refers to the frail elderly. Benefit schemes for young disabled people may therefore not be properly reflected in this typology. Coverage is often more comprehensive for young disabled people, relatively to older groups. In France, for example, disability benefits (*Prestation de compensation du handicap*) targeted to young people are higher than those under the dependency allowance (*Allocation Personnalisée d'Autonomie*) targeted to older people. Countries with no or very little public LTC coverage are not discussed.

The classification uses two main criteria to distinguish across country types:

- the *scope of entitlement* to long-term care benefits – whether there is universal[4] or means-tested[5] entitlement to public funding; and
- whether LTC coverage is through a *single system, or multiple benefits, services and programmes*.

Three broad country clusters can be identified based on these two criteria:

- universal coverage within a single programme;
- mixed systems;
- means-tested safety-net schemes.

It is also possible to distinguish additional sub-groups, depending for example, on: i) whether the sources of funds are earmarked taxes/contributions or general revenues; ii) whether the programme is or not part of health systems; and iii) in mixed systems, the nature of the programmes that constitute the mix.

Each LTC scheme has specific features, such as the target population group (the elderly only or the whole population), or the type of benefits provided (whether a cash subsidy/allowance or subsidised in-kind services), as summarised in Table 7.1.

Universal coverage within a single programme

Under this cluster, LTC coverage is provided through a single system, whether separate from health systems (*e.g.*, Nordic countries, social long-term care insurance), or part of health coverage (*e.g.*, Belgium). Systems with single universal LTC coverage provide publicly-funded *nursing and personal care* to all individuals assessed as eligible due to their care-dependency status. They may apply primarily to the old population (*e.g.*, Japan, Korea), or to all people with assessed care-need regardless of the age-group (*e.g.*, the Netherlands, Germany). Co-payments, user charges or up-front deductibles are required even in universal coverage systems. They are typically subject to income thresholds, with partial or full exemption from payments, or social-assistance mechanisms, for the poor, resulting, effectively, in a comprehensive collective coverage of LTC costs.

Table 7.1. Public LTC coverage: A summary

	Eligibility to coverage	Coverage programmes	Programme(s) name	Source of financing LTC	Target disabled population	Types of benefits provided	Public LTC spending, share of GDP (%)
Australia	Universal	Multiple programmes: Income-related benefits	Home and Community Care (HACC); Residential care by ACATs (aged care assessment teams)	Tax: 60% federal, 40% local, state and territorial governments for HACC; Tax-based	Old people	In-kind, home and institutional care	0.8
Austria	Two cash benefit systems, one universal, one means-tested	Multiple programmes: Income-related benefits	Pflegegeld (universal cash system); 24-hour care benefit	Tax: In 2006, federal (EUR 1.62 billion) and Lander (EUR 301.5 million)	All; Income criteria, Pflegegeld level 3	Cash, home and institutional care (in-kind benefits by Länders)	1.1
Belgium	Universal coverage within a single system (health-related and personal care); Social care (domestic care and other support)	Via the health system; Federal programme; Flemish programme; Regional programmes	Public health Insurance system (INAMI/RIZIV); Federal allowances for elderly/social welfare benefits; Flemish care insurance; Home help assistance	Social security contributions/payroll taxes (57%), general direct taxation (37%) and OOP (6%); Direct general taxation; Mandatory yearly contributions; General taxation and OOP (variable according to income)	All; 65+, low-income; All; At home	Cash and in-kind, home and institutional care; Cash, need-tested and income-tested; Cash, need-tested; In-kind, home social care	1.7
Canada	Set by each province	Mix of universal (for home care) and means-tested benefits (often for institutional care)	Varies by province	Provincial revenues from general taxes; Federal Canada health transfers to provinces	All	In-kind, home and institutional care	1.2
Czech Republic	Mixed system	Parallel cash benefit schemes	Care allowance; In-kind LTC services are divided across the social sector and universal health care system	Public budget from general taxation	All	Cash and in-kind, home and institutional care	0.2 (health); 1.2 (social)
Denmark	Universal coverage within a single system	Universal, tax-based		Block grants from federal government, local taxes, equalisation amounts from other local authorities	All	Cash and in-kind, home and institutional care	1.8
Estonia			Estonian Health Insurance Fund (EHIF) Health care; Personal care services mainly provided by local governments	Welfare services for mental disabilities: State; Nursing care services: Health insurance		Cash and in-kind, home and institutional care	
Finland	Universal coverage within a single system	Universal, tax-based		Government transfers to municipalities (31%), municipal and income tax (60%)	All	Cash and in-kind, home and institutional care	1.8

Table 7.1. Public LTC coverage: A summary (cont.)

	Eligibility to coverage	Coverage programmes	Programme(s) name	Source of financing LTC	Target disabled population	Types of benefits provided	Public LTC spending, share of GDP (%)
France	Mixed system	Income-related benefits	Sécurité sociale covers institutional and home care services (Ssaid); Allocation personnalisée d'autonomie (APA); Prestation de compensation du handicap (PHC)	Local and central taxes and social contributions; APA: 70% local level funding	All; Aged 60+, income-tested	Cash and in-kind, home and institutional care	1.7
Germany	Universal coverage within a single system	Public LTC insurance – Social insurance	Long-term care insurance	Tax, premiums, financing from Lander budgets	All	Cash and in-kind, home and institutional care	0.9
Greece	Mixed system	Mix of universal and means-tested (or no) benefits	Provision of social services by Ministry of Health and Social Solidarity and provision of care through Social Insurance Funds	Mixed: national budget, social security and private payments; Housing allowance for the elderly: national budget	"Any old person"	Mainly in-kind, institutional care	0.3
Hungary	Mixed system		Health care under the National Health Insurance System	National Health Insurance Programme: Contributions; Tax-based; Social care: Central government, local government contributions and OOP	All	In-kind, home and institutional care for individuals needing more than 4 hours of care	0.3
Iceland	Mixed system					Institutional care	1.7
Ireland	Mixed system	Parallel universal scheme	Nursing Home Support Scheme	Tax-based	All/no standard	Cash and in-kind, home care	
Italy	Mixed system		Institutional care: Residenze Sanitarie Assistenziali, part of health system; Care allowance: Indennita di accompagnamento		All	Cash and in-kind, home and institutional care	
Japan	Universal coverage within a single system	Public LTC insurance model – Social insurance	Long-term care insurance system	50% public contributions by those over 40, 50% governmental divisions (of which: 50% from national government, 25% from the prefectural government and 25% from the municipality)	Over 65, or 40-64 with age-related disease	In-kind, home and institutional care	1.4
Korea	Universal programme within a single system	Public LTC insurance model – Social insurance	National Health Insurance for the Elderly	Long-term care insurance fee, central and local government, budgets and out-of-pocket	Over 65 or under 65 suffering from geriatric diseases	Cash and in-kind, home and institutional care	0.3

Table 7.1. Public LTC coverage: A summary (cont.)

	Eligibility to coverage	Coverage programmes	Programme(s) name	Source of financing LTC	Target disabled population	Types of benefits provided	Public LTC spending, share of GDP (%)
Luxembourg	Universal long-term care insurance programme	Public LTC insurance model – Social insurance	Assurance Dependence, LTC programme part of healthcare insurance; Gerontological homes	Individual contributions, State contribution and electricity tax; Financed by the National Solidarity fund – EUR 7.6 million (2008)	All	Cash and in-kind, home and institutional care	1.4
Mexico	Mixed/Sub-national	Multiple programmes	Programme for older adults	Federal government (general taxes), contributions from employers and workers; Seguro Popular – Federal and state governments, households	65+	In-kind, cash subsidies, institutional care	
Netherlands	Universal programme within a single system	Public LTC insurance model – Social insurance	Exceptional Medical Expenses Act (AWBZ)	Contributions and additional tax contributions	All	Cash and in-kind, home and institutional care	3.5
New Zealand	Mixed system	Mix of universal and means-tested (or no) benefits	Health funding authority in charge of LTC provision; Residential care subsidy (RCS) pays the cost of contracted care	Tax-based, annual health care block grants from the District Health Boards		Mainly in-kind, home and institutional care	1.3
Norway	Universal programme within a single system	Universal, tax-based		National and local taxes	All	Cash and in-kind, home and institutional care	2
Poland	No separate system of LTC (2004)	Parallel universal scheme	Residential LTC by health care and social sector (Social Assistance System); National Health Fund (NFZ) Home care	Health services funded by a combination of general taxation and contributions to national health insurance schemes; Fully provided and financed by local authority	Over 75 years, disabled persons	Cash and in-kind, home and institutional care	0.4
Portugal	Mixed		National network for long-term care; Medium term and rehabilitation units	Health care: Ministry of Health, medium term and rehabilitation units– co-financed by Ministry of Labour and Social Solidarity (80%) and MoH (20%)	All	In-kind, institutional care	0.1
Slovak Republic			Municipalities and self governing regions provide social services including LTC	Cash benefits: state budget, social services: regional and municipal taxes	Age-related	Cash and in-kind, other: home and institutional care, government organises providers	0.2

Table 7.1. Public LTC coverage: A summary (cont.)

	Eligibility to coverage	Coverage programmes	Programme(s) name	Source of financing LTC	Target disabled population	Types of benefits provided	Public LTC spending, share of GDP (%)
Slovenia	Means-tested programme: No integral system for long-term care	Income-tested for in-kind benefits	Programme under health system and social security	Compulsory health insurance premiums; Pension and social insurance contributions; Tax revenue from Ministry of Labour, Family and Social Assistance; Municipality tax for care for disabilities	Over 65, disabled chronically ill	Cash and in-kind, home and institutional care	0.8
Spain	Mixed system	Mix of universal and means-tested	National long-term care system	Tax-based through central government and regional taxes, Grants	All	Cash and in-kind	0.6
Sweden	Universal programme within a single system	Universal, tax-based		84% local municipal taxes, 11-12% national government grants	All	Cash and in-kind, vouchers for care, Home and institutional care vary across municipality	3.6
Switzerland	Mixed system	Mix of universal and means-tested (or no) benefits	Mandatory health insurance (LAMal), means-tested complementary cash benefits under Law on Disability Insurance (LAI), benefits under the Law on Old Age and Survivors' Insurance (AVS)	Compulsory health insurance premiums, cash benefits: State budget, private payments by the persons needing care	All	Cash and in-kind, institutional care, home care provided predominately by private organisations	0.8 (1.3 including disability and survivors benefits)
United Kingdom	Mixed – means-tested social care system, with universal benefits for disability	Means-tested, safety net	Adult social care	Central taxation – given as block grants, local taxation (council tax)	All aged over 18	Cash and in-kind, home and institutional care	0.96 (2002)
		Universal benefit	Disability living allowance (DLA)	Tax-based	Under 65, disabled		
		Universal benefit	Attendance allowance (AA)	Tax-based	Aged over 65, disabled		
United States[1]	Means-tested system	Means-tested safety net	Medicaid	Federal and state funds	Low-income	In-kind mainly, mandatory institutional benefits, optional state community benefits	0.6
	Social insurance for the elderly	Universal for seniors	Medicare	Part A: Payroll, income tax; Part B: Medicare premiums and congress funds	Seniors	Post acute care in nursing homes	
	Voluntary insurance	Universal if employer opt in (opt out possible)	Community Living Assistance Services and Support CLASS (prospective)	Voluntary insurance	All	Cash benefits for home and institutional care	

1. Medicare is targeted towards those aged 65 and above or those people under 65 with certain disabilities. However, LTC or custodial care is not included in Medicare. Assistance for LTC may be sought, depending on eligibility from Medicaid, Programmes of All-inclusive Care for the Elderly (PACE) or in the future, the Community Living Assistance Services and Supports (CLASS) Programme; *www.medicare.gov/Publications/Pubs/pdf/10050.pdf*; *www.medicare.gov/Publications/Pubs/pdf/11396.pdf*; *www.pssru.ac.uk/pdf/rs040.pdf*.

Source: OECD compilation based on country replies to the OECD 2009-10 Questionnaire on Long-term Care Workforce and Financing.

Three main sub-models can be distinguished: i) tax-based models (e.g., Nordic countries); ii) public long-term care insurance models (e.g., Germany, Japan, Korea, the Netherlands, and Luxembourg); iii) personal care and nursing care through the health system (e.g., Belgium).

Tax-based models

Nordic countries are the most typical example. Norway, Sweden, Denmark and Finland provide universal, tax-funded long-term care services as an integral component of welfare and health-care services for the entire population. While the overall responsibility for the care of elderly and disabled rests with the state, a main feature of these countries is the large autonomy of local governments (e.g., municipalities, counties, councils) in organising service provision and in financing care, including the right to levy taxes (Karlsoon and Iversen, 2010). The state typically contributes to financing by paying non-earmarked subsidies either to municipalities (e.g., Finland) or to regional authorities (e.g., Denmark), adjusted to the population structure and need. Public long-term care services are broad and comprehensive, resulting in a relatively large share of GDP spent on LTC – ranging from 2% in Denmark to 3.6% in Sweden. Beside personal-care support in institutions and at home, they can include for example help with domestic care (Denmark, Sweden), as well as the provision of sheltered housing, home adaptations, assisting devises and transport (OECD, 2008; Ministry of Health and Social Affairs of Sweden, 2007). Out-of-pocket payments for LTC account for relatively low shares, for example around 4% of revenues in Sweden, and the private contributions to cost are capped in Sweden and Norway.

Public long-term care insurance model

A second model of universal coverage consists of stand-alone, dedicated social insurance arrangements for long-term care services. A number of countries, which typically finance health care via social health insurance, belong to this group (Germany, Japan, Korea, the Netherlands, and Luxembourg; see Table 7.2). Similar to the Nordic countries' model, service coverage is generally comprehensive – not just in reaching the entire population needing care, but also with respect to the scope of the covered services. As for Nordic countries, users are required to contribute to the cost of care, with very different level of cost sharing across country (see Box 7.1). Board and lodging in nursing homes may be partially covered in some countries, for example in Japan. As a share of GDP, long-term care spending is above or around the OECD average of 1.5% for this group of countries, apart from Korea (0.3%) and, at the opposite end of the spectrum, the Netherlands (3.5%).

These countries' arrangements share three main features. First, there are separate funding channels for LTC and health insurance, although they follow the same social-insurance model. Second, participation in the scheme is mandatory for the whole or a large section (i.e. those aged 40 and over in Japan) of the population. Third, the scheme is predominantly financed through employment-based, payroll contributions, but senior people can also be asked to pay contributions (e.g., all those above 40 years old in Japan; retired people out of their income in Germany) and a share of the cost is funded out of general taxation in most countries. There are some differences in the mix of financing sources, eligibility criteria, and benefit systems of these countries. For example, benefit values are fixed in Germany and were not consistently adjusted for inflation until the LTC reforms in 2008, which had led to a reduction in the purchasing power of LTC benefits until the stepwise increase in 2008. On the other hand, benefits statutory cover 90% of the cost

Table 7.2. **Universal long-term care insurance schemes in OECD countries**

	Year	Insurers/ purchasers	Financing sources	Contributions	Eligibility to benefits	Benefits	Providers
Germany	1995	Long-term care insurance funds	Payroll and income-related contributions (100%)	1.95% payroll tax (additional premium of 0.25% for those with no children). Paid by all working-age and retired population. Divided between workers and employers. 11% of the population opts out of social insurance and is obliged to buy a private LTC plan with equivalent benefits to social LTCI	Based on a need-assessment regardless of age	In-kind or cash, at user's choice. Fixed value, adjusted periodically	Providers on contract with the social long-term care insurance funds
Luxembourg	1999	National health fund (*Caisse nationale de santé*)	Taxation (about 45%). Contributions. Special tax	Paid by working-age and retired population. Contribution set at 1.4% of income	Disabled assessed as needing LTC, regardless of age	In-kind and/or cash, at user's choice	
Netherlands	1968	Regional insurers (private insurance companies)	Payroll and income-related contributions. Means-tested co-payments	Contribution rate is based on income. Paid by working-age and retired population (all citizens over 15 years old with a taxable income)	Disabled assessed as needing LTC, regardless of age	In-kind (institution, home care). Cash home (personal budgets)	
Japan	2000	Municipalities	Tax (45%). Contributions (45%). Cost sharing (10%)	Paid by over 40 year old population. Insured individuals between 40-64 pay 30% of total LTC costs. Income-related contributions for those aged over 65 years	Over 65 assessed as needing LTC. Over 40 with certain types of diseases	In kind	Competing services providers (private companies, consumers' co-operatives, and NGO) certified by the government
Korea	2008	National health insurance (NHI) corporation	Tax (37%). Payroll contributions (52%). Cost sharing (11%)	Paid by working-age population through contributions to health insurance scheme. 2011 NHI contributions set at 5.9% of wages, 6.55% of which goes towards LTC	Over 65 assessed as needing LTC. Younger people with geriatric diseases	In-kind or cash	Competing services providers (private companies, NGO, etc.)

Note: Korea: "Long-term Care Insurance for the Elderly" (*Noinjangjyoyangboheum*); Japan: Caregiving Insurance (*Kaigo Hoken*); Germany's *Pflegeversicherung* ("Care Insurance"); AWBZ (the Netherlands). All countries provide benefits for home and institutional care. Luxembourg and the Netherlands also include home adaptation and assistive devices.

Source: OECD compilation based on country replies to the OECD 2009-10 Questionnaire on Long-term Care Workforce and Financing.

of care in Japan. In Japan, the scheme is targeted only to the elderly population, while all individuals, irrespective of their age, are entitled to LTC insurance benefits in Germany and the Netherlands (Rothgang, 2010; Schut and van den Berg, 2010; Campbell *et al.*, 2010; Mot, 2010). Korea was the last of this group to implement LTC insurance, in July 2008 (Kwon, 2008; Campbell *et al.*, 2009) (see also Table 7.2).

Personal care through the health system

A third model is based on the coverage of long-term care cost entirely through the health system. In this model, not only skilled nursing care, but also help with daily activities (dressing, eating, washing, etc.) are financed within the universal public health system. Long-term care is hence viewed as a health risk, and institutional arrangements reflect a "medical model" of care delivery (as opposed to a social model), with care services being primarily performed by professional nurses. Belgium is an example. Belgium's public health insurance system (INAMI/RIZIV) provides for universal coverage of LTC cost both at homes and in institutions. The reimbursement is subject to a personal contribution (*i.e., ticket modérateur*), with ceilings on out-of-pocket payments (MAF, *maximum à facturer*). To face the non-medical costs of LTC, allowances are granted to low-income elderly people with care needs. Moreover, the local social welfare centre (CPAS) can provide assistance for board and lodging in homes for the elderly or in nursing homes. At the regional level, the Flemish government implemented a compulsory dependence insurance scheme, financed through mandatory yearly contribution of EUR 40 (in 2010) a year from each person aged over 25 years, which provides complementary cash benefits. LTC spending as a share of GDP accounts for 2% in Belgium.

Assessing universal coverage within a single programme

Single-programme universal arrangements are good in ensuring wide access to LTC services. They are typically comprehensive in relation to both the share of the cost publicly reimbursed, the number of people using care at home and in institutions (Figure 7.1), and the spectrum of services covered in institutional and home settings. In some cases, coverage also includes the cost of support/domestic care, home adaptations and assistive devices (*e.g.,* some Nordic countries). These systems do not discriminate access based on income or assets of users (or that of their families), although these may be taken into account to determine individual cost sharing up to a ceiling (*e.g.,* Norway, Sweden, the Netherlands, see also Box 7.1 later in this chapter) and there are significant differences across countries in the extent of out-of-pocket cost borne by users – from 4% of total LTC cost in Sweden to a third of total LTC cost in Korea. Often, care provision by nurses or caregivers is regulated to ensure minimum standards for the care purchased through public funds (*e.g.,* Japan, Belgium). In addition, the separation between health and long-term care budgets in all these countries but Belgium, generally reduces utilisation of more expensive health care services and professionals (*e.g.,* hospital care, doctors) for long-term care needs, for example by making "social hospitalisation" of frail people with LTC needs more difficult.

While universal LTC coverage can be achieve through different financing models, there can be advantages in having "dedicated" financing channels for LTC as in the case of social LTC insurance in Germany, Japan, Korea, Luxembourg and the Netherlands. It can ensure a reliable and predictable source of revenue streams, relative to non-earmarked taxation; it can also create a sense of entitlement for people, raising their willingness to pay for such an entitlement.

Figure 7.1. **Users of LTC services vary significantly across the OECD**

Older recipients of long-term care services as a share of the over 65 population, 2008

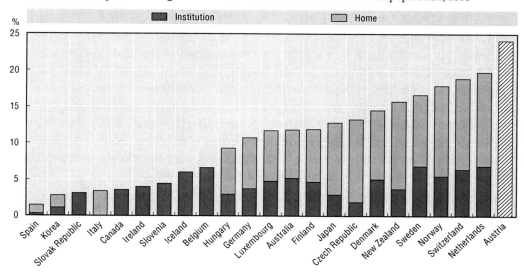

Note: LTC recipients aged over 65 years. Recipients refer both to home and institutional users. Data for Australia, Belgium, Canada, Denmark, Luxembourg and the Netherlands refer to 2007; data for Spain refer to 2009; data for Sweden and Japan refer to 2006. Data for Japan underestimate the number of recipients in institutions because many elderly people receive long-term care in hospitals. According to Campbell *et al.* (2009), Japan provides public benefits to 13.5% of its population age over 65 years. Austrian data represent recipients of cash allowances.

Source: OECD Health Data 2010.

StatLink ⏶⏷ *http://dx.doi.org/10.1787/888932401577*

On the down-side, these systems generally cost a larger share of national income and domestic budgets than the OECD average – typically above the OECD average of 1.5% of GDP, up to 3.6% of GDP in Sweden, in line with the relatively larger share of people eligible to care supports, the range of services covered and the relatively higher reimbursement rates compared with other systems. While comprehensive single-programme systems may still have incentives or mechanisms to support family carers, most such carers provide less intensive care in these countries. The separation of health and long-term care budgets may jeopardise the continuum of care and lead to cost-shifting incentives between different providers and require efforts to ensure co-ordination. Dedicated financing has cons, too, including the potential rigidities it can introduce in the way expenditures are allocated.

Mixed systems

Under mixed systems, LTC coverage is provided through a mix of different universal programmes and benefits operating alongside, or a mix of universal and means-tested LTC entitlements. Many of the countries in this group do not have a comprehensive single-programme LTC system, rather have multiple LTC benefits, programmes, or entitlements, depending on target groups, specific LTC cost component or setting covered, and, in some cases, jurisdiction. Some countries have cash-benefit systems in lieu of, or in addition to, in-kind services.

It is difficult to give a proper account of the variety and complexity of institutional arrangements belonging to this group. Nevertheless, one possible way to group countries – in decreasing order of universality of the LTC benefits – is the following: *i)* parallel universal schemes; *ii)* income-related universal benefits or subsidy; *iii)* mix of universal and means-tested (or no) benefits.

Parallel universal schemes

Parallel universal schemes rely on different coexisting coverage schemes, each providing universal coverage for a different type of care. Typically, universal nursing care is financed through the health system, while universal personal care is through a separate scheme.

Scotland is an example. Since 2002, all the counties of the United Kingdom have supported free skilled nursing care (i.e., the health component of LTC) for older people at the point of use. In addition, under the 2002 Scottish Health and Community Care Act, personal care (i.e., ADL support) for older people, which is part of the social-care system, is free in both institutions and at home (Bell and Bowes, 2007; Bell et al., 2007). Care is funded by the local authorities and is subject to an assessment of care needs, but it is irrespective of users' means. The system covers help with ADL, but it does not pay for accommodation costs in a nursing home, for which individuals are charged a fee.

Another example comes from some Southern and Eastern European Countries, which combine universal access to nursing homes (subject to available beds) or to skilled nursing care (often via the health systems), with universal, non income-related cash allowances to cover care cost, typically at home.

In Italy, specialised nursing homes for elderly and handicapped people (e.g., the *Residenze sanitarie assistenziali*) are part of the health system or receive a subsidy out of the health budget, while responsibilities for home care are shared between the health and social system. About half of total LTC spending consists of a care allowance covering a fraction of the cost incurred by users ("*indennita' di accompagnamento*", amounting to EUR 472 a month in 2009), which is often used to pay a formal LTC worker or a family carer (IRCCS-INRCA, 2009).

In the Czech Republic, responsibilities for in-kind LTC services are divided across the social sector and the universal health care system, and between different levels of government. As part of the 2007 Act on Social Services, a monthly care need-related cash allowance is granted to all individuals needing care, ranging from EUR 79 per month for those in the lowest category (slight dependency) to EUR 471 per month for those in the highest category. In Poland, a non means-tested national nursing allowance and supplement is granted to disabled children and seniors, while home-help services are the responsibility of local governments. Despite universal entitlement to LTC-related benefits, there is still significant need covered by family carers.

Income-related universal benefits

A second sub-group of countries has *income-related universal benefits or subsidies* (e.g., Ireland, Australia, Austria and France). In these countries, all those assessed as eligible on care-need grounds receive a public benefit, but the amount is adjusted to recipient's income and the adjustment can be very steep. There can also be additional benefits covered through the health systems (e.g., nursing care in France) or by local governments (e.g., in Austria and Australia).

Countries in this group have opted for a universal personal-care benefit but adjust the benefit amount to reflect the income of recipients. This approach works by progressively increasing the share of the cost paid for by the public system as the income of the recipient decreases. It is sometimes referred to as "tailored" or "progressive universalism" (Fernandez et al., 2009) and it is not intended to cover the full – or nearly full – cost of personal care. In the case of France, the recipient is required to complement public funding with a personal contribution, as a condition for receiving the public personal-care subsidy. Often, this *tailored benefit* applies to one care component *(e.g.,* home care; personal care), but different arrangements can apply for another components of the total LTC needed by the user. As in the previous group, this approach includes countries with both in-kind LTC services *(e.g.,* Australia), and cash allowances *(e.g.,* France).

Since the commencement of the *Nursing Homes Support Scheme, A Fair Deal of Ireland* in October 2009, all those with care needs are eligible to personal care in institutions, but everyone is required to contribute 80% of their assessable income and 5% of the value of any assets towards the cost of care (see also Box 7.1). In the case of long-term community services, eligibility is universal, although access is limited by resources and can result in targeting of services.

This is similar to the Australian approach. The majority of LTC cost (0.8% of GDP in 2009) is paid for by the government through consolidated, tax-based revenues (Ergan and Paulucci, 2010). Personal care is not free, however all individuals eligible to long-term care services through a care-need assessment process are entitled to a publicly funded subsidy. Recipients of residential and community aged-care services usually make a financial contribution to the cost of their personal care, whose amount is adjusted to user's income. In institutions, residents contribute to personal care cost via basic daily fees, income-tested fees, and fees for additional services, while the government subsidy accounts for about 70% (Productivity Commission, 2010).

Some European countries provide income-adjusted universal cash benefits or allowances to cover personal care cost. Austria has a mix of universal and income-related allowances, and in-kind benefits.[6] A universal cash allowance *(Pflegegeld),* co-financed through federal, Länder and municipality contributions, was introduced in 1993. It is provided regardless of income and assets, and its amount varies with the level of dependency, from EUR 154 to EUR 1 656 in 2010. Approximately 59% of those aged over 80 years and 9% of the 60-80 year old population receive Pflegegeld (Austrian Federal Ministry of Social Affairs and Consumer Protection, 2008). In 2007, a new income-tested grant for the most disabled recipients (so-called 24-hour care benefit) was implemented to complement the universal cash allowance. The two allowances do not cover the full cost of care and, for people unable to meet the remaining cost out of their pocket, public assistance organised by Länder comes into play. A key objective of Austrian LTC arrangements is to help individuals remain at home and live independent lives as long as possible. Another main goal is to formalise contractual arrangements between the care recipients and the caregiver, including (often undeclared) migrant carers. The law encourages care provided by family by not excluding family caregivers from entering in this kind of formal arrangement.

Another example is France. The health insurance programme *(Sécurité sociale)* pays for the health cost *(tarif de soins)* for all nursing-home stays (access is based on care need). In addition, the *Allocation personnalisée d'autonomie* (APA) is an income and need-adjusted cash benefit available to disabled people aged 60 years or older.[7] The monthly cash allowance varies according to the assessed level of dependence between EUR 530 and EUR 1 235 (April 2010), but depending on their income, beneficiaries are required to forgo a certain percentage of the assessed level of APA, up to a 90% reduction off the assessed floor. As a result, APA pays up to EUR 1 235 for high-need/low-income user, down to EUR 27 for higher-income users. For those living at home, APA provides support towards any expenses incurred, in line with a personalised support plan identified by a socio-medical team. It can include support for both ADL and IADL services and, in some cases, the employment of a caregiver (except for their spouse or partner). For those living in a nursing home, APA offsets a portion of the personal-care cost while the remaining is paid by the resident (about 33% of the dependence costs on average; Drees, 2008). APA is administered by local departments but it is financed by a mix of local and central-government funding.

Mix of universal and means-tested (or no) benefits

The third sub-group includes countries which have a *mix of universal and means-tested (or no) benefits*. Generally, universal entitlement tends to apply to one or both of the following:

● health-related, *skilled nursing care* (either at home or in institutions) *(e.g.,* Switzerland); and

● nursing and personal care in *home-care settings (e.g.,* New Zealand; some Canadian provinces).

In addition, in countries with limited formal service delivery, universal benefits may apply only to certain services, for example to *institutional care* (subject to available places) as in Greece, or to *cash benefits* (relative to in-kind alternatives) as in Spain.

Switzerland provides universal in-kind nursing care (both at home and in institutions) through mandatory health insurance (LAMal), but there are also means-tested complementary cash benefits towards the cost of personal care within the legal framework of the Law on Invalidity Insurance (LAI) and the Law on Old-age and Survivors' Insurance (LAVS). They include so-called supplementary benefits for old-age and disability, granted to recipients affected by permanent or long-term incapacity. A significant share of personal-care cost remains a responsibility of the users, who pay themselves about 60% of total health-related LTC cost. However, if all cash benefits are considered, the share of personal-care cost which remains the responsibility of the user would amount to around 36%. Disability allowances for retired persons with mild disabilities living at home have been introduced in additional to the allowances for those with middle and heavy disabilities.

In New Zealand, people assessed as needing home-based personal care services are entitled to these services, although, after an income threshold, they need to pay a co-payment. Eligibility to care in institutions is based on both needs and ability to pay. The residential care subsidy (RCS) pays the costs of contracted care (including board and lodging costs) above a maximum income-related co-payment. Around 71% of residential care inhabitants received the RCS in 2008. Since 2005, the New Zealand Government has been phasing out asset tests for determining eligibility for institutional care. This is similar to a general movement in some Canadian provinces/territories to eliminate the use of asset-testing (but not income-testing) for targeting government support to residents living in long-term care facilities.

Most Canadian provinces provide nursing and personal care coverage without charges in home-care settings but have income tests for admission to nursing care facilities. All provinces provide case management *(e.g.,* care assessment and service co-ordination) and nursing care without charge in home-care settings, although some provinces impose service maxima on nursing care. Some provinces provide personal-care coverage *(e.g.,* bathing and grooming), but fees may be imposed for other services such domestic care, meal preparation and shopping. As to institutional care, income testing is used in most provinces for admission, but there is a movement in many provinces to include public coverage for health-related services such as nursing and rehabilitation.

Another interesting case is Spain. Spain passed new legislation in 2006 introducing a tax-funded National Long-term Care System (Dependency Act, in force since 1 January 2007). The law guarantees a right to long-term care services to all those assessed to require care,[8] subject to an income and asset test. Entitlements to cash and in-kind services are slightly different, with cash allowances being universal, while not all individuals might receive in-kind services. Recipients are expected to pay one third of total costs of services. The system is intended to provide a "formal response" to societal and labour markets changes that are reducing the supply of family care in a context of ageing societies – and of growing need. It is expected to benefit 3% of the Spanish population in the short-term (a comparable percentage to that of some countries with fully universal benefits), and is to be phased in gradually until 2015 (Costa-Font and Garcia Gonzalez, 2007).

Finally, there are countries with less developed formal long-term care provision, which provide universal coverage for institutional care but no coverage for home care. The Greek long-term care system includes the direct provision of social services and care through health insurance funds. In theory, any old person, whether insured or uninsured, has access to long-term care where required by their disability status. There are no institutional discriminations or access restrictions, as long as people are legal residents of the country. On the other hand, there is limited formalised home-care provision in Greece, and no public funding for home care.

Assessing mixed systems

As for systems with single universal coverage, mixed systems generally do not cover long-term care cost in their entirety. Rather, income and, sometimes, assets of the care recipient can be taken into account to determine the subsidy level or the personal contribution to the cost of care (see Box 7.1). Several countries cap the benefit level (*e.g.*, France, Italy, Australia, Spain and the Czech Republic).

The level of the public subsidy relative to total LTC cost varies across the countries in this group. For example, in Spain users pay a third or the total LTC cost. In Australia, around 70% of residential care is covered by the Australian government subsidy, while 16% of the cost of the Community Aged Care Package (CACPs) is paid directly by users (Australia Government Productivity Commission, 2010). In France, APA private contributions represented about 20% of average APA entitlements for those receiving care at home and about 35% for those receiving care in an institution in 2008 (Dress, 2008). This cost is met by a number of different arrangements including funding from social assistance and other income-support mechanisms. In addition, the universal benefit or entitlement may refer to only one component of the care cost (*e.g.*, home care), but not to others (*e.g.*, care in institutions).

Mixed systems provide coverage for at least a share of LTC cost for all people needing care, and, therefore, offer a stable source of support for LTC dependent people. Generally, LTC benefits have been developed in recognition that long-term care can lead to catastrophic cost for users. Providing a universal entitlement is viewed as desirable both for equity reasons and for efficiency reasons – that is to offer insurance especially to those with high LTC need. The number of recipients as a share of the elderly population in this group varies from 1% in Poland to 10% in Switzerland, while *public* LTC spending as a share of GDP is below the OECD average of 1.5%, apart from France where it is above the average.

On the other hand, these systems can still leave a significant share of the cost to be paid out-of-pocket by users and their families. The lack of comprehensive coverage can be a disincentive to the growth of formal care supply in countries with less developed LTC delivery markets, with *de facto* reliance on family carers to shoulder high-intensity care. Where there is fragmentation – across different benefits or entitlements, across services governed by different programmes, across providers financed from different sources, across users entitled to different benefits depending, for example, on their age – there can be incentives for cost-shifting across providers and benefit systems, and it can be more difficult to quantify the overall support received by a user relative to the cost incurred. Some countries have set up mechanisms to facilitate co-ordination and help users navigate through the system, such as France.[9]

Means-tested safety net schemes

Under means-tested schemes, LTC coverage is provided through safety-net programmes. In these countries, income and/or asset tests are used to set thresholds for eligibility to publicly funded personal care. Only those falling below a set threshold are entitled to publicly funded LTC services or benefits, with care being prioritised to those with the highest care needs. This approach offers protection to those individuals otherwise unable to pay for the care themselves. The criteria for eligibility (*e.g.*, personal and/or family income and assets; availability or not of informal care), care-managers' flexibility in assessing needs, and thresholds for eligibility differ markedly and may or not overlap with prevailing social-assistance norms.

The United States belongs to this category. Medicaid – the public programme for the poor – is the chief public funder of long-term care services, paying for 40% of total LTC cost in 2010 (Kaiser Commission, 2010).[10] Medicaid is a social health-insurance programme funded by the federal and state governments, designed as a means-tested programme to assist people with limited income to pay for medical and long-term care expenses. States have mandatory benefits which must be offered, including institutional nursing-facility services, and home health-care services for individuals who are entitled to nursing facility services, but the majority of LTC services are at the discretion of the states, as are income and assets eligibility requirements. Means and asset testing is very strict. Commonly, in order for recipients to receive Medicaid coverage, participants will first have to exhaust personal resources. States may require Medicaid recipients to be responsible for a small co-payment. About 10 million people need long-term care in the United States, of which 3 millions are covered via Medicaid. LTC spending accounted for USD 115 billion in 2008 (Kaiser Commission, 2010), which accounted for around 0.8% of GDP.

England is often regarded as a means-tested system. Indeed, current policy discussion about reforming adult care coverage focuses around means-tested arrangements for personal care, although it is fair to say that there are also non means-tested benefits for severely disabled people in the United Kingdom. The Disability Living Allowance and Attendance Allowance are non-contributory, non means-tested and tax-free benefits, the former paid to severely disabled people who make a claim before age 65, the latter paid to those who claim from age 65. Social care is commissioned by local authorities, and is funded from a combination of central taxation, local taxation and user charges. Local authorities decide and set their own budget based on grants made from the central government, most of which are not earmarked. Access to nursing homes is both income- and asset-tested and users are required to deplete assets to be eligible for LTC nursing-home coverage. Conversely, for home care, eligible users receive an income-tested benefit, which can be granted in the form of a personal budget. As already mentioned, the health component of LTC is also free at the point of use. In 2006-07, slightly over 4% of the elderly lived in an LTC institution (UK Department of Health, 2009). LTC spending was estimated to account for 1.5% of GDP is 2006 (Comas-Herrera et al., 2010).

Coverage of personal-care cost in England has been subject to much discussion and reform proposal over the past few years. The previous Labour government proposed to provide free care at home for vulnerable elderly people. A White Paper released in April 2010 made proposals to extend the coverage of free care for people staying in residential care for more than two years (UK HM Government, 2010). The new (2010) government established the Commission on Funding of Care and Support, which is due to make its recommendations on reform to the adult social care system in July 2011 (Stone and Wood, 2010).

Assessing means-tested safety-net systems

Means-tested arrangements offer a safety net to those individuals that are otherwise unable to pay for the care themselves. Typically, coverage extends to support for daily living activities, but can also include board and lodging in nursing homes to the extent that people are required to deplete their resources before becoming eligible to public support. By targeting public funds to the poor, this approach can be effective at limiting costs, even though the cost per eligible user can be high. But it may also create inequities and incentives to use health care for LTC purposes, particularly where there are universal health-care services and targeted social-care services as in England. Means assessment can also be administratively expensive. These systems can result in unmet needs and leave families above the assets/income threshold vulnerable to high LTC expenditure (Fernandez et al., 2009).

Safety nets face similar challenges to those confronting poverty programmes and social-assistance systems. For example, they can leave elderly and disabled people impoverishing to become eligible for care. Setting thresholds is hard, particularly as it always implies creating a group not poor enough to qualify for public funding, and yet not rich enough to pay for care costs. When people are required to sell their homes and use such proceeds before being eligible to public coverage, the system can be seen as unfair, particularly given older people attachment to their homes. If there are no uniform criteria for eligibly across different jurisdictions, this can also lead to confusion over eligibility for public funding and reduce transparency.

Given that benefit entitlements tend to reach a more limited number of individuals and households, there can be under-funding and under-investment in these programmes. Especially during times of fiscal restraint, they are more vulnerable to budget cuts or cash-constrains. Finally, in light of expected increase in demand for care, the adequacy of such an approach is called into question as many people in need of care are denied access.

7.3. Even within universal systems, the comprehensiveness of coverage can vary significantly

The important variation in the share of GDP that OECD countries devote to long-term care cannot be solely attributed to the fact that some countries are older than others. For instance, the Netherlands and Sweden allocate relatively more resources to LTC than the OECD average and more than could be expected given the share of the elderly population,

Figure 7.2. **Variation in LTC expenditure is not strongly correlated to the share of the population aged over 80**

Share of the population aged over 80 and percentage of GDP spent on LTC in OECD, in 2008 or nearest available year

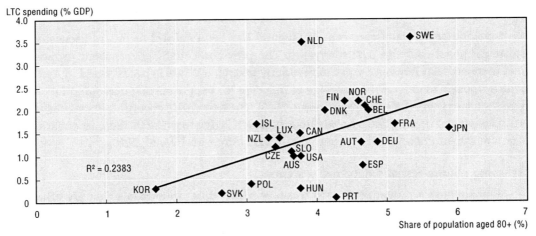

Note: Data for Denmark and Switzerland refer to 2007; data for Portugal and the Slovak Republic refer to 2006; and data for Australia and Luxembourg refer to 2005. Data include both public and private LTC spending. Expenditure data for Austria, Belgium, Canada, Denmark, Hungary, Iceland, Norway, Portugal, Switzerland and the United States include only LTC nursing care, and therefore exclude social LTC spending.

Source: OECD Social and Demographic Database, 2010, and OECD Health Data 2010.

StatLink http://dx.doi.org/10.1787/888932401596

while Portugal and Hungary allocate less (Figure 7.2). One possible explanation is that the comprehensiveness of a LTC coverage system – that is the extent to which a system finances/protects against LTC need – differs across country.

Assessing the *comprehensiveness* of a LTC coverage system is all but easy. Universality of entitlements to care is but one aspect, which has been used to derive the typology of systems presented earlier. But not all universal LTC systems are comprehensive. For example a significant share of spending is still paid out-of-pocket by users. In Switzerland, nearly 60% of total LTC spending is privately financed (36% if including cash benefits granted under the Invalidity and Survivors' insurance). In Portugal out-of-pocket LTC financing accounts for 45% total LTC cost, while the corresponding figure for Germany and Spain is around 30% of total LTC cost (OECD, 2000) (Figure 7.3). In the United States, out-of-pocket spending represents 22% of LTC cost (Kaiser Commission, 2010).

Eligibility rules – whether a system is universal or means-tested – are but one dimension to assess comprehensiveness of LTC coverage. In fact, three dimensions can be identified:

● *eligibility rules* – universal *versus* means-tested systems;

● the *basket of services* covered (breadth of coverage); and

● the extent of *private cost sharing* on public coverage (depth of coverage).

All countries have *eligibility rules* setting the care-dependency status and, in means-tested system, the income/assets levels triggering eligibility to public LTC support. Eligibility to care and the level of public support is determined on the basis of a care-need assessment based on physical and/or cognitive limitations (Table 7.3). Need assessment helps governments target care needs, and can follow more or less stringent rules depending on the country. While many of the functional capacities which are measured are similar, assessment systems and dependency levels on which eligibility is determined are not uniform across countries and, in

Figure 7.3. **Long-term care expenditures by sources of funding, 2007**

Countries ranked by decreasing share of out-of-pocket spending

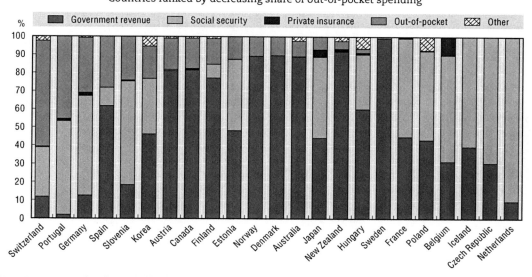

Note: Data on out-of-pocket spending for some of the countries are underestimated. For example, in the Netherlands, cost sharing on long-term care services is estimated to account for 8% of the total LTC expenditure. The share of out-of-pocket spending for Switzerland is overestimated as cash benefits granted for care in care facilities are not considered.

Source: OECD Health System Accounts Database, 2010.

StatLink ᴍᴤ￫ http://dx.doi.org/10.1787/888932401615

some cases, can vary across sub-national jurisdictions. For example, Germany provides public benefits to 10.5% of its seniors, whereas Japan provides public benefits to 13.5% of its population aged over 65 years (Campbell *et al.*, 2009). Health and/or social-care professionals are involved in the assessment process, although a medical doctor is involved in only a few countries, for example Belgium and France. For eligible people, the benefit amount is typically adjusted to need. An income and/or asset test may also be carried out to determine user cost sharing or the amount of the public subsidy (see below).

A number of countries – including the United States for Medicare and Medicaid, Canada for Chronic Care Funding (Ontario), parts of Switzerland, Iceland, Spain, Italy, and Finland – employ the International Resident Assessment Instrument (InterRAI) for assessing care needs and better target care support. InterRAI consists of a range of standardised assessment instruments that apply to different care settings such as residential care (RAI-LTCF), home care (RAI-HC), palliative care (RAI-PC) and mental health (RAI-MH). All InterRAI instruments include a comprehensive set of core-assessment items (*e.g.*, physical functions, locomotion, cognition, pain, relevant clinical complexity) that can be consistently used across care settings. To ensure consistency, each instrument is supported by a training and reference manual. The use of InterRAI can support efforts to ensure a continuum of care and better co-ordination through an integrated health information system. It can also play a complementary role in monitoring quality and care outcomes.

In terms of the second element – the *breadth of coverage* – LTC comprises multiple services (skilled nursing care, social work, personal care, medical equipment and technologies, therapies), delivered by different providers (nurses, low-skilled carers, allied health professionals) in a mix of settings (home, institutional, community care). While the

Table 7.3. **Long-term care need assessment process in selected OECD countries**

	Who can apply for care?	What is the assessment process?			Who is entitled to care?	
	Thresholds for eligibility to care	Assessment tool	Criteria and range	Assessor and process	Care categories assigned following assessment	Eligible users
Australia	Old people	For residential care: Aged Care Funding Instrument (ACFI)	12 care need questions. Diagnostic information about mental and behavioural disorders and other medical conditions is also collected	Aged care homes	Three need categories in activities of daily living (ADLs), behaviour, and complex health care	Based on the number of points allocated
Belgium	All ages (assessment for cash allowance)	APA-THAB Guidelines used to guide doctors assessment	ADL and risk awareness	Examination by a federal-government service doctor	Points are allotted based in the assessment	
	All ages (assessment for nursing care)	Standardised assessment tool and scale (KATZ) for care in nursing homes or home care	Assessment of six capabilities on a four-scale range and assessment of cognitive status	Examination by the nurse of the patient (+ public control by doctor)	Four to five need categories (home care/institutional care)	
Czech Republic	All ages	Defined in the law for the whole country	A 36 ADL/IADL checklist divides people into four groups, according to the number of "disability" points. Children need fewer points in order to qualify	Medical examination and social worker assessment of 36 ADL/IADL limitations	Four levels	Level 1: More than 12 points; Level 2: More than 18 points; Level 3: More than 24 points; Level 4: More than 30 points
France	People older than 60 years of age (for APA)	Standardised assessment tool (AGGIR – Autonomie gérontologie groupes iso-ressources)	ADL limitations. Assessment of ten capabilities on a three-range scale	Socio-medical team carries the assessment. Nationally standardised computer programme compiles the scores	Users assigned to six categories of care need	First four of six AGGIR categories. APA benefits are based also on applicants income
	Younger disabled people (Prestation de compensation du handicap, PCH)	Standardised assessment tool (GEVA, Guide d'évaluation des besoins de compensation des personnes handicapées)	Personalised plan	GEVA does not aim at grouping individuals in broad care categories; the assessment is individualised		All those with an handicap
Germany	All ages	Estimation of specific time of care-assistance needed, based on a pre-defined scale of time required for each ADL	ADL limitations. 20-25 minutes to wash entire body, 2-3 minutes for cutting food, 15-20 minutes for eating, and 4-6 minutes to take off clothing from entire body	Local councils responsible for determining care-allocation methods. Medical assessment service of the person's sickness fund. The assessor may deviate from the table, allowing for some flexibility	N.A.	If s/he needs a minimum of 46 minutes of ADL support (out of 90 minutes) per day

Table 7.3. **Long-term care need assessment process in selected OECD countries** (cont.)

	Who can apply for care?	What is the assessment process?			Who is entitled to care?	
	Thresholds for eligibility to care	Assessment tool	Criteria and range	Assessor and process	Care categories assigned following assessment	Eligible users
Japan	Citizens older than 65 years and aged 40-64 years with age-related illnesses (e.g. Parkinson's or Alzheimer's and terminal-stage cancer)	A national standardised tool based on a 74-item list is used for the assessment	Physical and mental status of the applicant	Applicants must contact their local municipality where the standardised questionnaire is administered. Standardised computer programme assesses replies to questionnaire, complemented by doctor assessment. Second stage review by an independent committee made up of local physicians, care managers and the applicant's doctor	Seven levels	The lowest two levels determines eligibility to preventive services. The higher five levels eligible to care
Netherlands	All ages	Nationally standard tool created by the Ministry of Health	Psycho-geriatric or physical limitations. Limitations assessed on a four-point scale	Independent governmental agency (Centre for Care Assessment, CIZ)	No specific categories; there are four steps to determine eligibly to care	Eligibility takes into account ADL limitations, alternative solutions (rehabilitation or home adaption), and ability of family caregivers to provide support
Sweden	All ages	No formalised measurement tool	N.A.	Professionals employed by the municipality carry out the assessment	No specific categories	Benefits are at the discretion of the assessor
United Kingdom	Older disabled people (social care)	Different tools are available, e.g. Resource Allocations Systems (RAS) and Single Assessment Processes (SAP)	National standard care categories based on dependency severity or risk (Fair Access to Care System, FACS)	Local council, the National Health Service (for health-related LTC) and, for working-age and younger people, the social security systems	Four levels of need	Set by local authorities
	Older disabled people (health care)	NHS checklist continuing care. NHS decision support tool	11 areas of care. Cognition, behaviour, communication, mobility, and continence	A health professional assesses health-care need based on the checklist	Four groups based on case severity	

Source: OECD 2009-10 Questionnaire on Long-term Care Workforce and Financing; Ros et al. (2010).

typology presented in this chapter has focuses on variation in coverage for personal care, reimbursement arrangements can differ, for example, on the following:

- health/nursing care;
- domestic care, practical help, assistive devices;
- board and lodging costs.

Health/nursing care, requiring medical acts typically provided by nurses *(e.g.,* administering medication and changing dressings), is generally covered under public health-financing arrangements. However, coverage rules may depend on care settings and on which worker is providing the care. For example, coverage is through the health system when nursing care is received jointly with and as part of other medical care, whether in hospitals or at home. When nursing care is received in an LTC institution, coverage systems differ across country. Countries belonging to the "universal coverage within a single programme" group tend to lump this cost together with personal-care cost (but not Japan). Conversely, countries with safety net systems and some of those with mixed systems tend to have separate billing and reimbursement procedures for health-related and personal care-related cost *(e.g.,* France, Belgium, the Czech Republic, United Kingdom, the United States for post-acute care cost). In home settings, coverage is often via the health system when care is provided by a nurse, while it follows the same rules as personal-care coverage when care is provided by a lower-skilled LTC worker.

Domestic care, practical help, such as cleaning and cooking and help with so-called instrumental activities of daily living (IADL) is often not covered by public LTC systems, apart from countries with comprehensive LTC coverage *(e.g.,* some Nordic countries). However, in some countries these services can be included in care plans designed to provide – as a package – the most suitable services for users, for example in Austria, Belgium, or the United Kingdom for home care. Similarly, the provision of equipment, assistive devices and technology is included in home-care coverage packages in some OECD countries, such as Australia, Sweden, Canada, the Czech Republic, Japan[11] and Slovenia.

As to *board and lodging costs* for residents in LTC institutions, these are often not included in public LTC-coverage schemes, apart from low-income people eligible to targeted assistance. Public support towards board and lodging in nursing homes is therefore typically means-tested. Even in countries with very comprehensive universal LTC coverage, significant cost sharing can be required for this cost component. For example, in Norway, municipalities can ask up to 80% of resident income in user cost sharing.

OECD countries can be clustered into three main groups in respect to this component of the LTC cost, on a continuum moving from less to more comprehensive systems (Table 7.4). In safety-net programmes, as already mentioned, users need first to deplete their income and assets before being entitled to care, including coverage in nursing homes. Many OECD

Table 7.4. **Approaches to covering board and lodging cost (B&L) in nursing homes in OECD countries**

Public support for B&L only available for eligible poor		Means-related cost sharing for B&L cost	
B&L cost treated as other LTC cost, as part of safety-net LTC programmes	B&L cost treated separately from other LTC cost, under social assistance	Income-related	Income- and asset-tested
United Kingdom, United States (Medicaid), Slovenia	Germany, Belgium, France, Switzerland, Italy, Poland, Slovakia, Czech Republic, Spain, Portugal, Korea	Norway, Sweden, Netherlands, Finland, some Canadian provinces, New Zealand	Australia, some Canadian provinces, Ireland

Source: OECD 2009-10 Questionnaire on Long-term Care Workforce and Financing.

countries – such as France, Belgium, Germany – consider board and lodging cost separately from personal and nursing care cost, requiring users (or their families) to pay for B&L themselves, unless they benefit from social assistance, targeted housing subsidies or other financial aid. Other countries include B&L as part of LTC coverage, but require income and, in some cases, asset-related contributions from users (*e.g.*, Netherlands, Nordic countries, Australia, New Zealand, Ireland). Last, in Japan, the cost of B&L is decided by contractual arrangements. There is a limit on the payment for low-income earners, making their share a flat fee, with the rest covered by the insurance benefit.

The third element of comprehensiveness – *cost sharing* – shows how deep is the protection of the public LTC scheme against long-term care cost. All public-coverage schemes across OECD countries require users to share part of the cost of the personal-care support they are entitled to. But countries differ markedly in method and extent.

Beside mains-tested systems, three main approaches can be identified (Box 7.1). A first one is to set (cap) the public contribution paid by the public system, leaving individuals

---

Box 7.1. Cost sharing in OECD countries follow three main approaches

Approach 1: Means-tested systems: Users have first to exhaust their means

Slovenia: For social care services, care recipients are required to cover the full costs. Exemption from payment is possible in exceptional financial circumstances and after a means test of household income. In such cases, the municipality will take responsibility for all charges.

United Kingdom: The national system of private contributions for residential care is means-tested such that an individual with over GBP 23 250 in savings are ineligible for public support with long-term care costs in a care home and must cover all care charges themselves. Individuals with less than GBP 23 250 are still expected to contribute to care costs but will receive some support from local authorities. Individuals with less than GBP 14 250 will have all their residential care costs paid for them by the state.

United States: Medicaid LTC services do not require user fees, but there are income and asset rules for eligiblity to Medicaid benefits.

Approach 2: Defined public contributions, cost sharing as residual

Australia: Institutional residents are asked to pay a basic daily fee towards accommodation costs and living expenses (*e.g.*, meals or heating and cooling). Maximum charges are regulated and set using a percentage of the basic single age pension (about 85% and equivalent to about AUD 14 000 a year). In addition, residents pay an additional fee for the care they receive, of up to about AUD 22 700 a year. The fee is income-tested such that residents with income less than about AUD 21 500 a year and assets less than AUD 37 500 do not have to pay it.

Austria: Those dependent on help with daily living activities are entitled to a needs-based universal cash benefit. The government can provide up to EUR 1 655 per month to the recipient. In 2007, a new income-tested benefit (so-called 24 hour care benefit) was implemented to complement the universal cash allowance.

France: In France, APA benefits are subject to national ceilings and the level of benefits is set to decrease as a proportion of income. Income includes a share of the imputed rent of non-financial income (*e.g.*, secondary residence) but does not include the imputed rent associated with a principal residence.

Box 7.1. **Cost sharing in OECD countries follow three main approaches** (cont.)

Germany: Cost sharing applies when the costs of LTC services go beyond the fixed public benefits. The family is obliged to help cover LTC costs that exceed statutory public benefits. For residential care, care recipients are liable for the costs of lodging and meals. In the event that care recipients are unable to cover LTC costs, social assistance may be available after an assessment of income, wealth and social circumstances.

Approach 3: Flat-rate cost sharing

Japan: User payments are set at 10% under of public LTC social insurance system and levied on all publically funded LTC services with the exception of LTC prevention services.

Korea: Under the national LTC insurance system, beneficiaries must pay 20% of total costs in institutional care and 15% of total cost for home-care services. Based on a means test on household income and assets, low-income recipients may pay half of the standard personal contribution rates. Social-assistance recipients are exempt from cost sharing.

Belgium: Private cost sharing for personal-care cost follows the same rules as for health insurance coverage. Payments for social care services received at home will vary according to eligibility for disability, and on income.

Approach 4: Income and/or assets-related benefits

Canada: In a number of provinces (British Columbia, Saskatchewan, Manitoba and Ontario), the level of co-payment for residential care services is set at different monthly rates according to one's income. In a number of provinces (Atlantic provinces) residents must pay the full cost of a nursing home, typically equivalent to board and lodging, unless their income is deemed not sufficient to pay for it.

Czech Republic: The level of cost sharing depends on the sector of provision of long-term care. In healthcare facilities, cost sharing consists only of the user charge for every day of hospitalisation (EUR 1.2 a day). In the social sector, the provider can charge up to 85% of the income (*e.g.* pension) of the client. There is no income testing or means testing to determine eligibility.

Finland: In home care, private contributions are set according to the amount of care needed and on the income of the care recipient and other household members, and cover about 15% of the total costs. In long-term institutional care, personal contributions are set at 85% of the recipient's net income. For institutions providing care to the elderly, user charges represent close to 20% of the total costs.

Hungary: Cost sharing is applicable to healthcare as well as chronic hospital treatment, social institutional care for the elderly and social support for IADL. Personal contributions are determined according to household income and the social situation of the care recipient. For institutional care, contributions cannot exceed 80% of a care recipient's total income and contributions for health-related services are fixed daily rates.

Ireland: In the case of institutional care, individuals contribute 80% of their assessable income and 5% of the value of any assets including land and property in excess of EUR 36 000 for an individual or EUR 72 000 for a couple. Assets include, for the first three years (also known as the "three year cap" deferral mechanism), the principal residence. For couples where one spouse continues to reside in the principal residence, the personal contribution of the spouse residing in the nursing home is determined according to half their combined income and assets.

Box 7.1. **Cost sharing in OECD countries follow three main approaches** (cont.)

Netherlands: LTC beneficiaries have to pay a fixed rate for each hour of care they receive, up to an income-dependent maximum amount. The minimum co-payment is set at about EUR 140 a month. The maximum amount varies according to the size of the household and to whether the disabled person is older than 65 years of age. As for those receiving care in an institution, two cost-sharing formulas are applicable. Under the low cost-sharing formula (during the first six months) private contribution equals to the lesser of EUR 1 700 or 12.5% of relevant income, up to EUR 9 000 a year. Under the high cost-sharing formula, private contributions can increase up to about EUR 24 000 (Mot, 2010).

New Zealand: Private contributions are determined by a means test, which evaluates income, capital savings and housing equity levels, with maximum annual amounts. A specific financial means test is applicable to persons over 65 years of age for residential care cost sharing.

Norway: Municipalities have the flexibility to set personal contributions consistent within a certain framework. Personal contributions are typically income-related, except for short-term stay in a nursing home, where contributions are set independently from one's income. For long-term stays in a nursing home, personal contributions cannot exceed 80% of a resident's income in excess of a given amount, while for home care, user charges are set so as to leave the recipient with a minimum income for extra expenses.

Poland: A recipient's income level will influence the amount of private contributions required but will not affect the recipient's eligibility for LTC services.

Slovak Republic: Each region has the flexibility to set private contributions which are applicable to all social services except for counselling, social rehabilitation and ergotheraphy. For individuals eligible for public LTC support (those who have less than EUR 39 833 in savings), cost sharing is determined by a means test, which typically considers income, assets and capital savings of the applicant and other household members.

Spain: Private contributions are determined by each autonomous region and differentiated according to care setting and type of service. The extent of cost sharing depends on an assessment of financial capacity which typically considers available capital, the estate of the beneficiary as well as household income. According to an individual's economic capacity, contributions for residential care range from 70 to 90% and 10 to 65% for home help.

Sweden: Municipalities can design cost-sharing structures flexibility, but consistently with some general principals established by the central government: fees should be fair, not exceed production cost and must leave users with a personal allowance (pocket money). As of 2003, central rules provide for maximum personal contribution amounts for both personal services and board and lodging as well as for minimum personal allowance amounts (pocket money). Maximum personal contribution amounts are set to about SEK 1 700 per month (about EUR 175) for personal services and about SEK 1 800 per month (about EUR 180) for board and lodging. Minimum personal expense allowances are set to about SEK 4 800 per month (EUR 490) for singles and SEK 4 050 (about EUR 415 per persons for cohabiting partners (Karlsson and Iversonm, 2010).

Source: OECD 2009-10 Questionnaire on Long-term Care Workforce and Financing, and other information collected by the OECD Secretariat.

responsible for paying the cost difference between the set public amount and the actual cost of LTC services (*e.g.*, Germany, Czech Republic, France, Italy, Austria). In Germany's LTC insurance one third of all funding is out-of-pocket and several LTC users are on social assurance. Flat cost sharing, where cost sharing is a given percentage of LTC cost, is applied in Belgium, Korea (20% in institutions, 15% at home), and Japan (10% co-payments), with upper ceilings on the user contributions in Belgium and Japan, but not in Korea. Last, private LTC cost sharing can be set according to disposable income and, in some cases, assets of the LTC user, with very diverse approaches regarding maximum amounts taken into consideration to calculate user cost sharing, the income/asset components taken into account, and the proportion of income/assets that cost sharing represent. For example, in Sweden, co-pays are income-relayed with a cap for home help services of EUR 180 per month, while in Ireland (from 2010) individuals contribute 80% of their assessable income and 5% of the value of any assets to nursing-home cost, and in the Netherlands, 9% of AWBZ expenditure is financed from income-related co-payments (with ceiling of EUR 1 800 per month).

As already said, it is difficult to draw a general assessment of systems' comprehensiveness. Despite limits to underreporting of private expenditure data on long-term care, the figures presented in Figure 7.3 gives a broad idea of the extent of private cost sharing for publicly covered long-term care services (depth of coverage), but it provides no indication on the difference in the range of services covered (breadth of services). Another way to look at the issue is shown in Figure 7.4, which represents:

● on the horizontal axis, the probability of an individual aged 65 years old to use LTC, measured as each country' distance from the average share of LTC recipients in the over 65 population;

Figure 7.4. **Comprehensiveness of public LTC coverage across the OECD, 2008**

Share of LTC recipients in the over 65 population (X axis) and LTC spending in GDP (Y axis)

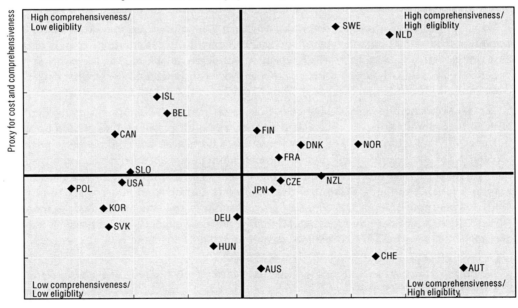

LTC recipients population over the age of 65

Note: Each country point shows the distance from the average share of LTC recipients in the over 65 population (in X axis) and the distance from the average share of LTC spending in GDP (in Y axis), across the OECD. Spending data are based on both public and private LTC spending. For Austria, Belgium, Canada, Denmark, Hungary, Iceland, Norway, Portugal, Switzerland and the United States, spending data are based on LTC nursing care only.

Source: OECD Health Data 2010.

StatLink ⟍⟍⟍ http://dx.doi.org/10.1787/888932401634

* on the vertical axis, LTC spending relative to GDP, measured as each country' distance from the OECD average, controlling for both the share of the population aged over 65 years using LTC, and for the share of a country's population aged over 65 years.

The horizontal axis can be considered an indication of system eligibility, while the position in the vertical axis can be regarded as an indication of the breadth and the depth of coverage. The position on the vertical axis also reflects differences in the relative high or low cost (unit cost and prices) of care in a country, as well as differences in the relative shares of the population aged under 65 using LTC.

7.4. Different approaches but similar directions: Universalism and choice-based models

The analysis of public LTC financing in OECD countries shows the complexity of existing arrangements. Coverage for long-term care does not follow pure models in many OECD countries. LTC-coverage schemes are the outcome of heterogeneous policy objectives, philosophies and institutional frameworks. Despite this mind-boggling diversity, LTC coverage schemes across the OECD are evolving in some common directions.

Coverage models reflect diverse motivations and institutional settings

OECD countries are at different stages of developing formal LTC delivery, partly because of ageing structures, partly because attitudes towards family responsibilities for caring are not the same, as well as the size of the economy. For example, there is relatively little formal-care supply and use in some low-income OECD countries (e.g., Mexico, Turkey), in central European countries, and in countries with strong family-care tradition (e.g., Mediterranean countries). This affects the development of LTC financing mechanisms (and vice-versa), and reflects in LTC spending figures.

Perhaps more than in the case of health care, there is considerable diversity in societies' norms regarding the appropriate balance between individual and collective responsibility for financing the cost of caring for elderly and disabled people. For example, Nordic countries have relatively broad and comprehensive systems with high reliance on public spending. Coverage of LTC can be seen within the context of an encompassing welfare system where the state – rather than the family – has the responsibility for making long-term care services available on a universal basis (Karlsson and Iversen, 2010). But in other countries the issue of LTC coverage is somewhat a "late comer" in welfare-state discussion. A consequence is that not all OECD countries have set up dedicated entitlements[12] for long-term care. This can explain the fragmentation across benefits, programmes, and funding sources for long-term care in some countries. A few OECD countries do not yet regard long-term care as a risk in and on its own. Others, which do, might have limited fiscal margins to play with, especially when "money is tight" as in the aftermath of the recent economic downturn.

There can also be other motivations behind the creation of similar LTC-coverage schemes. In Germany, the set up of LTC insurance in 1995 was partly motivated by limitations of social assistance for covering LTC users – such as the stigma on beneficiaries and growing cost for municipalities (Arntz and Thomsen, 2010). Informal care by family and friends continues to be regarded as an important complement. Indeed, users can choose between receiving benefits in-kind or cash, which can compensate a family carer in Germany. Conversely, a desire not to trap women into caring roles was behind the establishment of the Japanese LTC system and the choice to provide only in-kind benefits (services) (Campbell and Ikegami, 2000; Campbell *et al.*, 2009). Avoiding expensive, so-called social-hospitalisation of the elderly needing long-term care was another important goal for the creation of a stand-alone LTC insurance system in both Japan and Korea (Kwon, 2008). Expanding coverage to certain services can be a way to stimulate service providers to enter the market, or encourage particular settings. For example, one way to promote home care has been to push for more comprehensive/universal care provided at home (*e.g.,* Canada).

LTC coverage policies are not drawn on white canvas (Ikegami, 2010). Choice of financing sources and systems draws on the existing administrative structure. All countries with social long-term care insurance use similar social-insurance arrangements for health care, and similarly in the case of tax-based LTC coverage models. Different views regarding the nature of long-term care – as being a health or social risk – led countries to set up coverage arrangements that may in part overlap with health coverage, but the health-social boundaries are not uniform across the OECD. For example, nearly all LTC services are regarded as a component of the health system in Belgium, where a majority of care is delivered by nurses. Other OECD countries – such as Australia – regard personal care as entirely within the social sector. In many eastern European countries, support for LTC is largely perceived as a family responsibility, and public coverage approaches are characterised by fragmentation, mirroring the division between the health and social care sectors (Österle, 2010).

Finally, existing institutional arrangements are also reflected in the division of responsibilities among central and local authorities. Typically, local authorities have large autonomy in implementing programmes, assessing need, and delivering services, and often, have co-funding responsibilities. This governance structure has its logic and advantages. It enables services to be organised and delivered close to where the need is, and tailored to communities. It enables flexibility in spending decisions and allows sub-national government units to determine policy trade-offs. On the other hand, where there are no cost-sharing and equalisation arrangements across lower levels of governments, it can create inequities in the treatment of similar needs across different localities.

LTC systems are evolving towards common directions

Despite the diversity of approaches, looking back over time, long-term care systems in OECD countries are evolving in some common directions. The level of public coverage of long-term care cost is increasing in low-coverage or strict-targeting countries, although there is also greater targeting of public funding in the most comprehensive LTC systems. A desire for greater choice and consumer direction underpins recent reforms in a number of countries. LTC expenditure as a share of GDP is growing, and is projected to grow at a higher rate than other fast-growing areas of government, such as health care.[13]

At one end of the spectrum, some means-tested, safety-net approaches have been called into question, mostly on grounds of fairness and growing need. The use of asset testing for accessing a nursing home is being phased out in New Zealand, while Ireland introduced in 2009 a system of "tailored universalism" for coverage of institutional care. In England, despite universal disability benefits, means-tested social care leaves many people above the income eligibility threshold vulnerable to catastrophic LTC spending. A 2010 commission on long-term care will consider new ideas for reforming the LTC funding system, including a voluntary insurance scheme to protect the assets of those going into residential care and partnership schemes with an individual contribution matched by the public system (Wanless, 2006). The United States is introducing a voluntary publicly-managed LTC insurance programme as part of the new health-care legislation (so-called, Community Living Assistance Services and Supports, CLASS Act).

At the opposite end of the spectrum, in comprehensive universal coverage countries, the range of services eligible for coverage has been subject to scrutiny and increased targeting to those on most severe needs. Sweden has increased targeting of public services to the most sick and disabled (OECD, 2005). France has – at least in the medium-term – set aside discussion of creating a new social-security LTC pillar and is considering, among others, steeper targeting of APA. In the Netherlands, there have been proposals to re-introduce asset tests (Bureau Beleidsonderzoek, 2010). In Austria, the minimum amount of hours of care needed by those with milder disabilities to qualify for the universal cash benefit has been recently raised. In Japan, elderly assessed with the lowest care needs have been moved to a prevention scheme.

These trends result in a certain convergence in the "breadth" of eligible services covered and the "depth" of public coverage across countries. Ultimately, in a context of limited public funding, there can be trade-offs between providing broad eligibility and directing additional resources to those who need it the most, such as those with higher care needs or lower income. This is further examined in Chapter 9.

It is important to note that universal coverage for some share of the LTC cost does not mean that access to care is always provided in a prompt way. Even in universal benefit systems, eligibility can be targeted to those with the highest care needs, relative to those with milder care needs. There can be deviations from the universal model due to shortages of providers in semi-urban and rural areas and of specialised institutions (e.g. nursing homes, institutions of rehabilitation). If LTC programmes are funded through fixed budgets or if budgets are constrained (e.g., in lower-income OECD countries), coverage is limited to the services that can be funded, even when there is entitlement to some universal LTC benefit. Waiting lists – especially for access to nursing homes – are a way to match service supply with available resources. This means that there can be de-facto targeting of care based on (implicit or explicit) access and prioritisation rules.

Consumer choice and flexibility is another major goal of modern LTC systems. There is growing demand for better tailored and more responsive care. Within both universal and safety-net systems, several OECD countries have opted for providing LTC benefits in the form of cash entitlements or personal budgets in order to support family care and enhance autonomous choice for users and sometimes countries provide for both in-kind and in-cash benefits leaving users with the choice (e.g., Netherlands, Germany, Eastern European countries, Italy, England) (Da Roit et al., 2007; Glendinning, 2009). In some cases, the provision of a cash benefit is the sole care-coverage entitlement. While some central and eastern European OECD countries are far away from implementing an LTC system with extended coverage for nursing and personal care cost, Hungary, Slovakia, and the Czech Republic have set up cash-for-care schemes which can be used to compensate family carers and pay for a share of LTC cost (Österle, 2010). In Italy, use of the cash-for-care allowance, initially set up to provide income-replacement to disabled people unable to work, has grown to 4% of the population in 2004 (between 6 and 22% of the elderly, depending on the region), and is today the main and most significant source of financial support for elderly in need of long-term care (IRCCS-INRCA, 2009).

These direct payments bring more choice over alternative providers (including, in some cases between formal and informal carers) and can strengthen the role of households in the care-management process (Lundsgaard, 2005). Yet, it can be more difficult to exert control over the way cash benefits are utilised. If the value of benefits is not adjusted for cost inflation, it leads to a real loss in purchasing value of the benefit, exposing recipients to higher out-of-pocket expenses.

Maintaining cost growth within financially and fiscally sustainable limits[14] will be a key goal for the future. As the available pool of informal carers is likely to shrink, much in line with the overall working-age populations, there will be pressure to increase formal provision of LTC in OECD countries. Population ageing is pushing up public LTC expenditure, probably at faster rates than the growth in government revenues. Demands for better quality and responsive care systems are likely to continue. Although some goals of an LTC system such as broad access and ensuring equity can be achieved by expanding the comprehensiveness of coverage arrangements, these can rapidly lead to higher costs, and may have unintended negative impacts on the supply of (already shrinking) family carers. If costs grow more rapidly than the economy, this means that governments will either need to give up on spending in other areas or raise contributions/taxes to pay for higher LTC cost. Alternatively, and especially in the current economic and fiscal environment, governments will need to consider ways to ensure value from LTC spending. This means that private collective financing arrangements could have a role in complementing public coverage, at least in some countries. This also means that reforms in the delivery of long-term care services may need to consider improvements in productivity. These issues will be further discussed in the next chapters.

7.5. Conclusions

The fact that the cost of LTC can be high and an individual's need for LTC is uncertain, indicate the need for a LTC coverage mechanism, such as LTC insurance. LTC coverage pools risks and ensures protection against potentially catastrophic LTC costs. Although LTC involves a complex mix of services, several countries have similar LTC coverage approaches.

In ten OECD countries, LTC coverage is universal within a single programme while, at the opposite side of the spectrum, the United States and England use means-tested schemes. LTC coverage may also be provided through a mix of different universal programmes and benefits operating alongside, or a mix of universal and means-tested entitlements.

Assessing the comprehensiveness of a LTC coverage system is not easy. Several dimensions need to be taken into consideration, the first of which are the eligibility rules. The second dimension is the breadth of coverage, since LTC comprises multiple services, delivered by different providers in a mix of settings. The third dimension is cost sharing, showing the level of protection of the public LTC scheme against LTC costs.

OECD countries are at different stages of developing formal LTC delivery, due to ageing structures, attitudes towards family responsibilities for caring and the size of the economy. Nevertheless, countries are evolving in some common directions. Some means-tested approaches have been called into question, while, in universal systems, the range of services covered has also been subject to scrutiny. Consumer choice and flexibility have become a major goal of modern LTC systems. In the future, maintaining cost growth within financially sustainable limits will be a key goal.

Notes

1. In the past decade, the health component of total long-term care has increased, in per capita terms, at an annual average of over 7% in real terms across 22 OECD countries, compared to an average real per capita health spending growth of slightly over 4%.

2. The source of the information included in this section is the OECD 2009-10 Questionnaire on Long-term Care Workforce and Financing and other articles indicated in text. Country descriptions of LTC systems across the OECD are available at: *www.oecd.org/health/longtermcare*.

3. The classification presented here is not the only possible taxonomy of LTC coverage. For example, Kraus *et al.* (2010) classify 21 European LTC systems according to system characteristics, summarised in the dimensions of organisational depth and financial generosity.

4. The term universal means that all those needing LTC because of their dependency status would receive it, including higher-income groups, although individuals may still be required to pay for a share of the cost.

5. Means-testing refers to assessment of the financial "means" (income and assets) of a person to determine whether the person is eligible for LTC benefits.

6. Cash benefits made up 0.7% of GDP, out of the total expenditure on LTC in 2006 of EUR 3.3 billion, or 1.1% of GDP (BMSK, 2008). In-kind services can be bought, using the *Pflegegeld* to cover costs. According to local Länder arrangements, the beneficiary may opt for benefits in kind if they are better suited for care needs. In-kind nursing home-care benefits provided by Länder often require income and asset-related co-payments, depending on care needs.

7. In 2007, close to 1.1 million individuals received a total EUR 4.5 billion (about 0.25 of GDP) in APA benefits. About 40% of APA beneficiaries were living in institutions.

8. The system is implemented incrementally starting with provisions for those with the severest (degree III) disability from January 2007, with the aim of covering those with milder disabilities by the end of 2014.

9. This is the role of the *Caisse nationale de solidarité pour l'autonomie* in France.

10. Medicare pays for some post-acute care, accounting for 24% of spending. Private LTC insurance pays for 9%.

11. Although there can be differences across municipalities.

12. Such as obligations to provide LTC coverage written into specific laws or Acts (Merlis, 2004).

13. Under basic demographic scenarios, health spending (excluding long-term care) is expected to growth by just over 50% between 200 and 2050, while long-term care spending is expected to grow by 150% (OECD, 2001; and OECD, 2006).

14. See definitions in Chapter 9.

References

Arntz, M. and S.L. Thomsen (2010), "The Social Long-term Care Insurance: A Frail Pillar of the German Social Insurance System", *CESifo DICE Report*, Institute for Economic Research at the University of Munich, Vol. 8, No. 2, pp. 29-34.

Australia Government Productivity Commission (2010), *Caring for Older Australians*, Productivity Commission Issues Paper, May.

Austrian Federal Ministry of Social Affairs and Consumer Protection (2008), "Austrian Report on Strategies for Social Protection and Social Inclusion 2008-2010", Vienna, September.

Bar, N. (2010), "Long-term Care: A Suitable Case for Social Insurance", *Social Policy and Administration*, Vol. 44, No. 4, pp. 359-374.

Bell, D. and A. Bowes (2007), *Financial Care Models in Scotland and the UK*, Joseph Rowntree Foundation, York, accessed 28 February 2010 at *www.jrf.org.uk/sites/files/jrf/1859354408.pdf*.

Bell, D., A. Bowes and A. Dawson (2007), *Free Personal Care in Scotland. Recent Developments*, Joseph Rowntree Foundation, York, accessed 28 February 2010 at *www.jrf.org.uk/sites/files/jrf/2075-scotland-care-older-people.pdf*.

Bernd, B., Y. Doyle, E. Grundy and M. McKee (2009), "How Can Health Systems Respond to Population Ageing?", *Policy Brief*, No. 10, European Observatory on Health Systems and Policies, WHO Regional Office for Europe, Copenhagen.

BMSK (2008), *Mittel- und langfristige Finanzierung der Pflegevorsorge*. Präsentation der Studie des WIFO, Wien.

Bureau Beleidsonderzoek (2010), *Langdurige zorg. Rapport brede heroverwegingen*, Inspectie der Rijksfinanciën, The Hague, April, accessible at *www.minfin.nl/Onderwerpen/Begroting/Brede_heroverwegingen/12_Langdurige_zorg*.

Campbell, J. and N. Ikegami (2000), "Long-term Care Insurance Comes to Japan", *Health Affairs*, Vol. 19, No. 3, pp. 26-39.

Campbell, J.C., N. Ikegami and M.J. Gibson (2010), "Lessons from Public Long-term Care Insurance in Germany and Japan", *Health Affairs*, Vol. 29, No. 1, pp. 87-95.

Campbell, J.C., N. Ikegami and S. Kwan (2009), "Policy Learning and Cross-National Diffusion in Social Long-term Care Insurance: Germany, Japan, and the Republic of Korea", *International Social Security Review*, Vol. 62, No. 4, pp. 63-80.

Comas-Herrera, A., R. Wittenberg and L. Pickard (2010), "The Long Road to Universalism? Recent Developments in the Financing of Long-term Care in England", *Social Policy and Administration*, Vol. 44, No. 4, pp. 375-391.

Costa-Font, J. and A. Garcia Gonzalez (2007), "Long-term Care Reform in Spain", *Eurohealth*, Vol. 13, No. 1, accessed 28 February 2010 at *www2.lse.ac.uk/LSEHealthAndSocialCare/LSEHealth/pdf/eurohealth/VOL13No1/Costa-Font.pdf*.

Da Roit, B., B. Le Bihan and A. Österle (2007), "Long-term Care Policies in Italy, Austria and France: Variations in Cash-for-Care Schemes", *Social Policy and Administration*, Vol. 41, No. 6, pp. 653-671.

DREES (2008), "L'allocation personnalisée d'autonomie et la prestation de compensation du handicap au 30 juin 2008", *Études et Résultats*, No. 666, Paris, Octobre.

Ergan, H. and F. Paulucci (2010), "Providing and Financing Long-term Care in Australia", *Health and Ageing*, No. 3, October.

European Commission and the Economic Policy Committee (2009), *The 2009 Ageing Report: Economic and Budgetary Projections for the EU-27 Member States (2008-2060)*, Joint Report prepared by the European Commission (DG ECFIN) and the Economic Policy Committee (AWG), European Communities, Brussels, accessed 28 February 2010 at *http://ec.europa.eu/economy_finance/publications/publication14992_en.pdf*.

Fernandez, J.L., J. Forder, B. Trukeschitz, M. Rokasova and D. McDaid (2009), "How Can European States Design Efficient, Equitable and Sustainable Funding for Long-term Care for Older People?", *Policy Brief*, No. 11, European Observatory on Health Systems and Policies, WHO Regional Office for Europe, Copenhagen.

Gleckman, H. (2010), *Long-term Care Financing Reform: Lessons from the US and Abroad*, The Commonwealth Fund, New York, February.

Glendinning, C. (2009), "The Consumer in Social Care", in R. Simmons, M. Powell and I. Greener (eds.), *The Consumer in Public Services*, The Policy Press, Bristol, pp. 177-196.

Ikegami, N. (2010), "Japan's Long-term Care Insurance: Lessons from Ten Years' Experience", Presentation at the 9-11 September Conference on "Evidence-Based Policy in Long-term Care", London.

IRCCS-INRCA (2009), *L'assistenza agli anziani non autosufficienti in Italia*, Rapporto IRCCS-INRCA 2009, Maggioli Editore.

Kaiser Commission on Medicaid and the Uninsured (2010), *Medicaid and Long-term Care Services and Supports*, Kaiser Family Foundation, Washington, March.

Karlsoon, M. and T. Iversen (2010), "Scandinavian Long-term Care Financing", Health Economics Research Programme of the University of Oslo, June.

Kraus, M. et al. (2010), *A Typology of Systems of Long-term Care in Europe – Results of Work Package 1 of the ANCIEN Project*, Final Report, Institut für Höhere Studien (IHS), Vienna, August, accessed January 2011 at *www.ancien-longtermcare.eu/sites/default/files/Typology%20Report_Final%20Version_07.09.2010_postIHS2.pdf*.

Kwon, S. (2008), "Future of Long-term Care Financing for the Elderly in Korea", *Journal of Ageing and Social Policy*, Vol. 20, No. 1, pp. 119-136.

Lafortune, G., G. Balestat *et al.* (2007), "Trends in Severe Disability among Elderly People: Assessing the Evidence in 12 OECD Countries and the Future Implications", *OECD Health Working Paper*, No. 26, OECD Publishing, Paris, accessed 28 February 2010 at *www.oecd.org/dataoecd/13/8/38343783.pdf.*

Le Bihan, B. and C. Martin (2010), "Long-term Care Policy in France: Towards a Public/Private Complementarity", *Social Policy and Administration*, No. 4, pp. 392-410.

Lundsgaard, J. (2005), "Consumer Direction and Choice in Long-term Care for Older Persons, Including Payments for Informal Care: How Can it Help Improve Care Outcomes, Employment and Fiscal Sustainability?", *OECD Health Working Paper*, No. 20, OECD Publishing, Paris, accessed 28 February 2010 at *www.oecd.org/dataoecd/53/62/34897775.pdf.*

Manaaki, T. (2009), *How Should We Care for the Carers, Now and into the Future?*, National Health Committee of New Zealand, accessed 5 February 2010 at *www.nhc.health.govt.nz/moh.nsf/pagescm/7661/$File/caring-for-the-carers-nhc-2010.pdf.*

Merlis, M. (2004), "Long-term Care Financing: Models and Issues", Prepared for the National Academy of Social Insurance Study Panel on Long-term Care, accessed 5 February 2010 at *www.nasi.org/usr_doc/Merlis_LongTerm_Care_Financing.pdf.*

Ministry of Health and Social Affairs of Sweden (2007), "Care of the Elderly in Sweden", *Fact Sheet*, No. 18, Government offices of Sweden, September.

Mot, E. (2010), "The Dutch System of Long-term Care", CPB Document, The Hague.

OECD (2000), *A System of Health Accounts*, OECD Publishing, Paris.

OECD (2001), "Fiscal Implications of Ageing: Projections of Age-related Spending", *OECD Economics Department Working Paper*, No. 305, OECD Publishing, Paris.

OECD (2005), *Long-term Care for Older People*, OECD Publishing, Paris.

OECD (2006), "Projecting OECD Health and Long-term Care Expenditures: What Are the Main Drivers?", *OECD Economics Department Working Paper*, No. 477, OECD Publishing, Paris.

OECD (2008), *OECD Economic Surveys: Denmark*, OECD Publishing, Paris.

OECD (2010a), *OECD Health Data 2010*, OECD Publishing, Paris.

OECD (2010b), *Health System Accounts Database*, Paris.

Oliveira Martins, M.J. and C. de la Maisonneuve (2006), "The Drivers of Public Expenditure on Health and Long-term Care: An Integrated Approach", *OECD Economic Studies*, No. 42, OECD Publishing, Paris.

Österle, A. (2010), "Long-term Care in Central and South-Eastern Europe: Challenges and Perspectives in Addressing a 'New' Social Risks", *Social Policy and Administration*, Vol. 44, No. 4, pp. 461-480.

Ros, W., A. Van der Zalm, J. Eijlders and G. Schrijvers (2010), "How is the Need for Care and It's Allocation Determined in Europe?", UMC Utrecht (on behalf of the CIZ).

Rothgang, H. (2010), "Social Insurance for Long-term Care: An Evaluation of the German Model", *Social Policy and Administration*, Vol. 44, No. 4, pp. 436-460.

Schut, F.T. and B. van den Berg (2010), "Sustainability of Comprehensive Universal Long-term Care Insurance in the Netherlands", *Social Policy and Administration*, Vol. 44, No. 4, pp. 411-435.

Stone, E. and C. Wood (2010), *A Funding Settlement that Works for People, Not Services*, Joseph Rowntree Foundation, accessed October 2010 at *www.jrf.org.uk/sites/files/jrf/funding-care-services-full.pdf.*

UK Department of Health (2008), *Community Care Statistics 2007–08: Referrals, Assessments and Packages of Care for Adults*, National Summary, Health and Social Care Information Centre, London.

UK Department of Health (2009), *Shaping the Future of Care Together*, The Stationery Office, accessed 28 February at *www.dh.gov.uk/dr_consum_dh/groups/dh_digitalassets/documents/digitalasset/dh_102732.pdf.*

UK HM Government (2010), *Building the National Care Service – White Paper*, presented to Parliament by the Secretary of State for Health by Command of Her Majesty, 30 March 2010, accessible at *www.dh.gov.uk/prod_consum_dh/groups/dh_digitalassets/documents/digitalasset/dh_114923.pdf.*

Wanless, D. (2006), *Securing Good Care for Older People. Taking a Long-term View*, King's Fund, London, accessible at *www.kingsfund.org.uk/publications/securing_good.html.*

Chapter 8

Private Long-term Care Insurance: A Niche or a "Big Tent"?

Given the expected increase in total long-term care (LTC) expenditure, there is interest in some OECD countries in the potential role of private LTC insurance. Indeed, financial planning for retirement may include the subscription to a private LTC coverage product to protect one's income and assets against the risk of needing long-term care, in order to reduce the burden it would create on the family and provide more choices regarding the care received. But, there are very different views regarding the merit of private LTC coverage. For some, this could leverage new financial resources towards long-term care, thereby alleviating future potential pressures for governments to increase their support. For others, it could represent a less efficient and more costly way to ensure universal and comprehensive coverage, relative to public pooling. However, private long-term care coverage arrangements represent small markets in OECD countries. This chapter describes and analyses the role and size of private LTC coverage arrangements across OECD countries. It examines the potential factors affecting the size of LTC insurance markets and countries' initiatives to encourage its development. It then discusses the role that private insurance arrangements could play in LTC systems in the future.

The statistical data for Israel are supplied by and under the responsibility of the relevant Israeli authorities. The use of such data by the OECD is without prejudice to the status of the Golan Heights, East Jerusalem and Israeli settlements in the West Bank under the terms of international law.

247

8.1. A small number of OECD countries account for the largest markets

In OECD countries where private LTC insurance is sold, the market is generally small. As shown in Figure 8.1, private insurance arrangements play the largest role in the United States and Japan financing about 5 to 7% of total LTC expenditures; but they generally account for less than 2% of total LTC spending. Typically, private LTC insurance arrangements develop around a country's public LTC system, either to complement available public coverage, or provide benefits where there is no public LTC coverage. For instance, in Germany, private LTC insurance offers substitute cover to the population who opts out of the public LTC insurance. In the United States, most of the buyers of private LTC insurance are not eligible for Medicaid, which is targeted to the poor. Private LTC insurance can also offer complementary coverage for the portion of the LTC cost not covered under universal public plans, such as in France, Belgium, Japan and Germany.

Figure 8.1. **The private LTC insurance market is small**
Share of total LTC spending

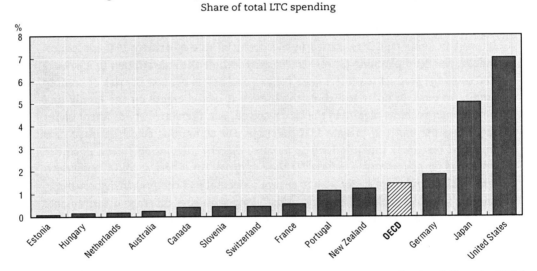

Note: Data refer to 2008 for Canada, Estonia, France, Hungary, Germany, New Zealand and Slovenia; 2007 for Australia, and Switzerland; 2006 for Japan and Portugal; 2005 for the Netherlands. Except in the case of the Netherlands, New Zealand, Slovenia and Spain, data refer to long-term nursing care only.

Source: OECD System of Health Accounts, 2010; and US Department of Health and Human Services, 2010.

StatLink ᴴᴥᴱᴾ *http://dx.doi.org/10.1787/888932401653*

Information on the proportion of the population covered by private coverage arrangements is limited; the literature points to the United States and France as two of the leading markets in terms of the population coverage. In the United States, about 5% of the population aged 40 and over holds a LTC insurance policy. In France, in 2010 about 15%[1] of the population aged 40 and over, held a LTC insurance policy.

A wide range of private LTC coverage arrangements with varying eligibility rules, benefit triggers and benefits paid can be found in OECD countries. Two main products have emerged over time, the reimbursement model, designed in line with private health insurance arrangements, and the indemnity model designed in line with annuity contracts.

Reimbursement policies are the dominant model of private insurance arrangements in the United States. Typically, they provide the eligible recipient with an indemnity up to a designated limit to cover for nursing home, home or outpatient care expenses. There is a wide selection of reimbursement policies in the United States in terms of, for instance, the maximum amount of benefits payable (per day, per week, per month or for a maximum number of years), waiting periods before one can receive benefits (duration of deductible) as well as benefits protection against inflation. Recently, indemnity policies have started being offered in the market.

In France, indemnity policies are the dominant model. Typically, they provide eligible recipients with a fixed level of monthly benefits for life, once the insuree meets criteria set in the policy regarding the level of dependency and waiting period. About 20% of indemnity policies solely cover the risk associated with severe or very severe levels of dependency, while about 80% also cover the risk associated with moderate levels of dependency (FFSA, 2009). Again, there is a wide array of indemnity policies available in France.

In Germany, two types of private long-term care insurance products have developed. First, as part of the implementation of the compulsory LTC insurance system established in 1995 and consistent with the structure of the health insurance system, a compulsory private LTC insurance pays for individuals who have opted out of social health insurance. This market provides coverage for about 9% of Germany's population and is highly regulated (Arntz et al., 2007). Second, voluntary LTC insurance insures eligible LTC expenses not covered by the social LTC insurance programme. In 2009, close to 1.6 million people held such supplementary private insurance, equivalent to about 3.5% of the German population aged 40 and over. In this market, the majority of policies sold are indemnity policies.

In Belgium – in line with the structure of its public LTC system, which is mainly provided as part of public health insurance – private coverage for the portion of health services not reimbursed by public health insurance can be obtained through complementary mutual health insurance, which are of a reimbursement type. As a stand-alone policy, private LTC insurance is not available in Belgium.

In Japan, private LTC policies are available either as principal coverage or as a rider to main life/medical insurance policies. Generally, they allow the insured to receive cash benefits once reaching a certain level of dependency.[2] Cash payments can take the form of a lump sum, an annuity or mix of the two. Some estimates suggest that since the introduction of the public LTC insurance, in 2000, the size of the private market has stagnated and remained low (Tachibanaki et al., 2006, Yasukawa and Inoue, 2007). In 2000, about 2 million individuals, equivalent to about 3% of the population aged 40 and over, had taken out LTC insurance (Taleyson, 2003).

In the United Kingdom, the market for long-term care financial plans is very small. Information from the Association of British Insurers (ABI) suggests that at the end of 2008, the total number of long-term care policies in force was of about 40 000, which is equivalent to less than 0.05% of the population aged 40 and over. Other private LTC insurance markets are emerging, such as Canada and Italy, predominantly based on indemnity policies.

Box 8.1. **Who buys and what products?** The case of the United States and France

In the United States, in exchange for an annual payment of about USD 2 100 to USD 2 500 per year (2008), a single 60-years-old could typically obtain an individual LTC insurance policy that would pay up to USD 150 a day for covered services including nursing home services, assisted living facilities, home-care services and adult day care for a maximum length of three years. Benefits would typically start to be paid 90 days after an insured individual qualifies for LTC. In addition, the policy would typically provide for inflation protection, such that the maximum daily amount would be increased by 5% compounded annually (Tumlinson et al., 2009).

A study prepared for the America's Health Insurance Plans provides information on some socio-demographic characteristics of individuals who purchased LTC insurance in 2005. More than 60% of buyers were between 55 and 70 years of age, more than 55% were female and about 60% were college graduates. More than 70% were married, with reported income above USD 50 000 a year and total liquid assets of USD 100 000 and over. In 2005, 90% of individual LTC insurance bought provided coverage for institutional and home services. The average daily benefit amount was slightly higher for nursing-home care (USD 142) than home care (USD 135) and the average policy duration was about five years. Average waiting periods before receiving benefits was 80 days and about 75% of policies bought had inflation protection. The average annual premium of individual LTC insurance policies was just above USD 1 900 per year representing about 7% of the average income of the elderly population age 65 and over (McDonnell, 2010). Close to 30% of the LTC insurance market in the United States consists of group insurance policies.

In France, in exchange of an annual payment of about EUR 400 and EUR 500 per year (2008), an individual of about 60 years of age could obtain an individual LTC insurance policy that would pay about EUR 600 a month in the event of severe or very severe dependency (dépendance lourde) and between about EUR 200 and EUR 400 a month in the event of moderate dependency (dépendance partielle). Generally, benefits would start to be paid three months after an insured individual qualifies for LTC. LTC insurance coverage can provide for inflation protection, but both the monthly benefit amount and the premium levels will typically be subject to annual increases (FFSA, 2009; Dufour-Kippelen, 2008).

In France, in 2008, the majority of subscribers to an individual LTC insurance policy were aged between 56 and 66 years (FFSA, 2009). An empirical study using the SHARE database has examined a number of factors affecting the probability of holding an individual LTC insurance policy in France. According to this study, among the population 50 years and over, those that are relatively younger, that are married or have children, that have attained a higher level of education or that expect to leave a relatively large estate/bequest are more likely to subscribe to an individual LTC insurance (Courbage and Roudault, 2007). In 2008, buyers of individual long-term care insurance policies, paid an average premium of about EUR 360 a year, while the average level of monthly benefits was about EUR 540 per insuree. In 2008, among individuals covered by insurance contracts still in force, about 45% solely had coverage for severe or very severe levels of dependency. Generally, individual insurance contracts include waiting periods before receiving benefits of about three months and about 75% of them offer inflation protection. The group LTC insurance market is large in France and represented about 45% of the LTC insurance contracts in 2009 (FFSA, 2009; 2010).

Recent market developments in some OECD countries suggest that insurance providers are moving towards private LTC indemnity policies providing a fixed cash benefit to qualifying insurees, which can be used according to the insurees' preferences. The main advantages of the indemnity model are the simplicity and flexibility it offers to subscribers and its conduciveness to facilitate the management of the financial risk associated with dependency for providers. More specifically, under the indemnity model insurance providers need to gauge the prevalence of dependency among a group of insurees over time, which can be defined in a more robust manner especially for severe and very severe level of dependencies. This contrasts with reimbursement policies under which an insurance provider typically needs to gauge both the prevalence of dependency among a group of insurees as well as the level of care that will be required at a given level of dependency over time, which is more uncertain and difficult to foresee (Cremer and Pestieau, 2009).

8.2. Market failures and "consumers myopia" explain why the private LTC insurance is small

In theory, the significant financial uncertainties in terms of potential need, intensity and duration of long-term care provide a powerful rationale for sharing this risk across individuals (see Box 8.2 for a conceptual assessment of private pooling arrangements). Yet, in countries where private LTC insurance is sold, population coverage remains low. The literature, mainly from the United States, points to a number of factors explaining the difficulty of developing comprehensive markets for private LTC coverage.

Box 8.2. **Assessment of private LTC pooling arrangements**

The role that private LTC insurance coverage can play is subject to debate among policy makers and experts alike. This section assesses the potential benefits and shortcomings of private LTC pooling arrangements with respect to access, comprehensiveness, financial sustainability, equity in financing and quality of LTC services.

While private LTC can increase the ability of most individuals to pay for potential future LTC expenses (Doty et al., 2010), it is generally not accessible to the whole population. For instance, private pooling arrangements typically exclude the most vulnerable segment of the population such as those who are currently using LTC services or those with a high risk of using them in the short term (e.g., individuals over 70 years of age).

Private LTC insurance plans, like many public coverage programmes, do not cover all expenses associated with LTC. Private LTC insurance typically provides for a pre-defined benefit package under which maximum benefit amounts are set. While individuals generally have the choice among more or less comprehensive policies at corresponding prices, modest and middle-income individuals may opt for less coverage at affordable premium levels, still leaving them at risk of facing significant LTC expenses.

Private LTC pooling arrangements could have the potential to leverage new financial resources and to alleviate future financial pressures on governments. But, thus far, their impact has been limited. Private pooling arrangements may also provide a framework to guide the financing of future LTC expenditures. Private pooling arrangements are, in principle, fully funded and include a pre-funding element thereby accumulating reserves to face the expected growing need for benefits pay-out in the future. Nevertheless, as the number of insurance providers increase, an increasing share of premium payment may be used for administrative purposes instead of financing future expected LTC expenditures and premium levels may still rise.

Risk-related pricing, which is predominately used for the management of private pooling arrangements, can alleviate some inter-generational equity concerns with respect

---

> Box 8.2. **Assessment of private LTC pooling arrangements** (*cont.*)
>
> to the financing of long-term care. In principle, under risk-related pricing, older eligible cohorts should contribute more to the pool given their higher likelihood to draw benefits from it in the short and medium term. However, risk-related premia typically do not relate to income, so that low and modest-income individuals are required to spend a relatively larger portion of their disposable income on private insurance. This may disproportionally affect women who typically have lower average income. This makes them more likely to not access private pooling arrangements on affordability grounds.
>
> It can be argued that by increasing enrolees' ability to pay, private LTC insurance can help some individuals access more quality care. In addition, private LTC benefits, predominately in the form of cash benefits, may foster personal choice by providing dependent individuals with more flexibility in their LTC decisions, which may lead to higher well-being. However, cash benefits alone are not sufficient and dependent individuals, especially those with cognitive diseases, would generally benefit from formal advice to guide them in the choice of services and to support them in navigating LTC systems. Furthermore, an increase in one's ability to pay will not guarantee an adequate supply of quality service.
>
> On a conceptual basis, while private pooling arrangements can bring about a number of benefits, they involve inherent drawbacks on accessibility and equity grounds. Public interventions can aim to mitigate these drawbacks but, in practice, the development of comprehensive markets for private LTC coverage remains a challenge due to the combination of supply and demand factors listed above.

First, well-known market failures due to asymmetric information in the private LTC insurance market, such as adverse selection and moral hazard, lead insurers to protect themselves by limiting access to coverage. Adverse selection would translate in only those with high-perceived LTC risk buying in or keeping the insurance policy, while moral hazard would translate in insures using more LTC services that they would have required because they are covered. With a view to mitigating adverse selection, insurers typically limit eligibility to a private LTC insurance to those with no pre-existing health conditions associated with dependency. This is often referred to as underwriting.[3]

Second, insurers face significant uncertainty regarding future costs, or the evolution of supply and organisation arrangements for long-term care. For instance, future trends in the onset of dependency are unknown, and there is uncertainty with respect to the costs of providing a unit of care as well as with the projected return from the invested accumulated reserves (Tumlinson *et al.*, 2009). This may result in insurers setting relatively higher premia or paying lower benefits. For instance, research in the United-States found that the typical LTC policy purchased marked premia substantially above expected benefits (Brown and Finkelstein, 2007), thereby reducing value for money for the subscriber. Premium mark-up may lead to lower demand for private LTC coverage as a result of its higher prices. In addition, the complexity of certain LTC insurance contracts makes it difficult for potential insurees to assess value for money.

Third, challenges associated with the ability of insurers to control the covered LTC risk might also lead to premium volatility. To ensure the financial viability of an insurance plan, insurance contracts include clauses that allow for the level of premia to increase if the overall level of risk shared within a pool of insurees increases. For instance, in the wake of the economic crisis, a number of existing LTC insurance policy holders in the United States have been subject to an increase in premium (Tergesen and Scism, 2010). Premium volatility makes the cost of private LTC coverage less predictable and may reduce the confidence in these types of insurance plans. Alternatively, low consumer confidence can also arise with respect to one's likelihood to benefit from such a plan.

Fourth, low demand for private LTC insurance may also reflect individuals' myopia in planning for the financial risk associated with long-term care. For instance, the risk associated with dependency is often deemed as too remote to warrant coverage starting at a relatively young age. Individuals' perceptions on the level of public support also affect the perceived need to hold private coverage. These may translate in individuals delaying until an older age decisions regarding the purchase of a private LTC coverage, when they are more likely to face high premia and less likely to pass underwriting tests.

Fifth, low demand may also reflect competing financial obligations and priorities faced by individuals and families, such as paying for children' education, schooling, and buying a house. It can be argued that for working-age households, the purchase of a LTC insurance should take place once a sufficient level of retirement savings have been accumulated and life insurance policies have been acquired. For households with low income, the cost of subscribing to a private LTC coverage can represent a high share of their disposable income. Some studies note the relatively small proportion (around 20%) of the United States population that can afford private LTC coverage (Melis, 2003).

Last, the availability of potential substitutes such as public coverage programmes can play a role in mitigating the demand for private LTC insurance. Given individuals' expected income and asset situation, and the comprehensiveness of public LTC coverage, willingness to buy private LTC insurance may be low. It could also be argued that the availability of family or friends providing care assistance may mitigate incentives to purchase insurance, although in France households with children have a higher probability to subscribe to private LTC coverage (Courbage and Roudault, 2007).

8.3. Policy and private-sector initiatives to increase take up

Regulations and fiscal policy

Regulatory intervention and tax incentives can be used to reach a number of policy goals such as fostering broader access to private LTC coverage, promoting the development of certain types of insurance schemes through, for example, standardisation of insurance contracts or the establishment of minimum requirements as well as promoting competition among insurance providers.

Tax incentives effectively aim at reducing the purchase price of a private LTC insurance, in order to stimulate demand.[4] Providing preferential tax treatment to private LTC schemes is often cited has a mean for governments to increase awareness of LTC risks as well as to signal the importance of advance planning. Preferential tax treatment for private LTC insurance exists in the United States, Spain, Mexico or Austria. Typical tax advantages include deductions or tax credits based on the level of private LTC insurance premium paid. In Mexico and in Australia, subject to limits, an individual may be eligible for a tax allowance equivalent to the amount of premium paid. In the United States, premia paid towards qualifying private LTC policies are considered as eligible health expenses which can be deducted when exceeding a given share of an individual's income. In the United States as well as in Spain, preferential tax treatment is also provided by excluding from an employee's taxable income the value of premia paid by employers as part of a group LTC insurance plan.

Generally, regulations aim at protecting individuals who purchase insurance as well as enhancing the quality of insurance products sold, for example by limiting the ability of insurance providers to cancel contracts or to alter premium levels following a change in an insuree's condition. Regulations also typically provide for risk-management frameworks to ensure the solvency of insurance plans.

For first-time purchasers, in many OECD countries, there are few limitations on an insurer's ability to impose exclusions on coverage based on pre-existing conditions as well as considering health-related factors as part of premium setting. For member countries of the European Union, EU law does not permit governments to regulate private insurance contracts and impose access-related standards, except in cases where private coverage plays a primary or alternative role to a compulsory social cover scheme. For instance, specific LTC regulations have been implemented in Germany as part of its compulsory private long-term care insurance market, which specify that premia and benefits be established in line with those of the social compulsory LTC insurance. Compulsory long-term care premia are also limited to maximum premium paid under the public social long-term care insurance system and providers generally cannot exclude or charge extra premia for those with pre-existing conditions.[5]

In the United States, as a complement to existing state regulations, the federal Health Insurance Portability and Accountability Act (HIPAA), outlines the requirements private LTC plans must meet in order to qualify for preferential federal tax treatment. Under HIPAA, coverage must begin when a person is certified as needing substantial assistance with at least two of the six ADLs due to a loss of functional capacity, or requiring substantial supervision because of a severe cognitive impairment. Functional limitations need to last for more than 90 consecutive days. Insurance providers must offer inflation protection and non-forfeiture benefits. Currently, most policies sold in the United States meet those requirements and are therefore eligible to the tax reduction.

Building public/private partnerships

In some OECD countries, the interaction between private LTC insurance coverage and public systems is regulated or specific programmes are designed to encourage complementarity between private and public coverage mechanisms.

In 1987, specific private-public partnership initiatives were established in four states (i.e. California, Connecticut, Indiana and New York) in the United States. The public-private partnership programmes have been designed to encourage individuals, especially moderate and middle-income individuals, to purchase LTC insurance. They were aimed at promoting higher quality insurance products. This was achieved by a better co-ordination between Medicaid assets eligibility rules and the level of benefits received under a private LTC insurance, such that if a policy holder received USD 100 000 in benefits from her Partnership-qualified LTC insurance policy, she could retain USD 100 000 worth of assets over and above the State's Medicaid asset threshold. Since the passing of the Deficit Reduction Act of 2005, which allowed for the expansion of the LTC Partnership Programme to all states, most states currently have active Long-term Care Insurance Partnership Programmes. On balance, the partnership has had mixed results. For instance, while the partnership did promote higher quality insurance products, it still only represents a small share of the overall LTC insurance market in the four initially participating states. In addition, the partnership has had mitigated success in attracting moderate and middle-income individuals to obtain LTC coverage (Alliance for Health Reform, 2007).

Singapore, which is not an OECD member, launched the Eldershield programme in 2002. Eldershield represents a different type of public-private partnership under which the programme is designed by the Government, but priced, sold and managed by private insurers (Hoffman, 2009). In 2009, three private insurance providers delivered and managed Eldershield. One feature of the Eldershield programme is that it provides for automatic enrolment, with an opting-out option (similar to the proposed Class Act in the United States). Enrolment is automatic for most aged 40 years, except for those already unable to perform three of the six defined activities of daily living. Individuals are provided with an initial window of three months to opt out of the plan. After opting out of the plan the option of opting-in remains but the individual will be subject to higher premia and underwriting. At the end of 2006, about 750 000 or about 50% of the population older than 40 years of age were covered under Eldershield. In addition, the opt-out rate has declined since the inception of the programme. In 2006, from those eligible and automatically enrolled in the programme, 14% opted out of the programme relative to 38% when the programme was first launched (Wong, 2007) (see also Box 8.3).

Box 8.3. **Public/private partnership, experience in the United States and Singapore**

As part of the Partnership programme, in the United States, a qualified policy is certified by the state. It typically provides for comprehensive benefits (at home and in institutions) and includes state specific provisions for inflation protection. Evaluation of the Partnership programme suggests that it had reached about 200 000 individuals by 2006, and that about 80% of those who purchased a partnership insurance policy would have purchased a "traditional" policy in the absence of the programme. In addition, the level of household income and assets of Partnership policy holders is comparable, on average, to the one of "traditional" LTC insurance policy holders (United States Government Accountability Office, 2007).

Under the Eldershield program, in Singapore, premia are typically age and gender-related and do not relate to income. Premia are fixed at the age of entry and payable annually starting from age 40 (i.e., for those who do not opt out) until age 65, unless they become eligible to benefit payout. After the premium paying period (typically up to 65 years of age), an individual is covered for life. In addition, Eldershield also includes a non-forfeiture feature that allows a policy member who fails to make a given premium payment to retain some benefit coverage as long as a minimum amount of the premium are paid.

Eldershield targets benefits to those with severe disability (unable to perform three of the six defined activities of daily living) and has been designed according to the fixed indemnity model. When first introduced, eligible individuals would receive a benefit of SGD 300 per month up to five years. In 2007, the plan was enhanced to SGD 400 per month up to 6 years. For comparison purposes, depending on one's functional status as well as the quality of accommodation (e.g., number of beds in one room) average nursing home charges can range from about SGD 1 000 to SGD 3 500 per month (Tan Ling, 2007).

Reaching the working-age population: The role of group LTC insurance

Group insurance coverage typically takes place in the context of employment and has the advantage of encouraging early subscription into a private LTC insurance plan. Group coverage can provide a number of benefits to enrolees, including the potential ability to negotiate better coverage solutions, as well as lower premia. Group plans may also result in fewer exclusions, based on the spread risks within a large group. For the insurance providers, group insurance mitigates the risk of adverse selection with the potential benefit of reducing the overhead costs associated with underwriting tests.

In France, the group LTC insurance market is large. In 2009, it represented about 45% of the LTC insurance contracts (FFSA, 2009). Employees covered under a group insurance plan are generally required to participate in the plan and employers may pay for a portion of the premia on behalf of the employees. Nevertheless, a portion of the group plans provides temporary annual coverage for the risk of dependency and does not provide coverage for future risks once an individual is no longer working (Gisserot, 2007).

Close to 30% of the LTC insurance market in the United States consists of group insurance policies (America's Health Insurance Plans, 2007). Some private employers offer group long-term care insurance coverage as a voluntary benefit. Contrary to group health insurance coverage, employers do not typically contribute to the premium cost. In March 2007, 12% of private industry workers were offered long-term care insurance coverage as part of a group plan (US Bureau of Labor Statistics, 2007).

In addition, in the United States, the federal government, as well as a growing number of state governments, also offer group long-term care programmes for their employees as a voluntary benefit. For instance, in 2002, the federal government began offering group long-term care insurance benefits for federal employees, retirees, and certain family members. As part of the federal plan, eligible individuals are provided with an enrolment period, during which they can voluntarily enrol into a group plan. Enrolees pay the entire premium associated with the plan. In 2005, the average age of federal enrolees was 56 years at the time of enrolment, compared with an average age of 60 for enrolees in individual products. Preliminary evaluation of the programme found that for a comparable level of benefits, premia paid as part of the federal programme were generally lower for both single individuals and married couples compared to similar products available in the individual market (United States Government Accountability Office, 2006). The evaluation also found that group insurance products, including the federal programme, expected to pay a higher percentage in claim payments and lower percentage in administrative costs compared with individual insurance products. Despite these benefits, participation rates in group insurance products are relatively low, with about 5 to 8% of the eligible population enrolling into such plans (United States Government Accountability Office, 2006).

Private sector innovations and mixed insurance products

A number of initiatives, mainly from the private sector, may have the potential to direct additional private resources towards long-term care. In most cases, initiatives aim at combining LTC insurance products with other types of financial products (Mayhew et al., 2010). These innovations generally seek to widen the range of products available and thereby can help meet the diverse needs of the population, but take-up has generally remained low across countries.

Some insurance providers offer LTC insurance policies as part of life insurance policies, which tend to have a much larger diffusion. Typically, these provide cash advances in the event that the policy holder requires long-term care for an extended period of time, paid out of the death benefit or the accumulated savings build into the policy. For elderly individuals, both life and LTC insurance policies can be seen as pursuing similar ends in terms of ensuring that there will be some assets left for transfer to survivors. This type of life insurance policy is available in a number of OECD countries such as the United States, France, Canada and Australia. In 2008, close to 150 000 individuals (about 5% of the market) was covered for LTC risk under such an insurance contract in France (FFSA, 2009).

Other financial products provide the possibility to convert home equity, which can represent a significant portion of the net-worth of elderly individuals, into cash. Reverse mortgage can provide a means to continue living in one's home while paying for required LTC services or to free up some cash in order to subscribe to a LTC insurance. These financial products have been available for some time in the United States and the United Kingdom and they are also available in Australia, Denmark, Ireland, Spain and Sweden. In the United States, two of the three main reverse mortgage products are government insured. In Ireland, a sort of public "reverse mortgage" programme, called the Nursing Home Loan, has recently been introduced for those who need long-term nursing-home care. The programme provides individuals with the flexibility of not selling assets such as their home during their lifetime in order to pay for their care. The loan can be repaid at any time but will ultimately fall due for repayment from one's estate upon death. The loan is provided according to the personal contribution towards the cost of receiving care in a nursing home. It also has relatively low upfront charges and applies preferential interest charges over the duration of the loan equivalent to the consumer price index.

Akin to reverse mortgage-type of financial products, closer ties could be established between private medical/general retirement savings accounts and the purchased of a private LTC insurance. This option is available only in a few countries such as the United States and Singapore. In Singapore, savings accumulated in a Medisave[6] account can be used to pay for Eldershield premia. In the United States a limited portion, depending on the enrolee's age, of the accumulated savings in a health account can be used to pay for a tax-qualified long-term care insurance. That said, as for private LTC insurance, evidence shows that individuals with relatively higher level of incomes are generally more likely to participate to private medical/general retirement savings account. In addition, it could be argued that increasing private savings to meet the private costs associated with LTC does not represent the most efficient means to pay for these costs, as it does not allow for the sharing of the risks associated with activity limitations across the population (Productivity Commission, 2011).

Long-term care insurance has also been combined with life annuities (Box 8.4). A life annuity provides for a series of regular payments over a specified and defined period of time in exchange for a single premium payment made at the outset. Relative to a traditional life annuity, a life/LTC annuity will typically provide for a reduced life annuity in exchange of an augmented one once the need for long-term care arises. The market for such annuities is fairly narrow as the purchase of an annuity requires a significant up-front single premium payment. Such life/LTC annuities are available for example in the United States and the United Kingdom.

> ### Box 8.4. **Additional information on reverse-mortgage and life/LTC annuities**
>
> The *"reverse mortgage"* or *"home equity conversion mortgage"* does not have specific income requirement, so that home owners with low and moderate income can borrow. In addition, a loan does not need to be repaid by the home owner unless they wish to sell and/or move. For example, individuals who move from their home to an assisted living home or a nursing home for more than a given period of time (*e.g.* 12 months) can be required to pay the loan back. Cash received from a reverse mortgage can be used for any purpose. Ultimately, the loan is payable from one's estate upon death. Lastly, reverse mortgage is not the only alternative available to elderly home owners to convert home equity into cash. Other alternatives can include selling one's home, downsizing to a smaller home or taking a home loan. Depending on individual circumstances and preferences, those alternatives may be preferable to subscribing to a reverse mortgage contract, which can be complicated and costly.
>
> There are two main types of *life annuity products* which include a LTC component. These can be referred to as "immediate LTC annuity" and "deferred LTC annuity". Under a deferred LTC annuity, a share of the single premium payment is allocated to LTC insurance funds, which can be accessed in the event that long-term care expenses are incurred. Generally, the rules of the annuity define how much can be accessed on a monthly basis from the long-term care fund. Depending on the annuity, underwriting test can be less stringent compared to those used in the private LTC insurance market. Immediate long-term care annuity plans are typically designed to cover the actual expenses associated with long-term care. Under such arrangement, an individual already in need of care can pay a single premium to buy a policy which will begin to pay for some or all of care expenses incurred for life. Under such arrangements, the "pool" of fund is shared among individuals who already are dependent so that risk sharing takes place over the period of time over which an individual will require long-term care.

Up to now, these innovations have had a limited impact in improving access to LTC coverage. Nevertheless, some are more promising than others. For instance, the combination of life and LTC insurance policies as well as "reverse mortgages" provide seniors with different avenues for mobilising additional liquidity out of their accumulated assets to pay for LTC-related expenses (see Chapter 9 for a more detailed discussion on this issue). Nevertheless, while these products widen the range of possibilities to direct resources towards LTC, the subscription to a private LTC insurance is likely to pay for a more significant share of LTC expenses.

8.4. Conclusions: Private long-term care insurance has some potentials but is likely to remain a niche product

As a pooling mechanism, private LTC insurance has the potential to help individuals and families manage more effectively the risk of facing significant out-of-pocket LTC expenses. In fact, as seen in Chapter 7, public LTC coverage systems across OECD countries require users to share a portion of the cost for their care, albeit at a different levels. Yet, even in countries where public LTC coverage is less comprehensive, people continue to rely predominantly upon out-of-pocket payments (and therefore upon their savings), or on family-based arrangements. This outcome reflects, in part, people's lack of awareness of the financial risk associated with LTC and understanding of what private LTC insurance can do in mitigating this risk. Given that the efficiency of LTC pooling mechanisms generally tend to improve through broad and early subscription, some OECD countries have intervened through regulation or fiscal policies to encourage broader coverage.

Public initiatives have ranged from enhancing the quality of LTC insurance products, to lowering the purchase price of a private LTC insurance, enhancing the complementarity between public and private LTC coverage, or making the subscription to a private LTC insurance automatic with an opting-out option. Thus far, in the context of voluntary pooling arrangements, public initiatives have generally had limited success in broadening access to private LTC coverage. But, some public initiatives seem to be less cost-effective than others. For instance, preferential tax treatment needs to be considered carefully in terms of its effectiveness to affect demand. More specifically, most of the fiscal cost of a tax measure can take the form of a "windfall" to those relatively better-off individuals, who would have purchased the insurance even in the absence of the tax reduction. Alternatively, support towards the purchase of a private LTC insurance could be targeted to lower-income individuals thereby compensating for the regressiveness of risk-related premiums.

Group LTC insurance can also represent an avenue for reaching working-age individuals so as to promote early subscription into a private LTC plan. While employers may see little benefit in contributing to an insurance covering the risk associated with dependency beyond an employee's working life, group insurance can still benefit employees through lower premia and higher-quality benefit packages. Still, not all workers are involved in paid employment. In addition, with increasing labour mobility and the onset of dependency typically arising well after retirement age, group LTC insurance can raise issues of portability and continued access to coverage. Portability features, either from one group-plan to another or from a group-plan to an individual plan, can play a role in ensuring continued access to LTC coverage as well as non-forfeiture benefit features, which allow policy subscribers to retain some LTC coverage even if they were to stop paying into the plan after retirement.

To date, evidence suggests that left on their own device, voluntary private LTC pooling mechanisms will remain niche products, which principally serve the segment of the population with relatively higher income and accumulated assets (Ergas and Paolucci, 2010). The market could potentially expand as younger generations become better aware of the financial risk associated with LTC based on the experience of their elders, and become more comfortable with LTC insurance products and their underlying features (Zhou-Richter et al., 2010). Nevertheless, unless mandatory, any expansion of the voluntary market will be subject to perennial supply and demand issues inherent to private coverage.

Notes

1. In 2009, about 1 million individuals had subscribed to an individual LTC insurance. In addition, close to 850 000 individuals had subscribed to a group LTC insurance coverage while about 150 000 had complementary coverage through a life insurance policy (Fédération Française des Sociétés d'Assurance, 2010). Furthermore in 2010, about 3 million individuals had coverage against the risk of dependency through mutual insurance contracts (Caisse Nationale de Solidarité pour l'Autonomie, 2010).

2. Private LTC insurance eligibility criteria can differ from the eligibility criteria of the public LTC insurance system.

3. Through underwriting an insurance provider determines the risk associated with an applicant, which can result in the provider declining to offer a policy.

4. Evidence on the elasticity of demand of LTC private insurance is limited and suggests that elasticity may be around 1.25 (Gopi Shah, 2010; Cohen and Weinrobe, 2000). Assuming that all policies sold are eligible to the tax incentive, more than 75% of the incentive would be targeted to individuals who would have subscribed to a policy in the absence of the tax reduction.

5. Insurance providers must also participate in a system of risk equalisation for premia.

6. Medisave is a mandatory saving scheme meant to help individuals pay for medical expenses after retirement.

References

AARP Public Policy Institute (2010), "Federal and State income Tax Incentives for Private Long-term Care Insurance", *In Brief*, Washington.

Alliance for Health Reform (2007), "Long-term Care Partnership, An Update",Washington.

America's Health Insurance Plans (2007),"Who Buys Long-term Care Insurance? A 15-Year Study of Buyers and Non-Buyers, 1990-2005", Document prepared by LifePlans, April.

Arnts, M. *et al.* (2007), "The German Social Long-term Care Insurance: Structure and Reform Options", *IZA Discussion Paper*, No. 2625, Bonn.

Assous, L. and R. Maheu (2001), "L'assurabilité de la dépendance et sa prise en charge par le secteur privé : Une mise en perspective internationale", *Health and Ageing*, No. 5, Geneva Association Information Newsletter, October 2001.

Brown, J.R. and A. Finkelstein (2007), "Why Is the Market for Long-term Care Insurance So Small?", *NBER Working Paper*, February.

Brown, J.R. and A. Finkelstein (2009), "The Private Market for Long-term Care Insurance in the United States: A Review of the Evidence", *Journal of Risk and Insurance,* Vol. 76, No. 1, pp. 5-29.

Caisse Nationale de Solidarité pour l'Autonomie (2010), "Évaluation des situations de perte d'autonomie pour personnes âgées – Des possibilités d'un partenariat public-privé pour l'évaluation des situations de perte d'autonomie des personnes âgées", *Rapport du groupe de travail animé par le CNSA*, October.

Cohen, A.M. and M. Weinrobe (2000), "Tax Deductibility of Long-term Care Insurance Premiums: Implications for Market Growth and Public LTC Expenditures", Health Insurance Association of America, Washington DC.

Courbage, C. (2010), "Insuring Long-term Care Risk", *Insurance Economics*, No. 61, December.

Courbage, C. and N. Roudault (2007), "La demande d'assurance dépendance. Une analyse empirique pour la France", Collège des Économistes de la Santé, Paris, 24 Octobre.

Cremer, H. and P. Pestieau (2009), "Securing Long-term Care in the EU: Some Key Issues", *CREPP Working Paper*, No. 2009-05, Liège.

Doty, P. *et al.* (2010), "Private Long-term Care Insurance: Value to Claimants and Implications for Long-term Care Financing", *The Gerontologist*, Vol. 50, No. 5, Oxford University Press on behalf of the Gerontological Society of America.

Dufour-Kippelen, S. (2008), "Les contrats d'assurance dépendance sur le marché français en 2006", *Working Paper*, No. 84, Direction de la recherche, des études, de l'évaluation et des statistiques, December.

Ergas, H. and F. Paolucci (2010), "Providing and Financing Age Care in Australia", *Health and Ageing*, No. 23, Geneva Association Information Newsletter, October.

European Observatory on Health Care Systems (2000), "Health Care Systems in Transition, Belgium", Copenhagen.

Evans Cuellar, A. and J.M. Wiener (2000), "Can Social Insurance for Long-term Care Work? The Experience of Germany", *Health Affairs*, Vol. 19, No. 3, May/June.

Feder, J. *et al.* (2007), "Long-term Care Financing: Policy Options for the Future", Georgetown University, Washington, June.

FFAS – Fédération Française des Sociétés d'Assurance (2009), "Les principales caractéristiques des contrats dépendance en 2008 – Contrats individuels", *Étude et Statistiques*, December, Paris.

FFAS – Fédération Française des Sociétés d'Assurance (2010), "Les contrats d'assurance dépendance en 2009 (aspect quantitatif)", *April 2010 Survey*, Paris.

Gisserot, H. (2007), "Perspectives financières de la dépendance des personnes âgées à l'horizon 2025 : Prévisions et marge de choix", Rapport à Monsieur Philippe Bas, ministre délégué à la Sécurité sociale, aux Personnes âgées, aux Personnes handicapées et à la Famille, 20 mars.

Gopi Shah, G. (2010), "The Impact of State Tax Subsidies for Private Long-term Care Insurance on Coverage and Medicaid Expenditure", NBER Working Paper, No. W16406, September.

Hoffman, J. (2009), "Singapore Long-term Care Plan. ElderShield Government Sponsored, Privately Sold", International News, Vol. 49, Society of Actuaries, December.

Lewis, S.J.D. et al. (2003), "Regulation of Private Long-term Care Insurance: Implementation Experience and Key Issues", Prepared for the Kaiser Family Foundation, March.

Mayhew, L. et al. (2010), "The Role of Private Finance in Paying for Long-term Care", Economic Journal, Vol. 120, November.

McDonnell, K. (2010), "Income of the Elderly Population Age 65 and Over, 2008", Employee Benefit Research Institute, Vol. 31, No. 6, June.

Melis, M. (2003), "Private Long-term Care Insurance: Who Should Buy It and What Should They Buy?", Prepared for the Kaiser Family Foundation, March.

Melis, M. (2004), "Long-term Care Financing: Models and Issues", Prepared for the National Academy of Social Insurance Study Panel on Long-term Care, 30 April.

National Clearinghouse for Long-term Care Information – Own Your Future, US Department of Health and Human Services, accessible at www.longtermcare.gov/LTC/Main_Site/index.aspx.

OECD (2003), OECD Reviews of Health Care Systems: Korea, OECD Publishing, Paris.

OECD (2004), "Private Health Insurance in OECD Countries", OECD Publishing, Paris.

Productivity Commission (2011), "Caring for Older Australians", Draft Inquiry report, Chapter 7, Canberra.

Riedel, H. (2003), "Private Compulsary Long-term Care Insurance in Germany", International Association for the Study of Insurance Economics, Cologne.

Tachibanaki, T. et al. (2006), "Koukyou shishutsu no jueki to kokumin futan ni kansuru ishikichousa to keiryou bunseki", RIETI Discussion Paper, No. 06-J-058, Research Institute of Economy, Trade and Industry, Japan.

Taleyson, L. (2003), "Private Long-term Care Insurance – International Comparisons", Health and Ageing, No. 8, Geneva Association Information Newsletter, March.

Tan Ling, L. (2007), "Nursing Home Charges", Singapore Ministry of Health, December.

Tergesen, A. and L. Scism (2010), "Long-term Care Premiums Soar", The Wall Street Journal, Weekend Investor, 16 October.

Thomson, S. and E. Mossialos (2009), "Private Health Insurance in the European Union", LSE Health and Social Care, London School of Economics and Political Science, 24 June.

Tumlinson, A. et al. (2009), "Closing the Long-term Care Funding Gap: The Challenge of Private Long-term Care Insurance", Kaiser Commission on Medicaid and the Uninsured, June.

United States Government Accountability Office (2006), "Long-term Care Insurance, Federal Program Compared Favorably with Other Products and Analysis of Claims Trend Could Inform Future Desicions", Report to Congressional Committee, March.

United States Government Accountability Office (2007), "Long-term Care Insurance, Partnership Programs Include Benefits that Protect Policyholders and Are Unlikely to Result in Medicaid Savings", Report to Congressional Committee, May.

United States Bureau of Labor Statistics (2007), "National Compensation Survey: Employee Benefits in Private Industry in the United States, March 2007", US Department of Labor, Washington.

Wong, H. (2007), "Eldershild Experience 2002-2007", Singapore Ministry of Health, Information Paper, No. 2007/21.

Yasukawa, F. and T. Inoue (2007), "A Primitive Study on the Relationship Between Public Long-term Care Insurance Policy Reform and the Performance of Private Long-term Care Insurance: How to Relieve the Burden of Care?", ITEC Working Paper, No. 07-32, Institute for Technology, Enterprise and Competitiveness, Doshisha University, December.

Zhou-Richter, T. (2010), "Don't They Care? Or, Are They Just Unaware? Risk Perception and the Demand for Long-term Care Insurance", Journal of Risk and Insurance, Vol. 77. No. 4, pp. 715-747.

Chapter 9

Where To?
Providing Fair Protection
Against Long-term Care Costs
and Financial Sustainability

For most individuals, it is difficult to foresee whether long-term care (LTC) will be required in the future, and if so, the type, the duration and the cost of that care. Over the next decades, public expenditure in most OECD countries is expected to grow rapidly, in most part because of the expected increase in age-related expenditure, such as public pension, health and LTC services. Generally, given current tax mixes and levels, expected revenues are set to grow at a slower rate than expenditures, with the potential risk of shifting their cost to future generations. The policy challenge can thus be framed as providing fair protection against the financial risk associated with long-term care, while ensuring that the way LTC revenues and expenditures is sustainable in the long-run. Targeted universalism and a forward-looking set of collective financing policies have the potential to help striking a reasonable balance between these two competing priorities. This is what this chapter will examine.

The statistical data for Israel are supplied by and under the responsibility of the relevant Israeli authorities. The use of such data by the OECD is without prejudice to the status of the Golan Heights, East Jerusalem and Israeli settlements in the West Bank under the terms of international law.

9.1. Why provide financial protection against long-term care cost?

For most individuals, saving enough money to meet the financial uncertainty associated with dependency is unattainable. Whether public or private, risk pooling mechanisms – that is, financial mechanisms to share the responsibility for financing long-term care (LTC) cost across a "pool" of individuals – provide them a means to obtain coverage against that risk at a lower cost. Despite improvements in coverage of LTC cost over time (see Chapter 7), formal LTC cost can still be high and represent a significant burden on users in several OECD countries. This chapter starts by arguing that there is a need to provide for a basic protection for all against the risk of LTC. Fair protection refers to the notion of ability to pay relative to the level of care needs.

The chapter then suggests that a universal policy design does not prevent the targeting of higher benefits and services to those who need it the most. In fact, the main challenge for LTC services and systems will be how to ensure that financing of the system is sustainable in the longer run. Fiscal sustainability refers to the extent to which a given set of fiscal policies for LTC does not shift too large a financial burden on future generations (i.e., intergenerational fiscal equity) and ensure that "ends meet". OECD countries use several mechanisms to align LTC revenues and expenditures. Yet, in the longer run, a set of forward-looking fiscal policies can help promote a fair sharing of LTC financing within and across generations.

While the policy challenge differs depending on how comprehensive existing LTC systems are, finding the right balance between fair protection and financial sustainability will ultimately depend on countries' views on an efficient and fair allocation of resources among the population and across generations.

9.2. Improving protection against catastrophic care cost calls for universal LTC entitlement

On both *fairness and efficiency grounds*, there is a rationale for providing some basic universal coverage for personal-care services regardless of individual financial means. This is why many countries have opted or are moving to universal coverage. But, as observed in Chapter 7, within the confine of universalism, there are many ways to target/direct support where the need is the highest, and thus ensure both fairness and value for money. Hereafter this concept will be generally referred to as *targeted universalism*.

Taking *fairness and access* first, the expenses associated with even relatively low care needs (i.e. ten hours per week) can exceed 60% of a senior's disposable income for low and moderate-income individuals, up to the fourth deciles (Figure 9.1).[1] In addition, these households typically have no or little savings to spend down on LTC. For those requiring a larger range of LTC services (i.e., 25 hours a week), the expenses associated with care can exceed 60% of the disposable income for those up to the 8th income deciles (Figure 9.2). Even for relatively higher income seniors, high-intensity LTC cost represents a significant burden requiring a rapid run-down of their savings. For most individuals with severe

Figure 9.1. **The cost associated with low-care need is significant
for low-income seniors**

Share of adjusted disposable income for individuals 65 years and over in different income deciles, mid-2000s

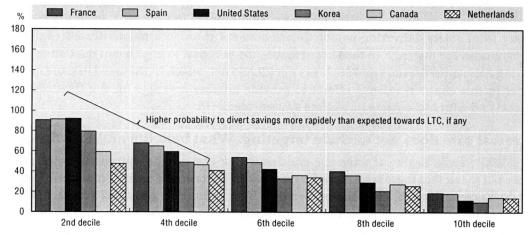

Note: Low-care need is defined as 43.33 hours of care per month, at the prevailing rate per hour, excluding public subsidies, in each respective country.

Source: OECD Secretariat calculation based on the *OECD Income Distribution and Poverty Database* (*www.oecd.org/els/social/inequality*).

StatLink ⫸ *http://dx.doi.org/10.1787/888932401672*

Figure 9.2. **The cost associated with high-care need is significant for most seniors**

Share of adjusted disposable income for individuals 65 years and over in different income deciles, mid-2000s

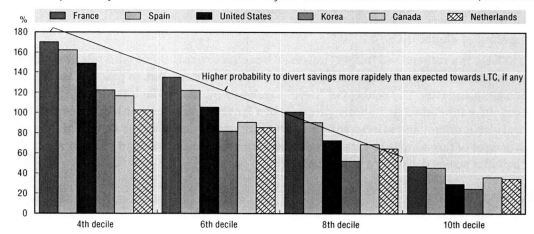

Note: High-care need is defined as 108.33 hours of care per month, at the prevailing rate per hour, excluding public subsidies, in each respective country.

Source: OECD Secretariat calculation based on the *OECD Income Distribution and Poverty Database* (*www.oecd.org/els/social/inequality*).

StatLink ⫸ *http://dx.doi.org/10.1787/888932401691*

functional limitations, long-term care cost can lead to a significant impoverishment and/or an overreliance on family carers or friends.

There are also good reasons on *efficiency grounds* for basic universal coverage of LTC cost. Delivering LTC benefits as part of welfare programmes or programmes of "last resort", where entitlement to coverage is subject to a "means" test, may have unintended effects such as shifting the allocation of benefits towards LTC/health services where public coverage is provided (*e.g.*, nursing homes or hospitals) as well as leading to potential abuse requiring additional administrative cost (*e.g.*, in the case of assets planning to quality for care in means-tested eligibility systems).

These are the main reasons why across the OECD there is some movement towards universal or more comprehensive coverage. As discussed in Chapter 7, most are moving away from solely delivering personal-care services through a means-tested eligibility programme. For instance, in the United States, the proposal to implement the Community Living Assistance Services and Supports Act (CLASS Act, which is discussed in more details later in this chapter) reflects efforts to provide broader coverage for the financial risk associated with LTC outside its welfare system, Medicaid.

9.3. Universal care does not exclude targeting: What benefits and for whom?

While some degree of universal entitlement *for care costs* is warranted, universality does not mean that there is no room for targeting benefits on the basis of care need. In fact, as OECD countries age, the trade-off between "fair" protection and fiscal sustainability is likely to become more difficult to bridge. Although views on the allocation LTC benefits (*e.g.*, to which disabled people, for what services or how much) differ among countries, *targeted universalism* has the potential to help striking a reasonable balance between these two competing priorities. Using the same framework for analysis of LTC coverage systems of Chapter 7, the targeting of benefits can take place on three fronts:

- the assessment/eligibility rules (entitlement);
- the basket of services covered (breadth of services covered); and
- the extent of cost sharing (depth of coverage).

Targeting of eligibility

There is a rationale to "target" universal benefits towards those with relatively higher care needs because of the significant financial cost LTC entails. But, in practice, targeting is not a simple matter. The concept of "need" involves a number of factors including physical or cognitive functional limitations, presence of a family carer or unique local circumstances (rural *versus* urban) and is inherently subject to interpretation. As a result, one of the main challenges of targeting is to establish assessment procedures that lead to a fair allocation of benefits across dependent individuals.

Defining the target

In the OECD, high-care needs are concentrated among the oldest age cohort, which is typically more likely to have severe or very severe functional limitations (Lafortune *et al.*, 2007). This means that in many OECD countries, the financial risk associated with LTC is generally the highest at a time when disposable income is typically the lowest over the lifetime (Figure 9.3). In 2008, about 50% of LTC recipients were older than 80 years old, of whom more than 75% were women who are also at highest risk of poverty.

Korea introduced in 2008 a universal LTC system for those aged 65 years and over.[2] With a view to containing cost, elderly Koreans with lower care needs are not eligible to LTC benefits unlike elderly living in countries with more comprehensive systems. Stringent assessment criteria are also in place in Germany, but not to the same extent as Korea (Campbell and Ikegami, 2010).

For countries that provide for "broader" universality, *better targeting within their universal system can represent an avenue to contain future expected cost.* For instance, Japan's

Figure 9.3. **Disposable income falls with age**

Adjusted disposable income of different age cohorts relative to the population average, mid-2000s

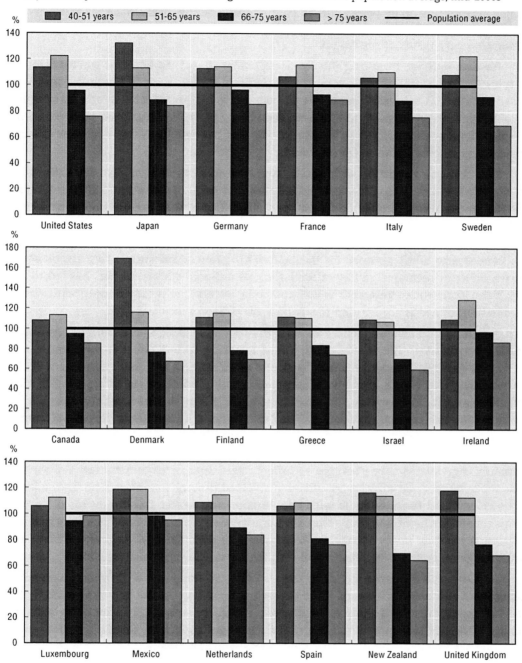

Source: Calculations from OECD Income Distribution and Poverty Database (www.oecd.org/els/social/inequality).

StatLink ⧉ http://dx.doi.org/10.1787/888932401710

public LTC system covers all individuals aged 40 years and older. As part of its 2009-12 planning cycle, and partly to mitigate future cost increases, seniors assessed with the lowest care needs have been moved to a prevention scheme with focus on encouraging healthy ageing (see Chapter 10). In 2010, Austria further targeted the allocation of benefits under their universal cash allowance (*Pflegegeld*) by increasing the minimum hours of help per month required to become entitled to an allowance for those with relatively lower levels of care need (level 1 and level 2). In the mid-1990s, Sweden also targeted services and therefore public expenditure on LTC more closely on the most sick and disabled (OECD, 2005).[3]

Assessing care needs of the target

Assessment for targeting purposes typically takes into account physical and (at varying degrees of importance) cognitive limitations. As discussed in Chapter 7, measuring instruments and especially methods for assessing long-term care needs and required levels of care vary across countries even though many of the functional capacities which are measured are similar. When looking at targeting of eligibility, three main issues related to assessment procedures seem important.

The first one has to do with access, and how to *reconcile local flexibility with national consistency*. Local municipalities are typically the first point of contact and often responsible for the assessment. The rationale for local flexibility is that the environment where a dependent individual lives (*e.g.,* rural or urban area) affects his/her needs. On the other hand, too much local flexibility can lead to inconsistencies with respect to who is eligible for care and to what services. In the United Kingdom, local authorities are ultimately responsible for setting eligibility criteria. Despite national standards, this has led to what has been sometimes referred to as "postcode lottery", whereby people with similar assessment of needs are entitled to significantly different levels of care.

A second and related issue concerns the extent to which assessors or assessment tools provide room for interpretation and tailoring to *individual circumstances*. Most countries (but not Sweden) have at least one standardised national assessment tool for determining LTC needs, along with complementary guidelines for interpretation of the assessment grid. In Germany, the assessment grid is very detailed, yet the assessor may deviate from it if necessary. Japan, on the other hand, does not allow deviations from the guidelines of care provision,[4] and, like France, utilises automated computer programmes to compile responses to the assessment grid and help standardise the assessment. While enabling individual's care packages to reflect users' unique circumstances, tailoring can also make budget planning less predictable and lead to some inconsistencies in the level of benefits granted to individuals with comparable care needs. Similar issues arise when people are classified into groups that are homogeneous in the level of care they need – an approach used by many countries. When there is considerable variance of care needs within a given group, categorisation of recipients can still raise fairness considerations.

A third issue concerns whom to target. With the exception of Germany, assessment procedures and benefits systems differ depending on the age of the applicant, such that the level of support provided tends to be relatively higher for younger than for older dependent adults. Generally, this reflects the fact that for younger applicants, assessment instruments take into account ability to work, training capacity, and aim at reintegration into society. Most countries – such as the United States under the Medicaid programme or the Netherlands – provide for additional funding for working-age handicapped citizens. Yet it is difficult to develop standard assessment of such needs, and the approach used for this category of care recipients is often tailor-made (Ros *et al.*, 2010). In addition, age criteria may be perceived as unfair, particularly by those just below the age threshold (*e.g.,* 65 years of age).

The reliability and accuracy of LTC care assessment systems also needs to evolve over time to reflect the changing nature of dependency and identify the right target groups.

Need assessments are increasingly challenged to better address cognitive limitations, for example. While taking into account ADL limitations, the actual assessment and related funding for services may not address adequately the needs of a population with growing incidence of dementia and Alzheimer. In France, there is ongoing discussion about developing different scales to better capture cognitive performance and address more appropriately the needs of future LTC recipients.

Targeting of the benefit package

Universal coverage can apply to a broader or narrower basket of LTC services. However, decisions about what services to include in the package need to balance the need for flexibility and control for the user with concerns about cost and effectiveness of the services included in the package, with respect to coverage for domestic help and to the mode of providing benefits (cash or in kind).

Support for domestic care or practical help (IADL) provides an example of how difficult it can be to decide what to include in the package. In a number of OECD countries, public support for domestic care or practical help (IADL) is subject to less comprehensive coverage relative to health/nursing care and personal care (ADL). For example, while in Sweden, Denmark and Luxembourg service coverage includes home adaptation, assistive devices and IADL support, in-kind benefits in Belgium, Korea and New Zealand focus on support for ADL. Also, LTC care assessment mechanisms give a significant weight to the inability to perform ADL relative to IADL (see Chapter 7).

It is typically easier to define the set of basic personal-care services (in terms of type, length and frequency) needed by a frail or dependent person than it is to define how much support for domestic care should be required by the user. Determining the basket of domestic-care services generally involves a greater element of subjectivity (e.g., over the frequency of shopping trips, where to and for how long). Support for IADL can also be more readily provided by family, friends or the community, since there is generally more flexibility with their provision. There is therefore a rationale for targeting support on nursing care and basic personal-care needs, since their assessment is less subjective and there are also cost-control considerations. To contain the growth in public LTC expenditures, support for IADL has for example been removed from the basic LTC coverage and devolved to municipalities in the Netherlands.

In practice, however, the distinction between personal and domestic help may not be as clear-cut as first suggested, especially for dependents with higher care needs, with cognitive limitations or with no or small family or community networks. The distinction can also be blurred by the fact that the services can be provided together by the same person or organisation (CIHI, 2007).

The inclusion of support for some IADL activities in the basket of services can also help delay institutionalisation or prevent a dependent individual with relatively high care need from moving to more expensive care settings. For instance, one of the main objectives of Denmark's LTC system is to encourage and enable the elderly to stay at home for as long as possible. To that end, support for ADL and IADL are generally available to all dependent individuals and not subject to co-payments.

Lastly, for the increasing number of dependent individuals with cognitive limitations, limiting the basket of services to support for personal care may not enable a recipient to live independently. But deciding the exact range of services needed and how this may vary over time can be very difficult. For instance, while a frail elderly with early stages of dementia might be self-sufficient in relation to personal care, his/her ability to perform IADL tasks associated with memory and cognitive performance such as using public transit or handling personal finance might be poor (Avlund and Fromholt, 1998). In recognition of the complexity of assessing these users' service needs, the basket of LTC services in Germany covers support for some IADL activities and, since July 2008, includes an extra benefit for those with cognitive disease such as those with dementia (Heinicke and Thomsen, 2010). In Luxembourg the basket of services includes support for official paperwork (Alzheimer-Europe, 2009).

Also relevant to the discussion about targeting of the benefit package is the mode of benefit provision. As users with relatively higher care needs continue to live at home, defining the "right" basket of services that recognises each individual's unique circumstances – including the presence of a spouse or the availability of children for caring – can be challenging. An increasing number of OECD countries – the Netherlands, Austria, Germany, France, Italy and the United Kingdom as well as eastern European countries (see Chapter 1) – are now providing *cash entitlements* to care, giving individuals and families more freedom to make decisions on the care they need, while fostering competition among different LTC providers. Cash benefits give users choice and flexibility and can help address difficult arbitrage in determining the composition of a basket of services, for example between personal care and domestic support. Depending on the level of user direction and users' specific circumstance, these cash entitlements can typically be used towards other type of services than ADL services, such as meal preparation and housekeeping.

One of the challenges with providing a cash benefit is to strike the right balance between safeguarding its proper use and providing personal choice. For instance, in England, take-up of the Direct Payment, a cash-benefit scheme, has been relatively low (only 0.2% of the older population, compared to 4.2% recipients in institution in 2006-07). Restrictions on the use of the payment were identified as one of the barriers limiting their use (Comas-Herrera *et al.*, 2010). In addition, the way cash benefits are structured plays an important role in setting expenditure levels over time.

Eligibility for cash benefit schemes can vary according to age, need and income. For instance, the cash benefit scheme in France (APA) is targeted to those 60 years and older and is income-related. While cash benefits in the Netherlands apply to all dependents, the amount is also income-related (Da Roit and Le Bihan, 2010). Typically, benefit levels increase with care need and can be set to a fixed amount (*e.g.*, Austria, Italy, Germany), subject to national ceilings (*e.g.*, France) or set according to a number of hours of care needed at a prevailing rate of care per hour (*e.g.*, Netherlands, Luxembourg). In Germany and the Netherlands, cash benefits are typically set at a lower level than if provided in-kind. While there is ample flexibility in determining eligibility criteria and benefit structure, once set cash benefits take the form of an entitlement and are generally managed through open-ended budgets. As for any benefits, the introduction of a "new" cash benefit scheme can be subject to uncertainty with respect to its take-up rate, such that higher-than-expected take-up can lead to higher- than-expected global budget. This happened recently in the Netherlands with respect to the personal budgets for dependent people. With a view to remain within the global budget set for 2010, entitlements to new personal budgets were halted (with some exceptions) once the spending had reached the global budget set for the year.

Targeting of private contributions towards the cost of care

Lastly, targeting within universal systems can take place on the extent of cost sharing. As reviewed in Chapter 7, all public LTC coverage systems across OECD countries involve an element of private cost sharing, albeit at significantly different levels. The rationale for using personal contributions can range from mitigating the risk of moral hazard, to recognising that ability to pay varies across users, and containing cost.

Private cost sharing can take the form of a flat cost-sharing formula (*i.e.*, flat percentage of LTC services cost). These are currently in place as part of universal public systems particularly in Japan, Korea and Belgium. One of the main objectives of flat cost-sharing formula is to provide a price signal such that demand for service is more likely to reflect the underlying need for that service (Finans Departmentet, 2009). It is also administratively simple. Nevertheless, flat cost sharing raises distributional considerations since lower-income dependent individuals as well as those with relatively higher need are typically required to spend a greater share of their income on those charges. In these countries, additional support is available through social assistance to compensate for the negative distributional impact of a flat cost-sharing scheme. In Japan and Belgium there are upper ceilings on the cost of care born by users.

Cost sharing can also be set as a given share (in some countries up to a given maximum amounts) of disposable income and/or assets. This is the case, for instance, in Finland, Ireland, the Netherlands and Sweden (see Chapter 7). The benefit of this approach is that it provides both certainty and predictability to individuals with respect to the maximum amount of resources they are expected to allocate towards LTC over time. Compared with flat cost-sharing schemes, they can be less regressive, especially for those with relatively higher LTC needs, but can be more complex to administer, since they require collecting information on income and/or assets and on how these evolve over time.

Cost sharing can also be set as a residual, if any, between the prevailing cost of LTC and the set amount of public coverage. In Germany and in the Italian disability cash benefit ("*indennita di accompagnamento*"), for instance, public coverage is a fixed support which depends on users' care need but not on users' income and assets and is subject to adjustments over time to reflect recent trends in LTC cost (*e.g.*, Germany in 2008). In Austria (combination of "Pflegegeld" and other LTC cash benefits) and France ("*Allocation personnalisée d'autonomie*"), on the other hand, the amount of support is capped but also varies depending on users' care level as well as income and/or assets. Although potentially more complex to administer, this approach can help control costs by capping benefits and increasing fiscal predictability for governments. It also takes into account ability to pay and is progressive. On the down side, it can leave users with uncertainty, especially for those with relatively lower income and higher care needs, particularly if the amount of public support does not keep track with the growth in LTC cost over time.

On equity and cost grounds, there is a rationale for requiring higher cost sharing from those with relatively higher ability to pay. That being said, the determination of the share of income and/or assets that should be allocated to LTC may depend on country's views regarding the balance between collective and individual responsibility for care cost and the notion of what constitutes "catastrophic LTC expenses" – for example whether LTC spending is deemed as catastrophic when it exceeds a given percentage of users' income and/or assets or a given maximum, or when it leaves a dependent individual with less than a minimum level of basic income and/or assets.

Potential interactions with targeted personal income tax measures and the structure of their pension systems also come into play. For instance, as shown in Figure 9.4, public transfers (*e.g.*, public earnings-related schemes as well as basic and resource-tested

Figure 9.4. **Public transfers provide the bulk of income in old age**

Public transfers as a share of the adjusted income of individuals 65 years and over, mid-2000s

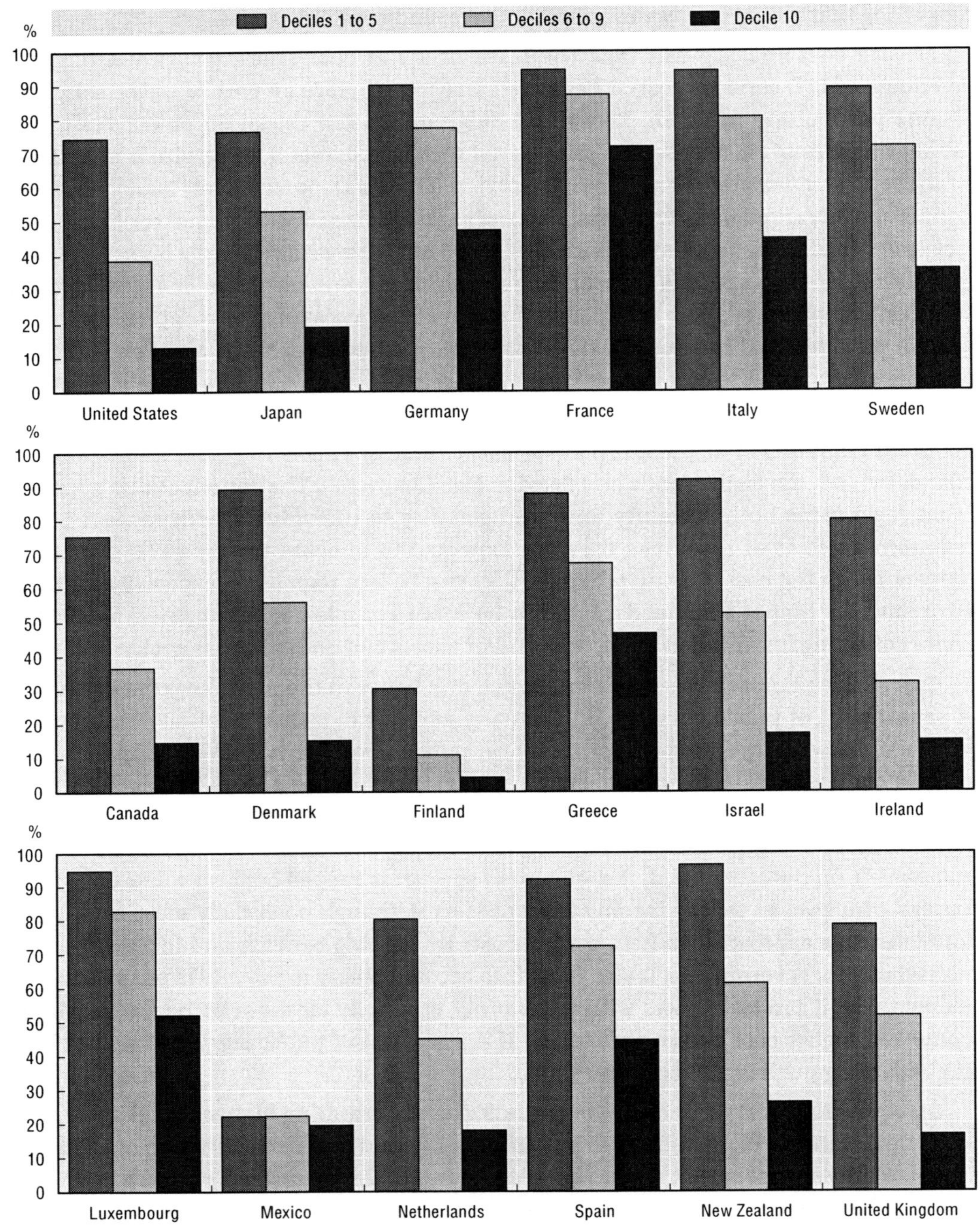

Note: Public transfers include earnings-related schemes, basic and resource-tested benefits as well as minimum programmes. In Finland, mandatory occupational pension plans are included as capital income and are therefore not accounted as public transfer.

Source: OECD Income Distribution and Poverty Database (www.oecd.org/els/social/inequality).

StatLink 🖳📊 http://dx.doi.org/10.1787/888932401729

benefits) generally represent more than 75% of income for half of the elderly with the lowest income. For elderly with intermediate income levels (those falling in the 6th to the 9th deciles) public transfers can range between 30 to 80% of income. This suggests that for seniors, a significant share of private cost sharing towards LTC is paid out of public transfers such that seniors' ability to pay for a share of LTC cost is related, in part, to the comprehensiveness of public pension systems.

9.4. Board and lodging costs in institutions are the main costs that LTC users face

A significant share of the costs associated with receiving care in a nursing home relates to board and lodging (B&L) costs. Depending on the standard and quality of accommodation (e.g., number of beds in one room), B&L costs can represent more than 50% of the total cost of residing in a nursing home (Fédération Hospitalière de France, 2010).[5] This cost can be prolonged over a long period of time: on average, dependent individuals reside between two to three years in a nursing home. B&L costs can be high relative to the ability to pay of senior dependent people. In most countries, the lion's share of a dependent disposable income can be used to pay for these costs (e.g. 80 to 85% of one's disposable income in Australia, Ireland, Norway or Finland) and may need to draw upon their accumulated savings to pay for them.

In most OECD countries, this component of LTC cost is generally viewed as a social/housing risk and is typically not included in public LTC coverage. Assistance is generally targeted to low-income people as part of existing social-assistance or housing subsidy programmes, with the exception of a few countries with comprehensive LTC systems (e.g., Japan and some Nordic countries), where cost sharing for B&L coverage can nevertheless account for a high share of residents' disposable income.[6] In Japan, the cost of B&L has been excluded from the insurance coverage since 2005, in order to ensure equity with people living at home.

High user charges or no coverage for the cost of B&L in a nursing homes contrast with the significantly lower charges paid for accommodation in hospitals or other short-stay acute care settings. The main rationale for the difference in cost treatment lies in the notion of what is considered as principal residence. Typically, for those receiving care on a temporary basis, either in a hospital or in a nursing home, one's principal residence continues to be the house or apartment. For those receiving care on a permanent basis in a nursing home, on the other hand, the former home or apartment is generally no longer considered as principal residence. In some countries, such as Norway and the Netherlands, the length of stay is taken into account to determine the level of private contributions towards the costs of residing in a nursing home.

In practice, moving into a nursing home is not akin to the usual accommodation choice within a community, since it is generally triggered by disability status. It is not only a difficult decision at the personal level but it also generally involves significant financial implications, at a time of life when disposable income is relatively lower, but accumulated assets can be high. This raises two main issues discussed below: first, how to calculate a "fair" level of cost sharing for B&L cost; and, second, how can policy makers help mobilise disposable cash (liquidity) to help users pay for the high cost of stay in nursing homes.

Settings cost sharing for board and lodging costs

It can be argued that all individuals should be required to pay at least for a minimum of their food and shelter-related expenses, regardless of the dwelling where they are living. It is also reasonable to expect that accumulated savings will meet some of the basic expenses related to food and shelter, including when a person move to a nursing home. The policy debate with respect to the B&L costs of a nursing home, then, is not on whether residents should pay for it, but how much and what type of expenses.

As board and lodging costs can be subject to significant variations depending on the standard and quality of the accommodation and services, a guiding principle may lie in ensuring that board and lodging cost reflects the market price of similar lodging and food services (Canada Healthcare Association, 2004). A difficulty, however, is that board and lodging costs often include the cost of other services, such as leisure activities provided in the home, or even the assignment of the capital cost associated with building or renovating a nursing home. As a result, board and lodging costs may be more akin to a "residence fee" consisting of the sum of all charges not publicly covered. This "residence fee" can represent a high burden for users and tensions may arise between them and the government on affordability grounds. Nevertheless, while public controls over residential charges and fees can help ensure their affordability – for both residents and governments – they may also have unintended impacts on overall investment decisions in the sector (National Seniors Australia, 2010).

The main question then relates to how public support for the cost of board and lodging could be targeted. A number of countries (see Chapter 7) rely on both income and assets testing to determine the level of public support – and conversely private contributions – for this cost component. The rationale for including assets in the means test is that it better reflects the distribution of economic welfare among individuals, leading to a fairer allocation of public support. This is particularly important for older people who have relatively higher "net-worth" – which is the difference between total assets owned and total debt incurred – than young people (Figure 9.5 in Box 9.1). On the other hand, asset

---

Box 9.1. **Evolution of net-worth across age groups**

For OECD countries included in the Luxembourg Wealth Study,* the median net-worth profiles exhibit a hump-shaped pattern, albeit at different levels of net-worth, in most countries. Typically, the young have less, the middle-aged have the most and the older have less than the middle-aged but more than the young (OECD, 2008a). Net-worth is defined as the difference between total assets owned and total debt incurred.

Figure 9.5. **Median net-worth by age of the household head**

Net-worth, values in 2002 USD

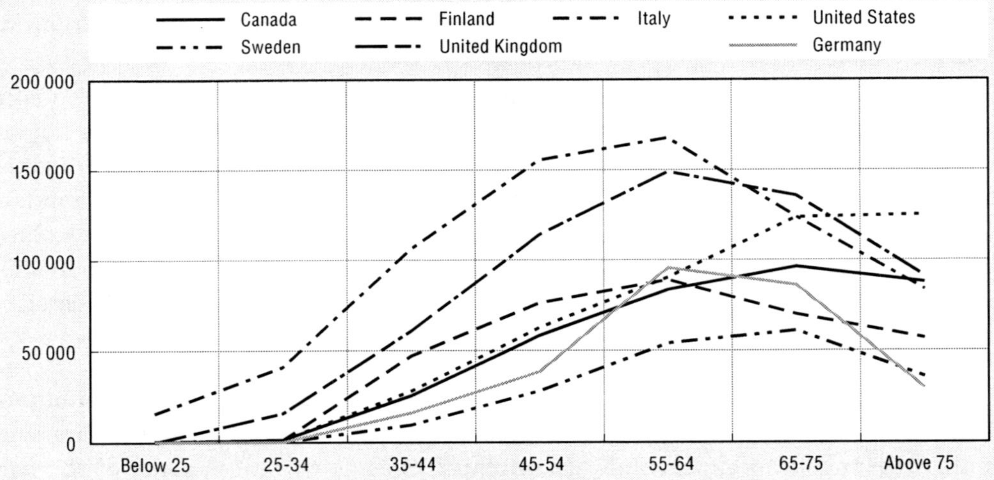

Source: Luxembourg Wealth Study (LWS) Database.

StatLink ⟶ http://dx.doi.org/10.1787/888932401748

Box 9.1. **Evolution of net-worth across age groups** *(cont.)*

As shown in Table 9.1, the majority of household's total assets comprise of non-financial assets, in the form of residential real estate. On average, the principal residence represents between about 45 to 70% of total assets.

Table 9.1. **Household composition of net-worth**
Percentage of total assets

Wealth variable	Canada	Finland	Germany	Italy	Sweden	United Kingdom	United States	United States
	SFS 1999	HWS 1998	SOEP 2002	SHIW 2002	HINK 2002	BHPS 2000	PSID 2001	SCF 2001
Non-financial assets	78	84	87	85	72	83	67	62
Principal residence	64	64	64	68	61	74	52	45
Real estates	13	20	22	17	11	9	14	17
Financial assets	22	16	13	15	28	17	33	38
Deposit accounts	9	10	–	8	11	9	10	10
Bonds	1	0	–	3	2	–	–	4
Stocks	7	6	–	1	6	–	23	15
Mutual funds	5	1	–	3	9	–	–	9
Total assets	100	100	100	100	100	100	100	100
Debt	26	16	23	4	35	21	22	21
of which:								
Home-secured debt	22	11	–	2	–	18	–	18
Net worth	74	84	77	96	65	79	78	79

Note: BHPS = British Household Panel Survey; HINK = Swedish Survey on Household Finances; HWS = Household Wealth Survey; PSID = Panel Study of Income Dynamics; SCF = Survey of Consumer Finances; SFS = Survey of Financial Security; SHIW = Survey on Household, Income and Wealth; SOEP = German Socioeconomic Panel Study.
Source: Luxembourg Wealth Study (LWS) Database.

StatLink ⧉ http://dx.doi.org/10.1787/888932401938

* The LWS is an international project to assemble existing micro-data on household wealth into a coherent database.

testing can be administratively more complex to implement and unduly punish those who carefully managed their budget over their lifetime. Given users – especially older people – attachment to their own home, there is resistance to inclusion of the value of the owned house into the assets test, even if this represents the core of older people net-worth (Table 9.1 in Box 9.1). There is also some evidence[7] suggesting that net-worth and disposable income are highly, albeit not perfectly, correlated. The distribution of disposable income may then represent a reasonable indication of the distribution of economic welfare or the base on which to allocate public support (Jantti *et al.*, 2008).

On balance, there is a rationale for considering a broad definition of income when setting the level of user cost sharing on B&L cost. But there are also arguments for relying solely on income testing. Countries decisions can be informed by considerations about administrative simplicity and the notion of what is regarded as "fair" by society, although no system will be entirely immune from criticism. In addition, public support for board and lodging costs can be heavily influenced by the way support for ensuring access to basic necessities, such as housing, is provided for the population at large. Transparency on how charges are set and on the reasons for charging is important, so that users know that they may incur significant B&L cost, even where there is "universal" coverage for personal care. These considerations also suggest that there is a role for governments to help mobilising resources to pay for what can rapidly become very high cost.

Delivering financial protection against board and lodging costs in institutions

Despite social assistance and other public support, moderate-income people residing in nursing homes are especially vulnerable to impoverishment due to high residential homes' cost. In addition, high nursing-home charges or cost-sharing requirements can force users to sell their homes to pay for care. Home ownership can provide a number of avenues to mobilise additional cash to pay, in full or in part, for expenses associated with LTC, such as board and lodging. These range from obtaining a loan against this cost, to trading it down, renting or selling it. Interesting public and private-sector initiatives can be found across OECD countries.

Some nursing homes are making use of *bonds/equity release* or loan schemes. For instance, in Australia, individuals with assets above a minimum threshold may be asked to pay for an accommodation bond when moving into a low-care home or entering an extra service place (at high or low-care level), where the level of care provided is the same as that provided generally in aged-care homes. An accommodation bond is like an interest-free loan to the aged-care home and by law it must be used by the aged-care home to improve building standards, and the quality and range of aged-care services provided. The aged-care home is allowed to deduct monthly amounts, called "retention amounts", from the bond for up to five years and up to a prescribed maximum amount (Australia Department of Health and Ageing, 2010a). Similar schemes are also used by some retirement homes in the United Kingdom (Collins, 2009). The benefit of those schemes is that they may foster a greater sense of ownership for residents. Nevertheless, they target those with relatively higher income and assets.

The ability to keep their own home and not have to divest it in order to pay for LTC is a sensitive matter for frail senior people. Measures to facilitate the mobilisation of non-financial assets towards some of the private cost associated with LTC, particularly B&L cost in nursing home, are especially relevant to people immediately above asset-testing threshold for public support.

Given the administrative complexity in valuing the stream of income stemming from an asset owned, especially with respect to non-financial assets such as a principal or secondary residence, asset testing typically takes the form of an asset cut-offs, which applies to the total value of assets owned at a given point in time. Typically, if an individual's total value of assets exceeds the given asset cut-off, s/he is not eligible for public support. For seniors having to move into a nursing home, the use of asset cut-offs to allocate public support can have important repercussion on their ability to keep their home. For instance, the inclusion of the principal residence[8] in a means-test may prompt a care-home resident to dispose of it to realise the property's capital and allow them to finance their care-home charges (Gheera, 2010).

While *private reverse-mortgage schemes* (see Chapter 8) may offer an avenue to mobilise cash to pay for care, these can be fairly complicated and expensive and not provide the necessary flexibility to keep one's home after moving into a nursing home. This is because private providers generally require the loan to be paid back once both spouses have moved out of the home for a given period of time. To date, such schemes have met with limited success.

Rather, governments in some OECD countries have set in place *public measures to defer payment* of nursing-home costs. These can provide greater flexibility to dependent individuals and their survivors to determine the composition of inheritances, which may include a dependent's home, while providing a means to meet immediate needs. For example, under the Irish Fair Deal Scheme introduced in October 2009, residents receiving care in a nursing home pay 5% of the value of any assets per annum in user fees. The value of the principal residence is included in the financial assessment, but only for three years. With respect to non-financial assets, such as land and property, the 5% contribution can be deferred to the time of residents' death. This provides individuals with the flexibility of not selling assets, such as their home, during their lifetime, in order to pay for their care. During the duration of the loan, preferential interest charges, equivalent to the consumer price index, apply. Since its introduction, about 15% of new nursing-home residents have taken advantage of this option (O'Regan, 2010).

In the United Kingdom, eligibility for public support for the cost of residing in a nursing home is subject to an asset test, which can take into account the value of users' principal place of residence (unless a partner or child still lives in the house). For those individuals who would meet the asset test if they did not own their home, some local councils provide a scheme that allows them not to sell the home immediately, and to move all or part of the nursing-home fees through a deferred-payment agreement. No interest generally applies on deferred payments over the period of the agreement and until a given number of days after the death of the resident. At that point, the deferred amount must be reimbursed or the residence sold. The New Zealand government also provide for interest-free Residential Care Loan to assist those not eligible to a residential care subsidy because of the value of their own home, but with limited cash or other assets, to pay for their care (New Zealand Ministry of Health, 2009). Similarly, in US Medicaid system, the value of a principal place of residence is generally excluded from the asset test, but can be subject to an estate recovery after the death of the resident, equivalent to the amount of support provided by Medicaid.[9] In essence, this is equivalent to a deferred payment scheme.

Deferral schemes have the virtue of permitting LTC users to keep their home, even if they have to move into a nursing home, although they can still raise considerations as to their impact on a dependent's inheritance to their survivors. Depending on the size of the deferred amount, the repayment or the recovery from users' estate after death can be perceived by survivors as a punitive inheritance tax targeted to the unfortunate few who required public support for paying for expenses associated with long-term care. However, it can be argued that, once a principal residence is no longer needed by the recipient, the recipient's spouse or a child, its equity should be used to cover some or all of expenses associated with LTC, such as board and lodging costs (US Department of Health and Human Services, 2005).

Private-sector initiatives, such as the combination of life and LTC insurance policies, can provide individuals with the opportunity of deferring (for some indefinitely) the decision of having to sell their home in order to receive the care they need. Typically, such hybrid policy provides for cash advances from the death benefit in the event that the policy holder requires long-term care for an extended period of time. For elderly dependents, this feature provides a way to mobilise additional liquidity thereby enhancing their flexibility to decide the type of assets that they intend to leave to their survivors. To date, these schemes still have limited diffusion, although life insurance is certainly a more diffuse product that LTC insurance in most OECD countries.

Board and lodging costs are high and will very likely remain high in the future. These costs can represent a significant share of the relatively low disposable income of the elderly. Nevertheless, elderly people typically have relatively higher level of assets and a portion of those should be used to help pay for basic necessities such as board and lodging. Most of elderly assets, however, take the form of non-financial assets (e.g., a house), and decision to turn this asset into cash can be more difficult. While some private initiatives, such as the combination of life and LTC insurance, can help mobilise additional liquidity towards the cost associated with LTC, their diffusion remains limited to date. Recent public initiatives, such as the one implemented in Ireland, suggest that governments can play a larger role in facilitating the conversion of non-financial assets into cash for residents receiving care in a nursing home.[10] Akin to public student-loan programmes, such public schemes can be designed to mitigate conversion costs through preferential transaction and interest rates. This type of public intervention could also help foster greater flexibility to dependents in determining the composition of assets that they would like to leave behind while providing a means to meet immediate needs.

9.5. Matching care need with finances: Policies for the future

OECD countries' experiences with matching LTC cost to funding point to public LTC systems being currently financed on a "pay-as-you-go basis". However, as a result of population ageing, public expenditure is expected to grow more rapidly than revenues over the next decades. Especially in the case of age-related spending such as LTC, it is important to build a set of financial policies that are more forward-looking, taking into account the potential impact on future generations.

Public LTC financing systems in OECD countries match cost on a year-by year-basis

With the general exception of countries with a dedicated social-insurance arrangement for long-term care services (e.g., Japan, Korea, Germany, the Netherlands), LTC financing typically represents a subset of a larger spending category such as health and/or social services.[11] In some cases, LTC financing cuts across different levels of governments. Comparing levels of LTC revenue and expenditure is a difficult exercise for countries relying on general revenue to fund LTC, typically requiring a broader fiscal perspective.

Countries use an array of mechanisms to ensure that revenues match the cost of LTC systems. In Japan and Korea, but also in Switzerland and Slovenia, for instance, contributions are generally raised to match expected expenditure of the LTC system.[12] In Japan, the process of matching revenues with expenditure takes place over a three-year cycle, while it takes place on an annual basis in Korea. As in Japan, a portion of the revenue raised is allocated to a financial stability fund, which can be used by municipalities to cover shortfalls arising because of inability to collect the premia or unexpected increases in utilisation. In Germany, while the contribution rate was kept fixed for several years, it was raised in 2009 to match growth in LTC cost.

In a number of countries – such as Belgium, Norway or Ireland – budgets for LTC services are set within larger global-budget envelopes that are set annually. In some cases, specific spending targets may apply to LTC expenditures, for example in France, New Zealand, Portugal and Slovenia. Generally, budgeting controls exist in most OECD countries, although many allow overshooting.

Another mechanism that has been used is to control entitlements. This can take the form of maintaining the value of LTC benefits over time or fixed pre-determined LTC entitlements (*e.g.* Austria, Czech Republic, Switzerland, New Zealand, Poland, Slovenia, Germany until 2007-08). All OECD countries also aim at controlling the demand for LTC care services to a specific target group of individuals, which is generally done through the assessment system.

Last, a number of countries contain LTC cost by exerting direct control on the supply of care services, either through the negotiation of salaries and fees paid to providers (*e.g.,* nursing homes, workers) or by controlling the number of subsidised beds or available workers. For instance, the Australian Government controls the supply of subsidised aged-care places through a provision ratio and determines the rate of residential care subsidy paid to approved providers for each person in their care, based on their assessed care needs. Belgium and other countries control the number of beds in nursing homes. In Japan, the number of LTC workers is indirectly controlled by requiring care workers to pass qualifications exams.

Each mechanism can have unintended impacts, for instance, most countries will face upward limits in their ability to raise revenue over time. Maintaining the value of LTC benefits can put some individuals at a greater risk of facing economic hardship, while controlling for the number of beneficiaries or the quantity of services provided may result in waiting times. This is why most countries currently use a combination of these mechanisms to ensure that LTC revenues are aligned with expenditures.

In line with general government budgeting processes, thus far the focus has been on matching LTC revenues and expenditures on a year-to-year basis. While such an approach is desirable to maintain public accounts in balance, it does not provide information on its potential impact on future generations. While still a relatively low share of GDP, evidence in some countries suggests that LTC cost is already exerting fiscal pressures on public budgets. In Japan, Korea, Germany, the Flemish government in Belgium and Luxembourg, LTC contributions have risen significantly since the introduction of public LTC coverage systems. For instance, contribution rates have about doubled in Germany from 1% in 1995 to 1.95% for people with children and 2.20% for people without children in 2009, while Luxembourg increased in 2007 its contribution rate from 1.0 to 1.4%. In France, central governments have reduced their respective share of LTC financing relative to local governments, while in the Netherlands the provision of IADL services was moved out of the public LTC insurance and devolved to the municipalities. Some administrations are attempting to reduce LTC spending as part of budgetary consolidation in response to the recent economic crisis. For instance, a number of states in the United States are cutting back on medical, rehabilitative, home care or other services needed by low-income people who are elderly or have disabilities, or are significantly increasing the cost of these services (Johnson *et al.*, 2010). Similarly, in New Zealand, some district health boards have been cutting hours of home help.

Promoting a fairer sharing of financing across generations

While ultimately an ethical concept, the notion of intergenerational equity has come to the forefront of policy discussions on LTC financing as a result of the expected reduction in the size of the working-age population compared to the elderly population (see Chapter 2 on demographic projections). Concerns are often raised with respect to the funding of age-related expenses, such as LTC, by requiring a relatively smaller future generation to pay for a portion of the care of a relatively larger previous generation (that is, on a pay-as-you-go basis). This concern can be examined, in part, using the concept of fiscal sustainability.

Fiscal sustainability is a multi-dimensional concept that incorporates an assessment of solvency, stable economic growth, stable taxes and intergenerational fairness (OECD, 2009). While not acting as target, the concept can help guide future changes to a given set of fiscal policies (i.e., expenditure and revenues) by informing the extent to which it may transfer liabilities to future generations in the long run. For illustrative purposes, if no change were made to the current set of fiscal policies, the gross-debt-to-GDP ratio for the 27 EU Member States would increase by about 80 percentage points and reach about 140% in 2030 (European Commission and the Economic Policy Committee, 2009). Similarly, for the United States, a no-policy-change scenario would result in the debt-to-GDP ratio to increase by about 50 percentage point and exceed 110% of GDP over the period of 2025 and 2040 (US Government Accountability Office, 2009). Those results suggest that the current set of broad fiscal policies is shifting a considerable amount of liabilities to future generations.

While the size of estimated fiscal-sustainability gaps[13] varies significantly across countries, most OECD countries have gaps typically arising as a result of both an unfavourable fiscal starting position and of the projected increase in the cost of ageing (European Commission and the Economic Policy Committee, 2009). For most OECD countries, the recent financial and economic crisis has deteriorated estimated fiscal gaps. In the case of OECD-EU countries, demographic ageing alone accounts for about half of the estimated fiscal gap[14] (European Commission and the Economic Policy Committee, 2009). Most of the projected increase in the cost of ageing arises from public pension and health expenditures. Nevertheless, on average, the increase in LTC expenditure is expected to contribute about 25% to the overall projected increase, with contributions above 40% in Sweden, Denmark, Italy, the Netherlands, Finland and Poland.[15]

The important contribution of age-related spending, including LTC, to fiscal sustainability gaps suggests that, in a number of countries it will be important to take a closer look at the way expected future expenditures and revenues are structured. The following section examines potential adjustments to help promote a fairer sharing of LTC financing within and across generations. While not all adjustments will be applicable or relevant to all countries, a menu of possible options is outlined.

Fostering intergenerational equity through pre-funding

One of the strategies that could be adopted to address the fiscal-sustainability gap includes the introduction of pre-funding, which essentially means building up assets to fund future ageing-related cost pressures, such as LTC (OECD, 2008a). There are a number of benefits associated with pre-funding, such as mitigating sudden increases in contribution and/or tax rates (also referred to as "tax-smoothing") in order to finance a stable set of benefits or services over time, as well as mitigating the risk of shifting obligations to future generations in the form of higher taxes or debt. The introduction of a pre-funding element would thus seek to extend the budgetary horizon to better take into account foreseeable LTC spending pressures.

In practice, pre-funding requires government to sustain budget surpluses over a given prolonged period of time, which can raise important political-economy issues since any surplus is typically subject to competing claims over funding alternative policy priorities, including tax reductions. Such political economy issues can be overcome by tying pre-funding to specific age-related costs (OECD, 2008a). For instance, some OECD countries (Japan, Switzerland, Sweden, Canada, France Ireland, New-Zealand and Norway) have introduced public pension reserves to pre-fund future public pension's obligations (Yermo, 2008). Although different circumstances apply depending on each country LTC funding system, consideration could be given to establishing similar public reserves with respect to LTC expenditures and to the appropriateness of moving towards partial or full pre-funding.[16]

The notion of pre-funding better applies to countries which finance its LTC expenditure from dedicated revenue sources, either as part of a LTC-coverage systems – such as Germany, Japan, Korea, the Netherlands, Luxembourg, France, and Belgium with respect to the Flemish LTC insurance (Chapter 7). Currently, most of these plans are financed on a "pay-as-you go" basis, with contributions and/or benefits typically adjusted to match revenue over pre-determined short-term cycles of typically one year (three years in Japan). In Germany and Luxembourg, the public LTC insurance scheme is mandated to accumulate a small reserve. In Germany, a small stock of savings of at least 50% of the monthly benefit spending designated in the budget must be withheld (Heinicke and Thomsen, 2010). In Luxembourg, the reserve has to represent at least 10% of annual LTC insurance expenses. In 2008, the reserve was equivalent to about 50% of annual LTC insurance expenses (ministère de la Sécurité sociale, 2009). Elements of pre-funding could also be introduced in countries which finance LTC as part of broad social-security systems, such as Belgium. For instance, in Germany, considerations are being given to financing reforms that would include an element of pre-funding through the introduction of a capital-based branch in the social insurance scheme. The objective would be to better ensure sustainable financing in the area of long-term care and take into account intergenerational equity. One shortcoming with this approach, however, is that unless accumulated funds are earmarked to LTC, it does not guarantee that some of the accumulated assets originally meant for LTC could not be diverted to larger expenditure posts, such as health or pension (Yermo, 2008).

For countries financing LTC from general revenues, such as the Nordic countries, Canada or Australia, the notion of pre-funding is a broader concept more akin to building a favourable fiscal position, generally through lower debt-to-GDP ratio. While savings in the form of public-debt reductions foster future fiscal flexibility, they may end up being used for other future outlays than for ageing-related expenses. Still, for these countries, the benefits associated with better taking into account future expected budgetary fiscal positions remain.

An outstanding question concerns what desirable degree of pre-funded for financing LTC – that is whether or not there could be full pre-funding in LTC insurance. The experience with premium setting in private LTC insurance can be of interest in this respect. As indicated in Chapter 8, in principle, private LTC coverage is fully funded as premium setting involves the establishment of reserves. Private LTC insurance is a lifelong contract over which the insurance provider guarantees a premium rate schedule. Typically, given a subscriber's age, gender or previous health conditions, the premium is set to cover future expected LTC benefit pay-outs, taking into account the income generated from accumulated premia (Riedel, 2003). In Germany, private LTC insurers have established an ageing reserve ("Alterungsrückstellung") for insurees to pay for the expected growth in LTC benefits due to ageing. Similar reserves, or "provisions constituées", are accumulated by France's assurance providers. In 2009, a total of EUR 2.6 billion (below 10% of France's public LTC spending) had been accumulated in reserves by French LTC insurance providers (FFSA, 2010). One lesson learned from the American LTC insurance industry, however, is that trends in the onset of dependency, the costs of providing a unit of care or the projected returns from invested reserves are all subject to high uncertainty. This can result in important year-to-year variations in premiums, with implications for the ability to fully fund a private LTC insurance scheme.

Under a public system, the move to a full-funding approach would not only be inappropriate due to uncertainty about the future need for LTC, but also be challenging to implement. It would raise fairness considerations in the way past unfunded LTC benefits of the current older segment of the population would be paid for. Potential ways to pay for past unfunded LTC benefits can range from a drastic increase in the level of contributions of the older segment of the population, which most would not be able to afford, to significantly reduce the level of LTC benefits provided to the older segment of the population in line with their level of contributions paid over their lives, or to require younger contributors to pay higher contributions to cover for both their and older people LTC benefits. Rather, the establishment of pre-funding could primarily aim at stabilising and/or minimising LTC contributions over time instead of ensuring the full-funding of the scheme (Office of the Chief Actuary, 2007). This could be achieved through partial pre-funding.

Under a partially funded LTC scheme, individual's LTC contributions would cover a portion of their expected future LTC benefits. Contributions and investment earnings would partially fund the scheme (Office of the Chief Actuary, 2007). One of the main advantages relative to full-funding is that it would be less sensitive to changes in the projected rate of dependency, the costs of LTC or the earnings from investment of reserve and thereby more conducive to stabilising contribution rates in the long run (Plamondon and Latulippe, 2008). The level of partial-funding depends on a number of variables, including the country's objectives in setting the level at which contribution/taxation rates should stabilise at as well as its age structure.

While the introduction of an element of partial pre-funding remains desirable to foster intergenerational fairness and stabilise contributions/tax rates within a public LTC scheme, its introduction may still be politically difficult because it would require individuals to pay an additional contribution/tax over the initial years of the financing scheme (e.g., 15 to 25 years).[17] To mitigate such concerns, the required increase in contribution/tax effort could be phased-in over a given period of time. Alternatively, other adjustments to the LTC financing model could be considered.

Who should pay?

Across OECD countries, the size of older cohorts will generally be larger than younger cohorts. This inverted demographic-pyramid structure challenges financing models primarily relying on the working-age population to support both the young and the old. As societies age, an increasing share of total disposable income will be in the hands of an older segment of the population (Figure 9.6),[18] mainly in the form of pension and capital income (Figure 9.7).[19] These demographic and economic trends suggest that the sustainability of LTC financing models could be fostered by either requiring LTC financing from more generations and/or through tax broadening.

The benefits of pooling the risk associated with LTC over as large a population as possible are well documented. But the inverted demographic pyramid can involve

Figure 9.6. **Increasing share of income in the hands of the older segment of the population**

Population aged 51 years and over

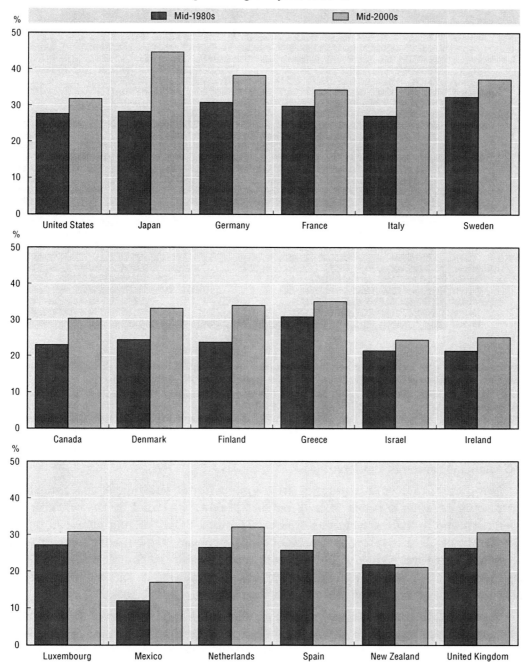

Source: OECD Secretariat calculations based on the *OECD Income Distribution and Poverty Database* (*www.oecd.org/els/social/inequality*).

StatLink ᘖᗅᔍ *http://dx.doi.org/10.1787/888932401767*

significant cross-subsidisation of this risk from a relatively small younger cohort to a relatively larger older cohort of individuals. Therefore, on inter-generational equity grounds, one way to mitigate this cross subsidisation is to introduce intra-generational pooling (St. John and Chen, 2010) by introducing a contribution starting from a certain age

Figure 9.7. **Elderly people's disposable income mainly consists of pension and capital income**

Percentage share of adjusted disposable income, individuals 65 years and over, mid-2000s

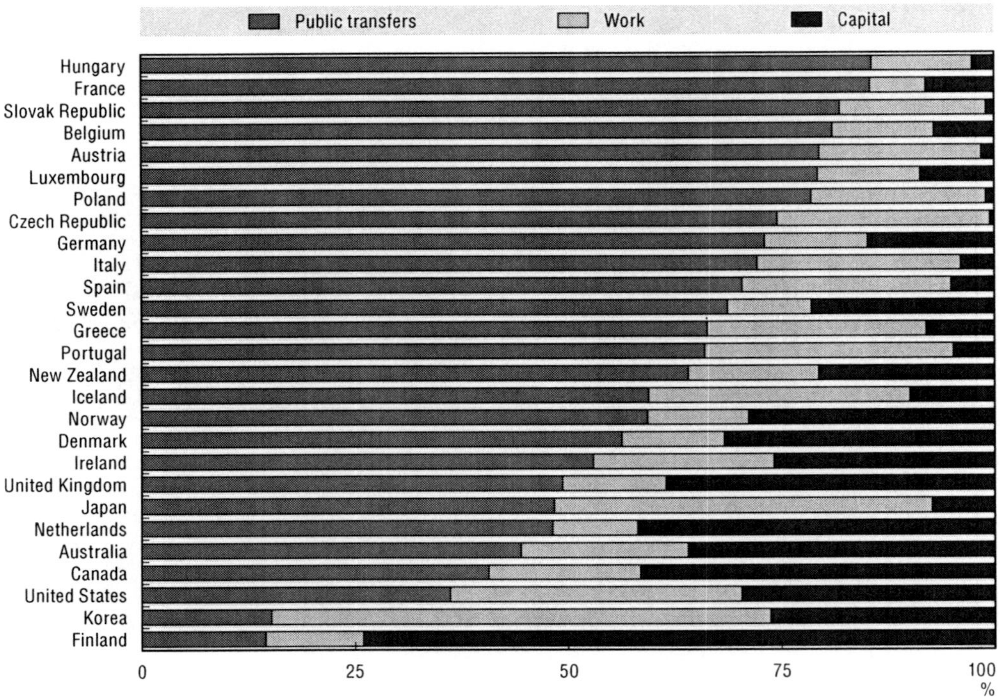

Note: Income from work includes both earnings (employment income) and income from self-employment. Capital income includes private pensions as well as income from the returns on non-pension savings.

Source: OECD Secretariat calculation based on the *OECD Income Distribution and Poverty Database* (*www.oecd.org/els/social/inequality*).

StatLink ⌨ http://dx.doi.org/10.1787/888932401786

of an individual or by requiring all people to contribute to LTC over their entire lifespan (LTC financing from more generations).

Complementary to introducing intra-generational pooling, is the concept of broadening revenue sources to look beyond revenues earned by the working-age population and include the retirees (tax broadening). Solely relying on social payroll contributions to finance LTC runs the risk of overly increasing the tax wedge on workers in the future. Large tax wedge would not only result in shifting the burden onto future generations but could also have negative impacts on employment. This is a main concern particularly for systems which rely on social insurance to cover LTC costs.

Japan's LTC financing system includes an element of intra-generational pooling and broadens revenue sources. In Japan, funding sources for the LTC insurance system are mixed. Of the overall budget, 10% is financed through user co-payments. The remaining 90% is equally shared between taxes (of which 25% from the central government and 12.5% each from prefectures and municipalities), and premia levied on the over 40 population. Setting aside cost sharing, 20% of the total LTC cost is covered from premia collected by the elderly and 30% from those aged 40-65.[20] Premia collected from retired people are income-related and those for individuals aged 40-65 are based on wages. Germany is also an example of extending LTC financing over more generations. Since 2004-05, pensioners have been required to pay the contribution entirely from their disposable income and no longer receive a contribution subsidy from the pension funds (Arntz et al., 2007).

Other OECD countries complement social payroll contributions with alternative sources of revenues either to specifically finance LTC insurance expenditures or more broadly to finance social security systems as a whole. In the Netherlands, while premia are laid only on the working-age population, LTC insurance is financed partly from general taxation. This share accounted for a fourth of the total budget of the Dutch AWBZ in 2008 (Schut and van de Berg, 2010). Similarly, in Belgium, the social security system is no longer solely financed through social payroll contributions and is partly financed through global budgets.[21] The financing of the Flemish long-term care insurance in Belgium provides for an alternative broad financing model. Of the overall budget, half is financed by a specific contribution paid by every adult resident[22] and the rest is financed by general taxes. LTC funding in France also comes from a mix of different revenue sources, most notably about two-thirds of the cash-for-care allowance (Allocation personnalisée d'autonomie) is generally financed from local property taxes.

In the case of LTC systems financed from general revenues, the same considerations apply, but more broadly. Tax broadening or adjustments to the composition of taxes can provide a way to extend financing of LTC over more generations, while maintaining the benefits associated with risk pooling. For example, this could be achieved by shifting the composition of tax revenues from taxing wages and employment to taxing general consumption (e.g., value-added taxes), recognising the inherent distributional impacts of such a shift.

Lastly, it could be argued that one of the central social functions of the family involves intergenerational transfers of time and resources (Osberg, 1997). For instance, as shown in Chapter 3, children represent a main source of family care to frail elderly. For parents, children provide a broad network of support, ranging from emotional to financial help, thereby potentially delaying a move into more expensive care setting such as a nursing home.

In Germany, the presence of children affects individuals' level of contribution to the public LTC system. Following a decision from Federal Constitutional Court, an additional premium of 0.25 percentage points has been required from childless people since 2005. In 2009, the level of contribution paid by people without children was equivalent to 2.20 percentage points compared to 1.95 for people with children. The rationale for the additional premium is that childless people are expected to receive higher benefits from the social LTC insurance relative to people with children (Heinicke and Thomsen, 2010). This situation may arise because of the higher likelihood of dependent people with children to opt for cash instead of in-kind benefit. In Germany, LTC insurance cash benefits are set at a lower level than in-kind benefits.

Similarly, different generations can also share income within the family. In some OECD countries, social-assistance systems include an obligation for children to contribute towards their parent's expenses associated with long-term care, such as board and lodging. This obligation is often referred to as the concept of "filial obligation". This is the case for instance of Germany, Portugal and France[23] (Casey, 2010). Under such system, the income and assets of a dependent individual's children are taken into account to determine the level of public support.

These provisions recognise the role and duties of family carers. However, the notion of family responsibility varies widely across countries and similar requirements may be regarded as unfair by childless households, or as impinging upon bequests of adult children. A simple and effective way to recognise the support of family carers is then by supporting them directly (see Chapter 4).

Considering partnerships and innovative approaches

Some recent initiatives or policy discussions have considered novel approaches to finance LTC, such as through forms of public-private partnerships, and automatic enrolment schemes.

Ideas of partnerships between the public and private sector have shown appeal in a few OECD countries. Public-private partnerships can mean different things depending on who are the "partners" of the public sector. For instance, as part of discussions currently held in France, considerations range from encouraging the take-up of voluntary private LTC to serve as a complement to the existing public LTC pillar, to moving towards compulsory private LTC insurance that would eventually replace the existing public scheme. At the time of writing, there is still uncertainty regarding how such public-private partnerships could be worked out in practice. Among the ideas proposed are introducing tax incentives to encourage voluntary private LTC insurance take-up, a targeted subsidy to compensate for the cost of compulsory private LTC insurance or encouraging combinations of private insurance and reverse mortgages (Le Bihan and Martin, 2010; Commission des Affaires Sociales, 2010).

In the United States, public-private partnerships have met with limited success, although the partnership in the United States applies to the co-ordination of private voluntary LTC coverage with means-tested public coverage (Chapter 8). Other ideas that have been floated for example in the United Kingdom regard partnerships between the public system and individual users, where public payers would match individuals' payments (Wanless, 2007) or the introduction of a mandatory social insurance system in which people would pay a single premium at a given age, for instance at age 65 (Barr, 2010). While the idea of partnership is attractive, making it work in practice can be challenging, and the jury regarding how best to structure partnerships is still out.

An interesting example of recent financing innovations from the United States is the so-called CLASS Act. The recently enacted federal health care reform legislation in the United States (the Affordable Health Care Act) creates a privately financed (there are no public subsidies), publicly provided, and voluntary insurance scheme that would pay a cash benefit to eligible dependent individuals to pay for long-term care services and support. Many of the specific features of the CLASS Act remain to be finalised and will be designated by 1 October 2012 (see Box 9.2).

The CLASS Act borrows some financing features from the private LTC insurance but the insurer is the government, enrolment is open for eligible individuals, and not subject to underwriting based on pre-existing conditions. Coverage – which is targeted to working-age individuals – is automatic for employees whose employers opt into the programme, but individuals have the option of opting out. Premia are generally set according to enrollees' age, regardless of income and health status, and include an element of pre-funding through the accumulation of reserves.

Automatic enrolment with the option of opting out – a feature that is akin to the Singapore Eldershield programme (see Chapter 8) – enables the government to signal the importance of individual planning for the financial risk associated with long-term care, while maintaining an element of individual responsibility. Relative to purely voluntary risk-sharing arrangements, automatic enrolment has the potential to provide for broader

Box 9.2. **United States: The Community Living Assistance Services and Supports (CLASS) Act**

The Affordable Health Care for America Act that was signed into law by President Obama in March 2010 includes the so-called Community Living Assistance Services and Supports (CLASS) Act. The CLASS Act is a national voluntary insurance plan that will be managed by the Department of Health and Human Services and solely financed through monthly premia paid by voluntary payroll deductions or payments made directly from individuals. The main goals of the Act are: i) to help dependent individuals maintain their personal and financial independence in order to live in the community; ii) to establish an infrastructure that will help address the needs for community living assistance services and support; iii) to alleviate burdens of family carers; and iv) to address the institutional bias by providing cash rather than in-kind benefits.

Eligible participants

Eligible participants in CLASS must be at least 18 years of age and earn a minimum level of earnings. For workers whose employers choose to participate in the programme, enrolment would be automatic through payroll deductions. For the self-employed, those with more than one employer or those whose employer does not elect to participate, an alternative enrolment procedure will be established. For the purposes of the opting-out option, annual enrolment and disenrolment period will be set. For those meeting the eligibility criteria, no underwriting test will apply.

Premia

Premia will vary by age, so that younger enrolees will pay lower premia than those choosing to enrol at older ages, but will not vary by medical condition, income or other factors. However, people whose income does not exceed the poverty line and working students younger than age 22 years old will pay a maximum of USD 5 per month (indexed over time).

At the age of entry, premia are set to remain level, unless, an increase in premium is necessary to ensure the solvency of the plan (calculated over a 75-year horizon). In this event, only the premia of those who have attained age 65 that have paid premia for at least 20 years and are not actively employed will not be subject to the increase. Premia will also increase if there is a lapse in payment of more than three months and the person wishes to reenrol. Premium payments will be placed in a "Life Independence Account" on behalf of each beneficiary.

Eligible beneficiaries

To receive benefits, enrolees will have to maintain enrolment in the programme by paying their monthly premia. In addition, before being eligible to benefits, premia must be paid for at least five years. Insurees will also be required to have worked for at least three years during the first five years of their enrolment into the plan. A person stopping to work after having met the three-year work requirement would still be enrolled in the scheme, as long as he or she continues to pay premia. The latter criteria implicitly exclude retired population. Those who did not pay premia for more than three months will need to pay premia for at least 24 consecutive months in order to be eligible again to benefits.

Eligibility will be based on care need. Eligible beneficiaries are those with a functional limitation expected to last for at least 90 continuous days and certified by a licensed health care practitioner. The limitation could be the inability to perform a minimum number (either two or three) of activities of daily living (ADL) without substantial assistance, or a substantial cognitive impairment requiring substantial supervision to protect the individual from threats to health and safety. Participants must continue paying premia to continue receiving benefits.

Box 9.2. **United States: The Community Living Assistance Services and Supports (CLASS) Act** (cont.)

Benefits

Eligible individuals will receive a cash benefit according to the degree of disability or impairment. The average level of benefits will be at least USD 50 a day. Between two to six benefit amounts could be designated. The benefit amount will be indexed to general price increases. There is no time limit on the number of years a participant can receive benefits.

The benefit will be put in a debit account available for withdrawals. It will be possible to use the benefit in a flexible manner, for example to purchase non-medical services and supports that the beneficiary needs to maintain his or her independence at home or in another residential setting of their choice (*e.g.*, nursing home or assisted living). Support and services can include home modification, assistive technology, accessible transportation, home help, home-maker services, respite care or personal-assistance services. Any surplus left at the end of the month can be rolled over to the next month, but not from year to year.

Tax treatment of the scheme

Premia and benefits of the programme will be treated in the same manner as tax qualified long-term care insurance, making the premia deductible, while, as for medical expenses, the benefits will generally be non-taxable.

Combination with other LTC programmes

The CLASS Act would operate as a complement to Medicaid and Medicare, without changing their eligibility rules. When a dependent individual will be eligible to benefits under both the CLASS and Medicaid, CLASS benefits could be used to reduce the costs of Medicaid. Specifically, 95% of the CLASS Act benefit could be used to cover the cost of a Medicaid beneficiary admitted to an LTC institution, with the beneficiary retaining 5% of the CLASS benefit. Those who receive home and community-based services may retain 50% of their CLASS benefits, which could pay for additional services and supports.

CLASS will help reduce the risk of (high) out-of-pocket payments and it could would reduce Medicaid payouts, while at the same time provide a new means for people to pay non-medical expenses and remain independent in their homes.

Source: Patient Protection and Affordable Care Act (enrolled as agreed to or passed by both House and Senate), Section 3201 to Section 3210. Richards and Walker (2010); O'Malley Watts (2009); Wiener *et al.* (2010).

---

access to private LTC coverage at a lower price by pooling risks across a broad group because of inertia. It continues, however, to be vulnerable to adverse selection (low-risk insurees choosing to opt out of the insurance pool) which could put upward pressures on premia (or create downward pressures on benefits) in order to maintain the viability of the plan.

Age-related premium structures can encourage early subscription into the plan by requiring late-comers to pay more. They also discourage participants from gaming the system through enrolment and disenrolment because individuals wishing to re-enrol into the plan would face higher premia, reflecting his/her age of re-entry. However, under age-related premia, low and moderate income individuals are generally required to allocate a relatively larger portion of their disposable income on premia in order to maintain coverage.

Evidence from the Eldershield programme with automatic enrolment (Chapter 8) is promising, but the voluntary nature of CLASS creates significant uncertainty with respect to the participation rate as well as the composition of the participants in the pool, especially over the initial years. Akin to private LTC insurance, the risk is that certain assumptions over enrolment rates might not materialise, translating into significant changes in premium levels.

Despite its limits, the CLASS Act has the potential to broaden access to some basic LTC protection, in a fiscally sustainable manner (the Act requires actuarial soundness for at least 75 years) while encouraging intergenerational equity. While benefits may not be sufficient to cover all the cost associated with dependency, such as board and lodging cost, the CLASS benefit will provide for a basic level of protection to all qualifying participants. By implicitly excluding the current cohort of retirees, CLASS is also in a position to avoid paying significant benefits early into its existence, therefore providing for a window of opportunity to accrue experience over the management of the plan.

9.6. Conclusions

This chapter discussed policies to address the challenge of providing fair protection against the financial risk associated with LTC in a fiscally sustainable manner. As most elderly dependents with relatively high care need likely face catastrophic LTC expenses, fair protection involves an element of universality of eligibility to care, which can be seen as a basic protection floor against LTC risk that potentially all citizens could face. Still, within the confines of a universal protection, important "arbitrages" remain with respect to targeting eligibility, a specific basket of services or the extent of cost sharing.

There is a rationale for targeting protection to the older segment of the population, those with lower ability to pay and those facing severe dependencies. Targeting the basket of services is a difficult exercise because it needs to address users' legitimate requests for users' choice, with appropriateness and flexibility over time. A special challenge will be posed by the growing number of users with cognitive dependencies, who may need a different package of services, relative to recipients with physical limitations, in order to support independent living. Assessment systems typically based on inability to perform activities of daily living may not adequately identify those with cognitive limitations. To address these difficult arbitrages in setting the basket of services and to enhance user choice, including between a formal and a family carer, a number of countries are providing services in the form of cash benefits.

Different considerations apply to board and lodging, a significant element of cost, which, strictly speaking, is not a "care" expense. For frail and disabled people living in nursing homes, expenses associated with board and lodging can be very high and rapidly force users to deplete all their accumulated income and assets. These costs are often not covered by public LTC coverage, or are subject to significant cost sharing where they are covered. While there is a rationale for the elderly dependents to pay for a share of these expenses, users with low and moderate income but accumulated assets may still find it difficult to turn some of these assets (e.g., a house) into cash in order to pay for such expenses. There is therefore a potential role for governments to facilitate mobilisation of cash to help users pay such cost. While outside the scope of this chapter, housing is a major issue for elderly, especially in a context of elderly preferring to live at home instead of moving in a nursing home (Haberkern, 2011). In fact, the supply of suitable housing for the elderly will be central to the development of future housing policies. This is an area that will deserve closer attention in the future years.

As showed in Chapter 7, the way a public LTC system is financed – through dedicated social contributions or through general taxation, has little implications on the way LTC benefits are ultimately structured. In fact, financing mechanisms generally build on existing institutional arrangements or reflects political considerations in raising additional public revenues. Existing institutional arrangements are also reflected in the division of responsibilities between central and local authorities, and the way these arrangements are set can have important impacts on the provision of public LTC services across a country.

Once a basic LTC protection has been designed, the question becomes how financing can be fiscally sustainable over the long-run. All OECD countries have budgeting mechanisms to align LTC revenues and expenditures, but focus is often short sighted, often going from one year to the next. These systems may also have unintended consequences – such as waiting times – or leave unmet needs. Given the expected increase in age-related spending, a set of forward looking financing policies could include elements of pre-funding, extending payments to more generations and broadening of the revenue sources. A number of countries have made progress in this direction, while an innovative approach recently enacted in the United States involves element of pre-funding and the accumulation of reserves.

As OECD countries age, addressing the trade-off between providing for "fair" basic universal coverage and fiscal sustainability will become more urgent. While the allocation of LTC benefits and its financing are subject to differing views and judgment, convergence towards targeted universalism on the benefit eligibility side and broad collective financing on the revenue side have the potential to strike a reasonable balance between these two competing priorities.

To conclude, this chapter focused on structural aspects of designing an LTC system on the benefit and the financing side. Nevertheless – while not neglecting the importance of policies to support and encourage family carers – the expected growth in demand for more and better care call for greater attention to policies to achieve value for money within formal LTC coverage systems. Chapter 10 provides an overview of different approaches.

Notes

1. Figure 9.1 shows the share of disposable income accounted for by a low-care basket of services (*i.e.*, ten hours a week at the prevailing rate per hour of LTC services), excluding public subsidies.

2. Individuals below 65 years of age with age-related (geriatric) disease are also covered under Korea's universal LTC system.

3. See detailed information on eligibility rules in Chapter 7.

4. Assessment includes a physician's report, which provides some personalised information to complement the computerised assessment.

5. For instance, in 2004-05, average board and lodging costs were estimated at about EUR 10 600 in Belgium, EUR 13 700 in France and EUR 21 000 a year in Luxembourg (Hartmann-Hirsch, 2007). In Belgium, more recent data for 2009 (2nd quarter), points to board and lodging costs being about EUR 14 200 a year (*http://economie.fgov.be*). In Australia, as of July 2010, basic daily fees for residential aged care were set up to about AUD 14 100 a year (Australian Government Department of Health and Ageing, 2010). In Canada, British Columbia, basic client rate is income-related and varies between about CAD 10 750 and CAD 35 200 a year (BC Ministry of Health Services, 2009).

6. See Chapter 7 for details on cost sharing in OECD countries.

7. From the Luxembourg study discussed in Box 9.1.

8. Typically, the value of the principal place of residence is not considered as an eligible asset if the residence is still occupied by a spouse/partner or a child under 16 years of age (*e.g.*, in the United-Kingdom and some states in the United States).

9. Medicaid estate recovery practices vary across US states.

10. As part of its Draft Inquiry Report, the Australian Productivity Commission also recently supported the introduction of a government-backed equity release scheme to cover the costs associated with LTC (Productivity Commission, 2011).

11. In Korea, while the long-term care social insurance covers care services separately, coverage for medical and rehabilitation services remains under Korea's national health insurance system.

12. In 2011, LTC insurance contribution rates will not be subject to an increase.

13. Fiscal-sustainability gap is an estimate of the adjustment needed to a country's primary budgetary position (*i.e.*, revenue minus non-interest expenditure) in order to keep a county's debt level on a sustainable path until some future dates.

14. The sustainability-gap analysis uses the projected changes in age-related expenditure from the European Union 2009 *Ageing Report*. The analysis includes the following spending categories, pensions, health, long-term care, education expenditures as well as unemployment benefits.

15. OECD calculation based on the European *Union Sustainability Report 2009*.

16. Contrary to the pay-as-you go approach, under which younger generations typically pay for the LTC benefits of older generations, full-funding would translate in each generation paying for its own LTC benefits.

17. In Luxembourg, the 2007 increase in the contribution rate from 1 to 1.4% allowed for the building of a reserve, as revenue raised in 2007 and 2008 exceeded expenses incurred by the plan.

18. As shown in Figure 9.6, over the last 20 years, the older segment of the population's share of total disposable income increased in all OECD countries. This reflects both the relatively larger size of this group as well as the relative increase in their level of income compared to the mid-1980s, especially for those aged between 51 and 65 years old.

19. As shown in Figure 9.7, public transfers and capital income, mainly from private pension, represented the bulk of disposable income for those aged 65 and over, in the mid-2000s, with the exception of Japan and Korea where work is an important source of old-age income.

20. These shares are subject to change over time, mainly as a result of changing demographic structure.

21. In Belgium, alternative financing comes from a share of its value-added tax.

22. The contribution is set at a lower amount for persons qualifying for lower co-payments in the compulsory health insurance system.

23. The administration of social assistance falls under the responsibility of the local governments ("Départements"), and the application of the filial obligation (obligation alimentaire) varies among them.

References

Alzheimer-Europe (2009), "Example of Good Practice", accessible at *www.alzheimer-europe.org/ Our-Research/European-Collaboration-on-Dementia/Social-Support-Systems/Examples-of-good-practice*, last updated, 8 October.

Arntz, M. *et al.* (2007), "The German Social Long-term Care Insurance: Structure and Reform Options", *IZA Discussion Paper*, No. 2625, Bonn, February.

Australia Department of Health and Ageing (2010a), "Accommodation Bonds for Residential Aged Care", *Information Sheet*, No. 16, Australian Government, September.

Australia Department of Health and Ageing (2010b), "Schedule of Residence Fees and Charges: From 1 July 2010", Australian Government, July.

Avlund, K. and P. Fromholt (1998), "Instrumental Activities of Daily Living: The Relationships to Self-Rated Memory and Cognitive Performance Among 75-Year-old Men and Women", *Scandinavian Journal of Occupational Therapy*, Vol. 5, No. 2, pp. 83-100.

Barr, N. (2010), "Long-term Care: A Suitable Case for Social Insurance", *Social Policy and Administration*, Vol. 44, No. 4, August, pp. 359-374.

BC Ministry of Health Services (2009), "New Rate Structure to Enhance Patient Care", Backgrounder, Ministry of Health Services, Victoria, 8 October.

Campbell, J. and N. Ikegami (2000), "Long-term Care Insurance Comes to Japan", *Health Affairs*, Vol. 19, No. 3.

Campbell, J., N. Ikegami and M.J. Gibson (2010), "Lessons from Public Long-term Care Insurance in Germany and Japan", *Health Affairs*, Vol. 29, No. 1.

Canada Healthcare Association (2004), "Stitching the Patchwork Quilt Together: Facility-Based Long-term Care within Continuing Care – Realities and Recommendations", Ottawa.

CIHI – Canadian Institute for Health Information (2007), "Public-Sector Expenditures and Utilization of Home Care Services in Canada: Exploring the Data", CIHI, Ottawa.

Casey, H.B. (2010), "Are We All Confucianists? Similarities and Differences between European, East-Asian and American Policies for Care of the Frail Older People", Presentation to the European Centre for Social Welfare Policy and Research, International Seminar Series, Vienna, 23 July.

CIZ Indicatiewijzer (2009), "CIZ Assessment Guide, Explanation of the Policy Rules for Needs Assessment under the Exceptional Medical Expenses Act (AWBZ) 2009", as determined by the Ministry of Health, Welfare and Sport, the Netherlands.

Collins, S. (2009), "Options for Care Funding: What Could Be Done Now?", Joseph Rowntree Foundation, York, March.

Comas-Herrera, A. *et al.* (2010), "The Long Road to Universalism? Recent Developments in the Financing of Long-term Care in England", *Social Policy and Administration*, Vol. 44, No. 4, August.

Commission des Affaires Sociales (2010), "La prise en charge des personnes âgées dépendantes", Rapport d'information présenté par Valérie Rosso-Debord, Députée, Assemblée Nationale, No. 2647, 23 June.

Da Roit, B. and B. Le Bihan (2010), "Similar and Yet So Different: Cash-For-Care in Six European Countries' Long-term Care Policies", *The Milbank Quarterly*, Vol. 88, No. 3, pp. 286-309.

European Commission and the Economic Policy Committee (2009), "Sustainability Report 2009", *European Economy,* No. 9/2009.

Fédération Hospitalière de France (2010), "Hébergement et services à la personne : Comment adapter l'offre aux besoins futurs", Présentation Conférence *Les Échos*, 10 March, Paris.

Finans Departmentet (2009), "Long-term Perspectives for the Norwegian Economy", Ministry of Finance, English summary, March.

FFSA – Fédération Française des Sociétés d'Assurance (2010), "Les contrats d'assurance dépendance en 2009 (aspect quantitatif)", Enquête, April 2010, Paris.

Gheera, M. (2010), *Financing Care Home Charges*, House of Commons Library, England.

Haberkern, K., T. Schmid, F. Neuberger and M. Grignon (2011), "The Role of Elderly As Providers and Recipients of Care", OECD/IFP Project on the "Future of Families to 2030".

Hartmannn-Hirsch, C. (2007), "Une libre circulation restreinte pour les personnes âgées à pension modique", *Population and Emploi*, Vol. 23, February.

Heinicke, K. and L.S. Thomsen (2010), "The Social Long-term Care Insurance in Germany: Origin, Situation, Threats and Perspective", *Discussion Paper*, No. 10-012, Center of Economic Research, 22 February.

Jantti, M. *et al.* (2008), "The Joint Distribution of Household Income and Wealth: Evidence from the Luxembourg Wealth Study", *OECD Social, Employment and Migration Working Papers*, OECD Publishing, Paris.

Johnson, N. *et al.* (2010), "An Update on State Budget Cuts. At least 46 States Have Imposed Cuts that Hurt Vulnerable Residents and the Economy", Center on Budget and Policy Priorities, updated 4 August.

Lafortune, G. *et al.* (2007), "Trends in Severe Disability Among Elderly People: Assessing the Evidence in 12 OECD Countries and the Future Implications", *OECD Health Working Paper*, No. 26, OECD Publishing, Paris.

Le Bihan, B. and C. Martin (2010), "Reforming Long-term Care Policy in France: Private-Public Complementaries", *Social Policy and Administration*, Vol. 44, No. 4, pp. 392-410, August.

Ministère de la Sécurité Sociale (2009), "Rapport général sur la Sécurité sociale au Grand-Duché de Luxembourg", ministère de la Sécurité sociale, Inspection générale de la Sécurité sociale, Luxembourg, November.

Mot, E. (2010), "The Dutch System of Long-term Care", CPB Document, The Hague.

National Seniors Australia (2010), "The Future of Aged Care in Australia", A public policy discussion paper prepared by Access Economics, National Seniors Australia, September.

New Zealand Ministry of Health (2009), "Changes to the Residential Care Loan Policy and Eligibility Criteria", *Fact Sheet*, August.

OECD (2005), *Long-term Care for Older People*, OECD Publishing, Paris.

OECD (2008a), *Growing Unequal? Income Distribution and Poverty in OECD Countries*, OECD Publishing, Paris.

OECD (2008b), *OECD Economic Surveys: Luxembourg*, Vol. 2008/12, OECD Publishing, Paris, June.

OECD (2009), "The Benefits of Long-term Fiscal Projections", *Policy Brief*, OECD Publishing, Paris, October.

Office of the Chief Actuary (2007), "Optimal Funding of the Canada Pension Plan", Actuarial Study, No. 6, Office of the Superintendent of Financial Institutions Canada, Ottawa, April.

O'Malley Watts, M. (2009), "The Community Living Assistance Services and Supports (CLASS) Act", Focus on Health Reform, Henry J. Kaiser Family Foundation, accessible at *www.kff.org/healthreform/7996.cfm*.

O'Regan, E. (2010), "Most Patients Reject State's Nursing Home Care-Cost Offer", *The Independent*, Tuesday 24 August.

Osberg, L. (1997), "Meaning and Measurement in Intergenerational Equity", Department of Economics, Dalhousie University, 14 May.

Plamondon, P. and D. Latulippe (2008), "Optimal Funding of Pension Schemes", *Technical Report*, No. 16, Association internationale de la Sécurité sociale (AISS), Genève.

Productivity Commission (2011), "Caring for Older Australians", *Draft Inquiry Report*, Chapter 7, Canberra.

Richards, R. and L. Walker (2010), "Understand the New Community Living Assistance Services and Supports (CLASS) Program", *Fact Sheet*, No. 183, AARP Public Institute, Washington.

Riedel, H. (2003), "Private Compulsary Long-term Care Insurance in Germany", The International Association for the Study of Insurance Economics, Cologne.

Ros, W., A. Van der Zalm, J. Eijlders and G. Schrijvers (2010), "How Is the Need for Care and its Allocation Determined in Europe?", UMC Utrecht (on behalf of the CIZ).

Schut, T.F. and B. van de Berg (2010), "Sustainability of Comprehensive Universal Long-term Care Insurance in the Netherlands", *Social Policy and Administration*, Vol. 44, No. 4, pp. 411-435.

St John, S. and Yung-Ping Chen (2010), "Aging of the Elderly: An Intragenerational Funding Approach to Long-term Care", *The Counter Ageing Society*, No. 15, European Papers on the New Welfare, October.

US Department of Health and Human Services (2005), "Medicaid Treatment of the Home: Determining Eligibility and Repayment for Long-term Care", Medicaid Eligibility for Long-term Care Benefits Policy Brief #2, Office of Assistant Secretary for Policy and Evaluation, April.

US Government Accountability Office (2009), "The Nation's Long-term Fiscal Outlook. March 2009 Update", Government Accountability Office.

Wanless, D. (2006), "Securing Good Care for Older People – Taking a Long-term View", The King's Fund, London.

Wiener, M.J. *et al.* (1990), "Measuring the Activities of Daily Living: Comparisons Across National Surveys", US Department of Health and Human Services.

Yermo, J. (2008), "Governance and Investment of Public Pension Reserve Funds in Selected OECD Countries", *OECD Working Papers on Insurance and Private Pensions*, No. 15, OECD Publishing, Paris.

Chapter 10

Can We Get Better Value for Money in Long-term Care?

It is well established that ageing populations will lead to increases in the demand for services in the years to come, thereby putting upward pressure on total expenditure on formal long-term care (LTC) systems in a context where large spending items such as pensions and health are also expected to grow. This may well create pressure on governments to ensure that spending in the sector is well worth the expenditure, or, in other words, that systems of long-term care deliver value for money. A review of OECD countries' experiences reveals different policies aimed at improving the efficiency of LTC systems and the "interface" between LTC and health care. However, it is evident that this is an area for further work: often, no definite conclusions can be drawn.

10.1. What is value for money in long-term care?

In theory, two different concepts of value for money would be relevant for long-term care (LTC) services. One relates to cost efficiency, which implies maximising output for a given amount of resources, and the other relates to cost-effectiveness or value for money, which implies maximising outcomes for a given amount of resources. However, in the social-service sector, the concept of value for money does not come easy. LTC services present complexities which make it difficult to evaluate efficiency – for example, what concept of efficiency to use, how to measure outcomes, or what elements of cost should be included. As a matter of fact, many OECD countries do not have at present operational concepts, measures or indications of efficiency in LTC systems. This chapter does not seek, therefore, to provide a quantitative assessment of efficiency in long-term care. Rather, it offers an overview of what OECD countries are doing under the broad umbrella of policies to improve efficiency in long-term care (Table 10.1). Often, there is no evaluation of impact of such policies, making it difficult to draw conclusions about how to improve value in long-term care.

The next section of this chapter concerns measures within LTC schemes, such as those seeking to balance institutional and home care, payment mechanisms, the impact of competition across providers in LTC, and productivity improvements linked to the use of technology in long-term care. The third part considers measures aimed at improving efficiency at the "interface" between LTC and health care. This section considers aspects such as the promotion of healthy ageing, co-ordination and integration between health care and LTC, and the incentives to avoid the use of acute care services for LTC needs. The last section of this chapter discusses challenges related to the governance of LTC systems and ways to improve administrative efficiency. Where it exists, the chapter points to evidence on the strengths and weaknesses of different measures.

10.2. Towards more efficient delivery of long-term care

Important measures to improve efficiency in long-term care services and systems have focused on three main areas: *i)* the choice of settings; *ii)* the incentives facing providers (payment mechanisms and incentives for provider competition); and *iii)* the impact of technology on productivity.

Encouraging home care

Over the past couple of decades, nearly all OECD countries have been encouraging "ageing in place" policies. The trend reflects the preference of older people to receive care at home. Institutional care can be associated with psychological and social costs for seniors. Home care, on the other hand, is believed to increase patients' satisfaction and their quality of life. Still, waiting times for admission to nursing homes can be quite long, for instance 7-8 weeks in the Netherlands and up to 2-3 years in Japan (Caris-Verhallen and Kerkstra, 2000; Byrne *et al.*, 2008; OECD, 2005). The trend also reflects policies to limit the cost of institutional care which causes a high financial burden on families and represents a significant cost for public payers. In 2008, institutional care accounted for over 60% of total LTC costs, while on average less than three every ten LTC users received care in institutions, across OECD countries. This is partly because of the lower labour and capital cost of home care, and partly due to the higher severity of institutionalised recipients.

Policies to encourage home care involve a mix of demand and supply-side interventions (see Table 10.2):

- direct expansion of home-care supply;
- regulatory measures;
- financial incentives.

Table 10.1. **Policies to improve value for money in long-term care in OECD countries: An overview**

	Encouraging home care	Ensuring care co-ordination and continuity of care	Discouraging use of acute care for LTC	Changing payment incentives for providers	Encouraging independent living and healthy ageing	Improving administrative/ institutional efficiency
Australia	No	√	√	No	No	No
Austria	√	No	No	No	No	No
Belgium	√	√		No	No	No
Canada	n.a.	√	√	No	√	No
Czech Republic	√			No	No	No
Denmark	n.a.				No	No
Estonia	√				No	No
Finland	√	√	No	No	√	No
France	√					
Germany	√		√			
Hungary	√	√	√	√	No	√
Ireland	√		√	√	No	No
Japan	√	√		√	√	√
Korea	√	√	No	√	√	No
Luxembourg	√	No	No	No	No	No
Mexico	√	No	No	No	√	No
Netherlands	√		√	No	No	No
New Zealand	√		No	No	√	No
Norway			√	No	No	No
Poland	√	√	√	No	√	No
Portugal				No	No	No
Slovak Republic	√	√		No	No	No
Slovenia	No	√	No	No	No	No
Spain	√			No	No	No
Sweden	√	√	√	√	√	√
Switzerland	√			No	No	No
United Kingdom	√	√	√	No	√	No

n.a.: not available.

Source: OECD 2009-10 Questionnaire on Long-term Care Workforce and Financing.

Direct expansion of home-care supply

Several countries have expanded community-based services, as well as home-care coverage and support, to enable LTC users to continue living in their own homes (*e.g.* Canada, Ireland, New Zealand, Sweden and Poland). The Japanese government passed in 2006 a reform emphasising comprehensive community support, organised by community members, LTC workers and volunteers, to enable seniors to continue living in a familiar environment. This has encouraged the development of alternative forms of home care, with professionals from residential homes visiting people at home. A similar programme also exists in Belgium. Other government strategies involve training and supporting informal caregivers to reduce demand for institutionalisation (*e.g.,* Mexico, New Zealand, Finland and the Slovak Republic).

Regulatory measures

Incentives related to regulations or institutional structures can take different forms. Finland[1] and the Czech Republic, for example, have developed guidelines to promote home care and enforce admission of those with high-care need only. Similarly, Hungary has restricted budgets and imposed stricter criteria for admission to nursing homes. In Sweden, the Act on Support and Service for Persons with Certain Functional Impairments (1995) moved a large number of people with functional impairments from hospitals into their own flats in the municipalities.

In the United Kingdom, the 2009 report *Use of Resources in Adult Social Carer* provided examples of the savings that could be achieved by promoting a better balance between institutional and home or community-based care. These included the development of new approaches to supported housing. The 2010 draft social care outcomes framework suggests a way for local authorities to benchmark their progress, including indicators on the proportion spent on residential care, and the proportion of older people who are still at home 91 days after discharge from hospital (UK Department of Health, 2010).

Another example is the 2007 Austrian Home Care Law. To avoid the proliferation of illegal or undeclared work, the Law established a legal basis for 24h home-care by legally qualified workers. Family members were also allowed to provide home care under formal arrangements.

Financial incentives

Financial incentives directed either at users or providers are increasingly used in OECD countries to enhance user choice and stimulate a rebalancing towards home and community-based care.

In the United States, where Medicaid mandatory benefits target institutional care, the 2010 Affordable Care Act (ACA) provides new incentives for the expansion of home and community-based LTC services (Reinhard *et al.*, 2010). The Home and Community-Based Services (HCBS) Plan Option provides states with flexibility to expand home and community-based services' benefits. Under the "Community First Choice Option", states providing supports and services for home carers can receive higher federal funding. States also receive additional funding for each Medicaid beneficiary transitioned from an institution to the community under the so-called "Money Follows the Person" initiative. Finally, the "State Balancing Incentive Program" incentivises states to increase the proportion of Medicaid spending on home and community care, through increased federal financial aid (Silow-Carroll *et al.*, 2010).

In several OECD countries, cash benefits have been increasingly used to promote home living for frail and dependent people. Cash benefits, including payments and individual budgets, help LTC recipients organise home care and promote choice (*e.g.*, Austria, the Netherlands, Sweden and the United Kingdom).

Table 10.2. Policies to promote home care in OECD countries

	Policies or incentives to encourage home care	Notes
Australia	N	
Austria	Y	The long-term care allowance should improve the opportunity for LTC patients to remain in their customary surroundings.
Belgium	Y	Policies include diversification, specification and innovation of home care services, for example, by broadening the eligibility criteria for admission to day-care centers, providing co-ordinated and personalised care for the patient, support of informal caregivers and financial incentives for palliative home care.
Canada	Y	The agreement between the federal and provincial governments 10-Year Plan to Strengthen Health Care in Canada states that governments are committed to provide first dollar coverage for various home-care services, based on a needs' assessment.
Czech Republic	Y	Residential facilities are motivated to accept preferably people with higher need for care and support and thus entitled to higher care allowance.
Finland	Y	Guidelines on services for older people are currently provided in many social and health care policy documents, all including the following key objectives: maintaining the functional capacity of older people, supporting living at home and prioritising non-institutional services.
France	Y	Home-care services are promoted by offering tax deductions. There are also benefits given to parents who stop working to take care of a disabled child.
Germany	Y	The 2008 Care Reform (Elften Buches Sozialgesetzbuch) further enforced the principle of "outpatient over inpatient" care.
Hungary	Y	Institutional care is restricted by budgetary measures and with stricter criteria of admission.
Ireland	Y	Expansion of community-based services for older people, in 2006 and 2007, was promoted through increased funding for home help, day and respite care.
Japan	Y	Establishments that succeed, through active support, in enabling a certain percentage of people who used to receive institutional care to return home can receive additional payments from the LTC insurance system.
Korea	Y	The Act on Long-term Care Insurance for the Elderly encourages home care. Also, institutional care is provided only to beneficiaries with the highest care need/disability level (1st and 2nd class).
Luxembourg	Y	Home care is promoted through regulation and legal provisions.
Mexico	Y	Government strategies promote active ageing and preventive care, thereby ensuring that the senior population minimises hospitalisation. In addition, training of care workers for elderly care has been targeted at families, in order to ensure that those taking care of a long-term patient have the basic knowledge needed.
Netherlands	Y	Personal care budgets encourage home care. The costs of living and the costs of care are going to be accounted for separately, to reimburse people just for care, while requiring them to pay the cost of lodging themselves.
New Zealand	Y	There has been a policy shift to encourage home care in lieu of institutional care, although with limited incentives. The aim is to keep people at home by assisting with home support, equipment and home modification. The (negative) incentive is that residential care is income and asset tested above a certain threshold.
Norway	Y/N	Municipalities are free to organise their LTC home-service as they see fitted.
Poland	Y	Within the social assistance system, some home services are offered to people in need of care due to sickness and/or old age. These services may include care and assistance in daily activities of life.
Slovak Republic	Y	The Act on Social Services and National Priorities promotes home care and the Act on Direct Payments supports informal carers, with the aim to retain the elderly in their home environment.
Slovenia	N	
Spain	Y	Article 3 of the Ley de Dependencia explicitly states that the elderly should remain in their home environments for as long as posible. Also, according to Article 14, home help and day-care centers receive financial benefits.
Sweden	Y	This is the prime policy direction at all levels of government in Sweden.
Switzerland	Y	At the federal level, the independence of older people is supported through subsidies given to institutions that provide courses for physical and cognitive maintenance and improvement of the elderly. Also, the level of allowance is higher for people living at home, than those residing in institutions. At the regional level, subsidies are also given to organisations that provide home care services.
United Kingdom	Y	The draft social care outcomes framework, which offers a way for local authorities to benchmark their progress, includes indicators on the proportion spent on residential care, and the proportion of older people who are still at home 91 days after discharge from hospital.
United States	Y	Home and Community-based Services (HCBS) Plan Option; Community First Choice Option; Money Follows the Person initiatives; and the State Balancing Incentive Program encourage home and community care via primarily financial incentives for states.

Source: OECD 2009-10 Questionnaire on Long-term Care Workforce and Financing.

Until 2006, the payment of LTC services in Japan differed according to the activity limitations of the resident; but the difference in payments from the severest to the lightest case was initially less than 20%, so providers had an incentive to admit patients with mild disability (Ikegami *et al.*, 2003). To correct that, the payment for those with the lowest level of care – who accounted for more than half of all patients in LTC beds – has been set below the care production cost since 2006. Additional payments are offered to institutions that have been successful in enabling a certain percentage of recipients to return home.

Evaluation of policies to encourage home care

The share of over 65 years old LTC users receiving care at home has increased in most countries, although trends in the share of old people living in an LTC institution vary across countries (Box 10.1).

Box 10.1. Trends of institutional and home care use among OECD countries

In the past decade, the density of beds in nursing homes has been reduced in nearly all OECD countries (Figure 10.1) (Reinhard, 2010; Barton Smith and Feng, 2010), while the share of home-care users increased (see Figure 10.2). These trends reflect policies to encourage home care, as well as measures to reduce cost. However, they have not necessarily been accompanied by a decrease in the number of old people receiving care in an institution, as shown in Figure 10.3. This apparently contradictory result can be explained by an increase in occupancy rates in institutions in many countries.

Figure 10.1. The density of LTC beds in nursing homes has decreased in the past decade

LTC beds in nursing homes per 1 000 people aged 80 and over, 1998-2008

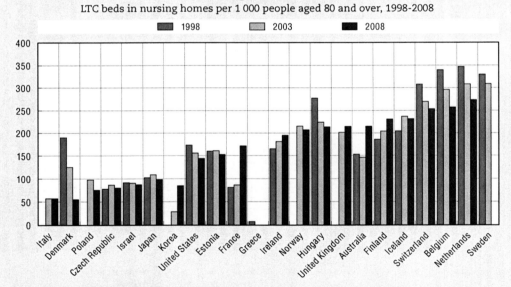

Note: 1998 data refer to 2000 for the Czech Republic and to 1999 for Germany. 2003 data refer to 2004 for Norway. 2008 data refer to 2006 for Belgium, 2007 for Luxembourg, Germany and Australia. OECD averages are based on data for 14 countries in 1998, 20 countries in 2003, and 22 countries in 2008.

Source: OECD Health Data 2010.

StatLink http://dx.doi.org/10.1787/888932401805

Box 10.1. **Trends of institutional and home care use among OECD countries** (cont.)

Figure 10.2. **The share of home-care users has increased accross the OECD**

Home care users as share of all LTC users, 2001 and 2008

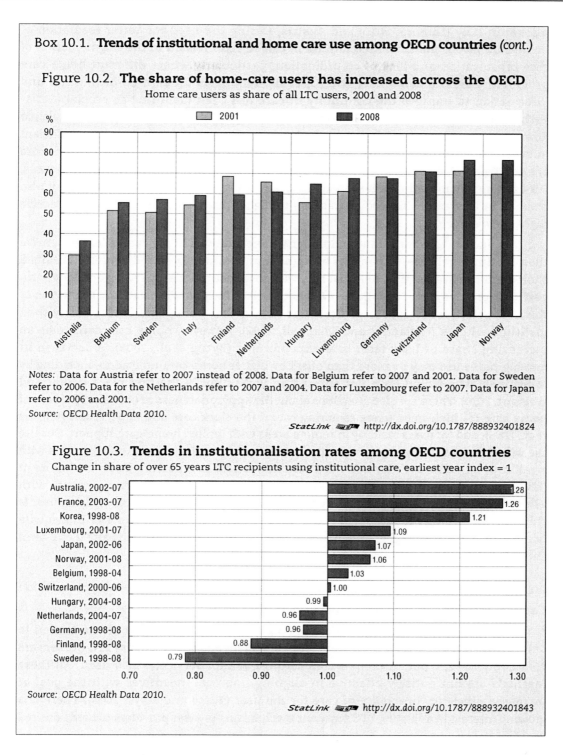

Notes: Data for Austria refer to 2007 instead of 2008. Data for Belgium refer to 2007 and 2001. Data for Sweden refer to 2006. Data for the Netherlands refer to 2007 and 2004. Data for Luxembourg refer to 2007. Data for Japan refer to 2006 and 2001.

Source: OECD Health Data 2010.

StatLink ⟜⟝ http://dx.doi.org/10.1787/888932401824

Figure 10.3. **Trends in institutionalisation rates among OECD countries**

Change in share of over 65 years LTC recipients using institutional care, earliest year index = 1

Australia, 2002-07	1.28
France, 2003-07	1.26
Korea, 1998-08	1.21
Luxembourg, 2001-07	1.09
Japan, 2002-06	1.07
Norway, 2001-08	1.06
Belgium, 1998-04	1.03
Switzerland, 2000-06	1.00
Hungary, 2004-08	0.99
Netherlands, 2004-07	0.96
Germany, 1998-08	0.96
Finland, 1998-08	0.88
Sweden, 1998-08	0.79

0.70   0.80   0.90   1.00   1.10   1.20   1.30

Source: OECD Health Data 2010.

StatLink ⟜⟝ http://dx.doi.org/10.1787/888932401843

While the shift towards home-based settings holds considerable promise, there are several potential challenges in rebalancing LTC away from institutional care. First of all, there needs to be a market for, or an adequate number of, home-care providers. In Greece, for example, there is universal eligibility to institutional care services, but few home-care providers. The lack of home-care providers has led to the growth of a migrant-carers market in Italy (Lamura, 2010) and Austria, raising the need for better regulation of home-care labour markets. Secondly, there can be risks related to the fragmentation of care organisation and lack of co-ordination, particularly where different home-care providers visit the same user (OECD, 2005). Emphasis on care co-ordination and information to improve the continuity of care has been identified as crucial (Caris-Verhallen and Kerkstra, 2000; Grabowski *et al.*, 2010). Thirdly, in cases where multiple home-care providers exist, choice can be hard for users, as they may not have sufficient information to base their choice upon, unless information support systems for home care are developed. The use of financial incentives can also create unintended consequences. For example, financial incentives in Japan lowered admission of low-need users, but also resulted in institutions up-coding patients to higher disability levels, in order to receive higher payments (OECD, 2009).

It is unclear to what extent and under what conditions home care is less expensive than institutional care. Expansion of home and community-based services entails a short-term rise in spending, followed by a decline in institutional spending and long-term cost savings (Kaye *et al.*, 2009). Some evidence, such as the Canadian National Evaluation of the Cost-effectiveness of Home Care, has shown that home care is less costly than institutional care (Hollander and Chappell, 2002). However, home care consumes an increasing share of long-term care expenditures (Byrne *et al.*, 2008). A decrease in nursing-home use may be more than offset by higher home-care utilisation, including by individuals who would have not entered an institution in the first place (Miller and Weissert, 2010). There are also questions about the appropriateness or cost-effectiveness of home care for high-need users requiring round the clock care and supervision (Wiener *et al.*, 2009), and for users residing in remote areas with limited home-care support. Despite the will of patients to live independently in their own homes and communities, users with significant impairments may still need continuous care in a nursing-home environment (Miller and Weissert, 2010) or in adapted-living, service-housing arrangements with 24h care, as in Finland. Indeed, some countries have cost threshold above which a user is shifted from home to institutional settings. In some cases, inappropriate or inadequate home care may lead to higher and more costly institutionalisation in the future (Long-term Care Reform Leadership Project, 2009).

Improving incentives for care providers: Pay-for-performance and provider competition
Can LTC providers be paid based on performance?

The issue of payment of providers in long-term care has received little attention to date. In institutional settings, per-diem reimbursement and salaries to pay LTC workers are commonly used, while in home-based settings, fee-for-service is also used. All these methods are not entirely effective in aligning financial incentives with the goal of increased efficiency or quality of care for the user (Busse and Mays, 2008). There is a growing interest in adjusting LTC payment mechanisms to steer providers towards desired goals for the system.

Fee-for-service schemes are not very frequent in LTC, particularly in institutional settings. Where they are used, incentives to provide as many reimbursable services as possible may arise. These can be mitigated by need-assessment procedures, which cap how much care the user will be provided with. However, if fees do not vary according to the user's dependency level or his/her place of residence, there can be incentives for providers to prefer easy-to-serve or lower-need users. Capitation payments[2] are used in managed-care schemes in the United States (Grabowski, 2007). While they can encourage underuse of services and "skimming" of high-risk individuals, the prolonged duration of LTC acts as an incentive to offer services that maintain or improve the population's health (Busse and Mays, 2008; Christianson *et al.*, 2007). The introduction of risk-adjusted capitation in the United States, whereby providers do not receive higher payments for patients with higher needs, may diminish the incentives for risk selection (Busse and Mays, 2008; Pope *et al.*, 2004). Salary payments are a common method for paying LTC workers. Often, these are accompanied by quality-related procedures and norms (Christianson *et al.*, 2007; Busse and Mays, 2008; Gold and Felt-Lisk, 2008).

Public LTC systems typically reimburse institutional providers (*e.g.*, nursing homes, organisations hiring LTC workers) on a per diem basis. In France per diem are flat rates, and it has been suggested that a case-mix payment would provide nursing homes with stronger incentives to treat more severely impaired patients. In Belgium and Canada, per diem payments are adjusted to reflect the risk of the LTC user. However, if the risk adjustment is made ex-ante on the basis of forecasts of users' need-profiles, providers may end up running a deficit if they admit a larger cohort of severely disabled users. This was a concern raised by nursing homes in Belgium, for example. Negotiated budget processes are commonly found among government administered LTC systems. This is an effective cost-control method, but it may result in unmet needs and leave providers at risk for budget over-runs.

An interesting new development is the idea to link payments to quality and efficiency in so-called pay-for-performance schemes (P4P). While there is much experimentation with P4P in health care, only a few examples can be found in nursing homes in the US Medicaid programme (Arling *et al.*, 2009; Briesacher *et al.*, 2009). Despite little empirical evidence that P4P programmes increase quality, one of the few evaluations in Iowa indicates improvements in resident satisfaction, employee retention rate, and nursing hours. Similar results were obtained from an analysis of Minnesota's P4P system, although a systematic evaluation has not yet been completed (Arling *et al.*, 2009).

Still, concerns have been raised regarding P4P programmes in LTC, for example regarding the incentives to focus only on particular services, the providers' self-reporting of performance data leading to unreliable or dubious results, or the incentives to admit users that will increase chances of achieving a good benchmark. Various programmes in nursing homes were terminated after a few years of operation, indicating that political or practical barriers hinder the implementation of P4P in this setting. Credible performance measures addressing a broad range of quality and quality of life indicators in long-term care are still under development (Arling *et al.*, 2009; Briesacher *et al.*, 2009).

Seeking efficiency gains from choice-based competition across providers

Providing users with choice over the carer they prefer can stimulate providers' competition and encourage them to deliver better care or care at lower cost. To date, however, there is limited evidence on the impact of such choice-based models on providers' efficiency. In the Japanese LTC insurance system, LTC users can choose freely among providers – including for-profit companies – and competition is regarded as one of the strengths of the system (Campbell and Ikegami, 2000; Campbell and Ikegami, 2003; Campbell *et al.*, 2010). A similar situation is also observed in Germany. In the Netherlands, personal budgets to pay for services or employ home carers, introduced in 1995, have increased users' control, autonomy and satisfaction over the care they receive. However, gains in efficiency and free competition have not yet been observed, mainly due to monopoly powers and the increased bureaucracy of the system (Kremer, 2006).

The use of voucher schemes for long-term care in Nordic countries is an interesting experience (see Box 10.2).[3] Generally, a voucher can be defined as a subsidy that can be used by the consumer to purchase restricted or regulated goods or services (Steuerle, 2000). It can, therefore, take the form of a printed check, electronic card or an authority's payment covenant (Volk and Laukkanen, 2007). Vouchers enable users to choose the provider that best meets their needs, leading, hopefully, to higher user satisfaction, improvements in quality and cost-effectiveness. However, concerns have been raised, for example, regarding the asymmetric and imperfect information available for consumers to make informed choices (Folland et al., 2001). Providers may discriminate prices among those who use a voucher and those who do not, or they may discriminate across different users (Volk and Laukkanen, 2007).

Box 10.2. Provider choice and the use of vouchers for long-term care in Nordic countries

Sweden. Sweden has encouraged LTC users' freedom of choice since the early 1990s, but this was further reinforced in 2009 under the act on "System of Choice in the Public Sector", which was implemented by approximately one fourth of the municipalities. According to this act, LTC clients can choose their service provider among those the municipality has contracted with. The municipalities then reimburse providers according to a timesheet that a user signs upon service delivery. Some fundamental acceptance criteria for providers are defined by the act and all applicants meeting the criteria have to be accepted. If a municipality decides to introduce such choice system, it has to disclose this decision on the national website, mentioning details on providers, acceptance criteria, quality information and contracts (Svensk författningssamling, 2008). Municipalities have the obligation to inform LTC customers about their freedom of choice and their right to change providers. They are also responsible for maintaining the same prices across providers. Enrolled individuals have the right to opt out of the voucher system and are guaranteed an alternative public service.

Finland. An optional voucher system was introduced in Finland in 2004, as part of a broader legislative change in health and social care. Subsequent changes in 2008 and 2009 made the system more uniform and expanded the range of available services (Paasivirta, 2009). In 2006, around 29% of the Finnish municipalities used a voucher service (Volk and Laukkanen, 2007). The voucher can be used to purchase only privately provided services, leaving the municipal production out of the system. The value of the voucher for purchasing regular home help and home-nursing services is determined by a formula that takes into account household size and income, with the service users paying the difference between the value of the voucher and the full price of the service. The amount of the co-payment also differs across providers, as they are allowed to price their services competitively (FINLEX). In temporary home help and home nursing, as well as in other social and health services, the value of the service voucher is not regulated. Broad criteria regarding the provider's eligibility are set in legislation. Although municipalities can set additional criteria, they do not discriminate against any provider. Similarly to Sweden, municipalities have the responsibility to supply individuals with information regarding suppliers, in the absence of a national registry (Volk and Laukkanen, 2007).

Box 10.2. Provider choice and the use of vouchers for long-term care in Nordic countries (*cont.*)

Denmark. Consumer choice and private provision of personal and practical help were introduced at the national level in 2003. In 2009, amendments to the Consolidation Act of Social Services made Denmark the only Nordic country where free choice of providers is mandatory for municipalities (Karlsson and Iversen, 2010). As early as 2005, 90% of individuals aged 65 years and over had the opportunity to choose between two or more home-help providers (Ankestryreseln, 2005). A municipality can choose three methods of implementing a consumer choice model. The first and most common entails a local council having a contractual relationship with each service provider that meets the locally defined standards, without an option to restrict provider's entry. In the second model, a municipality contracts with at least two but no more than five qualified service providers, by tendering (Government of Finland, 2009). The third model is a combination of the first two. It involves the first provider being found through a tender, and any other provider being allowed to enter the market, subject to price competition (Eriksen, personal communication). The municipality is responsible for setting the local quality standards (Ministry of the Interior and Health, Ministry of Social Affairs, 2005). These should be posted on two national webpages, along with other information regarding approved service providers and prices. The Consolidation Act gives the municipalities an additional option to increase freedom of choice by implementing a so-called "servicebevis" (service certificate). This certificate gives eligible individuals the opportunity to employ their own personal carers. The payment to the service provider is then made by the municipality. The size of the service certificate market is not known yet. Some local authorities were also allowed in 2003 to launch experimental systems with personal budgets for personal and practical care (Karlsson and Iversen, 2010).

Source: Viita (2010).

Customer surveys performed in Denmark and Finland indicate a general satisfaction among LTC voucher users, particularly among those who had chosen a private provider, although this satisfaction was related to freedom of choice rather than the service itself (Kaskiharju and Seppänen, 2004; Ankestyrelsen, 2005; Volk and Laukkanen, 2007). However, individuals are not always aware of the information provided by the municipality regarding the voucher system. For example, 16% of Danish users were unaware of the opportunity to choose a provider (Ankestyrelsen, 2005) and tended to choose a provider that had been recommended, rather than making their own informed choices (Kaskiharju and Seppänen, 2004). They rarely used their right to change providers, but more often opted out of the system altogether (Kastberg, 2001; Ankestyrelsen, 2005). Some evidence of providers' risk selection was also found in Finland (Volk and Laukkanen, 2007). In some rural areas in the Nordic countries, voucher schemes have proved unfeasible due to lack of private providers (Volk and Laukkanen, 2007). Some urban municipalities in Sweden are dominated by an oligopoly of private providers, hindering free competition (Sveriges Kommunen och Landsting, 2009).

Evidence of efficiency gains attributed to the voucher system in the three countries is not compelling. In many municipalities, the introduction of consumer choice lead to quality improvements and forced them to seek options for containing the cost of their service production. However, the design of services changed with the introduction of a voucher system, making it difficult to make comparisons across time, and across municipalities (Ankestyrelsen, 2005; Sveriges Kommunen och Landsting, 2009). Another drawback is the higher administrative work after the implementation of a voucher scheme

(Kastberg, 2001; Ankestyrelsen, 2005; Volk and Laukkanen, 2007; Kaskiharju and Seppänen, 2004), which could be overcome with technical solutions, such as electronic management tools (Ankestyrelsen, 2005).

In conclusion, studies on existing voucher schemes have shown greater satisfaction among participants, but provide limited evidence regarding efficiency increase. In most cases, free competition is hindered, either due to monopoly powers, or inability of individuals to make informed choices.

The impact of technology on productivity in long-term care

Caring for frail or disabled elderly can be a rich and emotionally rewarding task, but can rapidly become stressful and time consuming. Technological solutions could assist in reducing the workload and stress of carers and improve work co-ordination, allowing caregivers to allocate their valuable working time more efficiently (Valkila and Saari, 2010). Technology hence raises hopes for potential substitution of specific tasks and increased quality of life for the elderly and their carers (Haberkern *et al.*, 2011). The open question is to what extent this would result in productivity improvements. Some evidence can be found across the OECD, but it remains sparse at best.

Technology can have a wide range of applications in LTC (Haberkern *et al.*, 2011). To begin with, technology can be used to optimise medication, *i.e.* manage medication information, dispensing, tracking and adherence. Monitoring devices, such as glucometers and blood pressure monitors, help to manage care from a long distance. Assistive technologies can promote LTC users' independence and safety. Productivity of LTC workers could also be enhanced through remote training and supervision technologies. Newly emerging technologies include cognitive fitness and assessment games, as well as social networking programmes, enabling communication, organisation and sharing among older adults and their caregivers (Centre for Technology and Aging, 2009). The introduction and diffusion of information and communication technologies (ICT) could be particularly helpful in the future years.

Despite the large knowledge gap, some research results have shown a positive correlation between technology introduction, job satisfaction and productivity. A study in Australia indicated that paper work was perceived by LTC workers as time-consuming, keeping them away from their LTC recipients and contributing to diminished job satisfaction and productivity (Moyle *et al.*, 2003). A pilot voice-system linking frail elderly to their caregivers was introduced in a Finnish nursing home. The new technology made it easier and quicker for caregivers to complete their task without interrupting their work and arrange priorities, as they had instant voice contact with the resident in need of assistance. This led to better organisation and improved work productivity. Residents felt safer, too, leading to a 60% decrease in the number of alarm calls. This enabled caregivers to dedicate more time to attend to residents needing further assistance (Valkila and Saari, 2010).

In South Korea, the introduction of electronic equipment for home-care management was associated with better and more precise patient evaluations by nurses (Lee *et al.*, 2009). In the United States, the Green House Project offers an alternative to nursing homes. Among other features, Green Houses use sophisticated technology, such as smart technology computers, wireless pagers, electronic ceiling lifts, and adaptive devices. Although evidence on their effectiveness is preliminary, staff felt more empowered to assist residents and had greater job satisfaction (OECD 2009-10 Questionnaire on Long-term Care Workforce and

Financing; Kane *et al.*, 2005; Cutler and Kane, 2009). Hydraulic lifts reduce the time and effort required to transfer a frail elderly from the bed to a chair. A study from the United States showed that old people who do not use such technological equipment require approximately four additional hours of help per week, compared to those who use them, irrespective of the user's impairment level and LTC services received.

The use of ICT could result in a more productive time management for the caregivers (Hoenig *et al.*, 2003). A Swedish study demonstrated that the implementation of ICT in residential care for dementia leads to improvements in personal development, reduced workload, and higher worker motivation (Engström *et al.*, 2005). However, the introduction of ICT in community nursing in Slovenia lead nurses to spend more time on computers than with patients (Bitenc *et al.*, 2000). Similarly, home-care nurses in a Korean study evaluated electronic records as being burdensome and confusing (Lee *et al.*, 2009). ICT may be better suited for recipients with relatively mild disabilities. Evidence from Finland shows that reminders for taking medicine may be useless for mentally impaired people and telecare would be inefficient for the elderly needing cleaning and change of bandages (Söderlund, 2004).

The impact of ICT on family carers was also examined in Norway. ICT can facilitate contact with other carers, through which they can receive information and emotional support. Carers could increase their knowledge about the care recipient's illness and symptoms, and be better prepared to meet future changes in behaviour and care needs. Telecare technology implemented in Scottish community-care LTC services lead, among other things, to reduced pressure and stress on informal caregivers (Beale *et al.*, 2009). However, the effect of ICT on stress and mental well-being associated with caregiving were somewhat contradicting (Torp *et al.*, 2008).

In conclusion, evidence from OECD countries shows that there is a potential for greater use of technology in LTC. The majority of the studies remain pilot programmes, and further systematic assessment is needed to validate the findings. LTC remains a highly labour intensive sector, with technological assistance often being a help or supplement to labour force, rather than a substitute (Torp *et al.*, 2008). To facilitate the introduction and diffusion of technology, several main barriers need to be addressed, including infrastructural readiness and investment costs (Heberkern *et al.*, 2011), as well as resistance to change by workers (Virmalund and Olve, 2005).

10.3. Is it possible to optimise health and care?

Long-term care systems operate in close link with health care. However, it can be hard for the user to navigate the health and care crossroad, care continuum is not always guaranteed, and providers face inefficiencies and cost-shifting incentives. Three areas of "interface" between health and long-term care systems can be examined: i) incentives for appropriate use of LTC *vis-à-vis* acute-care settings; ii) co-ordination of health and care; and iii) healthy ageing and prevention. Table 10.3 summarises some countries' measures.

Appropriate use of LTC versus acute-care settings

For over 20 years, debates regarding the appropriateness of elderly's referrals to acute health-care services have flourished (Kurrle, 2006). Not only frail elderly may encounter risks of nosocomial infections or undergo unnecessary medical treatments during hospitalisation (Kurrle, 2006), but also acute care can be an unpleasant environment over an extended period of time. It is too costly of a setting for care of long duration. Estimates

Table 10.3. **Policies to avoid the inappropriate use of acute care services and co-ordinate LTC programmes in OECD countries**

		Policies/incentives to avoid inappropriate use of acute health care services for LTC needs	Co-ordination of LTC services provided by different providers or under different LTC programmes
Australia	Y	The Transition Care Programme helps older people complete their restorative process. The Long Stay Older Patients' Initiative targets older people whose care needs may be better met outside the hospital system.	The State and Territory Governments are responsible for the co-ordination and provision of programmes. In the area of home and community care services, client care co-ordination is delivered by the provider.
Austria	N		
Belgium	Y	The inappropriate use of acute health care services for LTC needs is limited by the provision of financial incentives, based on the AP-DRG system.	Care co-ordination for home-care services is ensured by the "Centers for Co-Ordination" (SIT) and the "Integrated Home Care Services" (SISD/GDT). Other pilot home care co-ordination initiatives include case management and crisis services.
Canada	Y	Explicit policies/incentives regarding the use of acute health care services for LTC needs do not exist on a national level as health care is primarily a provincial and territorial responsibility.	Co-ordinated access is used in all provinces to provide individuals with a single point of access to LTC information and services. Each province determines how they co-ordinate LTC in their jurisdictions.
Finland	N		
France			Care co-ordination takes place through the individual, the caregiver or through services such as SAD (Service à domicile) and SSIAD (Service de soins infirmiers à domicile). Also, Houses for the Autonomy and Integration of Alzheimer Patients have been developed for co-ordination purposes.
Germany	Y	Under the Competition Enhancement Act, rehabilitation services have been promoted. Further measures include on-time provision of rehabilitation services, financial incentives, improved management and counselling.	Since 2009, individuals are legally entitled to care consultant and case management services. This can take place at Nursing Points, which receive support and funding from the government. Training for the consultants is also provided.
Hungary	Y	Policies include active capacity reduction.	Care co-ordination has been attempted but faces various difficulties.
Ireland	Y	Under the Nursing Homes Support Scheme, a person who remains in an acute hospital bed when their acute phase of care is over may be required to pay charges.	
Japan	N		LTC services are provided by establishments designated by governors/mayors. The division of services is co-ordinated based on the work programme set out by the prefectural or municipal government.
Korea	Y	Based on needs assessment.	
Luxembourg	N		
Mexico	N		
Netherlands	Y	Although implicit, insurers bear the risk of acute health care services.	
New Zealand	N	Explicit policies or incentives do not exist, but there are recognised gaps and issues that will be worked on.	
Norway	Y	The Norwegian government has recently launched a strategy to combat such inefficient use in the public health sector.	The Ministry of Labour and Social Policy co-ordinates care support in the social assistance homes.
Poland	Y		
Slovenia	N		
Sweden	Y	Municipalities are legally obliged to take care of "bed blockers" in acute and geriatric hospitals. When the medical treatment ends at the hospital, the municipality has to arrange necessary further care, for those needing it.	Co-ordination of services and care by GPs, nurses and OTs/PTs working in primary health care and the home help services is recognised as an issue to address.
Switzerland	Y	The LAMal (Loi fédérale sur l'assurance-maladie) has been amended to contain a clear definition of acute care and transition needs. Following an acute care treatment, if a LTC patient continues to be hospitalised, compulsory health insurance will cover only the tariff for LTC services.	
United Kingdom	Y	Two of the main policies are "intermediate care" and "re-ablement". Intermediate care can promote faster recovery. Re-ablement is defined as "Services for people with poor health to help them accommodate their illness by learning or re-learning the skills necessary for daily living".	Services are co-ordinated at a national, regional and local level. At the national level, structures that enable partnerships of local authorities are put in place. At a regional and local level, services tend to vary as they become more locally focused.

Source: OECD 2009-10 Questionnaire on Long-term Care Workforce and Financing.

suggest that "inappropriate referrals" may range from 48% in the United States, to 36% in the United Kingdom, and 7% in Canada (Jensen *et al.*, 2009).

Several OECD countries have implemented explicit policies to avoid the inappropriate use of acute healthcare services, such as:

● *Health-system support measures.* For example, Australia, Hungary, Israel, the United Kingdom and Sweden arrange support of care outside the hospital. They also promote the acceleration of patient's recovery for those whose needs could be better met outside the hospital. Evidence from the literature suggests that increased involvement of primary care providers and GPs could result in fewer hospital admissions of frail elderly.

● *Financial measures to limit acute-care service use for LTC needs.* Ireland imposes additional charges for those who remain in acute hospitals when their acute care phase is over. Japan has introduced case-mix based payments in hospitals to reduce so-called *social hospitalisations.* However, results still lag behind the initial goals and there is evidence of patients up-coding by providers to receive higher reimbursements (OECD, 2009). In the United States, higher per diem reimbursement in some nursing homes seems to have contributed to lower hospitalisations from nursing homes. Pay-for-performance schemes hold some promises, too (see Box 10.3) (Intrator and Mor, 2004). In Sweden, under the Act on Support and Service for Persons with Certain Functional Impairments, municipalities receive a strong financial incentive to find care for the elderly outside hospitals (Trydegård, 2003).

Box 10.3. Avoiding unnecessary acute-care use for LTC needs: Some examples from the United States

In the United States, 19.6% of all Medicare beneficiaries were rehospitalised within 30 days of discharge to a post-acute care setting in 2004 – which includes rehabilitative services delivered by a skilled nursing facility, home health care, or inpatient rehabilitation facilities. About 90% of these readmissions were unplanned, with a cost of USD 17.4 billion to the Medicare programme. Between 2000 and 2006, the rate of rehospitalisations grew by 29% (Mor *et al.*, 2010).

A significant proportion of readmissions could be prevented. Payment reforms, such as bundling could help to reduce rehospitalisations, but they could also lead to providers' up-coding of patients' severity (Mor *et al.*, 2010). Pay-for-performance schemes exhibit some appeal, but Medicaid would not sustain the full cost of rewarding nursing homes with such an incentive-based system, and, at the same time, would gain little from any savings resulting from reduced hospitalisations. The lack of data sharing between Medicaid and Medicare also hinders the success of pay-for-performance schemes (Grabowski, 2007).

The Fallon Community Health Plan in Massachusetts launched the Healthy Transitions pilot programme in 2009. Under this programme, pharmacists are sent to patients' homes within 72 hours of discharge from hospitals, they review the prescribed medication and explain it both to the patient and to the caregiver. Pharmacists play an expanded role, serving as patients' care co-ordinators for a 30-day transition period after hospital release. Thereafter, patients have the option to enrol in LTC management schemes. The Healthy Transition programme has been so far well-received and the preliminary results indicate a positive impact on both preventable hospital readmissions and patient satisfaction (Bayer, 2010).

● *Changes in administrative responsibilities for care.* Again in Sweden, the Act on Support and Service for Persons with Certain Functional Impairments transferred the responsibilities for LTC to municipalities, who became financially responsible for older people remaining in hospitals (OECD, 2005).

● *The use of ICT.* The use of transfer sheets or electronic referrals can help overcome the problems associated with transfers of LTC users to acute-care settings (Kurrle, 2006). However, concerns have also been raised relating to the security and privacy of information, computer system response times, and operational costs (Soar *et al.*, 2007).

Table 10.4 shows a decrease in the average length of stay for acute care in hospitals for conditions linked to dementia and Alzheimer in most OECD countries. Given the information available, it is not possible to draw conclusions regarding the effectiveness of different interventions in reducing the use of acute care for LTC needs, but these data are encouraging.

Table 10.4. **Average length of stay for dementia and Alzheimer's disease in acute care (in days)**

	Dementia				Alzheimer's disease			
	1994	1999	2004	2008	1994	1999	2004	2008
Australia[1]	44.8	42.3	27.8	24.4	51.4	48.2	30.5	27.4
Austria	48.4	17.2	15.5	14.9	27.4	11.5	13.5	12.8
Belgium[1]			27.7	29.2			29.0	28.8
Canada[1]	48.6	33.2	36.5	41.2	47.8	33.5	34.6	42.3
Czech Republic				27.7				29.8
Denmark			14.2	10.3			11.3	8.8
Finland		121.9	116.3	118.7		89.7	68.0	83.9
France		12.9	14.0	13.1		11.0	12.7	12.2
Germany			17.7	16.1			18.7	17.5
Greece[2]		60.0	76.0	77.0				
Hungary			13.0	11.6			9.1	10.0
Iceland		17.1	26.2	28.6		16.0	24.4	22.1
Ireland		50.1	43.1	39.9		22.1	37.0	51.6
Italy[1]			11.2	10.7			8.6	8.7
Korea		58.1		128.0		55.8		101.3
Luxembourg[1]		20.5	17.4	21.2		19.7	15.7	19.0
Mexico		34.9	16.3	34.6		9.1	14.1	7.5
Netherlands	44.3	48.0	27.0	21.7	31.6	22.0	17.0	22.8
Norway			8.6	7.0			7.6	5.3
Poland			19.6	17.9			17.0	10.4
Portugal			13.0	17.8			10.5	14.3
Slovak Republic	27.7	33.8	28.4	28.0	14.0	12.4	31.3	15.9
Spain	90.1	104.5	63.7	66.3			38.1	37.1
Sweden[1]		19.8	16.4	14.6		27.7	23.7	21.8
Switzerland			54.3	42.6			99.8	72.6
Turkey				8.5				7.9
United Kingdom			74.3	62.2			77.5	66.9
United States[2]	13.4	11.3	10.5	9.0		8.2	8.4	8.0
OECD average[3]	**29.1**	**26.8**	**19.2**	**16.7**	**51.4**	**28.2**	**19.5**	**17.7**
OECD average[4]	*29.1*	*31.0*	*24.3*	*23.2*	*34.4*	*25.5*	*25.4*	*24.2*

1. Data for 2008 refer to 2007; data for Canada: A break in series in 2006 leads to longer reported average length of stay.
2. Data for 2008 refer to 2006.
3. Unweighted average on countries reporting data, per respective year.
4. Unweighted average for all countries that report data as of 1994 (six for dementia; five for Alzheimer's disease).
Source: OECD Health Data 2010.

StatLink ⬛ http://dx.doi.org/10.1787/888932401957

Co-ordinating or integrating health and care

The need to co-ordinate health and long-term care is obvious, but the way to achieve that is not. A key question is whether co-ordination would work better by keeping health and long-term care into separated systems, or by integrating settings and "silos".

There are several *co-ordination* challenges in long-term care. First, at the interface between health and social care, it can be difficult to organise continuity of care. Second, within LTC services themselves, there are often different coexisting payers, types of reimbursement, providers, and governing systems, acting as obstacles to care co-ordination (Pratt, 2010). For instance, as long-term care implementation is often left to lower-level jurisdictions, there can be important geographical variations from one area to the other. Care providers in some countries receive payments from various sources, and as a result face conflicting incentives for quality improvements and little incentives for cost-efficient delivery of care (Konetzka and Werner, 2010). In the absence of good information and direction for people needing care, consumers may end up interacting with different health and long-term care providers at the same time, unable to determine the best way to organise the services they need. When individuals do not receive timely care, they may end up in more expensive care settings, such as a hospital emergency departments, with increased costs imposed on the system and the patients (Long-term Care Reform Leadership Project, 2009). Indeed, hospitals are often a first point of contact for users needing LTC, but transfers across settings can be delayed or not optimised.

Most OECD countries have created co-ordination tasks or assigned responsibilities to guide users through the care process (see Table 10.3). These include mechanisms to provide individuals with single points of access to LTC information (Canada), the allocation of care co-ordination responsibilities to providers (*e.g.*, Australia, France, Sweden) or to care managers[4] (*e.g.*, Japan, Germany, Denmark, the United Kingdom), or the use of dedicated governance structures for care co-ordination (*e.g.*, Belgium, the French *Caisse nationale de solidarité pour l'autonomie*, Japan).

Even though much of the care co-ordination takes place at the local level, it is not uncommon to have national mechanisms or centrally-set regulations or guidelines. The Norwegian government, for instance, has issued policy suggestions to improve LTC co-ordination, including among others, better-defined priorities, focus on early intervention, changing the funding system, developing the specialist healthcare services and introducing new ICT and education for LTC professionals (Norwegian Ministry of Healthcare and Services, 2008-09). In the United Kingdom, LTC services co-ordination is primarily at the national level, where regulations are put in place. Local authorities, however, also work with LTC services to decide on the needs of each community, to make improvements and shape new developments. In the United States, an important feature of the March 2010 health reform legislation is the idea of Accountable Care Organisations (ACOs), involving health care providers in general, and LTC providers in particular. Their aim is to improve care co-ordination, benefit patients and minimise inefficiencies. They collaborate with private insurers and specifically focus on preventing chronic diseases, improving transitions between caregivers and avoiding preventable hospital re-admissions. Providers would share savings achieved through eliminating unnecessary expenses and improving quality. However, ACOs is a relatively new intervention, with cost and quality targets not having been established yet. Their diffusion is still quite limited, although an example can be found in the state of Montana. The policy implications of this intervention remain to be seen (Klein, 2010).

Despite these mechanisms, the challenge of how to organise the appropriate mix of health and long-term care services remains. Long-term and chronic care patients tend to be high users of health services, as they have numerous contacts with the healthcare system, usually not in the most cost-effective way. Patterns of care co-ordination change as individuals transfer from acute to LTC settings. This is sometimes due to the fact that LTC is the responsibility of local governments, while the oversight of acute care is at the regional or national level. Medical professionals discharge patients, and usually assess their needs and define care plans. During transitions from ambulatory to long-term care settings, neither ambulatory specialists, nor GPs, seem to have a leading role in many countries.

Around two thirds of the OECD countries have reported that they experience difficulties with transitions from ambulatory care to LTC; and four fifths face problems with transitions from acute care to LTC (Hofmarcher *et al.*, 2007; Oxley, 2009b). While care managers play an important role, there is little evidence on the cost-effectiveness of the care management or care co-ordination process (Hutt *et al.*, 2004). Care co-ordination could be improved by a better bridging of administrative and other obstacles that hinder easy transitions from acute care to LTC (Oxley, 2009b). Health care providers can also play an important role in giving support to family carers. This could range from providing advice and counselling to more specific interventions.

This discussion shows that while the separation of health and LTC can avoid the provision of LTC via the health care system, it can also lead to difficulties in organising care across a continuum of services. An alternative way would be to work through *integration*, for example by integrating funding and delivery of health and long-term care. The aim here is to combine care management, information systems, and incentives to minimise cost-shifting across health and care (Stone, 2000).

Examples of LTC integration can be found in Sweden, the United States, Canada and Japan. The Swedish government has developed a safe-care continuum especially for elderly with complex health problems and severe needs. As this group of frail elderly is a major user of LTC services and care, targeting this group is a key element of a value-for- money strategy. In the United States, integration of health and care for Medicare beneficiates takes place in the S/HMO, PACE and SNPs schemes. These, however, showed mixed results in terms of cost savings for Medicare and Medicaid, despite an increase in enrolees' satisfaction (Box 10.4). In Canada, the SIPA (French acronym for *System of Integrated Care for Older Persons*) is a

---

> ### Box 10.4. **Health and long-term care integration initiatives in the United States**
>
> The structure of Medicaid and Medicare creates conflicting incentives for the so-called dually eligible (for both Medicare and Medicaid) beneficiaries. These are among the most expensive beneficiaries, often requiring both acute and LTC services. It has been estimated that over one out of every five dually eligible person lives in nursing homes, compared 2% for Medicare beneficiaries. Both Medicare and Medicaid cover certain home and institutional care services. Medicare pays for acute care services for dually eligible individuals, while Medicaid pays for LTC services. There is evidence of some cost-shifting within home health care and nursing homes, and across chronic and acute care settings (Grabowski, 2007).
>
> To reduce cost and improve care co-ordination for this population group, several "integration" interventions have been suggested. These include federal managed care initiatives such as the Social Health Maintenance Organisation (S/HMO), the Programme of

Box 10.4. **Health and long-term care integration initiatives in the United States** (cont.)

All-Inclusive Care for the Elderly (PACE) introduced in the 1990s, and the Medicare Advantage Special Needs Plans (SNPs), such as the EverCare Programme. State managed care initiatives that combine Medicare and Medicaid financing also exist, such as the Minnesota Senior Health Options (MSHO) and others (Grabowski, 2007; Gross *et al.*, 2004).

Both PACE and S/HMO emphasise home and community-based services. S/HMOs were set up in 1984 to test whether providing LTC benefits to Medicare HMO enrollees could save money by co-ordinating care. S/HMOs provide both standard Medicare benefits, and restricted long- term care benefits to Medicare beneficiaries who voluntarily enrol. Despite the programme's almost 20-year history, its success is quite limited, with only four programmes currently operating, still as pilots (Gross *et al.*, 2004). Evidence suggests that S/HMO projects had lower levels of un-enrolment than Medicare's HMOs in general; but evidence that the S/HMOs were less costly than fee-for-service plans was mixed.

On the other hand, PACE has been more successful in integrating acute and LTC financing and delivery of care, as well as maintaining participants' independence. PACE receives capitated funding from both Medicare and Medicaid and is responsible for providing both primary and LTC to its participants. The combination of the patients' regular contact with the staff, and the integrated care delivery and financing, helps the PACE programme monitor chronic conditions, avoiding re-hospitalisations and deferring institutionalisation (Gross *et al.*, 2004). PACE enrolees have shown greater satisfaction with care services, as well as better functional status and fewer hospital admissions compared to their counterparts receiving the conventional fee-for-service care (Mui, 2002; Grabowski, 2007). This led to its designation as a permanent Medicare programme in 1997.

However, the PACE scheme has attracted a disproportionate number of healthy individuals. There is evidence that the total capitated payment to PACE beneficiaries was 9.7% higher during the first year of enrolment, compared to the corresponding Medicare and Medicaid cost, if the individuals had continued to receive care in the fee-for-service programme. It is estimated that PACE resulted in a 42% lower Medicare spending, but a 86% higher Medicaid spending. Possible reasons for these results could be the failure to target the appropriate services to enrolees through a stringent pre-admission process, or the inability to control expenditure on specific services (Grabowski, 2007).

One recent initiative to co-ordinate Medicare and Medicaid is the introduction of Medicare Advantage Special Needs Plans (SNPs) in 2003. SNPs work through private plans, which are most commonly health maintenance organisations. States have the opportunity to combine Medicaid's and Medicare's managed care, contracting for dually eligible beneficiaries (Grabowski, 2009). Despite the potential of SNPs to increase system's efficiency and strong entry into the market, there has been a rather modest enrolment, partly because SNPs offer little additional value to dual eligible beneficiaries, compared to the conventional Medicare Advantage plans (Grabowski, 2009). In addition, while the federal Medicare scheme emphasises consumer choice, state Medicaid programmes usually offer a limited number of plans. This may hinder care co-ordination if dually eligible individuals choose different Medicare and Medicaid plans. Misalignment of incentives may exist as well, since SNPs profit from any lower Medicare hospital costs, but the states do not directly benefit (Grabowski, 2007).

community-based scheme responsible for the provision of primary and secondary medical and social services. The scheme is publicly managed by the Provinces and financed by capitation. Evaluations of SIPA have shown that, despite being cost neutral, it can reduce acute care utilisation and increase community care (Bergman et al., 1997; Béland et al., 2006). The Japanese government tries to integrate LTC and health care in different ways. Emphasis is primarily placed on community-based care to ensure continuum of care. A GP's assessment is required as part of LTC needs' assessment. There are maximum separate monthly out-of-pocket payment ceilings for LTC and health care, but also another ceiling for those with high expenditure in both LTC and health care together.

It is difficult to draw firm conclusions from different country initiatives involving co-ordination and integration. In the United States, the PACE scheme has shown the most success in terms of quality of care and access to services. There are, however, concerns regarding its ability to contain costs. A similar programme in Canada shows promising results, but is only at an experimental stage. In Japan, the LTC insurance system includes co-ordination mechanisms, but there is relatively little evaluation of outcomes for users and costs. With growing LTC and health care cost, particularly for people with multiple chronic conditions, the co-ordination of health and long-term care deserves considerable policy attention in the future.

What can LTC systems do to encourage healthy ageing and prevention?

The most obvious way to reduce cost in long-term care systems would be to reduce potential dependency in later life through lifelong health promotion. Healthy ageing[5] corresponds to the notion of maintaining the older population in good physical, social and mental health, facilitating their autonomy and independence for as long as possible, throughout their remaining years (Oxley, 2009a). This is easier said than done, as demographic ageing is not always accompanied by good health (Thorpe and Howard, 2006; Lafortune and Balestat, 2007). Still, recent survey work by WHO indicates very large national variations in age-specific self-reported dependency rates, suggesting greater scope for fostering healthy and active ageing. Without entering in a discussion of the wide range of policies available to promote healthy ageing, some interesting recent country initiatives in long-term care are worth focusing on.

In 2006, the Japanese government introduced a community-based, prevention-oriented LTC benefit in their long-term care insurance system. The aim was to prevent seniors in need of low levels of care from becoming dependent, by providing services targeted at improving the individual's physical strength, mental health, oral function and nutritional status (Tsutsui and Muramatsu, 2007). All elderly requiring low-need care are eligible to receive this preventive benefit (so-called, Support Levels 1 and 2 in the LTC insurance). An estimated 40% (1.7 million) of the seniors certified as needing LTC support belong to these two categories (Tsutsui and Muramatsu, 2007). The benefit amount is lower than what people with similar care needs would have been entitled to before the 2006 LTC insurance reform (Morikawa et al., 2007). Services, such as strength training, nutrition management and mental education, are offered at day-care facilities (Morikawa et al., 2007). The management of prevention benefits is under the responsibility of local support centres established by municipalities for every community with a population of 20 000 to 30 000. These centres are responsible for the need assessment and care planning for people with Support Levels 1 or 2, the development of community support projects for seniors, and co-ordination between various professionals (Tsutsui and Muramatsu, 2007).

Evaluation of the preventive benefits scheme is encouraging, showing a drop in the enrolment and use of services by people with lighter care-need levels, after its implementation. The growth rate of total LTC beneficiaries in Japan now matches the growth in the population aged seventy-five and older, as they are the main users of LTC services. The reform also contributed to savings in the LTC insurance (Campbell *et al.*, 2010).

An interesting case of providing incentives for rehabilitation is the 2008 *Long-term Care Further Development Act* in Germany (Rothgang, 2010). Prior to the reform, both providers and sickness funds faced disincentives to finance rehabilitation, because successful rehabilitation resulted in the care level of an individual being downgraded, with subsequent reduction in reimbursements. Although there was a potential for rehabilitation among individuals receiving LTC services, the Medical Review Board would transfer only 6% of the cases to rehabilitation centres. Each sickness fund had to bear the cost of any rehabilitation measure it granted. However, savings from downgrading of an individual's level of care were spread among all funds, so that sickness funds still had few incentives to finance rehabilitation (Rothgang, 2010).

The 2008 reform introduced a financial incentive of EUR 1 536 when a resident is transferred from a nursing home to a lower level of care setting, as a result of rehabilitation. Sickness funds also face a EUR 2 072 fine, if they do not provide rehabilitation services, even though it has been recommended by the Medical Review Board. Still, it is too early to assess the effects of these financial incentives on the promotion of rehabilitation (Rothgang, 2010).

Another example can be found in Mexico, where the ISSSTE (Institute of Social Services for State Employees) began to promote healthy and active ageing among its beneficiaries aged over 40 years in 2008. This lead to the development of the *Active Ageing Program*, and, in 2009, of the *Healthy Ageing Program*, which is now being carried out in 35 geriatric centres across the country. The centres aim at providing rehabilitative services and physical therapy to the elderly.

Although several polices fall under the broad umbrella of healthy ageing *(e.g.,* increasing community activities, improving lifestyles and health literacy, as well as better adapting health care systems to the needs of the elderly) only few countries seem to have integrated specific healthy ageing objectives or interventions as part of their LTC systems. There is still uncertainty regarding which interventions aimed at keeping seniors in good health lead to better payoffs or are cost-effective (Oxley, 2009a). This uncertainty acts as a deterrent to implement potentially valuable initiatives in LTC systems. There is clear scope for more initiatives targeting health promotion for seniors and evaluation of practices.

10.4. Addressing long-term care systems governance

LTC services and systems are quite complex, posing significant difficulties for their management and regulation. When obtaining care services becomes too bureaucratic and imposes administrative burdens on users, this may undermine public confidence or inappropriately discourage individuals from seeking formal care (Fernández *et al.*, 2009).

A potential way of countering this complexity is the establishment of comprehensive information platforms, available to LTC users and providers. A study in the United States showed lack of public awareness and confusion regarding the availability of care services. Information databases defining more precisely the care eligibility criteria, the types of available care and financial support would be useful for users, and for providers, too, to assess the benefits and risks of various forms of care for patients with given characteristics.

Widely available information could improve users' informed choices and providers' decision-making (Fernández *et al.*, 2009; Miller *et al.*, 2008; Kane and Kane, 2001).

Explicit printed and audio material describing financial LTC entitlements can be found in Scotland and Ireland (Fernández *et al.*, 2009; Miller *et al.*, 2008). In Sweden, the need for better information platforms is well acknowledged, and specific initiatives already in place include "Open Comparisons" tools and "Guide for the Elderly" manuals, among others (Government of Sweden, 2010). Information support tools are more likely to gain widespread acceptance if they are more trustworthy than provider-generated web sites, and more comprehensive and less medically focused than reports from government regulatory agencies. It has been suggested that public-private partnerships may be tested to undertake such an information task, combining public and private data (Kane and Kane, 2001).

The implementation of evidence-based guidelines is another tool to support decision-making. This involves reviewing scientific knowledge and ranking by experts, based on different features such as patients' needs, benefit-risk ratios, cost-efficiency and the soundness of the evidence. Such clinical guidelines can be found in some OECD countries, as for example in Sweden and the United States. Structuring guidelines for the elderly population can be challenging, as they often need to address complex co-morbidities, and studies on younger populations without multi-morbidity may have limited generalisation value for older populations. Nevertheless, by encouraging standardisation among providers, the benefits to patients may be optimised (Ekerstad *et al.*, 2008; Boyd, 2005).

Another possible way to improve institutional efficiencies in LTC is care planning. One of the aims of LTC systems is to enable patients to receive tailored care, according to their needs. Those needs are determined by an assessment of the individual's current and past physical, mental and emotional condition. Collaborative work across health professionals is required. The definition of LTC care planning or care management differs across countries, however some core components include patient assessment, care plan development, monitoring, care co-ordination and responsiveness to crisis situations. In some cases, psychosocial support may also be included (Sargent *et al.*, 2007; Challis *et al.*, 2010).

Care planning programmes exist in several OECD countries, such as the United States, United Kingdom, Canada and Sweden (Sargent *et al.*, 2007; Challis *et al.*, 2010). In the United Kingdom, the National Service Framework for Older People (NSFOP) introduced in 2001 promoted individual care planning for the senior population, either in hospitals or in the community. Evaluations of this programme have shown that, although older people might not perceive improvements as a result of the NSFOP, they do observe improvements in the LTC systems as a whole (Manthorpe *et al.*, 2007).

Information sharing across government administrations may enhance the administrative efficiency of LTC services. These may include LTC financing, targeted personal-income tax measures and transfers, such as pensions, as well as existing social assistance or housing subsidy programs. In Japan, the introduction of LTC insurance in 2000 aimed, among other things, at promoting information sharing between LTC and other social sectors (Matsuda and Yamamoto, 2001).

A wide range of factors may influence inter-agency information sharing. For example, the policy and legislative context will have an effect on the balance of sharing and protecting information. The existing governance structures are likely to shape the links between LTC and social care systems, with respect to data sharing. Technical considerations play an important role as well; for instance, the degree to which computer systems are compatible and the extent to which one organisation has access to personal records held by another. Information exchange could be facilitated with the use of integrated records, including shared assessments and care procedures. The need of training and support to professionals on this issue is evident (Richardson and Asthana, 2006).

The organisation of health and LTC systems, as well as the presence of multiple payers, can lead to cost-shifting incentives for providers, which may in turn have negative implications on efficiency and other aspects of care. In order to address these problems, several policy initiatives, such as capitation payment and pay-for-performance, have been considered in the United States, although they all have strengths and weaknesses (Grabowski, 2007).

In sum, some possibly useful approaches to enhance institutional efficiency include the establishment of good information platforms, the setting of guidelines, the use of care planning processed, the sharing of data within government administrations and minimising the cost-shifting incentives. Given that all these interventions are dependent on other system features, this issue is likely to be a continuing focus of policy makers in the years to come.

10.5. Conclusions

Ageing populations will result in increased demand for LTC services in the future, placing a higher burden on the expenditure of formal LTC systems. Governments have, or should, become increasingly concerned with improving the value for money of their LTC systems. But there is still little measurement and evaluation of this important dimension of performance.

Nearly all OECD countries have been encouraging home care, in order to limit institutional costs and satisfy peoples' preferences to receive care at home. They have done so through the direct expansion of home care supply, and the implementation of regulatory measures and financial incentives. Obstacles such as limited home-care providers, fragmentation of care, and lack of incentives for providers and users have been identified in some countries. Some evidence suggests that home care may become more expensive than institutional care for severely disabled people.

LTC payment mechanisms can be used to steer providers towards desired goals for the system. Here, pay-for-performance initiatives may hold some promise, although their use in LTC is still limited. Efficiency gains could also be achieved from choice-based competition across providers, such as in the case of vouchers used in the Nordic countries to stimulate private providers. The introduction of new technologies could improve the productivity of LTC workers, but there is a dearth of evaluation of cost-effectiveness of many "smart" technologies and often technology appears useful as a supplement rather than a substitute of labour.

Inefficiencies may arise from the interactions of the LTC system with the health care system. Several OECD countries have targeted the inappropriate use of acute services for LTC needs via financial measures, changes in administrative responsibilities and the introduction of information technology. Many OECD countries have attempted to co-ordinate or integrate health care and LTC services, but the difficulties faced are not trivial. Policies promoting healthy ageing and prevention have been adopted, among others, in Japan and Sweden. There is still uncertainty regarding which interventions would generate the highest health gains for each dollar: this is an area where priority should be placed in the future.

LTC systems' governance is complex and can lead to institutional inefficiencies. Various approaches could be adopted for improvement, such as establishing comprehensive information platforms, implementing evidence-based guidelines to support decision-making, introducing care planning programmes, sharing of information across government administrations and minimising cost-shifting incentives of providers.

Finally, there is a need to engage with wider societal and public attitudes towards meeting LTC needs, since these often frame decisions about public funding. Population ageing requires a change of the "caring mindset", so that care for older people comes to be viewed as a priority for society as a whole. Without such a change in attitudes, older people with LTC needs may be left particularly vulnerable to domestic neglect and unwanted institutionalisation.

Notes

1. PAI (Plan, Assess, Invest) groups make the assessment.

2. Providers receive a fixed amount for the services provided over a specific period of time, irrespective of the volume.

3. The discussion on voucher systems in LTC in Nordic countries is based on an analysis carried out for OECD by Viita (2010) during the summer of 2010.

4. A care manager is typically involved in the screening, assessment, planning, implementation, and review of individuals living with long-term conditions. Often, the managers are in charge of organising the services. There is nonetheless variation in the role and tasks of care managers across countries.

5. *Active Ageing,* placing greater emphasis on prolonging labour market activity and functional capacity (WHO, 2002) and *Successful Ageing,* concerned more specifically with ensuring that individuals are in good physical and psychological health to endure tense experiences in later life, are also used in the literature (Oxley, 2009a).

References

Ankestyreseln (2005), "Frit valg i ældreplejen – landsdækkande brugerundersøgelse", Ankestyrelsens undersøgelser, accessible at *www.fritvalgsdatabasen.dk/indhold?system=fritvalg&id=fritvalg.publikation.*

Arling, G. *et al.* (2009), "Medicaid Nursing Home Pay for Performance: Where Do We Stand?", *The Gerontologist,* Vol. 49, No. 5, pp. 587-595, accessed 18 October 2010 at *http://gerontologist.oxfordjournals. org/content/49/5/587.full.pdf+html?ath_user=kclkkwi4196&ath_ttok=%3CTLxqlKMEQXdv77Eh9g%3E.*

Arntz, M. *et al.* (2007), "The German Social Long-term Care Insurance: Structure and Reform Options", *IZA Discussion Paper,* No. 2625, Bonn, accessible at *http://ftp.iza.org/dp2625.pdf.*

Barton Smith, D. and Z. Feng (2010), "The Accumulated Challenges of Long-term Care", *Health Affairs,* Vol. 29, No. 1, pp. 29-34.

Bayer, E. (2010), "Innovations in Reducing Preventable Hospital Admissions, Readmissions and Emergency Room Use. An Update on Health Plan Initiatives to Address National Health Care Priorities", AHIP Centre for Policy and Research, accessible at *www.ahipresearch.com/pdfs/innovations2010.pdf.*

Beale, S. *et al.* (2009), "Evaluation of the Telecare Development Programme. Final Report", Health Economics Consortium, York, accessed 24 November 2010 at *www.scie-socialcareonline.org.uk/ profile.asp?guid=84c830fd-7a8f-4f12-9ab7-84fc1aab5097.*

Béland, F. *et al.* (2006), "A System of Integrated Care for Older Persons with Disabilities in Canada: Results from a Randomized Controlled Trial", *Journal of Gerontology: Medical Sciences,* Vol. 61A, No. 4, pp. XXX, accessible at *http://biomedgerontology.oxfordjournals.org/content/61/4/367.full.pdf+html?ath_user=kclkkwi 4196&ath_ttok=%3CTKwvK6MsT6oIP7WiJQ%3E.*

Bergman, H. *et al.* (1997), "Care for Canada's Frail Elderly Population: Fragmentation or Integration?", *Canadian Medical Association Journal,* Vol. 157, No. 8, pp. 1116-1121, accessible at *www.ecmaj.ca/cgi/ reprint/157/8/1116.pdf.*

Bitenc, I. *et al.* (2000), "Critical Analysis of an Information System for Community Nursing", *Proceedings of the 8th European Conference on Information Systems*, Vienna, accessed 21 October 2010 at *http://is2.lse.ac.uk/asp/aspecis/20000145.pdf*.

Björkgren, M.A. *et al.* (1999), "Validity and Reliability of Resource Utilization Groups (RUGs) in Finnish Long-term Care Facilities", *Scandinavian Journal of Public Health*, Vol. 27, pp. 228-234, accessed on 19 October 2010 at *http://deepblue.lib.umich.edu/bitstream/2027.42/68924/2/10.1177_1403494899 0270030201.pdf*.

Boyd, C.M. (2005), "Clinical Practice Guidelines and Quality of Care for Older Patients with Multiple Comorbid Diseases. Implications for Pay-For-Performance", *Journal of the American Medical Association*, Vol. 294, No. 6, pp. 716-724, accessed on 17 January 2011 at *http://jama.ama-assn.org/content/ 294/6/716.full.pdf+html?ath_user=kclkkwi4196&ath_ttok=%3CTT78TqMYHKLI5j5O3Q%3E*.

Briesacher, B.A. *et al.* (2009), "Pay-For-Performance in Nursing Homes", *Health Care Financing Review*, Vol. 30, No. 3, pp. 1-13, accessed on 18 October 2010 at *www.ncbi.nlm.nih.gov/pmc/articles/PMC2758526/ pdf/nihms132435.pdf*.

Brizioli, E. *et al.* (2003), "Nursing Home Case-Mix Instruments: Validation of the RUG-III System in Italy", *Aging Clinical and Experimental Research*, Vol. 15, pp. 243-253, accessed on 19 October 2010 at *www.ars.marche.it/RUG/pubblicazioni/Aging_article(ART.INTERN).pdf*.

Busse, R. *et al.* (2006), "Editorial: Hospital Case Payment Systems in Europe", *Health Care Management Science*, Vol. 9, pp. 211-213, accessed on 19 October 2010 at *www.observatorysummerschool.org/ pdf/HCMS-DRG-Editorial.pdf*.

Busse, R. and N. Mays (2008), "Paying for Chronic Disease Care", in E. Nolte and M. McKee (eds.), *Caring for People with Chronic Conditions. A Health System Perspective*, European Observatory on Health Systems and Policies, Chapter 9, accessible at *www.euro.who.int/__data/assets/pdf_file/0006/96468/E91878.pdf*.

Byrne, D. *et al.* (2008), "Formal Home Health Care, Informal Care, and Family Decision Making", accessible at *www.iew.uzh.ch/institute/people/mgoeree/Research/fhhc.pdf*.

Campbell, J.C. *et al.* (2010), "Lessons from Public Long-term Care Insurance in Germany and Japan", *Health Affairs*, Vol. 29, No. 1, pp. 87-95.

Campbell, J.C. and N. Ikegami (2000), "Long-term Care Insurance Comes to Japan", *Health Affairs*, Vol. 19, No. 3, pp. 26-39, accessible at *http://content.healthaffairs.org/cgi/reprint/19/3/26*.

Campbell, J.C. and N. Ikegami (2003), "Japan's Radical Reform of Long-term Care", *Social Policy and Administration*, Vol. 37, No. 1, pp. 21-34, accessible at *http://onlinelibrary.wiley.com/doi/10.1111/ 1467-9515.00321/pdf*.

Caris-Verhallen, W. and A. Kerkstra (2000), "Continuity of Care for Patients on a Waiting List for Institutional Long-term Care", *Health and Social Care in the Community*, Vol. 9, No. 1, pp. 1-9, accessible at *www3.interscience.wiley.com/cgi-bin/fulltext/120716787/HTMLSTART*.

Center for Technology and Aging (2009), "Technologies to Help Older Adults Maintain Independence: Advancing Technology Adoption", *Briefing Paper*, accessed on 21 October 2010 at *www.techandaging. org/briefingpaper.pdf*.

Challis, D., J. Hughes, K. Berzins, S. Reilly, J. Abell and K. Stewart (2010), "Self-Care and Case Management in Long-term Conditions: The Effective Management of Critical Interface", Report for the National Institute for Health Research Service Delivery and Organisation programme, accessible at *www.sdo.nihr.ac.uk/files/project/201-final-report.pdf*.

Christianson, J.B. *et al.* (2007), "Paying for Quality: Understanding and Assessing Physician Pay-For-Performance Initiatives", *Research Synthesis Report*, No. 13, Robert Wood Johnson Foundation, accessible at *www.rwjf.org/files/research/no13synthesisreport.pdf*.

Consolidation Act on Social Services in Denmark (2010), accessible at *http://english.sm.dk/ MinistryOfSocialWelfare/legislation/social_affairs/social_service_act/Sider/Start.aspx*.

Cutler, L.J. and R.A. Kane (2009), "Post-Occupancy Evaluation of a Transformed Nursing Home: The First Four Green House Settings", *Journal of Housing for the Elderly*, Vol. 23, No. 4, pp. 304-334, accessed on 26 November 2010 at *http://pdfserve.informaworld.com/35051_713582246_917056901.pdf*.

Da Roit, B. and B. Le Bihan (2010), "Similar and Yet So Different: Cash-For-Care in Six European Countries' Long-term Care Policies", *The Millbank Quarterly*, Vol. 88, No. 3, pp. 286-309.

Dervaux, B. *et al.* (2006), "Assessing the French Nursing Home Efficiency: An Indirect Approach Via Budget-Constrained DEA Models", *Socio-Economic Planning Sciences*, Vol. 30, pp. 70-91, accessed on 19 October 2010 at *www.sciencedirect.com/science?_ob=ArticleURL&_udi=B6V6Y-4G63J8S-2&_user=*

946274&_coverDate=03%2F31%2F2006&_rdoc=1&_fmt=high&_orig=search&_origin=search&_sort=d&_do
canchor=&view=c&_searchStrId=1504075305&_rerunOrigin=google&_acct=C000049020&_version=1&_url
Version=0&_userid=946274&md5=b06b4bb6c5fe3cd7ccf69ae15dc79a39&searchtype=a.

Ekerstad, N. et al. (2008), "Characteristics of Multiple-Diseased Elderly in Swedish Hospital Care and
Clinical Guidelines: Do They Make Evidence-Based Priority Setting a 'Mission Impossible'?",
International Journal of Ageing and Later Life, Vol. 3, No. 2, pp. 71-95, accessed on 19 January 2011 at
www.ep.liu.se/ej/ijal/2008/v3/i2/a4/ijal08v3i2a4.pdf.

Engström, M. et al. (2005), "Staff Perceptions of Job Satisfaction and Life Situation Before 6 and 12 months
After Increased Information Technology Support in Dementia Care", Journal of Telemedicine and Telecare,
Vol. 11, pp. 304-309, accessed on 21 October 2010 at http://jtt.rsmjournals.com/cgi/reprint/11/6/304.

EU Discussion Paper (2007), "Healthy Ageing: Keystone for a Sustainable Europe. EU Health Policy in
the Context of Demographic Change", Health and Consumer Protection Directorate-General,
accessible at http://ec.europa.eu/health/ph_information/indicators/docs/healthy_ageing_en.pdf.

Fernández, J.L. et al. (2009), "How Can European States Design Efficient, Equitable and Sustainable Funding
Systems for Long-term Care for Older People", Health Systems and Policy Analysis, Policy Brief No. 11,
World Health Organization on behalf of the European Observatory on Health Systems and Policies,
accessed on 20 January 2011 at www.euro.who.int/__data/assets/pdf_file/0011/64955/E92561.pdf.

FINLEX, Finnish Legislation Database, www.finlex.fi.

Folland, S., A.C. Goodman and L. Stano (2001), "The Economics of Health and Health Care", 3rd edition,
Prentice Hall, Upper Saddle River, NJ.

Gold, M. and S. Felt-Lisk (2008), "Using Physician Payment Reform to Enhance Health System
Performance", Mathematica Policy Research Inc., accessible at www.mathematica-mpr.com/PDFs/
physpaybrief.pdf.

Government of Finland (2009). "Hallituksen esitys Eduskunnalle laeiksi sosiaali- ja terveydenhuollon
palvelusetelistä sekä sosiaali- ja terveydenhuollon asiakasmaksuista annetun lain 12 §:n
muuttamisesta", (Government bill to Parliament regarding an Act on Service Voucher for Social and
Health Services and an Act amending section 12 in the Act on Client Charges in Social Welfare and
Health Care), accessible at http://217.71.145.20/TRIPviewer/show.asp?tunniste=HE+20/2009&base=
erhe&palvelin=www.eduskunta.fi&f=WORD.

Government of Sweden (2010), The Future Need for Care. Results from the LEV Project (2010), Government
Offices from Sweden, accessed on 27 January 2011 at www.sweden.gov.se/content/1/c6/15/36/57/
d30b0968.pdf.

Grabowski, D.C. (2007), "Medicare and Medicaid: Conflicting Incentives for Long-term Care", The Millbank
Quarterly, Vol. 85, No. 4, pp. 579-610, accessible at http://onlinelibrary.wiley.com/doi/10.1111/j.1468-0009.
2007.00502.x/pdf.

Grabowski, D.C. (2009), "Special Needs Plans and the Co-ordination of Benefits and Services for Dual
Eligibles", Health Affairs (Millwood), Vol. 28, No. 1, pp. 136-146, accessible at www.ncbi.nlm.nih.gov/pmc/
articles/PMC2765211/pdf/nihms148139.pdf.

Grabowski, D.C. et al. (2010), "Supporting Home- and Community-Based Care: Views of Long-term Care
Specialists", Medical Care Research and Review, accessible at http://mcr.sagepub.com/cgi/rapidpdf/
1077558710366863v1.pdf.

Grieve, R. et al. (2008), "Evaluating Health Care Programs by Combining Cost with Quality of Life Measures:
A Case Study Comparing Capitation and Fee for Service", Health Services Research, Vol. 43, No. 4,
pp. 1204-1222, accessed on 19 October 2010 at www.ncbi.nlm.nih.gov/pmc/articles/PMC2517267/pdf/
hesr0043-1204.pdf.

Gross, D.L. et al. (2004), "The Growing Pains of Integrated Health Care for the Elderly: Lessons From the
Expansion of PACE", The Millbank Quarterly, Vol. 82, No. 2, pp. 257-282, accessible at http://onlinelibrary.
wiley.com/doi/10.1111/j.0887-378X.2004.00310.x/pdf.

Haberkern, K., T. Schmid, F. Neuberger and M. Grignon (2011), "The Role of Elderly as Providers and
Recipients of Care", OECD/IFP Project on the "Future of Families to 2030".

Help the Aged (2008), "The Case for Healthy Ageing. Why It Needs to Be Made", London, accessible at
http://policy.helptheaged.org.uk/NR/rdonlyres/C5EC6B06-8CCE-4760-89A0-854B84E1EE06/0/case_for_hea
lthy_ageing.pdf.

Hoenig, H. *et al.* (2003), "Does Assistive Technology Substitute for Personal Assistance Among the Disabled Elderly?", *American Journal of Public Health*, Vol. 93, No. 2, pp. 330-337, accessible at *www.ncbi.nlm.nih.gov/pmc/articles/PMC1447739/pdf/0930330.pdf.*

Hofmarcher, M.M. (2008), "Austria's New Home Care Law: An Assessment in the Context of Long-term Care Policy", Unpublished document, OECD Publishing, Paris.

Hofmarcher, M.M. *et al.* (2007), "Improved Health System Performance Through Better Care Coordination", *OECD Health Working Papers*, No. 30, OECD Publishing, Paris, accessed on 28 October 2010 at *www.oecd.org/dataoecd/22/9/39791610.pdf.*

Hollander, M. and N. Chappell (2002), "Final Report of the National Evaluation of the Cost-Effectiveness of Home Care", A report prepared for the Health Transition Fund, Health Canada; National Evaluation of the Cost-Effectiveness of Home Care, accessed on 31 January 2011 at *www.homecarestudy.com/reports/full-text/synthesis.pdf.*

Hutt, R. *et al.* (2004), "Case-Managing Long-term Conditions", King's Fund, accessible at *www.red-elaia.org/adjuntos/192.1-casemanagement.pdf.*

Ikegami, N. *et al.* (2003), "The Long-term Care Insurance Law in Japan: Impact on Institutional Care Facilities", *International Journal of Geriatric Psychiatry*, Vol. 18, pp. 217-221, accessible at *www3.interscience.wiley.com/cgi-bin/fulltext/104065479/PDFSTART.*

Intrator, O. and V. Mor (2004), "Effect of State Medicaid Reimbursement Rates on Hospitalizations from Nursing Homes", *Journal of the American Geriatrics Society*, Vol. 52, pp. 393-398, accessible at *http://onlinelibrary.wiley.com/doi/10.1111/j.1532-5415.2004.52111.x/pdf.*

Jensen, P.M. *et al.* (2009), "Are Long-term Care Residents Reffered Appropriately to Hospital Emergency Departments?", *Canadian Family Physician*, Vol. 55, pp. 500-505, accessible at *www.cfp.ca/cgi/content/full/55/5/500.*

Kane, R.A. and R.L. Kane (2001), "What Older People Want from Long-term Care, and How They Can Get It", *Health Affairs*, Vol. 20, No. 6, pp. 114-127, accessed on 21 January 2011 at *http://content.healthaffairs.org/content/20/6/114.full.pdf+html.*

Kane, R.A. *et al.* (2005), "Results From the Green House Evaluation in Tupelo, MS", Academy Health Annual Meeting, 26 June 2005, accessed on 26 November 2010 at *www.directcareclearinghouse.org/download/Boston%20Presentation%20at%20Academy%20Health%202005[1].pdf.*

Karlsson, M. and T. Iversen (2010), "Scandinavian Long-term Care Financing", *Working Paper*, No. 2010:2, University of Oslo Health Economics Research Programme, accessible at *www.hero.uio.no/publicat/2010/2010_2.pdf.*

Kaskiharju, E. and M. Seppänen (eds.) (2004), "Vaihtoehtona palveluseteli – Lahden seudun viiden kunnan palvelusetelikokeilu", *Report of the Ministry of Social Affairs and Health*, No. 2004:8, Helsinki (Service voucher as an option – Service voucher experiment in five municipalities in Lahti Region), accessible at *www.stm.fi/julkaisut/selvityksia-sarja/nayta/_julkaisu/1067339#fi.*

Kastberg, G. (2001), "A Tool for Influence – The Effects of Introducing a Voucher System Into In-Home Elderly Care", University of Gothenburg, School of Public Administration.

Kaye, H.S. *et al.* (2009), "Do Non-Institutional Long-term Care Services Reduce Medicaid Spending?", *Health Affairs*, Vol. 28, No. 1, pp. 262-272.

Klein, S. (2010), "Quality Matters in Focus: Building Accountable Care Organizations that Improve Quality and Lower Costs. A View from the Field", The Commonwealth Fund, accessed on 29 October 2010 at *www.commonwealthfund.org/Content/Newsletters/Quality-Matters/2010/June-July-2010/In-Focus.aspx.*

Konetzka, R.T. and R. Werner (2010), "Applying Market-Based Reforms to Long-term Care", *Health Affairs*, Vol. 29, No. 1, pp. 74-80.

Kremer, M. (2006), "Consumers in Charge of Care: The Dutch Personal Budget and Its Impact on the Market, Professionals and Family", *European Societies*, Vol. 8, No. 3, pp. 385-401, accessible at *http://pdfserve.informaworld.com/357654_713582246_757920324.pdf.*

Kumpers, S. *et al.* (2010), "Prevention and Rehabilitation Within Long-term Care across Europe", European Overview Paper, accessible at *www.euro.centre.org/data/1278594859_11573.pdf.*

Kurrle, S.E. (2006), "Improving Acute Care Services for Older People", *The Medical Journal of Australia*, Vol. 184, No. 9, p. 427, accessible at *www.mja.com.au/public/issues/184_09_010506/kur10200_fm.html.*

Lafortune, G. *et al.* (2007), "Trends in Severe Disability Among Elderly People: Assessing the Evidence in 12 OECD Countries and the Future Implications", *OECD Health Working Paper*, No. 26, OECD Publishing, Paris.

Lamura, G. (2010), "The Role of Migrant Work in LTC Sector: Challenges and Opportunities", Long-term Care in Europe, Discussing trends and relevant issues, Conference held under the project "Mainstreaming Ageing: Indicators to Monitor Implementation", accessed on 21 October 2010 at *www.euro.centre.org/data/1267541472_78930.pdf*.

Lee, E.J. *et al.* (2009), "Developing an Electronic Nursing Record System for Clinical Care and Nursing Effectiveness Research in a Korean Home Health Care Setting", *CIN: Computers, Informatics, Nursing*, Vol. 27, No. 4, pp. 234-244.

Long-term Care Reform Leadership Project (2009), "Achieving High-Quality Long-term Care: The Importance of Chronic Care Coordination", Vol. 2, No. 5, AARP, accessible at *www.ncsl.org/documents/health/carecoord.pdf*.

Manthorpe, J. *et al.* (2007), "Four Years On: The Impact of the National Service Framework for Older People on the Experiences, Expectations and Views of Older People", *Age and Ageing*, Vol. 36, pp. 501-507, accessed on 20 January 2011 at *http://ageing.oxfordjournals.org/content/36/5/501.full.pdf+html*.

Matsuda, S. and M. Yamamoto (2001), "Long-term Care Insurance and Integrated Care for the Aged in Japan", *International Journal of Integrated Care*, Vol. 1, pp. 1-11, accessed on 24 January 2011 at *www.ncbi.nlm.nih.gov/pmc/articles/PMC1484411/pdf/ijic2001-200128.pdf*.

McCutcheon, M.E. and W.J. McAuley (2008), "Long-term Care Services, Care Coordination and the Continuum of Care", in C.M. Mara and L.K. Olson (eds.), *Handbook of Long-term Care Administration and Policy*, Chapter 10, Taylor and Francis Group, accessible at *http://books.google.fr/books?hl=fr&lr=&id=cXExrXtf7YkC&oi=fnd&pg=PA173&dq=coordination+long+term+care&ots=8e2apRMWDH&sig=0to6qP7gPqR1YyozW8lJdJEOjE8#v=onepage&q=coordination%20long%20term%20care&f=false*.

Miller, E.A. *et al.* (2008), "Assessing Expert Views of the Future of Long-term Care", *Research on Aging*, Vol. 30, No. 4, pp. 450-473, accessed on 19 January 2011 at *http://roa.sagepub.com/content/30/4/450.full.pdf+html*.

Miller, E.A. and W.G. Weissert (2010), "The Commonwealth Fund Survey of Long-term Care Specialists", *Medical Care Research and Review*, accessible at *http://mcr.sagepub.com/cgi/rapidpdf/1077558710366864v1.pdf*.

Ministry of the Interior and Health-Ministry of Social Affairs (2005), "Report on Health and Long-term Care in Denmark", accessible at *www.sm.dk/data/Lists/Publikationer/Attachments/320/Report_on_health_and_long-term_care.pdf*.

Mollot, R.J. *et al.* (2008), "An Assessment of Pay-For-Performance for Nursing Homes with Recommendations for Policy Makers", *LTCCC Report*, Long-term Care Community Coalition, accessible at *www.ltccc.org/publications/documents/LTCCCP4Preportfinal08.pdf*.

Mor, V. *et al.* (2010), "The Revolving Door of Reshospitalization from Skilled Nursing Facilities", *Health Affairs*, Vol. 29, No. 1, pp. 57-64, accessible at *http://content.healthaffairs.org/cgi/reprint/29/1/57?ijkey=5swWrBs8cJbjY&keytype=ref&siteid=healthaff*.

Morikawa, M. *et al.* (2007), "Preventive Care or Preventive Needs? Re-Balancing Long-term Care Between the Government and Service Users in Japan", Fourth Annual East Asian Social Policy research network (EASP), Tokyo, accessible at *www.welfareasia.org/4thconference/papers/Morikawa_Re-balancing%20Long-Term%20Care%20between%20the%20Government%20and%20Service%20Users%20in%20Japan.pdf*.

Moyle, W. *et al.* (2003), "Views of Job Satisfaction and Dissatisfaction in Australian Long-term Care", *Journal of Clinical Nursing*, Vol. 12, pp. 168-176, accessed on 21 October 2010 at *http://onlinelibrary.wiley.com/doi/10.1046/j.1365-2702.2003.00732.x/pdf*.

Mui, A.C. (2002), "The Program of All-Inclusive Care for the Elderly (PACE): An Innovative Long-term Care Model in the United States", *Journal of Aging and Social Policy*, Vol. 13, No. 2, pp. 53-67, accessible at *http://pdfserve.informaworld.com/389048_713582246_903288273.pdf*.

Norwegian Ministry of Healthcare and Services (2008-2009), "The Co-ordination Reform. Proper Treatment at the Right Place and Right Time", Report No. 47, accessed on 14 February 2011 at *www.regjeringen.no/upload/HOD/Samhandling%20engelsk_PDFS.pdf*.

OECD (2005), *Extending Opportunities. How Active Social Policy Can Benefit Us All*, Chapter 8, OECD Publishing, Paris, accessible at *http://publications.oecd.org/acrobatebook/8105051E.PDF*.

OECD (2009), *OECD Economic Surveys: Japan*, Vol. 2009/18, Chapter 4, OECD Publishing, Paris.

Oxley, H. (2009a), "Policies for Healthy Ageing: An Overview", *OECD Health Working Paper*, No. 42, OECD Publishing, Paris.

Oxley, H. (2009b), "Improving Health Care System Performance Through Better Co-Ordination of Care", *Achieving Better Value for Money in Healthcare, OECD Health Policy Studies*, Chapter 3, OECD Publishing, Paris.

Paasivirta, K. (2009), "Palveluseteli sosiaali- ja terveyspalvelujen järjestämistapana" (Service voucher as a way to organize social welfare and health services), accessible at *www.kunnat.net/k_perussivu.asp?path= 1;29;353;135218;57267;62601*.

Pope, G.C. et al. (2004), "Risk Adjustment of Medicare Capitation Payments Using the CMS-HCC Model", *Health Care Financing Review*, Vol. 25, No. 4, pp. 119-141, accessed on 19 October 2010 at *www.cms.gov/HealthCareFinancingReview/downloads/04Summerpg119.pdf*.

Pratt, J.R. (2010), *Long-term Care. Managing Across the Continuum,* Chapter 1, 3rd edition, Jones and Bartlett publishers, pp. 27-28, accessible at *http://books.google.com/books?id=5hJLvPie2OUC&pg=PA29&lpg= PA29&dq=coordination+long+term+care&source=bl&ots=U4cufW8Cqr&sig=I0rXxBftJBUeTXR0o6e7hrcbhYA&h l=fr&ei=vvwhTOeWHpa8jAebxv2uAQ&sa=X&oi=book_result&ct=result&resnum=3&ved=0CB8Q6AEwAjhQ#v =onepage&q=coordination%20&f=false*.

PSA Delivery Agreement 17 (2010), "Tackle Poverty and Promote Greater Independence and Well-Being in Later Life", HM Government, accessible at *http://webarchive.nationalarchives.gov.uk/+/http://www.hm-treasury.gov.uk/pbr_csr07_psabetterqualityoflife.htm*.

HM Government UK (2007), "Putting People First. A Shared Vision and Commitment to the Transformation of Adult Social Care", accessible at *www.dh.gov.uk/prod_consum_dh/groups/dh_digitalassets/@dh/ @en/documents/digitalasset/dh_081119.pdf*.

Reinhard, S.C. (2010), "Diversion, Transition Programs Target Nursing Homes' Status Quo", *Health Affairs*, Vol. 20, No. 1, pp. 44-48.

Reinhard, S. et al. (2010), "Weathering the Storm: The Impact of the Great Recession on Long-term Services and Supports", AARP Public Policy Institute, accessible at *http://assets.aarp.org/rgcenter/ppi/ltc/ 2010-10-hma-nasuad.pdf*.

Richardson, S. and S. Asthana (2006), "Inter-Agency Information Sharing in Health and Social Care Services: The Role of Professional Culture", *British Journal of Social Work*, Vol. 36, pp. 657-559, accessed on 24 January 2011 at *http://bjsw.oxfordjournals.org/content/36/4/657.abstract*.

Rothgang, H. (2010), "Social Insurance for Long-term Care: An Evaluation of the German Model", *Social Policy and Administration*, Vol. 44, No. 4, pp. 436-460, accessible at *http://onlinelibrary.wiley.com/doi/ 10.1111/j.1467-9515.2010.00722.x/pdf*.

Sargent, P., S. Pickard, R. Sheaff and R. Boaden (2007), "Patient and Carer Perceptions of Case Management for Long-term Conditions", *Health and Social Care in the Community*, Vol. 15, No. 6, pp. 511-519, accessible at *http://onlinelibrary.wiley.com/doi/10.1111/j.1365-2524.2007.00708.x/pdf*.

Silow-Carroll, S. et al. (2010), "States in Action", The Commonwealth Fund, accessed on 26 October 2010 at *www.commonwealthfund.org/~/media/Files/Newsletters/States%20In%20Action/2010_10_15_ StatesInAction.pdf*.

SNIPH – Swedish National Institute for Public Health (2006), "Healthy Ageing – A Challenge for Europe", accessible at *www.fhi.se/PageFiles/4173/Healthy_ageing.pdf*.

Soar, J. et al. (2007), "Reducing Avoidable Hospital Admissions of the Frail Elderly Using Intelligent Referrals", *Electronic Journal of Health Informatics*, Vol. 2, No. 1, pp. 1-6, accessible at *http://eprints.usq. edu.au/2608/1/Soar_Yuginovich_Whittaker_Publ_version.pdf*.

Söderlung, R. (2004), "The Role of Information and Communication Technology in Home Services: Telecare Does Not Satisfy the Needs of the Elderly", *Health Informatics Journal*, Vol. 10, No. 2, pp. 127-137, accessed on 21 December 2010 at *http://jhi.sagepub.com/content/10/2/127.full.pdf+html*.

Steuerle, C.E. (2000), "Common Issues for Voucher Programs", in C.E. Steuerle, V.D. Ooms, G. Peterson and R.D. Reishauer (eds.), *Vouchers and the Provision of Public Services*, Brookings Institution Press, Washington DC.

Stone, R.I. (2000), "Long-term Care for the Elderly with Disabilities: Current Policy, Emerging Trends and Implications for the Twenty-First Century", Millbank Memorial Fund, accessible at Swedish National Institute for Public Health, *www.milbank.org/reports/0008stone/LongTermCare_Mech5.pdf*.

Svensk författningssamling (2008), "Act on the System of Choice in the Public Sector", accessible at *www.notisum.se/rnp/sls/sfs/20080962.pdf*.

Sveriges Kommuner och Landsting (2009), "Valfrihetssystem, erfarenheter från ett antal kommuner och landsting", accessible at *http://brs.skl.se/brsbibl/kata_documents/doc39646_1.pdf*.

Torp, S. *et al.* (2008), "A Pilot Study of How Information and Communication Technology May Contribute to Health Promotion Among Elderly Spousal Carers in Norway", *Health and Social Care in the Community*, Vol. 16, No. 1, pp. 75-85, accessed on 21 October 2010 at *http://onlinelibrary.wiley.com/doi/10.1111/j.1365-2524.2007.00725.x/pdf*.

Thorpe, K.E. and D.H. Howard (2006), "The Rise in Spending Among Medicare Beneficiaries: The Role of Chronic Disease Prevalence and Changes in Treatment Intensity", *Health Affairs*, Vol. 25, No. 5, pp. 378-388, accessible at *http://content.healthaffairs.org/content/25/5/w378.full.pdf+html*.

Trydegård, G.B. (2003), "Swedish Care Reforms in the 1990s. A First Evaluation of their Consequences for the Elderly People", RFAS 4, pp; 443-460, accessed on 24 November 2010 at *www.sante-sports.gouv.fr/IMG/pdf/rfas200304-art14-uk.pdf*.

Tsutsui, T. and N. Muramatsu (2007), "Japan's Universal Long-term Care System Reform of 2005: Containing Costs and Realising a Vision", *Journal of American Geriatric Society*, Vol. 55, pp. 1458-1463, accessible at *http://onlinelibrary.wiley.com/doi/10.1111/j.1532-5415.2007.01281.x/pdf*.

UK Department of Health (2010), *Transparency in Outcomes: A Framework for Adult Cocial Care. A Consultation on Proposals*, Department of Health – Social Care, accessible at *www.dh.gov.uk/prod_consum_dh/groups/dh_digitalassets/@dh/@en/documents/digitalasset/dh_122037.pdf*.

Valkila, N. and A. Saari (2010), "The Productivity Impact of the Voice Link Between Elderly and Nurses: An Assisted Living Facility Pilot", *Archives of Gerontology and Geriatrics*, accessed on 21 October 2010 at *www.sciencedirect.com/science?_ob=ArticleURL&_udi=B6T4H-506YWTR-1&_user=946274&_coverDate=06%2F02%2F2010&_rdoc=1&_fmt=high&_orig=search&_origin=search&_sort=d&_docanchor=&view=c&_acct=C000049020&_version=1&_urlVersion=0&_userid=946274&md5=d4f5edd282642c86312b94e0a3d7881f&searchtype=a*.

Viita, A.M. (2010), "Introducing Consumer Choice in the Delivery of Long-term Care. Experiences from Voucher Systems in Denmark, Finland and Sweden", Dissertation for the MSc Health Economics Program 2009-10, University of York.

Vimarlund, V. and N.G. Olve (2005), "Economic Analyses for ICT in Elderly Healthcare: Questions and Challenges", Vol. 11, No. 4, pp. 309-321, accessed on 21 October 2010 at *http://jhi.sagepub.com/content/11/4/309.full.pdf+html*.

Volk, R. and T. Laukkanen (2007), "Palvelusetelin käyttö kunnissa", Reports of the Ministry of Social Affairs and Health 2007:38, Helsinki, accessible at *www.stm.fi/julkaisut/selvityksia-sarja/nayta/_julkaisu/1064619#fi*.

WHO (2002), *Active Ageing. A Policy Framework*, accessible at *http://whqlibdoc.who.int/hq/2002/WHO_NMH_NPH_02.8.pdf*.

Wiener, J. *et al.* (2009), "Why Are Nursing Home Utilization Rates Declining?", Real Choice System Change Grant Program, US Department of Health and Human Services, Centres for Medicare and Medicaid Services, accessed on 26 October 2010 at *www.hcbs.org/files/160/7990/SCGNursing.pdf*.

Zhang, N.J. *et al.* (2008), "Has the Medicare Prospective Payment System Led to Increased Nursing Home Efficiency?", *Health Services Research*, Vol. 43, No. 3, pp. 1043-106, accessible at *http://onlinelibrary.wiley.com/doi/10.1111/j.1475-6773.2007.00798.x/pdf*.

ORGANISATION FOR ECONOMIC CO-OPERATION AND DEVELOPMENT

The OECD is a unique forum where governments work together to address the economic, social and environmental challenges of globalisation. The OECD is also at the forefront of efforts to understand and to help governments respond to new developments and concerns, such as corporate governance, the information economy and the challenges of an ageing population. The Organisation provides a setting where governments can compare policy experiences, seek answers to common problems, identify good practice and work to co-ordinate domestic and international policies.

The OECD member countries are: Australia, Austria, Belgium, Canada, Chile, the Czech Republic, Denmark, Estonia, Finland, France, Germany, Greece, Hungary, Iceland, Ireland, Israel, Italy, Japan, Korea, Luxembourg, Mexico, the Netherlands, New Zealand, Norway, Poland, Portugal, the Slovak Republic, Slovenia, Spain, Sweden, Switzerland, Turkey, the United Kingdom and the United States. The European Commission takes part in the work of the OECD.

OECD Publishing disseminates widely the results of the Organisation's statistics gathering and research on economic, social and environmental issues, as well as the conventions, guidelines and standards agreed by its members.

OECD PUBLISHING, 2, rue André-Pascal, 75775 PARIS CEDEX 16
(81 2011 03 1 P) ISBN 978-92-64-09758-2 – No. 58059 2011

9 789264 097582